1817
ARTES
VERITAS
SCIENTIA
LIBRARY OF THE
UNIVERSITY OF MICHIGAN
TUEBOR
SI QUAERIS PENINSULAM AMOENAM
CIRCUMSPICE

FINAL REPORT

OF THE

COMMITTEE ON TAXATION.

OF THE

CITY OF NEW YORK

NEW YORK
1916

THE O'CONNELL PRESS
176 Park Row
New York

330—2,000—'16

COMMITTEE ON TAXATION

OF THE CITY OF NEW YORK

APPOINTED APRIL 10 1914

BY

HONORABLE JOHN PURROY MITCHEL, MAYOR

ALFRED E. MARLING, Chairman
EDWIN R. A. SELIGMAN, Chairman, Executive Committee
FREDERIC C. HOWE, Secretary

ROBERT S. BINKERD
GEORGE CROMWELL*
FRANK HARVEY FIELD
JOSEPH N. FRANCOLINI
JOHN J. HALLERAN
HAMILTON HOLT
JEREMIAH W. JENKS
ARDOLPH L. KLINE
FREDERIC C. LEUBUSCHER
WALTER LINDNER
CYRUS C. MILLER
GEORGE V. MULLAN
LOUIS HEATON PINK
LAWSON PURDY
DAVID RUMSEY
OSCAR R. SEITZ
FREDERIC B. SHIPLEY
ROBERT E. SIMON
FRANKLIN S. TOMLIN
CHARLES T. WHITE
DELOS F. WILCOX
COLLIN H. WOODWARD

LAURENCE ARNOLD TANZER, Executive Secretary

---

*Resigned January 12, 1915.

TABLE OF CONTENTS

EXHIBITS ACCOMPANYING REPORT.

UNTAXING OF BUILDINGS.

Answers to Questions.

Briefs Submitted on the Untaxing of Buildings.

TESTIMONY TAKEN AT HEARINGS ON THE UNTAXING OF BUILDINGS.

Hearing Held November 8, 1915.

Hearing Held November 10, 1915.

Hearing Held November 15, 1915.

Hearing Held November 17, 1915.

Hearing Held November 22, 1915.

Hearing Held November 24, 1915.

Appendix.

BILLS PREPARED BY COMMITTEE.

COMMITTEE ON TAXATION

FINAL REPORT

January 5th, 1916.

HON. JOHN PURROY MITCHEL,
Mayor and Chairman of the Board of Estimate and Apportionment,
City of New York.

Sir:

Pursuant to a resolution of the Board of Estimate and Apportionment, adopted February 20, 1914, an advisory body of citizens was appointed by you by letter, dated April 10, 1914, requesting them "to make a comprehensive and exhaustive study of the several methods of taxation in use here and in other cities of this country and abroad, and of such methods and devices as have been, or may be, during the continuance of your investigation, suggested as calculated to effect an improvement in the ways and means of creating revenue for payment of the cost of the city government."

The Committee met and organized, electing Mr. Marling Chairman, Prof. Seligman Chairman of the Executive Committee, Mr. Howe Secretary, and the following additional gentlemen as members of the Executive Committee: Messrs. Lindner, Jenks, Purdy, Rumsey, Simon and Wilcox. Mr. Mullan was subsequently added to the Executive Committee.

Mr. Cromwell, on being elected State Senator, resigned from membership in the Committee. Otherwise there has been no change in the composition of the Committee.

Various sub-committees were appointed, and Mr. Laurence Arnold Tanzer was chosen as Executive Secretary.

It was understood from the Mayor's original letter, as well as from subsequent letters to the Committee, that the Committee would deal chiefly with two distinct lines of inquiry. The one was the question of the advisability of reducing in whole or in part the tax on improvements, which forms a part of the ordinary local general property tax. This involved simply a proposed change in the methods of raising the existing amount of public revenue. The other problem had to deal with the question of the best available method for an increase of the city's revenue.

On the question of untaxing buildings, various studies were initiated immediately on the organization of the Committee. One expert, Dr. Robert Murray Haig, Instructor in Economics in Columbia University, was entrusted with the responsible duty of making a thorough study of the experiments with the so-called single tax in Canada and in the few American cities where the plan has been tried.

Dr. Haig spent about three months in personally visiting most of these cities and in ascertaining at first hand the facts regarding the working of the experiment. The results of his investigations were embodied in a report which has been published by this Committee entitled: "The Exemption of Improvements from Taxation in Canada and the United States." This report contains not only a full account of the experiments but also much information regarding the conditions, financial, economic and social, affecting their operation.

Subsequently the Committee, with the assistance of the Department of Taxes and Assessments, collated a large quantity of data, taken principally from the assessment rolls of the City of New York, bearing on the probable effects in the City of New York of the exemption of improvements. Dr. Haig was employed to study and analyze this information. The results of these studies have been embodied in another report published by this Committee entitled: "Some Probable Effects of the Exemption of Improvements from Taxation in the City of New York."

After a year and a half of preliminary investigation and discussion, a series of public hearings on the proposal was held. A sub-committee, appointed for that purpose, prepared a list of questions, analyzing the problem in its various aspects and submitted them to a large number of individuals and organizations interested in the problem of the untaxing of buildings. Answers to these questions were received from several individuals and organizations and a number of briefs were filed with the Committee. The hearings took place on November 8th, 10th, 15th, 17th, 22nd and 24th. About 40 advocates and opponents of the plan were heard and ample opportunity was given for the discussion of all sides of the problem.

After the hearings, further discussion took place within the Committe itself on the proposal, the result of which is stated below. Appended hereto, in addition to the conclusions of the Committee and the reasons therefor, are the questions submitted, the answers and briefs received and the testimony taken at the hearings.

The question of new sources of revenue became acute, because of the financial situation arising in the Summer of 1914, shortly after the Committee was appointed. The Mayor communicated with the Committee directing its attention particularly to this situation, and asking it to make at the earliest possible date such recommendations as might be possible, looking toward an early increase of the city's financial resources.

The Committee, in response to this call, devoted its time during the Winter of 1914-1915 very largely to this problem.

In January, 1915, it tentatively recommended to the Mayor as possible means of raising the required revenue, an abilities tax, composed of a habitation tax, an occupation tax and a salaries tax, to be accompanied by an increment tax. These proposals are substantially the same as are discussed more fully below. Bills embodying these measures were prepared by the Committee and submitted to the Mayor and are appended to this report.

The attention of the Committee was in the early part of 1915 especially called by the Mayor to proposals then pending for a low rate tax on intangible or tangible personal property and for a municipal income tax. The Committee went further into studies on these subjects and called a number of experts into consultation. As a result of these conferences, the Committee, in April, 1915, tentatively reported against either of these proposals. Later the Committee took up the question of a state income tax. In this study it has enjoyed the valuable assistance of Professor Thomas S. Adams, of Cornell University.

Throughout its consideration of this subject, the Committee has been in conference with other bodies engaged in the same study. In February and March, 1915, it engaged in conferences with the Mayor, the Comptroller, the President of the Board of Aldermen, the Chamber of Commerce, the Merchants' Association, the City Club, the Allied Real Estate Interests, the Bureau of Municipal Research, and other organizations, to consider generally the financial problems before the City administration.

At the 1915 session of the Legislature, a Joint Legislative Committee on Taxation was appointed, of which Senator Ogden L. Mills is Chairman. The Committee on Taxation has been in frequent consultation with the Legislative Committee with a view to co-operation in the interest of the city as well as of the State.

Other phases of the problem of new sources of revenue considered by the Committee are referred to in the discussion on that subject, which follows this report.

In January, 1915, when the Committee made the tentative recommendations mentioned above regarding new sources of revenue, it also recommended the adoption of certain changes in the existing tax laws, which seemed to it calculated to simplify and improve their administration and, at the same time, moderately to increase the revenue. These recommendations are repeated below, and are more fully treated in a memorandum on administrative changes accompanying this report.

In addition to the two principal lines of inquiry mentioned above, the Committee has given its attention to a number of other topics. The subject of excess condemnation has become one of special practical interest in the City of New York, through the adoption, in 1913, of an amendment to the State Constitution legalizing that practice. The Committee undertook a study of this subject and secured from the National Municipal League an unpublished report on that subject, prepared for one of its committees two or three years ago by Herbert S. Swan, and which, with the assistance of the National Municipal League, was revised and brought up to date. It contains important information not generally accessible in regard to the use of excess condemnation in London and other English cities, and also a history of the development of the movement of excess condemnation in this country. Pending the deliberations of the Committee, the Legislature, in 1915, passed an act empowering the City of New York to exercise the power of excess condemnation. On May 20th, 1915, this Committee transmitted to the Mayor a report on this subject. This report, together with Mr. Swan's report mentioned above, the text of the New York City Excess Condemnation Act, and photographs and maps showing the operation of the system heretofore used in New York, have been published under the title of: "Excess Condemnation, A Report of the Committee on Taxation of the City of New York, With A Report Prepared by Herbert S. Swan for the National Municipal League."

Another subject to which the Committee has given consideration is that of the methods of paying for public improvements by assessments on property benefited. Dr. Haig, in the course of his investigations, mentioned above, secured valuable information as to the operation of the system in the cities visited by him. The Committee employed Mr. Mitchell P. Talmage to visit a number of other cities in the United States and obtain, at first hand, information as to the actual workings of the system. The Committee secured in this manner and through correspondence with other cities, as well as by consultation with officials in the various city departments in the City of New York, much valuable information. The time and attention required for the consideration of the great problems with which the Committee has principally been concerned, and the desirability of concluding the Committee's labors at an early day, have made it impossible for the Committee to carry its studies to the point of being able to make a definite report on this subject. The Committee believes that the question of raising additional revenue from special assessments is one of great importance and should be studied and reported upon with the aid of material already gathered by this Committee. This can, in the opinion of the Committee, best be done by the appointment of a smaller committee to report upon this subject.

Many other topics bearing on the general subject of taxation as affecting the City of New York have been brought to the Committee's attention and many helpful suggestions from various sources have been received by it, which the pressure of time and the practical requirements of the situation have made it impossible to report upon.

The Committee desires to express its appreciation of the assistance given it in its investigations by individuals and organizations so numerous that individual mention might appear invidious. The Committee is under special obligations to the Comptroller, to the Register of the County of New York, to the Department of Taxes and Assessments and to the Municipal Reference Library for assistance in securing information.

As a result of its deliberations, the Committee makes the following recommendations:

1. The Committee recommends against the adoption of the principle of untaxing buildings, gradually or otherwise.

2. The Committee recommends a state income tax as a partial means of securing the additional revenue required in the immediate future.

3. The Committee recommends that, in the event of the adoption of a state income tax not proving feasible, an abilities tax, composed of a habitation tax, an occupation tax and a salaries tax for the City of New York, be adopted as a partial means of securing the additional revenue required in the immediate future.

The adoption of either of the recommendations numbered 2 and 3 would, in the opinion of the Committee, require the abolition or superseding of the personal property tax as it exists at present as a part of the general property tax; a result which this Committee would regard as in every way highly desirable.

4. The Committee recommends against the adoption of a low rate tax on intangible or tangible personal property as a means of securing additional revenue required in the immediate future.

5. The Committee recommends the adoption of the principle of a tax upon the increments of land values as a partial means of securing the additional revenue required in the immediate future.

6. The Committee recommends against a supertax on land values as a means of raising the additional revenue required in the immediate future.

7. The Committee unanimously recommends the following changes in the existing tax laws as calculated to simplify and improve their administration, and at the same time moderately to increase the revenue:

(a). An amendment to Section 4, Subdivision 7, of the Tax Law by omitting the words: "or is in good faith contemplated" so that real property shall not be exempt when vacant, though owned by a charitable or other similar corporation.

(b). An amendment to Section 12 of the Tax Law, by omitting the provision for the deduction of surplus and the provision for the deduction of the assessed value instead of the actual value of real estate.

(c). An amendment to the Tax Law inserting a new section requiring the state board of tax commissioners to furnish the local assessors throughout that state with full particulars concerning the real property of public service corporations exclusive of their special franchise.

(d). The repeal of Section 48 of the Tax Law which provides for the deduction from a special franchise tax of the amount paid by the owner of the special franchise as rental for the franchise and any sums paid which are in the nature of taxes, such as car licenses, etc.

(e). An amendment to Section 204 of the Tax Law requiring the Secretary of State, who is now required to report to the State Comptroller certain details concerning all certificates of incorporation and amendments to such certificates filed with him, to send a duplicate report to the assessors of the town, city or village named in the certificate of incorporation, as the principal place of business of the corporation.

(An additional recommendation adopted by the Committee, for an amendment to Section 926 of the Greater New York Charter, changing the date for sending unpaid personal taxes to the Marshal for collection from January to the preceding August, was enacted into law by Chapter 600 of the Laws of 1915.)

8. The Committee unanimously recommends that the Mayor appoint a committee to report upon the question of raising additional revenue from special assessments and of possible improvements in the laws relating to special assessments.

There is great diversity of opinion among members of the Committee with respect to most of the foregoing recommendations. While each of them represents the views of a substantial majority of the Committee, those favoring one recommendation were, in several cases, not those voting in favor of another. The recommendations adopted by the Committee are, therefore, set forth above without discussion. Appended hereto is a separate statement with respect to each recommendation requiring any further discussion, signed by the majority favoring it, stating their reasons therefor, followed by a statement of the views of those members of the Committee who dissent or who concur only in part or with qualifications.

Respectfully submitted,

ALFRED E. MARLING,
Chairman.

STATEMENTS ACCOMPANYING REPORT.

PART ONE.

UNTAXING OF BUILDINGS.

Majority Report.

Your Committee believe that it would conduce to a clearer understanding of the problem if the arguments on both sides were presented in summary. If we characterize those who advocate the plan of untaxing of buildings as the affirmative, and those who are opposed to the untaxing of buildings as the negative, it may be convenient to discuss the arguments under four heads:

I. The alleged advantages of the scheme as advanced by the affirmative;

II. A rebuttal of these arguments by the negative;

III. The alleged disadvantages of the scheme, as propounded by the negative;

IV. A rebuttal of these arguments by the affirmative.

I. THE ALLEGED ADVANTAGES OF THE SCHEME AS ADVANCED BY THE AFFIRMATIVE.

The advocates of the scheme for the untaxing of buildings who appeared before the Committee may be divided into three classes: (1). The out-and-out single taxers who espouse the views of Henry George, and who consider private property in land to be an anachronism; (2). The social reformers who allege that taxation must be used primarily, or even incidentally, for social purposes, and who think that great social benefits would accrue from the change; (3). Those who, while not single taxers, believe that largely for fiscal reasons alone, there is some warrant for considering the propriety of the untaxing of buildings. Of the arguments herewith submitted, some would appeal to one of these three classes, and some to another. The arguments themselves have been urged with insistence before your Committee. They may be summed up under seven heads:

(1). Land is something entirely different from the products of labor. Land is a gift of nature; ordinary commodities are the product of human energy. Land values are entirely the creation of the community; all other values are labor values. Since land value is a social product or a community product, land rents should go to the community, or, at all events, all taxes should be derived, in the first place, from land. Houses, being products of labor should, therefore, be exempted from taxation. This exemption of houses from taxation will lead to an increased production of buildings, and this increased production of buildings will tend to increase wages and to diminish unemployment.

(2). Land is essentially a monopoly, since the supply of land available for building cannot be increased. Buildings, like all other products of labor, are subject to the influence of competition, and their value, therefore, will be limited to the cost of production. Since land is a monopoly, its price, like that of all monopolies, ought to be controlled by the government; and the best method of such control is through the agency of taxation. Buildings, being subject to the ordinary competitive law, do not need this control. Therefore, buildings should be exempted from taxation, while land alone should bear the burden.

The existing monopoly of land, both of acreage and of land value, in New York City, make the proposed change especially just and appropriate. There are, in New York, one hundred families who were the owners of record of land, assessed in 1915 for $473,808,075, approximately one-ninth of the total assessed value of land in the city. The assessed value of their improvements was only $157,515,235, or less than a third as much, while the value of the building of a small home owner is usually about three times as much as the value of his site.

It is estimated that eight hundred families are the owners of record of land assessed for about eight hundred millions, between one-fifth and one-sixth of the total assessed value of land; and that less than three thousand families own, directly or through real estate corporations which they control, approximately two-fifths of the assessed value of land in the city. Assuming even eight persons to a family, twenty-four thousand people, out of a population of five million three hundred thousand, own about two-fifths of the total assessed value of land in the city.

Most of these families acquired their land years ago for a small part of the present selling price. Almost every wealthy family in the city owning a mansion would pay more taxes under the proposed change. The Astor family alone are the owners of record of land assessed for nearly as much as the total land owned by nearly all of the smaller home owners of the city. Several families or corporations own from one hundred to several thousand lots in the outlying boroughs, which they are holding for high prices.

(3). Land speculation is one of the great evils of modern city life. People who buy land in order to keep it out of use until some future time when its value should be considerably enhanced are the real enemies of society. Their profits are exorbitant. They take for themselves what really belongs to the public, with the result of giving to our American cities that straggling appearance which is the despair of the reformer. Land speculation results in large tracts of land held out of use, and is one of the chief causes of high rents, and one of the chief reasons for the need of exorbitant sums for supplying rapid transit facilities.

Moreover, in the City of New York, the normal annual increase of land values is very great. During the past decade, for instance, land values have increased by over a thousand million dollars, while business in general is very poor. It is only fair that the chief beneficiaries of our economic system should be compelled to suffer the burden.

Increases in the selling price of land are a waste in the cost of production, irrespective of whether one land speculator loses what another gains, or whether it is a net clear acquisition of any one land speculator. The average annual increase in the selling price of land in New York has been for the last decade about $125,000,000. The total increase for the decade has been about $1,250,000,000. Calculating interest at five per cent., and net ground rent also at five per cent., this means an annual charge of $125,000,000 on a decade's increase in land values, to be paid by manufacturers, business men in general, tenants and home owners. This constitutes a dead weight fixed charge upon the workers of the city, of no use to any one except land speculators.

Gradually transferring taxes from buildings to land values, during a period of ten years, would prevent most of the speculative increase in the selling price of land, and would save the community this fixed but wasteful charge, which tends to increase the cost of living and interest rates, and to keep land out of use longer, thus restricting employment.

Speculation in land differs from speculation on the stock market. Speculation in land lays a burden in perpetuity upon the city; speculation on the Stock Exchange is a game in which only gamblers lose or gain. Those who complain of their heavy burdens on real estate ignore the fact that, while in 1880 real estate paid 87 per cent. of the taxes for the city, in 1913 real estate paid only 75 per cent.

(4). The untaxing of buildings will lead to the lowering of rents. More houses will be built, and the competition of these houses will bring down rents, not only in the outskirts, where the new houses are built, but in the city's slums and centers. These lower rents will apply not only to the tenants of residential apartments but to the tenants of commercial structures. In either case, there will be an economic saving, due to the lower rent. In the case of tenements, the lower rents will mean an increased surplus to be divided for general purposes, which will tend to increase wages and to lessen unemployment. In the case of lower rents for business purposes, it will make New York City more attractive to industrial ventures, and will, to the extent of lessening of taxes, increase the funds available for the payment of wages or the investment of capital, and thus contribute to general prosperity.

(5). The untaxing of buildings will tend to lessen congestion in the City of New York, either by the lowering of rents or by providing larger rooms and better accommodations at the same rental. The untaxing of buildings will tend to replace the dark and noisome rookeries by improved, light and airy dwellings; it will help to stamp out tuberculosis; it will better the physique and the morals of the whole population.

(6). The untaxing of buildings will lessen the tendency that is now seen in New York to the erection of tenement houses and flats. It will make it more profitable, and therefore more attractive, to intending owners of small homes in the suburbs to build their own homes, and will thus help to prevent the repetition in the outskirts of the city of the slum conditions in the center.

The change would save the smaller home owner of the city about $50 a year taxes on the average, and would only retard the rate of increase in the selling price of his land.

(7). Finally, apart from any of the above considerations, buildings ought to be exempted from taxation because the financial benefits of city expenditure accrue exclusively to the land owner. The building of a school house increases the value of the adjoining lands. The construction of a new subway creates or augments land values. Everything that is spent by the city ultimately accrues to the advantage of the land owner, and if there are any advantages at all that come from city expenditures to other members of the community, they have to pay for these advantages in the increased rent that they give to the owners of the real estate. For these reasons buildings should be exempted from taxation.

II. REBUTTAL OF THESE ARGUMENTS BY THE NEGATIVE.

On every one of these points opposing arguments are advanced, and either the benefits are alleged to be chimerical or the arguments are declared to be inconclusive. Let us take them up in order:

(1). As a general philosophy of economics and social life, it is denied that land is so entirely different from other kinds of wealth. It is true that land is a gift of Nature; but it is also true that a great part of the so-called products of labor are also gifts of Nature. The wood that goes into a table, the wool that goes into a suit, and the pearl that goes into a necklace, are all gifts of Nature. Furthermore, it is denied that we can, at all consistently, distinguish between land values as community-made values, and other values as man-made values. What gives value to everything is demand. Without demand no labor product would have any value whatever. If people spend their time in making things for which there is no demand, those things will have no value. The demand is as important and insistent in the case of labor values as it is in the case of land values. Again, in reply to the contention that values depend upon the relation between demand and supply, it is an error to state that the supply of land cannot be increased while the supply of other things can be increased. To all intents and purposes the supply of land can be increased. Assuming that there is sufficient demand, land will be taken from the outskirts, and turned into building sites. Finally, and above all, value in modern life comes not so much from the application of labor as from all sorts of relations and privileges. These speculative relations and actual privileges enter so importantly into all forms of modern income that it would be illegitimate to draw so hard and fast a line between land and other things.

(2). Land monopoly exists only in the imagination of the affirmative. As a matter of fact, land in the City of New York is not held out of use for any appreciable length of time. The vacant parcels in the Borough of Manhattan, for instance, apart from those used for coal or wood yards, and so forth, are so insignificant as to be entirely inappreciable. As a matter of fact, any attempt to hold land out of use would, under existing conditions of taxation in New York, be a losing venture. It is not denied that under other conditions vacant land is not assessed at all, or assessed at only a fraction of its value, and where the system of special assessments is not in vogue, this might become a serious problem. Even then the proper solution of the difficulty is by levying a special tax on vacant land. In the City of New York, however, such conditions are practically non-existent, as land is brought into use just as soon as it will pay the land owner to put up a building thereon. To speak of land monopoly is a great mistake. Moreover, it must be remembered that in the City of New York land, as a rule, changes hands frequently. In the City of Chicago it was shown by a recent investigation that each parcel of land changed hands on an average every twenty-seven years. There is no reason to believe that the average is far different in New York City. It is true that there are some large holdings of land by individuals, but the fortunes of even these large land-owners are insignificant to-day as compared with the fortunes of our capitalists, financiers, and captains of industry. While no careful statistical investigation has been made, it is fairly demonstrable that there are about 200,000 individual land owners in New York City. On the general assumption that the head of the family represents his wife and three children, and on the further assumption that the great majority of land-owners are married men, there would be one million people directly or indirectly owning land. Moreover, it was brought out in the testimony that by far the greater part of New York City lands is mortgaged, and that the quantity of real estate owned free and clear is exceedingly small. Since, therefore, the equity is slight, the owners of the mortgages are, to all intents and purposes, part owners of the land. Real estate mortgages in the City of New York are held to an overwhelming extent by savings banks, life insurance companies, and similar institutions, so that the real owners of the greater part of New York real estate are the depositors in savings banks and the policy-holders of the insurance companies. To speak of land monopoly in such a case, it is contended, is absurd.

(3). Speculation in land is not the bugaboo that has been made of it. Speculation in land is not essentially different from speculation on the Stock or the Produce Exchange. It is not denied that abuses exist in the one case as in the other; but, as every careful thinker knows, speculation is an essential element in all modern business enterprises. Without speculation, there would be far greater fluctuations in the prices of ordinary commodities. The speculative expert is the one who takes the risk for the community. The speculator in land is, therefore, just as legitimate and as necessary as the speculator in anything else. Moreover, two great misapprehensions should be removed. The first is the idea that land speculators, as a class, or land owners as a class, whether they speculate or not, make any more money than any other members of the community. We are often presented with the picture of the man who invests a certain sum in land and then travels and leaves the land alone for years or for decades, in order, finally, to reap the immense increment in its value, a value which, we are told, is produced by the community. As a matter of fact, if the same man, instead of putting his $10,000 into a piece of vacant land, had put it into the bank and allowed it to increase at compound interest, he would find that, at the end of a term of years, he would be better off than if he had invested the same amount of money in a piece of vacant land subject to increasing taxation and to all kinds of special assessments. The large profits of land owners and land dealers are fanciful. As a class, they do not earn any more than any other class in the community. During the past few years, in New York City, at least, they have earned far less than the other classes of the community. Speculative profits in land in New York City, as a social danger, are a myth.

The other misapprehension comes from a failure to understand the real function of the owner of real estate. In the City of New York, as in most American cities, the same man who owns land owns the building. Investments in real estate, therefore, constitute one of the productive industries of the United States, and, in many respects, the most important productive industry. In lieu of being a menace to, or a drag on, the community, the land owner—the land speculator, in the better sense of the term—is really one of the indispensable classes in the community. We must be careful to distinguish between the use and the abuse of a system. The Stock Exchange may have its abuses, but no sensible man would desire to do away with the Stock Exchange.

In answer to the contention that land values have increased during the past decade disproportionately to everything else, two points are made. In the first place, a large part of the so-called increase of land values is due to the arbitrary raising of assessed valuations which was resorted to during the years 1910-1911, in order to make possible a broader basis for addition to the city debt, required primarily by the new expenditure for subway construction and by other permanent improvements.

In the second place, it must be remembered that in not a few sections of the city the nominal increase in the value of the land which has been normally improved is due to improvements on the adjoining land, such as the Woolworth and other skyscrapers. In reality, the owner of the adjoining property which is already covered by the normal improvement, instead of enjoying a benefit from this ostensible increase in valuation suffers a detriment, and this detriment will continue, at all events, up to the time when the actual value of the land increases to such a point, making allowance for a proper amortization of the buildings, as to make it profitable to destroy the existing improvement. Finally, it must be remembered that a not inconsiderable part of the ostensible increase in land values has been offset by the accumulated taxes and by the payment of special assessments of all kinds that may have been levied upon the lands. It not infrequently happens that the burden suffered by special assessments is in itself made the basis for an increased valuation, and, therefore, an increased payment of taxes to the city.

Finally, the claim that in 1880 real estate paid 87 per cent. of the taxes for the city, while in 1913 real estate paid only 75 per cent., is specious. What has happened, as a matter of fact, is that a number of taxes have been added to the general property tax, thus reducing the proportion paid not only by real estate but by all property in general under the general property tax. As a matter of fact, in 1913, real estate paid a much larger percentage of the general property tax than it did in 1880, and entirely apart from percentages the actual burden of real estate has increased enormously. Not only have the tax rates themselves increased very greatly, but assessed valuations have been raised from 60 per cent. or 70 per cent. to 100 per cent., so that there can be no question about the very much greater burden upon real estate at present as compared with that of a generation ago.

(4). In answer to the contention that rents will be lowered as the result of the untaxing of buildings, it is pointed out that while it is true that the incidence of a tax on buildings is different from the incidence of a tax on land, it does not follow that in actual life rents would really be lowered. Entirely apart from the argument to which attention will be directed below, showing that there would be countervailing forces tending to more than over-balance the influence of the remission of taxes, it is argued that in actual life we must consider the influence of friction. In many portions of New York City, for instance, it has been pointed out that the rate of taxation has been going up for the past five or ten years, but that there has been in those quarters no increase of rent. If an increase of taxation has so slight an influence on the rent, why should a remission of taxation have any greater influence? Far more important than any change in the rate of taxation are the other economic factors involved, such as general conditions of industry, rapid transit, et cetera. Even if it be conceded that, in the long run, lower taxes on houses might lead to lower rents, the results would be slow in showing themselves, and the changes would be far less than are imagined. Again, it must be remembered that there are countervailing influences at work in preventing a decrease of rents. One of the most important facts here is that house owners in New York City count upon a future normal appreciation of land values to make good the inevitable deterioration in the value of the building; in other words, the expected growth in land values takes the place of a deterioration fund or amortization fund for the house. If, now, by a change in the methods of taxation, this virtual amortization fund disappears, it will be necessary to put into operation an actual amortization fund. This, however, will pro tanto increase the carrying charges of the building and will tend to augment rather than reduce the cost. So far as this point is concerned, therefore, the tendency of rents would be to increase rather than to decrease.

Moreover, the benefits, so far as the question of wages and employment are concerned, are entirely exaggerated. Wages and rents move along together. It is absurd to claim that since all wealth is divided into rent, wages and interest, if more goes to the payment of rent less will be available for wages and interest. This may be true of a hypothetical static condition; that is, where there is a given sum to be divided; but it is not true of actual life, which is a dynamic condition and which continually changes. If rents rise because of greater population and greater prosperity, it is just as likely that wages will rise at the same time, because of the greater prosperity and the greater demand for the products of industry. The only correlation between rents and wages that is at all sure is that if rents go up, wages must go up also. The scale of wages and professional earnings is far higher in the City of New York than in the small neighboring towns, and the difference is very largely measured by the difference in house rents. If, therefore, rents were to fall in New York as the result of the untaxing of buildings, it is probable that wages would also fall. The untaxing of buildings would, therefore, not benefit wages.

Again, there is no truth in the contention that the untaxing of buildings will lead to greater employment. It may be true, it is conceded, that the immediate result of the untaxing of buildings might lead to an overbuilding of the city; but as soon as the first impetus had spent itself after a year or two, and a new equilibrium had been reached, there would be only the normal increase in building due to the normal increase in population, which would come with or without the change in building operations. There would, therefore, be no continuous tendency to more employment.

Moreover, there is a fallacy in the argument that the savings of the merchant and manufacturer in his store or factory, assuming that rents would fall, would lead to more employment. The surplus, it is true, would now go into the hands of the merchant or manufacturer instead of into the hands of the land owner; but in the one case, as in the other, the surplus would either be spent unproductively in riotous living, which would give little or no employment to labor, or it would be turned into the bank and then invested in some productive enterprise. For the purposes of the community, it is immaterial whether this capital is productively employed through the medium of the land owner, or through the medium of the merchant or manufacturer. In every case it is an addition to social capital.

Thus, it is a gross economic fallacy to argue that the untaxing of buildings would be of any benefit to the laborer in the way of greater employment. It is the old fallacy of Henry George, which has not been accepted by any modern economist of repute.

(5). With reference to the argument as to congestion, it is replied that the affirmative regards only one kind of congestion, the congestion of population per room. The other kind of congestion is the congestion of population per acre. Whatever good results might ensue from diminishing congestion of the first kind would be more than outweighed by the congestion of the second kind. It is indubitable, for instance, that the untaxing of buildings will lead to a more intensive use of the land, simply because it will pay better to economize in the use of the land. The results will be, without any doubt, that all vacant land, so far as there is any, will tend to be covered with buildings, and that there will also be a tendency to replace all low two- or three-story structures by skyscrapers in tthe business districts, and by lofty tenements in the slums. In so far as this will lead to the destruction of some of the poor and outworn tenements, it may be conceded that this is a good thing. But the benefits of this are far more than overbalanced by the conversion of whole sections of comparatively low buildings into sections of high and densely-populated structures. The congestion per acre would be enormously increased and all the dangers to life and safety which would be removed in one way would be reintroduced in another.

The affirmative argues that all this might be prevented by proper laws limiting the height of buildings and by proper zoning systems. The attempt, however, to carry out this scheme, if made at all, ought to be made after and not before these laws are passed. To permit the untaxing of buildings now and to hope that the other laws will come subsequently is a very naive argument. We must consider the proposition on its merits. If it is true that the untaxing of buildings will of itself increase congestion of the second kind, the argument of the affirmative is pro tanto weakened.

(6). The alleged advantage to the small householder is largely illusory. Almost all improvements in New York City are made through mortgage loans. The decrease in the capital value of land, due to the increased rate of taxation on land, will so impair the security for loans that either the rate of interest will rise or a smaller percentage of the capital will be loaned at the same rate of interest, since it is customary in this city to increase the rate of interest on loans with the proportion of the loan to the real value of the property. In either case, there will be an increased expense to the intending home-builder, which will tend to offset whatever advantage might accrue to him from the decrease in taxes.

In the second place, the point is made that just as in the country at large it is the expected increment in land values which was chiefly responsible for the settlement of the West by individual farmers, who sold out and moved on whenever the value of their farms reached a certain figure, so it is the anticipated increase in the value of the land that forms the greatest inducement to intending home-builders. When a man builds a house of his own and borrows most of the capital necessary, he hopes that, while in the course of time the value of the house will depreciate, the value of the land will appreciate to a much greater extent, so that when land values have gone up to a certain point, he can then sell out and, by reason of his profits on the land transaction, pay off his mortgage and come out clear. Even if, as a matter of fact, many small home owners do not sell out under these conditions, it remains none the less true that the knowledge that the capital value of their investment has risen prompts them to bear with greater ease and equanimity the annual burden of the mortgage debt. If, now, we take away from the intending house-builder this expectation of being able ultimately to finance his building operations without difficulty, we manifestly decrease the inducement to build.

Combining these two points, the increased interest rate and the removal of the anticipated increase in land value, we have a very decided obstacle to building small homes. This obstacle will more than outweigh the advantage both of the remission of taxes and of the decrease in the cost of the land. The net result of all these factors will be the decrease and not the increase in the inducement to build small homes.

(7). Finally, the argument that the benefits of city expenditure accrue exclusively to the land owner is completely false. Most of the city expenditures redound to the benefit of the community as a whole. The expenditures for fire protection redound to the benefit of people who own houses and to people who live in structures; the benefit of the police is to protect every property owner, whether his property consists in land or in personal property, from theft, and to protect every individual, whether he owns any property or not, from violation; the benefit of the courts is to dispense even justice between individuals, whether or not they are land owners; the benefit of the school system is to give advantages primarily to the children of the poor; the benefit of the city departments of Charities and Corrections goes to the weak and the suffering; the benefit of the city hospitals accrues to every one, whether or not he owns land; the benefit of the subways goes to every one who uses the subways, and especially in the case of the large mass of wage-earners increases opportunities for work. In short, even from the narrow point of view of monetary compensation, it may be said that the expenditures of a great metropolis like New York result in increased opportunities for gain. Laborers, merchants and manufacturers would not flock to New York unless they made more money here than they would elsewhere.

It is not denied, of course, that with increasing prosperity there comes an increase of land values. But it is denied that the land owners are the only beneficiaries. It is true, indeed, that the value of property does not normally increase as land values do, but it should not be forgotten that the opportunities for increased income grow in about the same proportion as the increase in land values. The greater the city, the higher the wages; the greater the city, the higher the profits of the merchants and manufacturers, and the greater the income of the salaried and professional classes. It is contended by the affirmative that even though some benefits accrue to the public at large, these benefits are swallowed up in the higher rentals paid to the land owners. To this there is a double answer: First, it is not true that the benefits to the community are swallowed up in higher rents. Rents indeed are higher, but unless there was a growing surplus or margin over and above these higher rents, there would be no inducement for merchants, manufacturers, professional classes, or even laborers to congregate in New York. The very fact of the gradual increase of population shows that there is a margin or surplus over and above the increase of rents.

Secondly, even assuming that the foregoing is not true, there is no reason why the burdens of taxation should be put exclusively on the land owners; for then, even according to the arguments of the affirmative themselves, the community at large, such as merchants, manufacturers, professional classes and laborers would receive a benefit from city expenditures, but would pay nothing at all, even in the rentals, since buildings would be untaxed. That is to say, the community at large would have a double exemption; they would pay no direct taxes of any kind to the city, nor would they pay any taxes indirectly to the land owners, since it is conceded by the affirmative that a tax on land values would not be shifted to the tenant. The net result, then, would be that all the expenses of the city would be borne by the land owner alone, although a large part of the benefits would accrue to other classes as well.

We have now considered the arguments advanced by the affirmative, and the rebuttal of these arguments by the negative. We now proceed to consider the alleged positive disadvantages of the scheme advanced by the negative, and shall then discuss the rebuttal of these arguments advanced by the affirmative.

III. DISADVANTAGES OF THE SCHEME AS SET FORTH BY THE NEGATIVE.

(1). The first point made by the negative is the so-called confiscation-of-property argument. It is pointed out that under our laws, as they have existed, people have been encouraged to invest in land as well as in other things. What possible reason is there for the government now to step in and, by utilizing the engine of taxation, to take away from present owners a part of their property? Here is a man who has worked hard for years, gotten together the sum of, say, ten thousand dollars, and invested it in a piece of real estate, where the improvements, as frequently happens, are worth far less than the land. He works hard, perhaps, in managing his piece of property and in keeping the building in good condition and in looking after the continually changing tenants. Here is another man who has inherited ten thousand dollars from his father, or has made ten thousand dollars by a lucky plunge in Wall Street, and who buys corporate stock, or deposits his cash in a bank, and runs off to Europe to have a good time. The land owner finds, as a result of the untaxing of buildings, that the value of his property falls to eight thousand dollars. He loses not only a fifth of his capital invested, but must pay more money out every year in taxes. The successful stock speculator enjoys in perpetuity the full amount of his property and, perhaps, pays no taxes at all. This is a travesty of justice. It is an unendurable utilization of governmental powers, and results in practical confiscation. Several of the witnesses who appeared before the Committee, who were owners of vacant land, have testified how anxious they were to improve the property, and how impossible it was for them to secure the large loans needed for this purpose under the circumstances. They have called our attention to the fact that the change contemplated would simply wipe them out. Owners of more modest houses in the Borough of Manhattan, on both the east and west sides, have claimed that, as a result of the untaxing of buildings, they would be unable to keep their heads above water, and that they would have to sell out at a great loss.

It has been contended that a large part of the two hundred thousand owners of real estate, representing about a million of the population in New York City, are in a condition where the value of the land considerably exceeds the value of the structures. In all such cases, and they are far more numerous than is supposed by those who think simply of the Astor Estate, the result would be disastrous. This objection would only be slightly weakened by the proposition to decrease the rate on buildings gradually for a term of years. This would be like pulling a man's teeth out one by one instead of pulling them all out together. The net result in the end would be equally unfortunate.

The exemption of buildings is defensible only on the theory that property in land is unjust, and that all land ought to be confiscated by the government. Only an infinitesimal number of people in the City of New York, less than one-hundredth of one per cent., hold any such opinion. How absurd, then, to make such a change in the fundamental principles of the city tax policy in order to satisfy the misguided demands of a minute fraction of the population.

(2). The immediate result of the adoption of the scheme would be a great real estate panic. It would lead to the instant stoppage of the loan of mortgage funds by the great investing companies, and would produce such an apprehension that there would be a calling in at once of all existing loans. This would mean a wiping out of all existing equities, and would lead, under actual conditions in New York, to an unheard-of disaster. All panics are psychological in character, and are often the result of unreasoning fear. Whether or not the actual contemplated injury to property would ensue is immaterial. The apprehension or the fear of such injury, either at once or in the future, would be enough to bring about the panic. This apprehended injury, moreover, would not be confined to the idea of any immediately-added burdens, but would consist to a large extent of the apprehension that the present project was simply an entering wedge for a much more complete scheme of confiscation of land values for the benefit of the community.

(3). Entirely apart from the question of confiscation of property, the scheme would lead to an undue and unjust burden on all property owners where land values were greater than building values. Under existing conditions in New York, immense sums of money are invested by people of small means in modest shares of real estate parcels. It is unjust to add to the existing burdens on real estate. Real estate, as a business, is in a most depressed condition in New York. To increase the burdens at this time would be suicidal policy.

(4). The untaxing of buildings would tend to increase the city expenses, as it would increase the congestion per acre. Immense sums would have to be expended for breathing spaces and city parks; streets would have to be widened to permit of the increased traffic; fire hazards would be augmented, and in every way the difficulties in the cost of municipal administration would be increased.

(5). The general financial condition of the city would also be rendered more difficult. It is an acknowledged maxim of taxation never to narrow the base in the face of an anticipated increase in the amount to be levied. Under actual fiscal conditions in New York, there is great need of increased revenue, yet the proposition is to reduce the base in the face of this needed increase. The Constitution provides that the amount to be raised by taxation, exclusive of debt service, shall not exceed two per cent. on the value of the property. The contention of the affirmative that the assessed value of the property will remain the same, notwithstanding that, as is proposed, the rate on buildings should be reduced to one per cent. of the rate on land, is erroneous. As a legal proposition, it is clear that if the tax rate on buildings is reduced so as to be only one-hundredth of the rate on land, the courts will undoubtedly hold that, for the purposes of this constitutional provision, either the assessed or the selling value of the buildings should be estimated as only one-hundredth part of their real value.

(6). A similar argument is advanced with reference to the city debt, which, by the Constitution, is limited to ten per cent. of the assessed valuation of real estate. Here, however, the argument is even stronger than in the preceding cases. If, as is conceded, the higher tax rate on land will lead to a diminution in the value of the land, the margin for future debt will be wiped out, and there may even be an impairment in the city credit owing to a lessening of the underlying security for the present debt. To make such needless experiments with the city finances is reprehensible in the extreme.

IV. REBUTTAL OF THESE ARGUMENTS BY THE AFFIRMATIVE.

(1). The affirmative contends that there is nothing in the confiscation argument. The cry of confiscation has been raised whenever any improvement in the condition of the working classes is suggested, from tenement house laws to the abolition of child labor. The more extreme advocates of the scheme go so far as to say that all land owners are thieves, and that they ought to be well content to get off with only a slight loss; for, in reality, the community ought to take back all of their ill-gotten gains. The process must be considered not as confiscation but as a resumption by the community of what has been taken by extortion.

The less extreme advocates of the scheme do not characterize land ownership as robbery, but contend, nevertheless, that there is really no confiscation. They concede that the value of the land may be diminished, but they say that there is no divine right guaranteeing the owner forever in his property. They call attention to the fact that a sudden change in the tariff or in the system of internal revenue taxes may, under certain circumstances, bring about a loss to the owner of certain kinds of goods or property, and we do not recognize this as an essential injustice.

Still another class of advocates of the scheme concede that there will be a loss and deplore this loss in the case of what they confess to be innocent holders; but, say they, in any great change we must always weigh the good against the evil. If, as they claim, the adoption of the scheme would lead to very great social benefits, the property loss to owners of land, while regrettable, must not be deemed sufficiently important to interfere with the greater good to be accomplished.

Finally, still another class of the advocates of the scheme think that there will be no loss to property owners at all, because, in their opinion, land values will really increase rather than decrease, owing to the greater demand for land which will come from the increase in building, and from the additional incentive to the gross population.

The assertion that there is no general interest in the subject is belied by the fact that over 40,000 voters in the City of New York have asked for a referendum on the question.

(2). With reference to the alleged panic, this is a mere figment of the imagination. The affirmative rely especially on the opinion of the head of a large loaning company, and upon a certain other gentleman connected with a savings and loan association. They quote the testimony of these two gentlemen, to which they attach more importance than to all the other real estate experts who testified. Their argument, in short, is that as more houses would be built, it would be to the interest of the lenders, through pressure of competition, to supply funds for the same, while money, now sunk in speculative increases in the selling price of land, will be available for buildings.

(3). The argument as to the injustice of increased expense to the owner is sought to be rebutted by the affirmative by the statement that an increase of expense is only the fair return for what will sooner or later be an increase of revenue.

(4). The argument that the expenses of the city will be increased is denied. It is conceded that more money may have to be spent for parks, etc., but it is claimed that there will be a saving in expense by a more compact city, which will, among other things, diminish the need of very expensive subways, etc.

(5). The argument as to the constitutional dangers in taxation is sought to be met in a double way. In the first place, we ought not to be prevented from accepting the change because of constitutional doubts. If the change is a good one, the Constitution can easily be altered. In the second place, the legal argument is incorrect, and no matter what the rate of taxation is, as long as the assessed values are not changed, the fiscal conditions are not altered.

(6). As to the debt, several points are made in rebuttal. In the first place, it is held that it is a good thing to put obstacles to the creation of further debt. It is claimed that the huge debt that has already been piled up is utterly unnecessary, and even if necessary it has been contracted for the sole benefit of the land owners, therefore, it is held that either we should stop short in adding to the debt, or that we should make the land owners pay for it. In the second place, others who take a slightly different view of the debt and the city credit, contend that we must not be deterred by the constitutional provision, but that contemporaneously with the change proposed, we must seek to secure an amendment to the Constitution.

It is contended by others, finally, that no change in the Constitution is needed, and that notwithstanding the diminution of the value of the land, the enormous increase in land values to be expected from a growth of the population would give the city all the leeway that is needed, and that, therefore, no impairment of the credit is to be expected.

CONCLUSIONS OF THE COMMITTEE.

Your Committee have carefully weighed all of the above arguments and counter arguments. Three conclusions have been forced upon us: (1) The complexity of the situation is apparent. As regards each particular point, the arguments both for and against have been very vigorously presented and in not a few cases the issue of fact or probability seems to be in more or less doubt. (2) Many of the arguments on each side are inconclusive and are destroyed by opposing arguments on the same side. (3) Many of the arguments, as to both the advantages and the disadvantages of the scheme, have obviously been exaggerated by each side. As in almost every controverted question, where much bitterness has been engendered, it is important to estimate both the benefits and the dangers that are advanced.

Another point that ought to be disposed of at once is the appeal by both sides to the experience of Canadian or American towns that have tentatively made the experiment. On this phase of the subject, the Committee concur with the conclusions of its expert, Dr. R. H. Haig, who has made a thorough study of these experiments. Dr. Haig sums up the Canadian experience as follows:

"It has been customary to think of Western Canada as a region where single tax measures have been uniformly and conspicuously successful. Such is not the case. In some places the measures have been conspicuously unsuccessful from practically every point of view. * * * In some places the plan has worked well; in other places it has worked poorly. In particular cities it has given satisfaction at one time, and dissatisfaction at another."

Dr. Haig tells us again that even in those cases "where the system was successfully introduced, land values were increasing enormously," but that with the stoppage of the boom the situation changed entirely. He tells us again that "the Canadian experiments have been confined to young cities," and that "the Canadian experience offers no evidence as to what the effect may be where land values are increasing unevenly, or where the margin between loans and securities is narrow." He says, furthermore, that the system is, even "under favorable circumstances, neither a plague nor a panacea." While he concedes that "certain definite and desirable social ends can be gained through its adoption," and that they "may be gained, under certain conditions, without an appreciable burden upon property owners," he also writes: "These conditions were present when the transition was made in the cities of Western Canada. They were not present when the change was made in the Alberta towns. These conditions do not obtain to-day in New York

City." Again, as regards the American experiment, Dr. Haig's conclusion is, after careful investigation, "that there is little basis for drawing conclusions either in favor of or in opposition to the plan of exempting buildings from taxation." Finally, as to the situation in Pittsburgh and in Scranton, Pennsylvania, owing to the fact that the gradual exemption of buildings was only a very incidental feature in the great reform of abolishing the old classification scheme, Dr. Haig calls attention to "the hopelessness of expecting clear-cut immediate results under these circumstances."

In considering the evidence that has been submitted to the Committee, both in writing and at the public hearings, the Committee have been impressed by the following facts: The witnesses may be divided into five classes, viz., the single taxers, the real estate dealers and the loaning interests, the representatives of the laboring classes, the owners of small parcels of real estate, and scholars and publicists.

The single taxers, as was to be expected, were all in favor of the scheme as a matter of general principle. The real estate dealers and the experts in the loaning interest were all, with a single exception, opposed to the scheme because of the anticipated dangers, and there was one other prominent expert who, although not inimical to the proposition as a matter of theory, declared himself opposed to the scheme as a practical proposition at present. The representatives of the labor interest were in favor of the scheme because of their belief that it would lead to lower rents and more employment. The more modest owners of property were divided; that is, those who were owners in the suburbs, where land values are still less than building values, were in favor of the scheme. Those in other parts of the city, and especially in the Borough of Manhattan, where land values are greater than building values, were opposed to the scheme. Finally, while the scholars and publicists, who might be supposed to take an impartial attitude, were divided in their judgment, the preponderance of opinion was opposed to the scheme, either as a matter of general principle or as a matter of immediate application.

As a final result of a careful weighing of all the evidence in the case your Committee have come to the following conclusions:

We believe, in the first place, that both the advantages and dangers of the scheme have been exaggerated by each side. We believe that there still remain, as a matter of principle, certain advantages as well as certain disadvantages. We think it entirely possible that there may be a temporary decrease of rents. We believe, however, that the extent of this decrease has been grossly overestimated. Moreover, we think that even if there should be a tendency to a permanent decrease of rents, it is not at all improbable that the result of decreased rents will be in the direction of lower wages. We also believe that there will not be any substantial final difference in the demand for labor.

On the other hand, we cannot but be sensible of the disadvantages of the scheme, both as a general proposition and in its practical application to the City of New York. We think that it has been clearly proved that the tendency of the scheme would be to a more intensive use of land and that, therefore, it would be out of the question to adopt the scheme without first enacting laws to regulate the height of buildings and to provide for a proper zoning system. Without such preliminary measures the scheme would not be defensible, even as a general proposition. In the second place, while we think that the financial dangers have been somewhat exaggerated, we believe that it would also be prudent to provide for a change in the constitutional provisions affecting the tax rate and the debt limit before we could even think of recommending the scheme in general.

Apart from these general doubts as to the advisability of the scheme, there are particular circumstances in the City of New York which afford ground for serious hesitation. New York is the greatest metropolis of the New World, and is probably destined soon to be the greatest metropolis of the entire world. Business operations of the greatest delicacy and the greatest magnitude are common. The complexity of property interests is enormous and the conditions of landholding differ from borough to borough and almost from street to street within the same borough. In our opinion, the probable result of the contemplated change would be to benefit some property owners and to injure other property owners. After careful investigation, our expert, Dr. Haig, has pointed out that, while the anticipated benefits to the home owners in the outlying boroughs might be very slow of realization, there is no doubt as to the effect of the change on the magnitude of taxes payable by the owners of the single-family dwellings in Manhattan, and that it would lead to a depressing influence upon land values. It has, moreover, been proved to our satisfaction that, in the Borough of Manhattan, at least, the burden would be relatively heavier upon the owners of the less expensive parcels of real estate, and that in a not inconsiderable number of cases the actual diminution of value to the owners of property would be considerable.

This is, in our mind, the chief consideration that impels us to doubt the wisdom of the contemplated change. Even if the anticipated benefits of the scheme were to be immediate and unquestioned, it would still be doubtful, in our opinion, whether these benefits on the one hand would not be outweighed by the added burdens on the other. But where, as is undoubtedly the case here, the benefits of the scheme have been much exaggerated and would be slow in coming; where, in other words, the extent of the benefits is questionable, and the fact that the added burdens to certain classes is unquestionable, the conclusion in our minds is irresistible. It would, in our opinion, be neither fair nor wise to cause the owners of real estate, and especially the owners of the more modest parcels of real estate, to suffer diminution in the amount of their invested capital because of vague and uncertain benefits to other classes that might ultimately be expected. As in every practical problem of statesmanship, the losses and the gains must be weighed against each other. In the opinion of this Committee, the losses to the community as a whole, under existing economic conditions in New York City, would outweigh any probable gains. We have, therefore, come to the conclusion that it would be unwise in the City of New York to exempt buildings from taxation.

ALFRED E. MARLING,
EDWIN R. A. SELIGMAN,
FRANK HARVEY FIELD,
JOSEPH N. FRANCOLINI,
JOHN J. HALLERAN,
JEREMIAH W. JENKS,
ARDOLPH L. KLINE,
WALTER LINDNER,
CYRUS C. MILLER,
GEO. V. MULLAN,
DAVID RUMSEY,
OSCAR R. SEITZ,
ROBERT E. SIMON,
CHARLES T. WHITE,
COLLIN H. WOODWARD.

UNTAXING OF BUILDINGS.

Concurring Memorandum by Messrs. Pink and Holt.

The theory of untaxing buildings is logical and right. Many who believe in the principle view the practical application of the plan here with grave apprehension.

The chief arguments for the untaxing of buildings are the social benefits that would accrue; cheaper rents, encouragement to ownership of small homes, participation by the community in the values created by the community.

On the other hand, it is not denied that the property of many would be confiscated, and that the change would take money out of the pockets of owners of unimproved and underimproved land and put it into the pockets of those whose property is highly developed.

Most real estate owners are to-day facing a loss, and the introduction of this change in taxation would still further discourage owners of vacant and underimproved property, reduce values and result in considerable decrease in the city revenue. The city has so lavished its credit on subways and water supply that a huge bonded indebtedness confronts us, and to decrease taxable values and contract the base of taxation would be foolhardy.

But cannot the social benefits of the plan be largely realized without confiscating the property of innocent people and placing the city in a precarious situation?

The increment tax will take from those who are able to pay and will bring back to the city part of the value the people create.

Exemption of the first $2,000 from taxation in the case of one- and two-family detached or semi-detached houses will encourage the building of workingmen's homes and home ownership. It will tend to bring to market land now idle but within the reach of transit and public improvements.

If we remove the tax on all buildings we encourage congestion in thickly-populated districts where high land values prevail. If we remove or lessen the tax on a specific kind of building, we encourage that form only. Is it necessary to apply a general formula which admittedly will do harm as well as good when we can, by specific applications of the remedy, accomplish what is desirable, escape confiscation, and avoid congestion?

If we desire to encourage industries to locate here and the building of factories, we should rebate a percentage of the tax on new factory buildings.

The entire population of New York can be accommodated in one-family houses within its present borders and much vacant land will be left for the millions to come. It is imperative that, so far as possible, we give the workers an opportunity to live in homes instead of four-story tenements, our children the run of the yards and fields instead of the paved court and crowded street.

Abroad it is considered good business for government to provide fit housing for the toiler and the day is not far off when America must give serious consideration to this problem.

In Belgium, workmen's dwellings are exempt from a number of the local taxes, and societies whose object is the erection of such homes are not compelled to pay stamp duties or registration fees.

France gives partial exemption to workingmen's dwellings, and substantial encouragement to building and loan associations.

In Germany, the taxes differ greatly in the various governmental divisions, but the policy of granting some encouragement to owners of small homes has been generally adopted. Many cities, among which Ulm is notable, build artisans' dwellings and sell and rent them at cost.

Hungary exempts from state taxes company houses complying with the sanitary laws, rented or sold to workingmen on easy instalments. An allowance is also made from municipal and communal taxes.

Massachusetts has recently adopted an amendment to the Constitution, authorizing cities and towns to acquire land, improve it, and sell the buildings for the purpose of relieving congestion and providing homes for workers. It is provided, however, that the State shall not sell the land and buildings at less than cost.

CONCLUSION.

We are agreed with the minority that, theoretically, the exemption of improvements from taxation is desirable. We hold with the majority that it would be inadvisable to alter radically the base of taxation on real property in the City of New York at the present time. We favor strongly an increment tax on land values, to go into effect as soon as possible, and the exemption of the first $2,000 of the cost of one- and two-family houses, detached or semi-detached.

We believe that the partial exemption of new factory buildings from taxation should receive serious consideration.

If the exemptions prove socially beneficial, the City will be in position to make further experiments in the direction of untaxing improvements.

LOUIS HEATON PINK,
HAMILTON HOLT.

UNTAXING OF BUILDINGS.

Minority Report.

The undersigned dissent from the conclusions of the majority as to the untaxing of buildings, and regard the summary of the arguments, pro and con, contained in the majority report as incomplete and inadequate. Although the burden of proof rested upon the affirmative, less than one-third of the space devoted to the summary is taken up with the elaboration of the arguments in favor of the proposition and in rebuttal of the arguments against it. The Committee was at work for eighteen months collecting data on this subject, but the subsequent time devoted to a study of this data and to a consideration of the many intricate issues involved was altogether too short to enable the Committee as a whole to reach definite conclusions based on the evidence before us.

In order that the case of those who favor the untaxing of buildings may be fairly and fully presented, it will be necessary for us to restate the arguments. The question at issue is not altogether a new, and by no means a local, one. A man does not have to live in New York in 1915 to think of this question: "When I make an improvement, why should the city fine me for doing it?" or this other question: "If my land gets to be worth a great deal more by reason of the growth and activity of the community, why should not the city take a larger share of the increment, instead of levying taxes on buildings and other products of individual industry?" All the world is thinking about these questions, and in many parts of the world action is being taken more or less similar to that proposed here. The cities and provinces of Western Canada have exempted buildings from taxation with the results set forth in part in Dr. Haig's admirable report on "The Exemption of Improvements from Taxation in Canada and the United States." Bulletin 158 of the United States Department of Labor, in discussing "Government Aid to Home Owning and Housing of the Working People in Foreign Countries," shows that the production of workingmen's homes is encouraged either through direct exemption in whole or in part from taxation or through the levy of a special tax on unused building sites or on the increment of land values in Austria, Germany, Hungary, Italy, Switzerland, Belgium, France, Roumania and Chili.

In England, the Land Enquiry Committee, appointed by the Chancellor of the Exchequer, reporting in 1914, stated, among its conclusions, that:

"Owing to the inclusion of the value of buildings and other improvements in the basis of assessment, the present rating system hampers industry in general and agriculture in particular.

"In towns the discouragement of improvements is felt most by small tradesmen and others who work on a small margin of profit.

"Both in urban and in rural areas the rating of buildings is an obstacle in the way of providing good working class houses at reasonable rent.

"The total or partial exemption of buildings and other improvements from rates would stimulate the development of industry and agriculture and encourage the provision of working class houses.

"All future increases in local expenditure that are chargeable on the rates should be met by a rate upon site values."

Prof. Thomas Nixon Carver, the celebrated Harvard economist, in his new book, "Essays on Social Justice," issued in 1915, in concluding his discussion on the subject, says:

"Because a considerable extension of the land tax would tend to force into productive use a certain amount of land which is now held out of use for speculative purposes; because it would tend to relieve active production from the repressive burdens of taxation, and because it would tend to cut off the incomes which now support capable men in idleness, thus forcing a certain amount of talent into action, we must conclude that an extension of the land tax would work well for the nation."

Moreover, Dr. Haig, this Committee's expert, whose conclusions are quoted at some length and relied upon by the majority, in his oral testimony stated unequivocally that he believes the tendency of the scheme to untax buildings on the whole to be *in the right direction,* and in his report on its application to New York conditions said that *"the change promises ultimate benefits of considerable importance to all tenants and to many of the home owners in the outlying boroughs."*

The general principle involved in the partial or complete exemption of buildings from taxation is supported by its advocates on grounds both of justice and of expediency. These grounds may be summarized as follows:

ARGUMENTS FOR UNTAXING BUILDINGS BASED ON JUSTICE.

1. Land, in the broad sense of the term, is different from all other species of property. Its situs is fixed. It can neither come nor go. It is neither made nor destroyed. Its quantity cannot be either increased or decreased by use or by human effort. Its value, for city purposes at least, is wholly dependent upon advantages of location with reference to the needs and uses of population. As people come to a particular spot and invest labor and capital there, the value of the land is created and increased by community effort and community use. Even the birth of a child or the advent of a stranger or an immigrant, by increasing the business of the community, adds to the value of the land. While it may be said that land values are created by labor, by investment and by human activity generally, it is clear that in their creation human efforts and activities are so intermingled as to make these values a community product. The increment of land value created by the presence or activity of the individual may be regarded as his indivisible but inalienable share in the community wealth. The rental value of the land is the income from this common fund and should be devoted, as far as may be required, to the payment of necessary community expenses. Until this income is completely used up, it is both prodigal and unjust to let it be appropriated by private individuals while the community expenses are met in part by the levy of oppressive taxes upon buildings which are the direct product of individual labor and investment and which are the direct instruments of industry and social activity.

2. Not only are land values created by the general activities of the people, but they are especially the product of governmental expenditures Every dollar wisely spent by the city government either increases land values or prevents their fall. This fact is recognized in the case of ordinary street improvements, which are paid for in whole or in part by special assessments upon the property directly benefited. This principle is almost universally recognized in America, but in some cities it is more widely applied than in New York. Special assessments are frequently used for the acquisition and development of park systems and, in some cases, for the extension of water mains. In New York, a few years ago, the Rapid Transit Law was amended to make possible the use of special assessments for the construction of rapid transit lines, but the jealousies of the different sections of the city and the fact that some lines had already been built out of the general funds prevented the use of this plan in connection with the tremendous system of rapid transit development now under way. But everybody knows that this public improvement will add immensely to the value of lands situated in many parts of the city. It cannot be successfully disputed, either,

that the building of bridges, the extension of water mains, and other improvements frequently add direct and ascertainable benefits to certain lands. But in the case of many improvements, such as the rapid transit system, the benefits are so widely diffused that it would be impossible to locate all of them even by the most elaborate special assessment scheme. It is contended that more general improvements and services, such as the construction of schoolhouses and the maintenance of schools, the installation and maintenance of a system of fire protection, the maintenance of an efficient health department, and the furnishing of adequate police protection, and all the other expensive functions of the government, by increasing the advantages of location in New York, are reflected directly in the increase of site values here. It is urged that land gets the exclusive net financial benefit of city expenditures and that, therefore, land should pay the taxes.

3. Moreover, it is pointed out that every purchaser of land buys himself free from all future taxes at the established rate. The taxes are discounted in the price he has to pay for the land. He is merely the collecting agency for the city and even the cost of collection is discounted. If the tax increases by reason of an increased assessment based on an increased value, still the owner is only giving up a percentage of what comes to him *gratis,* and in reality he escapes the burden of taxation altogether unless the *rate* of taxation is increased. It is urged, therefore, that the transfer of the tax on buildings to land values would not be unjust even if it should result in some decrease in the capital value of land as reflected in the selling price, as this is the only way in which any real share at all of the burdens of government can be placed on the present owners of land, as such.

4. Land ownership in New York City tends to be a monopoly. It is alleged that one hundred families are the owners of record of land assessed in 1915 at $473,808,075, which is approximately one-tenth of the total assessed value of land in the city. The improvements on the land so held were assessed at only $157,515,235, or about one-eighteenth of the total assessed value of improvements in the city. This indicates that many large land owners are keeping their holdings wholly or partially unimproved, expecting to profit from the unearned increment at the expense of the community. It is further alleged that 800 families own land assessed at 800 millions, which is more than one-sixth of the aggregate assessment of land values, and that 3,000 families own, directly or through real estate corporations, about two-fifths in assessed value of all the land in the city. These figures, though not officially verified, were not disputed by any witness or by any member of the Committee. It is contended that these semi-monopolistic conditions would justify the policy of levying a heavier tax on land values for the purpose of equalizing tax burdens and restricting the advantages of private monopoly in the most fundamental of all human necessities. It is pointed

out specifically that real estate paid 87 per cent. of the city budget in 1880, but only 75 per cent. in 1913.

ARGUMENTS FOR UNTAXING BUILDINGS BASED ON EXPEDIENCY.

5. The untaxing of buildings and the corresponding increase of the tax burden upon land values would tend to compel the owners of the most valuable sites, which in general are those nearest the business center of the city, to improve them if vacant, or, if already partly improved, to improve them more fully. This would do away with the long stretches of vacant land now held out of use past which home-seekers are compelled to go to the suburbs in search of cheap lands for use. It would also tend to do away with the old ramshackle buildings in lower Manhattan and lower Brooklyn and compel their replacement with commodious modern buildings. The whole tendency would be toward the development of a compact, symmetrical city, and consequent great economies in public expenditures for streets, sewers, water mains, transit lines, fire and police protection, public lighting, garbage collection, etc. While, on the other hand, the city might be compelled to acquire more parks and breathing places to take the place of private lands now held vacant, the cost of the park lands to be acquired, as well as the cost of lands for all other city purposes, would be reduced by the partial or complete elimination of speculative values. Moreover, when the city depends on private owners to maintain open spaces for public benefit, it is leaning on a broken reed; for sooner or later these places will be improved, and then the city, at enormously greater expense, will have to acquire other lands and, perhaps, destroy expensive improvements located upon them. To depend on private forbearance for the satisfaction of this public need is only saddling the inevitable burden on the future and permitting an irregular and unsymmetrical development for the present.

6. The untaxing of buildings and the further penalization of owners who hold vacant land out of use would stimulate the erection of buildings. On vacant land ripe for improvement appropriate structures would be erected. On used land, where the buildings were already old and inadequate, the day of their replacement by fit structures would be hastened. This would tend to eliminate the slums, make a better built city and increase its real wealth and prosperity.

7. Through the competition of more and better buildings, rents per unit of space occupied would fall and the people would have the choice of taking better accommodations for the same money or of devoting the margin saved in the decrease of rents to other uses. This relief, even if it were comparatively small in amount in the individual case, would, in the aggregate, represent an immense social benefit.

8. The increase in building activity would reduce unemployment

and tend to an increase in the rate of wages, and thereby benefit the workingmen.

9. Through the cheapening of vacant land by the elimination of speculative values, and through the exemption of buildings from taxation, it would be made easier for mechanics and men of moderate means to acquire homes in the suburbs. Generally, the cost of a modest home in the outlying sections is two or three times the cost of the land, even under present conditions. It is well known that realty development companies capitalize the expected future increase in the value of the land and fix their prices on this basis, especially where the purchaser buys the property on the easy-payment, instalment plan. Speculative values of land are poor security for loans in any case. The home-seeker has to furnish or borrow the price of the land the same as the cost of the building. If the price of the land were less, its stability of value would be greater and the amount of the investment required would be less. All this decrease would come off the amount of the loan required, and therefore the owner, putting in the same amount of money, would have a larger proportionate equity in the property. On the other hand, the relief of the building from taxation would, in the case of practically all small home owners, result in a considerable net decrease in tax burdens, and would pro tanto increase their ability to pay the interest on their loans. It is well known that the ability of the individual borrower to pay interest and ultimately liquidate his debt is one of the chief elements of security taken into consideration in the loaning of money, even on real estate mortgages. Hence, the rate of interest to be paid on loans would be reduced on account of the greater security or the proportionate size of the loans obtainable at the present rate of interest would be increased. In either case, house-building would be encouraged. This would result in drawing people out of the crowded tenements in the slum districts, thus helping to solve the problems of disease incident to congestion, and particularly the tuberculosis problem.

10. The general effect of a reduction in rents and of the exemption of buildings from taxation would be to attract population and industries to New York, and thus increase the city's general prosperity. This would tend to restore on the basis of actual use value the selling price of land which now contains a speculative or unreal element.

We have given what we believe to be a fair statement of the serious arguments in support of the general principle here under discussion. It will now be necessary to take up the arguments made by the opposition. Following the plan of the majority report, we may first consider arguments advanced to disprove the claims of those who favor the plan, and then take up the specific objections urged by its opponents. But we shall not content ourselves with a mere summary of assertions, but shall attempt to analyze the arguments as they are presented.

ARGUMENTS TO DISPROVE THE CLAIMS OF THE AFFIRMATIVE.

1. The opponents of the plan deny that land is essentially different from other species of property, or should be treated differently. They say that land values are the product of human labor and the investment of capital just as much as other values are, but they do not answer the argument that the land value of any particular parcel is not created by the labor and capital of the owner, but by the general growth and activities of the communty. However, they say as to owners who have purchased land with their own savings that the investment represents labor and capital the same as any other investment, and is entitled to the same protection from the State. This is true, but it must be remembered that the State does not guarantee private investments except in enterprises devoted to public service and subject to public regulation. When the slaves were freed the government did not pay for them. When prohibition laws are enacted the government does not pay for the liquor in stock or for the saloon fixtures and the good-will of the business. When men put money into speculative enterprises and stand to lose either through the ordinary course of competition or through changes in governmental policy, they are not protected from loss. This is not intended as a complete answer to the confiscation argument, which will be discussed further on, but it shows that even if the actual existing investments in land were accumulated by the savings of labor and capital before they were put into land, this fact does not entitle the present owners to protection from loss if they run foul of a change in governmental policy under the taxing power or the police power.

2. As to the claim that land gets the exclusive financial benefit from governmental activities, this is vigorously denied by the opponents of the proposed measure. While it is admitted that land gets benefit from governmental expenditures, it is claimed on the other hand that good schools, adequate police protection, health service, public charities, parks, etc., confer financial benefits upon all individuals in the city, and that therefore everybody should be called upon to help pay for these services. Speaking of the advantages of life in New York City generally, it is urged that the unearned increment shows itself in higher salaries, greater professional earnings and increased business profits, as well as increased land values. It is contended that if there were no margin of financial benefit in coming to New York, not absorbed by increased rents, people would not come and the city would not grow.

But, as stated in the summary given as a part of the majority report, the arguments advanced on this point seem to destroy each other. In one place it is said that "the opportunities for increased income grow in about the same proportion as the increase in land values. The greater the city, the higher the wages; the greater the city, the higher the profits of the merchants and manufacturers, and the greater the income of the salaried and professional classes." In another place, where the argument is being made that a decrease in rents would bring about a fall in wages, it is said that "the scale of wages and professional earnings is far higher in the City of New York than in the small neighboring towns, *and the difference is very largely measured by the difference in house rents.*"

Those who favor the measure state that, of course, people will not come to a city except in hope of increased financial profits or other advantages deemed equally important, but that they do, in fact, have to pay for these financial advantages in higher ground rents. Everybody has to have a place to live and work, and for that place he pays a larger rental by reason of the benefits conferred by governmental action. Having paid once, he ought not to be taxed a second time on any margin of advantage accruing to him. It is not just to tax him on the increased product of his labor while the tax paid in rents is still unexhausted. As proof that the land gets benefits in excess of the total cost of government, it is pointed out that the valuation of land as measured by the assessments, in spite of an increasing tax rate, has increased more than twice as much as the total increase in the public debt during the past ten years. It is urged that after making allowance for any possible advance in the ratio of assessments to real values, we should certainly find a large margin of excess in the increase of land values over the increase in the city's debt. And so it is urged that even if individuals do receive a certain surplus of the financial benefit accruing from governmental expenditures, the initial benefit goes to land and is a community benefit which is more than ample to pay all the expenses of government. When this ceases to be true, it is an evidence that a city has reached or is closely approaching the economic limit of its growth, and that it will not pay for it to get any larger.

3. No direct answer is made to the contention that the only way to tax present land owners at all is by an increase in the tax *rate* on land, but it is claimed that if the tax rate is raised above a certain point it will result in the impairment of capital values and that this would be unjust. Most of the opponents of the proposed measure declare that all classes in the community should be taxed. They ignore the argument that every person in the community is already taxed by the landlord and that the proper way to get a contribution from everybody for governmental purposes is to levy a tax on land values which the landlord will have to pay out of the ground rents already collected by him. It is commonly stated that the tax on land must be paid by the owner of the land and cannot be shifted to the tenant, but the opponents of the proposed measure forget that the tenants have already paid the tax, and that land values as such are only the capitalized privilege of collecting this tax from the tenants and keeping a portion of it instead of paying it all over to the government. The only way the land owner

as such can be made to bear any portion of the tax burden is by taking away from him a larger percentage of his collections than he figured on when he bought the land, or, in other words, when he invested in tax-collecting privileges.

4. As to the claim that there is a land monopoly in New York, the opponents of the exemption of buildings from taxation allege that there are about 200,000 owners of real estate in the city and that these owners with their families represent a million people, to say nothing of the individual holders of mortgages and the depositors of savings banks and the policyholders of life insurance companies whose investments are largely in real estate loans. They say that under these circumstances the talk of a land monopoly is ridiculous. To the allegation that certain families have enormous land holdings they reply that these families now have to pay a correspondingly large share of the taxes, and if their properties are left vacant or unimproved the burden upon them is relatively heavier because their income from rentals is proportionately less. Moreover, they say that the advantages of land ownership in New York, with the heavy tax already imposed on land, do not constitute a special privilege. In short, they maintain that there is no land monopoly, and if there is, it is an unprofitable one which cannot justly be saddled with a special burden of taxation. To these negative arguments it may be replied that if only one-fifth of the families of the city have any direct or ascertainable share in land ownership, although *every* family and *every* individual uses and must use land all the time as a base of operations, this fact in itself proves the existence of a land monopoly. While it is clear that in New York, where land values are so enormous, it may never be practicable for the majority of families to have a direct share in land ownership, this makes it all the more necessary that indirectly everybody should share in the benefits of land ownership through taxation. The use of the term "monopoly" moreover is proper because the quantity of land is fixed and its ownership is subject to all the conditions of monopoly ownership regardless of the number of owners. Things capable of reproduction may be owned by one person without that person being the owner of a monopoly because there is always potential competition. On the other hand, land may be owned by millions of persons and yet their ownership is a monopoly. It is for this reason that a tax on land cannot be shifted and a tax on things capable of reproduction tends to be shifted to consumers. As to the allegation that no larger profits are made in the real estate business than in other lines of business, the opponents of the proposed measure seem to confuse *land* speculation with real estate development. In the cities of Western Canada the real estate men, those engaged in the development of land for use, were generally in control of the municipal governments when buildings were exempted. The untaxing of buildings is not calculated to kill the real

estate business or reduce its profits so far as it is concerned in actual development rather than mere speculation in land values.

5. As to the claim that the untaxing of buildings would tend to a more intensive use of valuable lands and the development of a more compact city, there is no substantial difference of opinion. However, the opponents of the measure think that the cost of acquiring the additional breathing spaces made necessary by the enforced improvement of private lands previously held vacant, would more than offset the economies to be effected in other ways, and that street congestion and new expenses would result from the overdevelopment of the downtown sections. If through more intensive development of the most valuable parcels of land more business should be transacted or more people have their dwellings on an acre than at present, this would not be congestion, but organization on the basis of the greatest economy. The capacity of the streets puts a limit upon the intensive use of land at the business center, and if certain property owners, by building skyscrapers and thus absorbing all of the surplus capacity of the streets in their vicinity, condemn their neighbors to the maintenance of low buildings, that difficulty can be solved under the new system only as it can under the old, namely, by the limitation of the heights and dimensions of buildings with relation to lot areas and street widths. The necessity for such control has long been urgent and it could hardly be made greater by the proposed change in the tax plan. The opponents of the proposed plan to untax buildings say that, in any event, this change should be preceded by a system of zoning and limitation of building heights. They overlook the fact that plans for these reforms are already far advanced and can be put into effect in a year, while the untaxing of buildings will take a series of years. If the adoption of building limitations were recognized as a condition precedent to the untaxing of buildings, the opponents of the latter would doubtless be found opposing the former.

6. The opponents of the measure are divided as to its probable effect upon building operations. Some think that it would start a building boom which would last until the city was overbuilt, and be followed by a severe reaction. Others maintain that it would make real estate investments so hazardous as to paralyze immediately the business of land development. They say that money-lending institutions would shut down tight, or that the rate of interest would be raised so as to bring building to a dead stop. The wide variation in the views of experienced men who oppose this measure tends to the conclusion that in all probability the effect of its adoption, so far as building operations are concerned, would be a mild stimulation which would lead neither to a boom nor to immediate or future paralysis.

7. The opponents of the measure minimize its probable effect on rents. They generally maintain that the reduction in rentals would be small, while at the same time insisting that the effect upon land values

would be disastrous. The seeming discrepancy in this argument is explained in part by the claim that confidence is the basis of land values and that such a measure as this, even though it did not reduce the earning power of land, would so undermine the confidence of the investing public as to greatly reduce the selling value of land. It is also explained in part by a misapplication of well-established economic principles. Particular dependence is placed on Dr. Haig's analysis of the probable effects of the proposed plan as applied to New York conditions, in which he maintains that the maximum reduction in rents obtainable by the tenants in any given building as a direct result of the change in the taxing system would be the amount of the tax taken off the building, and that the probable decrease in the value of the land would be the amount of the increase in the tax on the land as such, capitalized. The fallacy lies in the assumption that the shifting of the tax on buildings to the tenants is in any degree a direct process, independent of competition. This assumption is in direct conflict with the accepted theory of the incidence of the tax on buildings, which is that the tax is shifted to the tenants *through the curtailment of competition* and likewise that any decrease in the tax is passed on to the tenants in the form of lower rents *through the encouragement of competition.* Except for competition, neither the increase nor the decrease in the amount of taxes levied on buildings would affect rents at all. The land, as the residuary legatee of the buildings, would absorb all the injury or the benefit. But with competition, the aggregate amount of the taxes taken off buildings bears no ascertainable relation to the aggregate amount of the saving due to a decrease in rents. In like manner, Dr. Haig draws a fallacious conclusion as to the effect of the proposed plan on land values. Assuming that the tenants will get the benefit of the reduction in the taxes on buildings, he necessarily follows this assumption with another, namely, that the selling price of a given parcel of land will be decreased by the capitalized amount of the increase of the taxes levied directly upon it. It seems clear that if rents are not reduced and if the total amount of the tax payable on the land and the building together is decreased, the value of the land will tend to rise, no matter what the nominal rate of taxation applied to the land value as such may be. Thus the *direct* effect of the transfer of the tax should be, not a decrease in the aggregate selling value of all land, but a readjustment of land as between improved and unimproved or underimproved parcels. The decrease in the aggregate selling value of land would be brought about only by a reduction in the aggregate amount of net rentals actually or prospectively paid, and this, as we have already seen, will be brought about only through a lowering of rents resulting from the competition of new buildings, which properly may be regarded as one of the *indirect* effects of the proposed plan.

The opponents of the measure also maintain that real estate owners, under present conditions, usually depend on expected increases in the value of their land to offset the depreciation in their buildings, and that therefore depreciation is not now included in rents. They claim that the effect of the exemption of buildings from taxation would be to decrease land values, or at the very least to prevent or seriously check their increase. They maintain that the result would be to compel owners to add depreciation to the rentals charged their tenants. It may be urged in reply, that the increase in rentals due to this cause would not in any event more than offset the decrease due to a shrinkage in land values, unless land owners are now playing a losing game. Depreciation is a legitimate part of the cost of furnishing building accommodations, and not to provide for it is poor business policy for everybody concerned. The analogy of the public utilities holds good here. It is for the ultimate interest of both investors and users that depreciation should be provided for as it accrues. No matter what the effect on rents may be, it certainly would be a great advantage to real estate owners if they were compelled to provide for depreciation.

8. As to unemployment and wages, the opponents of the measure maintain that the reduction of unemployment and the increase of wages through scarcity of labor could, in any case, last only through the period of the boom in building, should one ensue, and that as soon as things had reached a new equilibrium unemployment would reappear and wages settle back to their old level. Moreover, they claim that high rents make high wages and that if rents should be lowered, wages would have to fall with them, all according to the iron law formulated by Ricardo. In reply to this claim, the advocates of the measure maintain that the effect of the exemption of buildings from taxation would not exhaust its force in an immediate riot of building activity, but would be a continuing incentive to a liberal building policy. Furthermore, as to wages, attention is called to the modification of Ricardo's law effected by the unions. With wages once up, organized labor can be depended upon to maintain them, certainly during periods of reasonable prosperity. In any case, the workingmen would share in the general prosperity of the city, and would not have to pay their taxes twice—once in ground rents and a second time in house rents and the prices of commodities.

9. As to the building of small houses or any other kind of houses, opponents of the measure foresee dire consequences from its adoption. They claim, but have not proven, that there are some 200,000 land owners in the City of New York, and that the equities of a very large proportion of these owners would be wiped out by the shrinkage in land values. They claim that a panic would ensue upon the adoption of the policy of untaxing buildings, that existing mortgages would be called, that new loans would not be made, that in any case the necessity of intensive development would multiply large tenement and apartment houses, that the heavier tax on land would banish gardens and lawns from the city, and that home owners who now depend on the

expected increase in the value of their lands to pay off their mortgages would be deprived of this support. They ignore entirely the benefits to the small householder whose improvement is usually worth two or three times the value of his land. On the matter of home ownership, Dr. Haig makes these significant comments:

"The cities of Western Canada show a large percentage of home owners. Certainly the tax system has not prevented home ownership on a large scale. Probably it has encouraged it. The decreased carrying charge is an item which appeals to the man in moderate circumstances. It should be remembered, however, that under the conditions present in Canadian cities the reduction of the tax on buildings has been a net reduction in taxes payable on residence property, the weight of the burden being largely assumed by the vacant and underimproved real estate."

So far as the wiping out of equities is concerned, there is no good reason to believe that it would take place, except possibly in a few isolated instances where the equity is a very narrow one or the shrinkage of the particular parcel substantial. But even if there should be a general decrease in land prices, the effect upon the small owner would certainly be very much less serious than the opponents of this measure predict. Small home owners with mortgages on their property would not suffer foreclosure. With the decreased tax charges they would be in a better position than before to pay off their mortgages, and when they had them paid would be in possession of property which for purposes of actual use would be at least as valuable as it is now. All they could possibly lose would be the theoretical reduction in value due to the elimination of the speculative element in the value of their land based upon its prospective theoretical net income on a hypothetical rental basis. They would not have to pay any more to complete their purchases than they would have to pay under existing conditions, and they would be in a better condition to pay it. As to the limitation of garden space, it seems clear that the intensive development of the downtown centers, where gardens do not belong anyhow, would tend to relax the demand for and diminish the price of outlying lands must suitably located for garden purposes. Gardens would undoubtedly stick to the fringe, and would be pushed gradually further out as the intensively developed business center expanded. As to increased congestion on account of the more intensive development of the land, it is to be remembered that the tendency to intensive development affects only the more expensive centrally located sites, and the value of these sites would be checked by the competition of cheaper sites for separate houses. As to the dependence of home owners on the future increment in land values to liquidate their mortgages, it is clear that an increase in land value will not actually pay off a mortgage unless the land is sold. This brings the home owner who depends upon the increment into the speculative class. No convincing evidence has been produced to show that the mechanics and small home owners in building and loan associations belong in this class. Moreover, the testimony of those opposed to the untaxing of buildings, if true as to the average profits from real estate speculation, would tend to show that this is no sort of business for a poor man to indulge in. When this consideration is combined with the fact that in selling lots and houses the realty development companies usually succeed in capitalizing any foreseeable increment in value, it seems clear that prospective increases in land value, while good talking points for the salesmen, cannot safely be relied on by buyers for the payment of their mortgages.

10. The opponents of the measure do not deny that if rents fell and buildings multiplied the effect might be to attract more population to the city, but they allege that if this should happen it would immediately increase rents again, increase land values and stimulate speculation, thus depriving the people of the very advantages claimed as resultant from the adoption of this plan. However, they do not pay attention to the fact that values restored on the basis of larger population and more intensive use would be real values, and nobody would be injured by them. The advocates of the measure do not claim that rents can be reduced indefinitely. They recognize that as cities grow and the demand for locations increases, rents must go up to correspond with the more intensive use and the greater value of particular sites. What they do claim is that rents at the present time contain an element of fictitious value based on the speculative factor in the value of land. They also point out that if the plan does result in bringing more industries and more people to New York with the effect of stiffening land values and increasing rents, at least the prognostications of disaster given out by the opponents of the measure will not be fulfilled. In regard to land speculation, the opponents of the measure say that human nature is unchangeable, and that the only effect of the measure would be to scale values down a certain amount to a new base line, from which speculation would be resumed as vigorously as ever. They ignore the fact that the increased *rate* of taxation, applying to increases in value as well as to existing values, would tend to retard the increase in value and reduce its amount. Thus, even if the full effect of the proposed plan could be discounted in order to form a new base line of values for speculative purposes, the stakes would thereafter be smaller and the incentive to speculation correspondingly less.

The objections to the plan, most strenuously advanced by its opponents, in so far as they have not been fully stated in connection with the preceding discussion, are the following:

ALLEGED OBJECTIONS TO THE EXEMPTION OF BUILDINGS FROM TAXATION.

(a). It is claimed that the plan would result in the confiscation of a portion of the capital value of land, and that it is therefore both unjust and dishonest.

(b). It is predicted that the adoption of the plan would bring on a terrible real estate panic, in which multitudes of small investors would lose their all, the great financial institutions which have their money invested in real estate mortgages would be shaken to their foundation, improvements would stop, taxes would be largely uncollectible, and the city and its people would pass through a period of great inconvenience and suffering. Nobody would invest in real estate, and real estate speculation, one of the most necessary and productive occupations, would be suspended. The alleged land monopoly, now non-existent, would become a reality as an outgrowth of the ruin of the small investors.

(c). It is pointed out that the city's tax rate, except for the debt service, is limited to two per cent. of the assessed valuation of taxable real and personal estate, and it is predicted that the adoption of this plan, with the resultant depression in land values, would force the tax rate up beyond the constitutional limit.

(d). It is pointed out that the city's net indebtedness, excluding exemptions, is hugging the constitutional debt limit of ten per cent. on the assessed valuation of real estate, and that a small shrinkage in land values would wipe out the margin of credit entirely, and put the city in a position where it could not borrow a penny for general public improvements, no matter how pressing the necessity might be.

(e). It is urged that the adoption of the proposed plan, no matter in how mild and tentative a form, would be a step in the direction of the single tax, would admit its principle and would probably lead to its ultimate adoption in toto. This is regarded as an inconceivably bad outlook, to which not more than one-one-hundredth of one per cent. of the population of the city (some 530 people) would at the present time be willing to give assent.

(f). It is urged that however well this plan might work in a new community, it ought not to be put into effect in New York City, the financial metropolis of the New World, with its immense vested interests and its delicate relations with the commerce and finance of the entire country, certainly not until it has been thoroughly tried out and proven good in smaller communities. If experiments must be made, let them not be made here.

(g). Finally, it is urged that if the plan is to be put into effect at all, it should be put into effect on a rising real estate market, where the shock can be absorbed. It is maintained that now, of all times, would be the worst time to inaugurate the plan in New York, with real estate in the trough of a wave, with the city's financial needs expanding, and with the demand for new sources of revenue acute.

These are serious objections which were urged upon the Committee with deep conviction and great insistence. To them the advocates of the plan make the following answers:

HOW THE OBJECTIONS ARE ANSWERED.

(a). As to the confiscation argument, it is pointed out that any other form of taxation is a species of confiscation. It is urged that when additional revenue is needed to pay the expenses of the government, the least offensive form of confiscation is to take for community uses a portion of the value created by the community and temporarily the subject of private investment. It would be much more unjust to confiscate the individual products of labor and capital or the income from labor and capital. If the taking of an additional portion of the annual earnings of land sites is unjustifiable confiscation, what is to be said of the taking of a percentage of a man's income or salary, or of the addition of an excise tax to the prices he pays for goods? It is urged with great force by some that land values are not an appropriate subject for private ownership and never were, that they belong to the community at large, and that present owners, no matter what their actual investments may be, are in the position of men who have bought "stolen goods." It is not necessary to take this extreme position. We may admit that private property in land values has been sanctioned by modern law and custom, and that the owners of land are no more reprehensible than the owners of anything else. But even if we admit all this, it is clear that the plan here under discussion would not affect vested interests in land so seriously as to differentiate it from other fiscal measures and governmental policies that are never questioned on moral grounds. For example, right under our very eyes the city, by its deliberately adopted rapid transit policy, is spending vast sums of money for improvements which, it is known in advance, will destroy values in certain sections, and create them in others. The city is making some men poor while it makes others rich, and, what is more, is making those who are injured by them help pay for the improvements that are destroying their property. In fact, there is reason to believe that the present unsettled condition of real estate and the depression of values, particularly in Manhattan, of which we have been reminded so insistently, are not so much due to any increase in taxation as to these very public improvements in transit to which the city has committed itself. The proposed plan would doubtless cause a mild readjustment of values, but this readjustment would tend to offset and correct the tremendous shaking up now going on, by checking the rise in value of vacant suburban lands and by checking the fall in value of improved lands in older sections of the city just outside the central business district.

(b). As to the claim that the adoption of the proposed plan would bring on a real estate panic, the advocates of the measure maintain that this fear is wholly imaginary. They point out that the change proposed is less radical than the change effected without harm some years ago when the standard of assessments was changed so as to bring vacant land on a parity with improved lands. It is stated that improved lands were jumped from a 60 per cent. to a 100 per cent. valuation, while vacant lands were jumped from a 30 per cent. to a 100 per cent. basis at the same time. No panic followed, and even the opponents of the present plan admit that the change then effected was both just and expedient. It has not been made clear just what is meant by the predicted refusal of people to invest in real estate, or the evil effects that would follow therefrom. It is clear that the land itself will not run away or slip into the sea merely because investors refuse to "hold" it. It will remain right where it is and its potential usefulness will in no way be diminished. The same is true of existing buildings. They cannot run away and they will not fall down or disappear until they are worn out or destroyed. As to new buildings, while there was a marked difference of opinion among the opponents of the measure as to what its effect would be, the great weight of the entire testimony at the hearings and of the opinions expressed in the Committee's own discussions pointed to an increase in the number and size of buildings. If this increase should materialize, the argument that nobody would invest in real estate falls to the ground so far as buildings are concerned. Even the radical advocates of the measure admit that the *immediate* transfer of the total tax now levied on buildings to land values would cause considerable hardship and perhaps temporarily unsettle business conditions. But nobody proposes to make the change in a shorter period than ten years or by steps more radical than ten per cent. per annum.

In regard to this general point, Dr. Haig reports from Western Canada:

"There is general agreement that the special land taxes had no unfavorable effects upon credit conditions. Loanable funds have not been withheld or mortgages foreclosed to any considerable degree because of the pressure of the tax system."

While he pointed out that certain conditions as to loans prevail in the Canadian cities which do not prevail to the same extent in New York, the Committee had the benefit of the testimony of Mr. Richard M. Hurd, a profound student of New York land values and president of one of the great loaning institutions of the city, who stated that in his opinion credit conditions on the whole would be improved as a result of the untaxing of buildings, if this policy were carried out in connection with a comprehensive town-planning scheme to limit the height of buildings and stabilize values by a proper zoning system. As a lender, he expressed himself as opposed to very high land values, and as believing that a moderate reduction in them would benefit the loan market. He saw no reason to expect a panic as the result of the adoption of the new tax plan.

So far from starting a panic, it is probable that the adoption of this measure would administer a corrective to the depression already on our hands, which has been brought on for the most part by causes quite other than taxation. Certainly, if the plan were once put into effect, those who now oppose it, and predict such disastrous results from it, would be the last to participate in an artificially-engendered panic to prove their point. Loaning institutions would certainly be very slow about instituting a general call of mortgages. There would be no panic.

(c). As to the claim that the transer of the tax on buildings to land values would increase the tax rate beyond the limit prescribed by the Constitution, it is pointed out that the Constitution does not limit the tax rate as such, but merely provides that the *amount* to be raised for city purposes, in addition to debt charges, "shall not exceed in any one year two per centum of the assessed valuation of the real and personal estate" of the city. The increase of the tax rate on *land values,* which are and will remain under the proposed plan only a portion of the tax base, has no constitutional significance. But even if the constitutional inhibition were interpreted to apply to the rate of taxation on land values, it is pointed out by the advocates of this plan that the debt service, amounting to about one-third of the total tax levy, falls outside the two per cent. limit, and that therefore the tax rate could go to more than three per cent. without violating the Constitution. Moreover, it is pointed out that the proposed plan would be put into effect gradually and that the constitutional arguments certainly would not apply to the early stages of the experiment or to the partial exemption of buildings if it should be determined later not to carry the plan through to its full extent. This would give ample opportunity, if the plan met with favor and if, in fact, the tax levy for municipal expenditures outside of the debt service approached the two per cent. limit, to secure any constitutional changes that might be considered necessary or desirable. It is pointed out, moreover, that the proposed plan has no direct relation to an increase in the total amount of taxes collected from real estate. While some of the advocates of the plan might favor the levying of all additional taxes upon land values, the determination to do so is not a part of this proposition, and if it were thought best to look for other sources of revenue so as to limit the contribution of real estate to the relative amount now raised from this source, such a policy would, in itself, prevent the tax rate on land under the plan proposed from exceeding the two per cent. limit. The merits of this particular plan are not necessarily dependent upon the theory that all additional burdens of taxation should be laid upon land.

(d). As to the claim that the untaxing of buildings would so depress the value of real estate as to wipe out the city's margin of credit under the constitutional debt limitation, it is maintained that the proposed plan contemplates carrying buildings on the assessment roll at their full value as a part of the property base for the city's credit. It is pointed out that there is no reason to expect, as a direct effect of the proposed plan, any immediate reduction in the aggregate value of land, but only a shifting of value from vacant land to improved land. If, however, as expected and hoped, the indirect effect of the plan would be to eliminate in large part the existing speculative element in the value of land, this would only be done by the increase in the value of buildings which would, at least, partially offset the decrease in the value of the land itself. Moreover, this speculative element in land values has even yet, at least, in many parts of the city, not been fully assessed. Furthermore, with the increase of population and business, as already pointed out, the value of the land itself would be restored and the aggregate value of buildings would be greatly increased. It is admitted, however, that the city's present debt margin is very narrow and that the fluctuations in value now going on as a result of subway expansion and the general real estate depression may be sufficient to wipe out this margin entirely. The proposed plan, if introduced gradually, would not add materially to the existing shrinkage and might, as already shown, partially check the violent readjustment now going on and tend to restore stability of values. It is urged, however, that even if the debt margin should be wiped out as a result of the introduction of the proposed plan, no disastrous effects would follow. It is commonly believed that the city is now suffering from extravagance in expenditures and especially from extravagance in past years in the piling up of debt against the future. The pay-as-you-go policy recently instituted by the Board of Estimate and Apportionment is sound in theory and necessary in practice. Land has temporarily benefited in the past by the postponement of legitimate burdens until a future time. The day of reckoning has now come, and while it may be burdensome upon the present owners of real estate to pay for the dead horse whose services they enjoyed for less than cost while it was alive, it cannot be said that this burden is unjust or other than inevitable. Moreover, every dollar that is paid in taxation to prevent the incurring of debt is a double advantage to real estate. In the first place, it subjects public expenditures to a much more severe test of economy and necessity than is possible where borrowed money is being spent. In the second place, it strengthens the foundations of public finance, increases the city's assets and decreases the future burden upon the taxpayers. Both as a matter of justice and as a matter of good business policy the land owners should not object to the severe limitation of the city's borrowing habits.

In any case the city's outstanding obligations will not be impaired and the stocks and bonds already issued will have as good security as ever. The constitution is perfectly clear on this point and there is no excuse for any misunderstanding or misstatements in regard to it. The section of the constitution limiting municipal debt specifically provides that "no indebtedness of a city valid at the time of its inception shall thereafter become invalid by reason of the operation of any of the provisions of this section." Whatever effect the proposed plan might have upon the city's borrowing capacity it would apply only to the future and, as already pointed out, the absolute stoppage of any increase in the city's debt, especially at this time, might be a blessing to everybody concerned rather than a calamity.

(e). To the claim that the proposed plan would be only an entering wedge for the Single Tax, the principle of which is approved by only an infinitesimal proportion of the people, the reply is made that this plan does not, in itself, commit the city even to the principle of the Single Tax, and that as the exemption of buildings is to be brought about only gradually, if the results are unsatisfactory and the people see the Single Tax coming, they can stop the project by new legislation any year and go back to the old system or stay where they are at the time. The fact that a man starts west by the Hudson tubes is no proof that he is bound for San Francisco, much less that he will get there. Indeed, the very fear of the opponents of this plan that once it began to be tried it would lead ultimately to the Single Tax seems like a confession that the results of the plan would commend themselves to the people, and surely, in this democratic country, the opponents of the plan would not maintain that the people ought not to be trusted to determine for themselves the fundamental policies of government. The plan cannot be killed by calling it an entering wedge for the Single Tax any more than the expansion of social services rendered by the government has been stopped by dubbing it a movement toward Socialism.

(f). To the argument advanced by many, even by some who favor the principle of the untaxing of buildings, that the change should be initiated on a rising market, not in the midst of a depression such as now exists in New York, it is replied that in boom times when other forces even stronger than taxation are at work the social and economic effects of the plan are obscured, as they were in the western Canadian cities, and indeed may be lost altogether for a time in the inevitable collapse which follows an overdevelopment, temporarily stimulated by a combination of forces. It would seem, on the whole, that there could be no better time than in the midst of a depression to begin putting this plan into operation. It would gently stimulate building and thus revive legitimate real estate development. It is urged that the only effect of the plan on land values would be to squeeze out the "water" in them, their speculative as distinguished from their use elements. When, in the midst of a depression, these speculative elements are largely absent any way, the new system would have a less disturbing effect and cause less distress than would be the case in normal times. Moreover, as already argued, the plan might well have the effect of mitigating the violence of the readjustments in values now going on; and if, as many realty operators assert, the real estate business is on the verge of a healthy revival, the effect of the proposed plan might well be slightly to retard and hold in check the upward movement so as to prevent it from assuming boom proportions. In other words, a heavy tax on land is as steadying as it is inescapable. The violent increases and decreases in land values are primarily due to speculation, and this plan would tend to curtail speculation. All things considered, it is urged, now is as good a time as ever to begin the gradual introduction of the proposed plan into our tax system.

In answer to the specific objection that the tax base should not be curtailed in the face of increasing needs for revenue, it might be said that the exemption of buildings would not, in any real sense, decrease the base. All the tax that could be levied on land and buildings could be collected from the land alone. The land is the base for the building tax now.

(g). Finally, to the argument that the plan might be a good one if we were starting a new city, or even now in a smaller city, but that it should not be introduced into a great city like New York, with its enormous vested interests and its intimate relations with the financial business of the country, it is said in reply that because a city has grown up with a wrong system is no sufficient reason why it should run on the wrong track forever. Moreover, as New York is the greatest of American cities, so the evil effects of congestion, unsymmetrical development and an unjust system of taxation are most marked. If the proposed plan will produce the effects claimed for it, then New York, of all places, needs to have it put into effect. The fact that there are great vested interests here is no reason against it, especially as the ownership of land, and even the investment in buildings, are highly speculative business in New York. The shifting of values through the working of powerful social forces already takes place on so large a scale that the unsettling effect of the proposed exemption of buildings from taxation would be mild and innocuous compared with what is going on already. A change in the shopping center, a diversion of traffic by a new transit line, the building of a new bridge and many other forces now at work are making tremendous shifts in values. Of all times and of all places this time and this city are the most favorable for instituting the change. Everything is in a state of flux. While we are all shaken up anyhow is the time to prepare to settle down on right lines if we hope ever to do so. The people of New York themselves do not half appreciate what a tremendous crisis they are going through. Values in portions of Manhattan are depressed and it appears that Manhattan's resident population has come to a standstill or even commenced to decline. Because of our habits of thought and because of the preponderant weight of Manhattan values, many people tend to judge the condition of the city, as a whole, by what is going on in Manhattan. In fact, Manhattan constitutes only seven per cent. of the area of the city and now contains only 42 per cent. of the total population, although fifteen years ago it contained 54 per cent. The cry of half a century for relief from the dreadful congestion of population on Manhattan Island is at last being heard. In 1904, prior to the opening of the Williamsburg Bridge, there were only four transit tracks across the East River connecting Manhattan with Long Island. Within the short space of fifteen years, of which eleven are already past, the number of transit tracks across the East River will have increased to thirty-eight. During the same period the number of local transit tracks across the Harlem River will have increased from ten to thirty, and the McAdoo tubes with four tracks crossing the Hudson have been opened during the same time. It is no wonder that Manhattan land values are upset and Manhattan land owners quaking in their boots. While the patient is in the hospital is the very best time to perform another operation on him that will tend to relieve him of a long-standing ailment and help him recuperate more completely.

If the plan is a good one, it would seem that New York's need for it is the greatest, and the present time is the best. Here, better than anywhere else, and now, better than at any other time, can the merit of the plan be demonstrated, and the manner of introducing the new system is so conservative that the "shock" can readily be absorbed.

Vancouver, which has fallen upon evil times, following the collapse of the boom in Western Canada, and which is now suffering a depression, reported to be much more severe than any New York has seen in recent years, refuses to take a backward step in the matter of the exemption of buildings from taxation. Mayor Taylor, who was returned to office about a year ago largely on this issue, in a recent published article, makes the following statement:

"The City of Vancouver, like many individuals, has had to curtail its expenditures in every direction, but notwithstanding this, when the council brought down the estimates for the current year and struck the tax rate, the resolution to exempt improvements carried for the sixth time, without a dissenting vote."

CONCLUSIONS AND RECOMMENDATIONS.

We believe that the weight of the evidence placed before the Committee, when properly valued in the light of practical experience and sound economic theory, is distinctly in favor of the proposition to differentiate between buildings and land values in taxation by transferring all or a portion of the tax now levied on buildings in New York City to land values.

We are of the opinion that the untaxing of buildings properly applied would result in great benefits to the city and its people.

It would tend to discourage speculation in land as distinguished from the actual development of real estate for use.

It would tend to bring land values down to their actual use value.

It would tend mildly to stimulate building operations, and particularly to cause the replacement of obsolete and inadequate buildings with more modern and better ones.

It would tend to bring symmetry into the city's development.

It would tend to a decrease in rents.

It would encourage the building of small homes in the suburbs.

It would tend to increase the city's prosperity and thereby reduce unemployment, increase wages, and add to the profits of capital productively invested.

It would institute a fundamental change for the better in our taxing system, which in the long run would bring benefits, small in detail, but immense in the aggregate, to many millions of human beings.

For practical reasons we would not recommend the actual removal of buildings from the assessment roll, and would recommend that the proposed exemption be put into effect gradually.

We should accept with equanimity a law requiring a progressive reduction of the tax rate on buildings, continuing until the rate on buildings should be one-half the rate on land. We regard the establishment of the principle and its continuous exercise as more important than the rate at which the particular reduction should proceed. In our judgment a moderate reduction of the tax rate on buildings will prove so satisfactory that when the public is accustomed to the decrease a more rapid reduction may be almost unanimously demanded.

FREDERIC C. LEUBUSCHER,
DELOS F. WILCOX,
LAWSON PURDY,
FREDERIC C. HOWE,
FREDERIC B. SHIPLEY.

UNTAXING OF BUILDINGS.

Dissenting Memorandum By Mr. Shipley.

I dissent from the majority recommendation against the principle of untaxing buildings, and concur substantially with the views expressed in "The Minority Report on the Untaxing of Buildings." However, recognizing that the stability of realty values are, and for the calculable future must be, vital to any scheme of municipal revenue, I emphasize the importance of spreading this change over a long term of years in order to avoid any possible danger of unsettling price values which might otherwise indirectly result from ill-advised fears.

FREDERIC B. SHIPLEY.

UNTAXING OF BUILDINGS.

Dissenting Memorandum By Mr. Binkerd.

Circumstances which arose after I accepted service on this Committee made it impossible for me to meet with it, or to participate in its public hearings, in the final and most important stage of its work. The only fair thing I can do, therefore, is to file an individual statement.

Without intending any criticism as to the intention of the majority report to be fair, I agree with slight reservations in the minority report on untaxing buildings.

It follows that I believe in raising additional local revenue by a super tax, or an unearned increment tax, on land.

ROBERT S. BINKERD.

UNTAXING OF BUILDINGS.

Dissenting Memorandum By Mr. Tomlin.

I do not agree with the majority in recommending against untaxing buildings and a super tax on land. Practically all the argument against an increased tax on land is based on the claim that it will injure the business of land speculation, and there is very little doubt that this is true. Injuring or benefiting any special business or interest is something with which we, as a Committtee, have nothing to do. The only question that concerns us, in considering any proposed measure, is: Will it promote the welfare and prosperity of the people of the City at large, immediately or ultimately? When a new system or method or machine is introduced into an industry which causes hundreds or thousands of people to be thrown out of employment, we do not stop to inquire what will become of these people. We simply say: The change is in the line of progress and these people must seek other employment, and so if putting a better system of taxation into operation incidentally causes injury to any special interest those who are injured must submit to the same fate that causes injury to the working people, by introducing new and improved methods or machines. I am of the opinion that untaxing buildings will very materially improve the welfare of the people of the city, but I am not so much of an enthusiast as to imagine that this measure will, of itself, bring about a municipal millennium.

FRANKLIN S. TOMLIN.

PART TWO.

SOURCES OF ADDITIONAL REVENUE

PRELIMINARY STATEMENT.

During the Autumn of 1914, your Committee were made acquainted with the fiscal emergency which suddenly confronted the city because of the probability of the imposition of a large direct State tax, and of the burdens added to the city by the adoption of the new plan of financing public improvements.

On January 18, 1915, your Committee made a preliminary report, in which they tentatively advanced the plan of a presumptive income or ability tax. Several months later, the State Joint Legislative Committee on Taxation was appointed to consider the entire problem of public revenues.

On November 15, 1915, that Committee issued a statement in which there were briefly brought to public attention three proposed taxes, viz.: The Income Tax, the Classified Personal Property Tax, and the Ability or Presumptive-Income Tax. In view of this statement of the Joint Legislative Committee, your Committee deem it wise to define their attitude to these three suggested projects, and to add such other considerations as seem to be pertinent.

We have been informed by the municipal authorities that even if we assume that the cost of government can be kept at its present level, the city will have to raise, exclusive of the State direct tax, the following amounts over and above the budget for this year:

1917	$10,137,000
1918	19,400,000
1919	34,719,000
1920	34,554,000

If to this we add New York City's share of the probable State direct tax we are confronted by the staggering situation that within a few years New York City will, if the estimates are correct, need an additional revenue of between $40,000,000 and $50,000,000. On the other hand we have the unquestioned fact that real estate is in a condition of depression which has rarely been equalled in the history of New York. A proposal to meet these large additional expenditures wholly by an increase in the general property tax would necessitate so enormous an increase in the tax rate on real estate as to be both destructive and impracticable. Many owners of real estate are even now on a narrow margin and such an immense increase in the tax rate as would be needed to raise the additional revenue would cause widespread ruin, and would, in some cases, be completely unenforceable. It must be remembered that a property-tax rate of over two per cent. on full valuation is something which greatly exceeds what is found in other parts of the United States, and is absolutely unheard of in the remainder of the world. The additional revenue ought not, and cannot with safety, in the opinion of your Committee, be provided from an increase in the general tax rate.

A second possible alternative is the attempt to secure the additional revenue from a more rigid enforcement of the personal property tax. This possibility is eliminated by the conviction that, under existing administrative methods in the United States, it is wholly impracticable to secure any substantial additional revenue from the personal property tax. Throughout the United States, the larger the city the more complete is the breakdown of the personal property tax; and every one of the tax committees or commissions of the past half century in New York has been unanimous in agreeing upon this point. The recent experience of New York City with the attempt to enforce more rigidly what is left of her personal property tax has resulted in the more widespread and definite conviction on the part of the community that far from developing the present system of personal property taxation, an attempt must be made, if possible, to get rid of its absurdities and inequalities. Your Committee, therefore, have studied these possible new sources of revenue not only from the point of view of providing more income, but also from the point of view of serving as a substitute for the wholly ineffective and vicious personal property tax.

The next alternative was to impose a multiplicity of taxes on all sorts of commodities, businesses, and other subjects of taxation. Your Committee realize that some revenue could indeed be secured from such taxes as those on automobiles, theater tickets, moving picture shows, bill-boards, telephones, commercial transactions, and the like. The alternative, as a whole, however, was dismissed by the Committee for three reasons: First, these indirect taxes, almost without exception, have been reserved in the past for the purposes of Federal government. The Federal government has again very recently begun to utilize these indirect taxes, and it is entirely probable that it will do so to a greatly increasing extent in the near future. In the second place, each particular interest sought to be subjected to tax would raise the cry that it should not be singled out for special burdens, and would thus seriously impede the elaboration of any comprehensive measure. In the third place, the revenue from all these sources combined would, in the opinion of the Committee, be entirely inadequate to meet the present emergency and some more comprehensive scheme would, at all events, have to be adopted. It, therefore, seems to your Committee wiser to concentrate attention upon this more comprehensive scheme.

In considering the situation, your Committee were impressed by the fact that the City of New York is the wealthiest city in America, and one of the wealthiest in the world. The ability of the inhabitants of the City of New York to defray the expenses of the city is undoubted. The real problem is to find an equitable and expedient method of reaching this ability. The most obvious solution of the problem is through an income tax.

I. INCOME TAX.

Majority Report.

When your Committee originally considered the advisability of an income tax, they were confronted by the fact that as the problem was a purely local one we could not discover any administrative machinery which would make a direct municipal income tax feasible. Under existing conditions, we thought, and still think, it impracticable to localize income for the purposes of a municipal income tax.

An entirely different complexion has, however, been given to the problem by the creation of the Joint Legislative Committee of the State, and by the possibility of instituting an income tax under general state law.

Your Committee have always been of the opinion that, in principle, the direct income tax is one of the fairest of all taxes. They believe, furthermore, that a bill can be drawn which, if passed, will make the income tax entirely workable under general state law, and they agree that such a tax, carefully devised, would go far towards solving the fiscal problem of New York City as well as that of New York State. While your Committee do not deem it proper, in view of the anticipated report by the Joint Legislative Committee, to present any definite bill, and while they reserve the right to criticize or even to oppose any special provisions of the project which may be submitted by the Joint Legislative Committee, your Committee believe that the following general principles ought to be observed in an income tax applicable to the conditions of New York:

First. All incomes ought to be taxed, whether they accrue to residents of New York or whether, if they are within the State of New York, they accrue to non-residents. The adoption of this principle, which, in the opinion of your Committee is legally entirely possible, would completely differentiate the income tax from the personal tax.

Second. Only so much of the income tax should be taxable within New York as fairly belongs to New York in the face of interstate relations. A just system of allocating income both within and without the State, and within and without the localities of the State, ought to be devised.

Third. The exemption from income tax ought to be reduced below the level of that existing in the present Federal tax. The exemption, however, ought not to be so low as to trench on the income of the wage earner who is compelled to spend virtually his entire income.

Fourth. The rate of income tax ought to be proportional and not graduated, as the larger incomes are already reached at a higher rate by the Federal tax. A very low rate, as will be seen below, will be adequate to yield a substantial revenue.

Fifth. The administration should, as far as possible, be in the hands of central authorities so as to ensure both expertness and impartiality.

Sixth. The returns ought to be made, as far as possible, duplicates of the returns for the Federal income tax, with such minor additions as may seem necessary.

Seventh. Use should be made, as far as possible, of the principle of information at source, in preference to the system of collection at source.

Eighth. Complete secrecy should be required of all the officials and employees with regard to any details disclosed in any income returns.

Ninth. The personal property tax should be abolished, or if that be found to be impracticable, the amount paid as a personal property tax should be deducted from the amount payable as income tax.

With the observance of these principles, your Committee believe that an income tax would be desirable.

Two possible methods of safeguarding the fiscal interests of the City of New York might be adopted. In the first place a 2% income tax might be levied by the State, of which 50% or 75% might go to the localities. We believe that an income tax on the lines sketched above, even if all public-service corporations were exempted from income tax and continued to be taxed as at present, would yield at the rate of 1% from $20,000,000 to $25,000,000. Allowing for the deduction of the personal property tax a 2% income tax would yield net not far from $40,000,000. If 50% went to the localities, the share of the City of New York would be somewhere around $15,000,000, and if we were to add to this the remission from the direct State tax there would accrue to the City of New York about $30,000,000. If, instead of giving to the localities 50%, the share of the localities were to be increased to 75%, the advantage to New York City would naturally be greater.

On the other hand, if, for some reason, it seemed unwise or impracticable for the State to levy a direct income tax, your Committee would recommend that by State law there should be given the privilege to the City of New York to substitute for the direct State tax on property, an income tax to be levied according to general rules laid down in the State law, and with such additions to the rate of income tax for municipal purposes as might be recommended by the municipal authorities. To this extent, we are in favor of the plan of local option even in taxation, for it would be an option carefully guarded.

ALFRED E. MARLING,
EDWIN R. A. SELIGMAN,
FRANK HARVEY FIELD,
JOSEPH N. FRANCOLINI,
JOHN J. HALLERAN,
HAMILTON HOLT,
JEREMIAH W. JENKS,
WALTER LINDNER,
CYRUS C. MILLER,
LOUIS HEATON PINK,
DAVID RUMSEY,
OSCAR R. SEITZ,
CHARLES T. WHITE.

INCOME TAX.

Concurring Memorandum By Mr. Simon.

If the State Income Tax can be made absolutely workable, I am strongly in favor of it. If not, I would prefer, as my second choice, the Ability or Presumptive Income Tax.

ROBERT E. SIMON.

INCOME TAX.

Concurring Memorandum By Messrs. Purdy and Kline.

We concur in the conclusion that under existing conditions an income tax is preferable to the personal property tax. If an income tax should be imposed, the tax, in respect of income from shares and bonds of corporations doing business in this State, should be collected at source by requiring such corporations to pay in proportion to dividend and interest disbursements. Natural persons would then deduct the tax so paid on their behalf. Such corporations should be exempted from the provisions of Section 182, and would not be required to make any statement as to income other than the statement as to disbursement of dividends and interest and such statement as might be required to apportion the tax in case part of the property of the corporation is without the State.

The State should collect the tax and distribute all of it to the cities and towns in proportion to the equalized assessed value of real estate.

LAWSON PURDY,
ARDOLPH L. KLINE.

INCOME TAX.

Concurring Memorandum By Mr. Binkerd.

I should be glad to see an income tax adopted for State purposes, so that the property tax would be used exclusively to support local government. I am opposed to a local income tax as a part of the city's permanent revenue system.

ROBERT S. BINKERD.

INCOME TAX.

Concurring Memorandum By Messrs. Mullan and Woodward.

In concurring with the majority of the Committee in its recommendation of an income tax, we restrict ourselves to an endorsement of the bare principle of that plan, as, in the first place, we are unable to subscribe to many of the specific recommendations contained in the majority report, and, in the second place, we do not believe the plan can be successfully operated at this time by a State, certainly by a State like New York, in view of existing legal and economic conditions.

As to the first ground for our dissent, we will cite only one example, the suggested proportional rate. Just why it should be a reason against a progressive tax that the Federal income measure contains that usual feature of the direct income plan, we fail to see. Such force as there may be in that species of argument could be equally employed against the adoption of any State income tax.

As to the second ground, we will mention merely a single administrative difficulty, that of so apportioning sources of income as to refer to this State only such income as is derivable from activities and property located here.

We believe that a direct income tax is, under the right conditions, the most just and scientific of all plans yet devised for the raising of the revenue needed to maintain social organization. It is with reluctance, therefore, that we feel compelled to express the opinion that, although we may in time come to the adoption of the income tax for State purposes, that device offers to us no prospect of success in the performance of the task that has been set us, that of providing the revenue needed to meet the existing financial crisis in this city. We believe that a long period of experimentation, with possibly an amendment of the Federal Constitution, will be required in order to make of a State income tax in this State a workable and money-producing scheme; and, in our judgment, we must turn to some other plan that promises better and more immediate results.

GEO. V. MULLAN,
COLLIN H. WOODWARD.

INCOME TAX.

Dissenting Memorandum By Mr. Leubuscher.

I dissent from the majority report recommending:

1. The Income Tax.

2. The Presumptive Income or Ability Tax (including the Habitation, the Occupation and the Salaries Taxes).

3. The Land Increment Tax.

All of these taxes and the general system of local and State taxation must be considered in connection with the Federal system of raising revenue. Nearly all of the $700,000,000 expended last year by the Federal Government (exclusive of the Post Office deficit) was raised by tariff and internal revenue taxes. The greater part of these were paid by the poor and those in moderate circumstances. Prof. Seligman, in his book on "The Income Tax," states:

"In a country of the prodigious wealth of the United States it is no exaggeration to say that the entire expenses of the National Government could be easily met by a system of internal excises which would even then be moderate in both rate and extent. Instead of reckoning our internal revenue by the few hundreds of millions, we could, without great difficulty, reckon it almost by the thousands of millions."

The majority plan to raise such vast sums from the workers. Every dollar which they propose to get through the income and ability taxes for local purposes, should be secured by the Federal Government to meet increases in Federal expenditures and to reduce the tariff and internal revenue taxes on the hundreds of thousands of families in the United States whose total income is from $100 to $300 less than that required to maintain a reasonable standard of efficiency. In New York City this standard has been estimated to be nearly one thousand dollars.

The avowed purpose of the income and the presumptive income taxes is to reach those who do not pay their fair share of the cost of local government. The majority have, however, entirely overlooked the absentee landlords. Probably about a tenth of the value of land in the city is owned by people who do not live here, or live here for only a few weeks in the year. The most conspicuous example is William Waldorf Astor, who is the owner of the record of land in the city assessed for $33,522,100. The net ground rent, calculated at only 4%, is $1,330,880. Mr. Astor pays the British Government 34% on his income in excess of $500,000. Even supposing that he had no other income, he pays the British Government an income tax on $830,880, amounting to $282,500, all derived from his land holdings in New York City. As he has a large income from house rents, bonds, mortgages, etc., it is likely that he pays the British Government an income tax on an amount in excess of the ground rents ($1,330,880), such tax probably exceeding a half million dollars.

I oppose an income tax for local and State purposes for the following chief reasons:

1. The amount of revenue that can be secured by an income tax is limited, and every dollar obtained in this way is needed by the Federal Government. If revenue is derived through this method by cities and states, the Federal Government must tax the industry and ultimately the workers of the country more heavily.

The Federal Budget will be at least $850,000,000 next year, exclusive of the postal deficit.

Last year only $41,046,000 was secured from the individual Federal income tax. Should the Federal Government take a third of the total income of those who have an income of $1,000,000 a year, counting the average income of those individuals of $3,000,000, and tax the total incomes of those now receiving incomes of $500,000 to $1,000,000, 25%, and all large incomes at the war rates of European countries, taking 3 per cent. of the total incomes of those receiving $3,333 to $5,000 and 1 per cent. of the total incomes of those receiving $2,500 to $3,333, this would yield only about $350,000,000, which is approximately one-third of the revenue the Federal Government will doubtless have to secure within a few years.

2. The majority do not recommend any particular rate but approve the proposal of the Joint Legislative Committee, which is to levy a State and local income tax of 1 per cent. on small incomes and only 2 per cent. on large incomes. This violates every principle of justice. The 1 per cent. income tax will be levied chiefly upon small salaried persons and others dependent upon their daily toil, or exertions, for their living.

The majority of the 102 persons in this State who have an income of $500,000 or over, derive most of it from secure investments. It would be fairer to tax these 102 persons 10 per cent. of their income for State and local purposes than to tax the professional men, small shopkeepers, clerks, etc., at one per cent. on their incomes under $10,000 for these purposes, because they are now paying a vastly larger proportion of their earnings, for the cost of local, State and Federal Governments, than those receiving $50,000 and over, and it would chiefly be a tax upon unearned, instead of earned, incomes.

The majority say of the local income tax: "The rate of income tax ought to be proportional and not graduated, as the larger incomes are already reached at a higher rate by the Federal tax." The maximum Federal rate is only 6% on the excess of $500,000, while our present tax system costs many workers nearly a fifth of their earnings. No distinction is made between the man who earns his salary of $3,000 and the man who draws $3,000 a year from city bonds and lives in leisure. Both have the same "income." Assume that each man has a wife and three children; the first one must save for the future, but the other inherited leisure and income. It is obviously most unjust to tax both at the same rate.

3. The majority state in effect that they wish to prevent the workers of the city from saving anything, and to tax those who earn as soon as they begin to save; but they have the most tender solicitude for those who have amassed fortunes. They say: "The exemption from the income tax ought to be reduced below the level of that existing in the present Federal tax. The exemption, however, ought not to be so low as to trench on the income of the wage earner who is compelled to spend virtually his entire income."

The assumption of the majority that government should take more taxes as soon as a wage earner begins to save a little in order that he and his family may not be dependents, is a new concept of the science of government. It is similar to the suggestion of a professor of economics who has urged a tax of $1,000 for every child. Of course, he opposed the untaxing of buildings.

4. Whether designedly or not, the plan of the Joint Legislative Committee, which is endorsed by the majority of our Committee, may, if adopted, play into the hands of those who believe in a higher tariff. State Senator Mills, the Chairman of the Joint Legislative Committee, stated that cities and states should adopt an income tax before the Federal Government dries this up as a source of revenue. New York State now pays 42% of the Federal income tax. If a State income tax be levied, it will be urged with great insistence that it would be confiscation, so far as the people of New York State are concerned, to increase the rates of the Federal income tax; and that, therefore, the greatly increased revenue required for national "preparedness" and other purposes must be raised by increasing the tariff charges on imported commodities.

5. We agree with Prof. Seligman's opinion, as stated in his work on "The Income Tax" (1914 Ed.), as follows:

"If any one lesson is to be learned from Swiss experience, it is that a system of State income taxes, resting, as do the general property taxes, upon methods of local assessment, even when modified by a central state control, is bound to fail. It is a conclusive proof of the fact that the way out of American difficulties is not to be sought in the direction of any kind of local or state income tax. (p. 363) * * So that even at the very best a state income tax would not be apt to succeed unless it was controlled and regulated by the Federal Government, either in the formulation of the principles to be adopted or in the choice of the administrative methods to be employed; for, in no other way can the incomes derived from interstate business be reached." (p. 427.)

It is claimed that the above mentioned desiderata for a successful state income tax are incorporated in the majority report—first, by requiring the tax to be a state and not a local one, and the administration to be "as far as possible in the hands of the central authorities so as to ensure both expertness and impartiality;" and secondly, by the requirement that "the returns ought to be made as far as possible, duplicates of the returns for the Federal income tax, with such minor additions as may seem necessary." It seems to me, however, that neither of these meet the above criticisms that "the way out of American difficulties is not to be sought in the direction of any kind of a local or state income tax," and that "a state income tax would not be apt to succeed unless it was controlled and regulated by the Federal Government." Merely copying the forms used by the Federal Government and the returns made to that government by the taxpayers surely is not tantamount to a control and regulation by the Federal Government, even were such control and regulation constitutional or desirable.

FREDERIC C. LEUBUSCHER.

INCOME TAX.

Dissenting Memorandum By Messrs. Wilcox and Howe.

We dissent from the majority recommendation in favor of an income tax to be levied by the State for the benefit, in part, of the City of New York, for the following reasons:

1. For administrative reasons and on account of equity, the income tax is especially appropriate to the needs of the Federal Government and should be developed much more extensively for Federal purposes. We deem it inexpedient, at least for the present, that the State of New York should attempt to share the benefits of this tax.

2. The proposed plan would tend to tie up the city finances too closely with the State finances, and make the city too dependent upon changing State policies for the revenues needed for municipal purposes. The practice of turning over to the city a fixed share of certain taxes levied and collected by the State may not be objectionable in cases like the mortgage tax and the excise tax, where the rate of the tax is the same from year to year, but in the case of a State income tax the rate would very likely fluctuate with the needs of the State, with the result that the amount to be derived by the city from this source would be determined every year by the Legislature, not by the local authorities. The municipal budget, at least, so far as revenues for local purposes are concerned, ought not to be dependent from year to year upon the action of the Legislature.

3. The particular plan suggested provides for a flat rate instead of a graduated rate on the plea that the larger incomes are already reached by the Federal tax, which is graduated. It is hard to see why the same rule as to graduation should not apply in both cases. If it is just to require the wealthy to pay according to their ability for Fed-

eral purposes, that is all the more reason why they should also pay according to their ability for local purposes.

4. We do not believe that the exemption should be lower than that now or hereafter provided in the Federal income tax. Otherwise the State income tax would be designed to offset the graduation feature of the Federal tax by imposing for State and local purposes a special tax on small incomes.

DELOS F. WILCOX,
FREDERIC C. HOWE.

INCOME TAX.

Dissenting Memorandum By Mr. Tomlin.

I am opposed to the levy of an income tax by either the city or State, at the present time, for the reason that in all probability the national government will need a largely increased revenue in the near future, and this revenue should be obtained by increasing the rate of the Federal income tax and not by taxing the industries of the country. It seems to me any attempt to levy a State income tax would embarrass the National Government.

FRANKLIN S. TOMLIN.

INCOME TAX.

Dissenting Memorandum By Mr. Shipley.

I dissent from the majority recommendation of "A State income tax as a partial means of securing the additional revenue required in the immediate future." While agreeing to its superiority to the present personal property tax, I believe it to be impracticable as an emergency measure because of administrative and legal difficulties.

FREDERIC B. SHIPLEY.

2. CLASSIFIED PERSONAL PROPERTY TAX.

Majority Report.

The second project mentioned by the Joint Legislative Committee is the classified personal property tax, or the low rate tax on intangible personality, to be followed later by a low rate tax on tangible personality. Your Committee see no reason to depart from the conclusions at which they arrived several months ago, and which were embodied in a special report made to the Mayor. Without repeating all the considerations which have been previously urged, your Committtee content themselves by summing up the objections to a low rate tax on personalty, as follows:

1. It will require for its successful operation a listing system, which has always been repugnant to the citizens of New York. The listing system as applied in other states to the property tax, has always resulted ultimately, with the publicity that has by law everywhere attended it, in an increase of perjury rather than of revenue.

The schedules required to be filled out for the existing Federal income tax cannot be considered as a counter argument. Secret returns of income are in their practical operation very different from the public listing of personal property, including assets of all kinds and thus necessarily disclosing business secrets.

2. The low rate on personal property would only slightly diminish the temptation to evasion. A rate of four or five mills represents a 10% income tax on 4% or 5% bonds, and an additional income tax of 10% is not likely to remove temptations to evasion, especially in a state like New York where, under the law, residence for the purpose of taxation can be so easily changed.

3. Even a low rate of taxation on personal property would jeopardize the interests of New York City. If levied upon securities it will be an intolerable burden upon all of these interests that deal in securities and whose profits are in very slight relation to the amount of securities they may hold for sale.

In the case of merchandise, a law-rate tax will be a tax on assets and on stock in trade which will bear with peculiar hardship upon merchants, as in the large wholesale centers stock in trade has no net direct relation to profits.

4. A low-rate tax on personalty is confronted by the problem of debts. If no allowance is made for indebtedness, the tax is clearly unjust. If allowance is made for indebtedness, inducement is given to the creation of fictitious debts, which will again result in inequality.

5. No system of taxation, whether low rate or high rate, can be profitably levied upon property as such with the exception of a local tax on real estate. The whole tendency of modern times is to estimate tax-paying ability in general in terms of profit or income, not in terms of property.

6. A low-rate tax will entirely fail to reach those who are in possession of large incomes from salaries or professional exertions.

7. A low-rate tax will not begin to yield the revenue that is required. In the few states where the low-rate tax has been employed, the increase in revenue has been only moderate and far from what would be needed in New York. In some of these states, like Iowa, there has even been an actual and considerable diminution of the revenue.

We believe, therefore, that in the existing situation of New York, a classified personal property tax would be a step backward and not a step forward. It would scarcely, if at all, help us in the fiscal emergency and it is based upon an erroneous principle of public finance.

ALFRED E. MARLING,
EDWIN R. A. SELIGMAN,
FREDERIC C. HOWE,
FRANK HARVEY FIELD,
JOSEPH N. FRANCOLINI,
HAMILTON HOLT,
JEREMIAH W. JENKS,
ARDOLPH L. KLINE,
FREDERIC C. LEUBUSCHER,
WALTER LINDNER,
CYRUS C. MILLER,
LOUIS HEATON PINK,
ROBERT E. SIMON,
LAWSON PURDY,
DAVID RUMSEY,
OSCAR R. SEITZ,
CHARLES T. WHITE,
DELOS F. WILCOX.

CLASSIFIED PERSONAL PROPERTY TAX.

Dissenting Memorandum By Messrs. Mullan, Halleran and Woodward.

We dissent. While we do not believe that the classified low-rate personalty tax offers an ideal solution, we do believe that it offers the only real and practical solution of the immediate and pressing problem of securing revenue additional to that derived from real estate. Other plans may accomplish the same purely fiscal result, but none, to our mind, will produce a like result in that respect with a like minimum of the dissatisfaction and disturbance that must inevitably accompany any radical change in, or readjustment of, a taxation system.

Eventually we must come, we think, to what many of those who have given serious thought to the subject conceive to be the most just and equitable system of taxation, a tax based directly upon income. But whether the people of the State are ready to adopt a State income tax, and whether, if they are ready for it, that system can be so planned and operated under existing conditions as to reach any substantial part of the vast wealth that finds lodgment and opportunity here, are questions that remain to be answered. The economic, legal and administrative difficulties that lie in the way of a State income tax may not be insuperable, but they are undeniably great, and it must be conceded that the adoption of such a system at this time would be at best a step in the dark, as the much-referred-to example of Wisconsin offers but little in the way of encouragement, and sheds practically no light upon the probable result of an income tax in this State, in view of the very different and infinitely more complex business and social conditions that obtain here.

At the present time it seems to us that as Hobson's choice, if for no other reason, recourse must be had to the classified low-rate plan. And it would be idle to deny to that plan the many and great advantages it possesses.

One of the most important of these advantages is that there is nothing new about the taxation of personalty. The only educational effort needed would be to show the taxpayer that, instead of being taxed, or of being in danger of being taxed, at a confiscatory general property tax rate, he would be required to pay at a fixed rate of only two or three mills, and to many this information, however unpopular taxation must from its very nature be, would go in the category of good news. The wisdom of the inheritance tax lies in the fact that it causes a mere lessening of the sum received, the loss of the amount of the reduction being to a large extent lost sight of by the beneficiary because of the simultaneous receipt by him of a sum many times greater. The likeness to the mental attitude of a man facing a greatly reduced personalty tax burden is, of course, not exact, but the underlying psychology is not essentially different.

Nor would the principle of taxing personalty at a fixed low rate be a new departure in this State. There are several kinds of personal property that we have for years taxed in this way, and the opponents of the plan in question have shown no particular anxiety to bring about a repeal of the statutes fixing certain and low rates for those special classes. We refer to bank shares, the shares of trust companies, mortgages, and secured debts; and other examples of the extension of the principle might be named. Indeed, some of those who are strongest in their opposition to all plans to change the general personalty tax laws for the better were active in the efforts to secure the passage of the measures we have instanced.

Not the least of the merits of the fixed low-rate plan is that under it we would commence operations with a body of decision law ready to hand for immediate application. The change of the rate would leave undisturbed the now thoroughly settled and well-understood body of law on the subject that it has taken many years of litigation to create. On the other hand, our entry into any new field of taxation must of necessity involve us in the tangles and mazes of a new and bewildering mass of decision that will expand and change and harass the taxpayers during all the many years required to bring about a settlement of the many mooted problems that may confidently be anticipated. Even under the comparatively simple conditions that prevail in Wisconsin, the administration of its income tax has been hampered by perplexities and doubts on all sides, and although that system has been in operation there for nearly five years, the people of Wisconsin have not yet begun to see legal daylight.

It would appear, though, from the majority report opposing the fixed low-rate plan, that there is either something inherently wrong about the taxation of personal property, or that there is no way in which personal property can be taxed. We will waste no time on any supposed sacrosanct character of personalty but will come at once to the question of its availability for providing tax revenue.

The majority report is a direct descendant of the old taxation papers written in the days when government was more simple and land could furnish all the needed revenue. The same familiar arguments of by-gone days are marshaled against the classified low-rate plan as were so effectively employed against the taxation of personalty at the general property tax rate. The draftsman of the report adheres to the time-worn custom of those opposed to the taxation of personalty, and erects the bugaboo of the administrative breakdown of personalty taxation as part of the system of a general property tax, and then points to that breakdown as if the evils of that old and vicious system were necessarily incident to the administration of any other system that included personalty as a subject matter of taxation.

It has been said for years that personal property taxation was in its essence a maker of perjurers and tax-dodgers. Men would make false oath about their property, they would create fictitious debts and fictitious legal residences, they would even move their homes to another state and from one state to another in quick succession, sooner than obey the law and pay their share of the cost of government. Some of this criticism was just, some of it was exaggerated, and some of it was without basis, but all of it referred to the always high and often confiscatory general property tax. And, in our judgment, none of it can be fairly made to apply to a fair and just low-rate plan.

That there will always be some tax-dodgers requires no denial. That the vast majority of men, treated fairly and equally by the government, would not pay their proper proportion of the government's cost, we do deny, and we have not yet been given any evidence that the contrary is probable.

If, under a fair and just low-rate law, properly classified as between tangibles and intangibles, and classified within those main classes, some men would become residents of other states in order to escape payment, it would not be long before those other states sought them out and made them pay. The same increasing burdens of government are pressing upon all the states and communities alike, and all are reaching out for additional sources of revenue. The low-rate plan is spreading from state to state and in a little while there will be no safe asylum for the weary tax-dodger, and, in our opinion, it would be good riddance for any state or community to be free of him.

Rhode Island was formerly a haven of refuge for some of our rich men. And Rhode Island has recently adopted a four-mill personalty tax.

In so far as concerns corporations, there need be no great fear of their being able to escape; they are creatures of the state and thoroughly within its control, and laws can be amended from time to time so as adequately to forestall dodging by them.

Were we to rely wholly upon the majority report, we would be forced to believe that personal property taxation has been practically discarded throughout this country, and that in the few states in which serious effort is being made to reach personalty under more modern methods, and at a low rate, the attempt has, in all cases, been signally unsuccessful. The precise contrary seems to us to be the fact. We take the liberty of quoting from the memorandum submitted to the Joint Committee on Taxation of the New York Legislature, in November, 1915, by A. E. Holcomb, Treasurer of the National Tax Association, generally conceded to be one of the foremost taxation authorities in the country:

"The plan (classified low-rate tax) is one which has had the endorsement of practically all tax investigating bodies, all students of taxation and all experienced tax administrators as shown by the literature on the subject during recent years. In very many states the constitutional limitations have been such as to require the same general rate upon all classes of property and in these states preliminary work has been necessary to secure amendments to the constitutions, but the avowed purpose has uniformly been to adopt a classified tax system. In New York itself reference may be made to the report of the Commission on New Sources of Revenue submitted to the Mayor of the City of New York, in January, 1913, which recommended a 3-mill rate on personalty with no debt offset. Furthermore, the tax has been in practical operation in very many states and has demonstrated itself as a revenue producer and what is equally important, as an efficient agency in bringing about greater equality in distributing the burdens of taxation.

"Of perhaps most immediate interest in this connection are the results of the system as applied to intangible personalty in various states. Thus it has been applied to this class of property with satisfactory progress in Connecticut, Pennsylvania and Maryland for many years and more recently in Minnesota, Rhode Island and Iowa. It has been recognized by statute and applied to some extent also in Michigan, Massachusetts and North Dakota. It is probably safe to say that if constitutional provisions had not prevented, the system would now be in operation in Kansas, Kentucky, Illinois and Indiana as evidenced by recent agitation and current comment in those states. In fine it represents the almost universal trend of public opinion and popular judgment, so far as such a technical and at the same time highly 'personal' subject may be said to express itself in a definite way."

The short experience of Maryland with a very defective low-rate plan is to us peculiarly significant as showing that with even the slightest attempt at efficient admisintration the property sought is reachable, and makes practically no attempt to evade. We were told that in those parts of the state where the personalty is not reached it is wholly because its assessment is left to local assessors who make no attempt to enforce the law. In some counties, it was stated, the assessors did not even know of the law's existence.

The main reason for the failure to reach personalty, in our judgment, is that while persons of wealth and influence have, for perfectly natural reasons of selfish concern, been doing their utmost to make the taxation of personalty odious and impossible, it has been left to no one in particular to do what he individually might to obtain the substitution for the archaic general property tax of an administratively workable tax at a reasonable fixed rate. Let us consider for a moment the conditions that exist in New York.

The existing body of personalty taxation law in this State is a hopeless jumble of unequal statutes, passed in spots, and wholly unrelated either to one another or to any traceable scheme of tax legislation. One man has his property in notes, or credits, or stock in trade, or monies in bank, and he pays at whatever the rate for the year may be, as for realty, say $1.90. Another has his property in bank shares, and he pays .50, collected at source. Another has his property in railroad bonds and he pays whatever may be .50 divided by the number of years the bonds have to run, as once he pays the .50, the bonds are exempt for all time. (Secured Debt Law referred to later.) Another has his property in capital stock, and he pays nothing. Neither do some of the others mentioned if they have "just debts" to offset.

Due largely to the necessities of the case, caused by the absence of any law requiring men to assess themselves on their own personalty by means of compulsory returns, with penalties for default, the scheme of administration of our personalty tax laws is not short of laughable. The City Directory and the telephone book have been our main sources of information as to possible quarry. A high-sounding name or a fashionable address produces a high assessment. One of the undersigned never was assessed except when he lived for a while on Fifth Avenue, and then he was put down for $50,000. He found that the colored janitor was assessed for the same sum.

The law practically requires the continued performance, year after year, of the monstrous farce popularly known as "swearing off."

The whole sorry business is a travesty on law and justly breeds a contempt for law.

This condition has existed and has been notorious for years and yet there has been no real attempt made to correct it.

Now, either there was some quality in personalty that made it naturally exempt from taxation or there was not. If there was not, it should have become a question merely of what the rate should be, or what the various rates should be, in case of classification. If there were, on the other hand, the situation should have been frankly faced with insistent demands that all personalty tax law be abolished. Neither of those courses was adopted. Instead, the administrative breakdown continued, as was inevitable, and the destructive tinkering at the law itself went on. The most serious of these statutes was that creating the Secured Debt Law, passed in 1911. When it was passed, the vast majority of personalty had been put out of reach, in one way or another, except that in which the great wealth of very rich men is most apt to be invested. Though it was not, in fact, paying taxes, the great volume of income-producing property known generally as "bonds" was subject to taxation as was other property, and the possibility of a day coming when they would be forced to pay on this property was a sword hanging over the heads of many affluent citizens who were not paying their just share of the burdens of government. And for them, or if not for them the result is quite the same, was passed this law allowing them to pay a tax of one-half of one per cent. on their bonds and thus secure exemption during the life of the securities, and more extraordinary still, even that pitiful contribution to government goes wholly to the State and not one penny of it to the cities and towns where these men live and enjoy security of life and protection of property at the cost of the other citizens.

To cite a concrete example. Mr. Carnegie, who is a resident of New York City, pays not a dollar to the city treasury except as owner of a residence here. He took immediate advantage of the Secured Debt Law and has since enjoyed immunity from taxation on his vast wealth in United States Steel bonds and other securities. On his examination by the New York City Tax Board, in 1912, there developed the grotesque situation that although the real body of his wealth was exempted under the Secured Debt Law, he had a few millions lying around uninvested, but that this was beyond the reach of the tax assessor, as Mr. Carnegie had offsetable "just debts" in a greater sum in the form of "agreements to make gifts," probably for some of his justly famous libraries, though that is not stated.

Now, Mr. Carnegie's case is merely referred to as illustrative. There are thousands of men and women in this city, not so conspicuously rich, of course, who, in the same way, escape payment of their share of the cost of maintaining the city. We do not mean to impute to that distinguished gentleman or the others even the slightest degree of dishonesty or of lack of civic spirit. They are only doing what any normal human being would do in the circumstances.

The history of the statute known as the Secured Debt Law, to which we have referred several times, shows how alert are the possessors of personal wealth to secure statutes of exemption, and how their efforts have been successful chiefly because it has been no one's particular business to see that personal wealth does not escape. The Secured Debt Law was passed in 1911. It did not get before the Legislature in the regular way, but came before both houses under an emergency message from the Governor, a device so fruitful of harm that the constitutional delegates in 1915 voted to abolish it. There was no publicity given to the measure, nor was there any real opportunity afforded the public of opposing it. When, however, last spring, a small but determined opposition to the law manifested itself before the Legislature, and the act was forced out into the open, it was substantially repealed, although those who were profiting by it succeeded in continuing the exemption of bonds already taxed under it, and in procuring an amendment under which bonds paying a tax of three-fourths of one per cent. prior to October 1st, 1915, would secure an exemption for five years. We do not believe that the law, either as originally passed or as it has been amended, is constitutionally valid, but that is not a matter in point here. We are merely citing this statute and its short history as illustrating much that we have said in the way of general statement.

It must be admitted that as wealth, for reasons that no one could in fairness condemn, has been consistently arrayed in this State in the effort to prevent the taxation of personalty, it is only reasonable to expect that the bitterness of the attack upon any proposed modernization of personalty taxation, founded upon sanity and a desire to be fair, will be equalled only by the fear that such a reconstruction of the personalty taxation laws will prove not only popular but productive of vast revenue. It is unfortunate that this opposition must be encountered, but as additional revenue must be raised, the issue cannot be avoided, and we think there can be but one outcome. And the low-rate plan is the logical way, because it is the way of least novelty and, therefore, of least resistance. There has been much foolish over-statement in the opposition to the taxation of property as such; it may not be the best way, but we are used to the idea in general, and quite content with the system in practice as it affects realty. When we go about leaving the taxation of property behind us, let us do it in the reasonable way of following the line of normal departure.

To quote from the report of the Mayor's Commission of New York City made in 1913:

"The most equitable conclusion in regard to the matter appears, therefore, to be that the personal property tax should be retained on the basis of a low uniform rate, until, at least, some very desirable substitute which is not yet in sight has been found."

In our judgment, no "desirable substitute" is yet in sight.

We will now answer the specific objections made to the low-rate plan in the majority report.

1. The so-called listing system. This is the objection most strongly urged against the adoption of modernized personalty taxation. Because the only person who really knows what he possesses is required to inform the assessor as to his taxable holdings it is claimed by many that a heinous crime against personal liberty is to be committed in the name of the law! This species of attack reacts against itself, for it must be obvious that the only personal liberty really threatened with invasion is the liberty to dodge taxation, as there can be no genuine fear that the secret information of the return will be spread broadcast. Provisions for drastic punishment effectually prevent that. No one complains that his Federal income tax return has become common property, and no reason is given in the majority report why the return need be less secret than in the case of the Federal income tax. In point of fact, the really feared possessor of the information is none other than the tax assessor. Furthermore, many of those who urge this so-called objection are not consistent, as they favor an income tax founded on the Wisconsin model, and this is what the Wisconsin Tax Commission says upon the subject in its report of 1912:

"No tax measured by ability to pay can be administered without asking searching questions. The more thoroughly these questions are asked the more certain honest people can be that the tax dodgers are paying their fair share. If taxation is confined to visible things alone, the assessor can get along without asking questions; but such procedure would exempt from taxation many of the wealthiest and ablest members of the community. When an assessor is trying to ascertain a man's income, or the value of his personal property, he must ask either the man himself or the man's neighbors. The second method is obnoxious. The open way is to put the taxpayer himself on record. This procedure is the honest man's only protection against the tax dodger.

"The old personal property tax would have been much more inquisitorial than the income tax if it had been enforced. It failed largely because questions were not asked; and its failure resulted in large financial burdens being shifted from the shoulders of certain classes of the community onto the shoulders of other classes far less able to bear them. The income tax will be a farce if searching questions are not asked and answers insisted upon."

We also deem worthy of quoting here the following excerpt from a statement made by the present Attorney General of this State, Hon. E. E. Woodbury, when he was Chairman of the State Board of Tax Commissioners (Vol. 2, N. T. A. Reps., page 153):

"I am aware that the cry will at once go up in opposition to a listing plan or requirement, that it is inquisitorial in character, but we have the system and have operated under it for years as affecting corporations made up of individuals, and will soon be preparing lists under the Federal income statute of the most inquisitorial nature.

"It is an anomalous condition of our taxing system that we subject properties of varying character to taxation, and require our taxing officials to value them for taxation purposes and at the same time deprive those officials of the power to obtain information from practically the only source from which it can be obtained—the owner. In reality there is no difference in principle between requiring an owner to furnish a list of his securities and credits, and in requiring him to furnish a statement of the true consideration paid for his real estate, which is now being advocated by many of those who oppose a listing of securities."

2. The suggeston that a man subject to a four-mill tax is almost as likely to want to evade as if he were subject to a twenty-mill tax is not convincing. Further, we think a two-mill rate would prove sufficient.

3. The claim that the low-rate plan would jeopardize the commercial interests of the city is a familiar assertion as to anything new, is never supported by attempt at proof, and could apply equally well to any new kind of taxation. A similar claim was made when the stock transfer tax was enacted, but Wall Street has not yet gone to Jersey City, and we do not believe it ever will. The City of New York is not a boom town that is made or unmade overnight.

4. There is no genuine "problem of debts." We believe there is only one state other than New York which allows general debt deduction. Some states allow the deduction of debts against credits, and stop sharply there. The New York debt deduction is not a breeder of perjury; it is much more. It is an invitation to swear off. If it can be shown that in certain classes of mercantile cases there might be some hardship due to the elimination of debt deduction, such proof could be met by proper special treatment in any bill that may be enacted. A like special treatment may be accorded to dealers in securities. But general debt deduction is a device of exempters and not of taxers.

5. The statement that no property is reachable except realty may be substantially accurate in so far as it refers to the confiscatory high general property rate, but it is negatived as to a low rate by the experience of Maryland and other states. The experience of Iowa, referred to in the majority report, is of no significance to those familiar with the

statute in that state. The plan there in use is bad in many important particulars, as, for example, that large and unnecessary debt deductions are allowed, the rate is comparatively high (5 mills), and many classes of property are exempted. We agree with the statement that the tendency of the present day is to tax according to ability, but we assert that a proper low-rate plan is based upon the same theory of ability as that upon which the direct income tax plan rests, and would, in the opinion of many who believe in taxation according to ability, work out as fairly in that respect as would a direct income scheme. And we do not believe that a direct state income tax is now feasible. The problems created by the nature of the form of government in the United States, under which a state is sovereign within certain limits, and very powerless beyond those limits, have convinced many, if not most, men who have studied the subject that a state income tax cannot be operated successfully, if at all, without years of experimentation and adjustment to the peculiar conditions encountered, and possibly without amendment to the Federal Constitution.

6. If "those who are in possession of large incomes from salaries or professional exertions" (and presumably accumulating nothing, as otherwise we do not get the point of the objection) spend all they receive, the community is not harmed as the money becomes invested in other hands and thus does not escape taxation.

7. The claim that the low-rate plan will yield no substantial revenue is as unsupported by proof as are the confident assertions made in the other direction on behalf of the income tax. Mr. Holcomb and many other authorities believe that a very large revenue would be produced by the low-rate tax. The State Tax Commissioner of Massachusetts has figured that in his state the amount of personalty is three and a half times greater than that of realty. In the City of New York, it is generally conceded, the proportion in favor of personalty would be much greater. Figured at five to one, we would have forty billions in this city alone. The probable yield at a two-mill rate for the city alone has been variously estimated at from $20,000,000 to $40,000,000, but we are dealing with such vast possibilities that no one can do more than guess. If we would measure probable results by the fear of those results, the yield would certainly be large.

In conclusion, we wish to point out that no claim is made by the majority that the modernized personalty tax would be an administrative failure because of the necessity, under our State Constitution, of assessment by local officials. While we formerly had some doubt upon the subject, we do not now believe that in the case of the low-rate plan such an objection actually lies. The local assessor is quite capable of dealing with the situation, if he wants to. Hitherto, he has not wanted to. But the compulsory return feature would oblige him to deal with the matter, whether he wanted to or not. This would make it useless for a resident of New York City to move to Nassau or Westchester or some other county where they do not need much revenue. And a simple amendment vesting in the State Tax Commission or other body power to act as investigators of the local assessors, without authority to change an assessment, but with power to report and prosecute charges, would undoubtedly accomplish any needed change in the point of view of the local official without violating the rights he has under the State Constitution. A few removals and prosecutions for nonfeasance or malfeasance would bring about whatever might be needed in the way of reform. Furthermore, the person assessed may be relied upon to desire to keep himself out of trouble.

GEO. V. MULLAN,
JOHN J. HALLERAN,
COLLIN H. WOODWARD.

CLASSIFIED PERSONAL PROPERTY TAX.

Dissenting Memorandum By Mr. Tomlin.

Nothing that has been said in our discussions, nor have I read anything that convinces me a personal property tax cannot be collected. The collection of this tax should be prosecuted with the same vigor as any other kind of tax. Judging from the evidence no such attempt has ever been made in this or any other state. Proper laws, a loyal attitude on the part of the courts and efficient administration would, I believe, result in collecting a four-mill tax on personal property. I am in favor of such a tax.

FRANKLIN S. TOMLIN.

CLASSIFIED PERSONAL PROPERTY TAX.

Dissenting Memorandum By Mr. Shipley.

I believe that a tax of from two to four mills upon variously classified tangible and intangible property, without deduction, but with certain equitable exemptions, would be very simple of administration and easily provide the needed revenue, as well as bear evenly and lightly upon the city's activities. The success of the present one per cent. tax upon bank's capital, surplus and undivided profits may be cited as an example. This is the simplest and relatively the most profitable of all of our present forms of taxation.

FREDERIC B. SHIPLEY.

CLASSIFIED PERSONAL PROPERTY TAX.

Memorandum By Mr. Binkerd.

If the personal property tax, which is iniquitous in theory and practice alike, must be retained, then I certainly concur in the proposal to lower the rate.

ROBERT S. BINKERD.

3. THE ABILITY OR PRESUMPTIVE INCOME TAX.

Majority Report.

If the direct income tax is found to be impossible, your Committee would repeat its recommendation of last winter, viz., that the State permit the City of New York, as well as the other cities if they so desire, to reach incomes indirectly rather than directly by the so-called Ability or Presumptive Income Tax. Several members of your Committee would even go so far as to prefer, under actual conditions in New York, the Ability Tax to the Income Tax.

What is here called the Ability Tax is a tax on the abilities of those who benefit from the opportunities afforded by the City of New York. Conceding that the fairest test of ability to pay is income, the proposition here is to reach the income indirectly and by outward signs or criteria, utilizing certain definite facts of expenditure as affording some indication of relative income. The Ability Tax as a presumptive income tax would, therefore, be composed of three parts, viz.: (I) the Habitation Tax, (II) the Occupation Tax, and (III) the Salaries Tax, with provisions by which only one of these taxes would be payable by any particular person.

I. THE HABITATION TAX.

The Habitation Tax is a tax upon individuals occupying habitations —that is, houses or apartments for residential purposes. The tax proceeds upon the theory that what a man spends for rent is a rough indication of his ability to contribute to the public burdens. Inasmuch, however, as the ratio of house rent and income decreases as the amount of rent increases—that is, inasmuch as people with smaller incomes must spend a relatively larger share of their income for rentals, it is obvious that in order to secure approximate justice the tax must be rather sharply graduated, so that the tax will increase not only in proportion to the rental, but more than in such proportion.

The schedule of the tax ought to be so arranged that every individual will pay a sum that is about equivalent to one per cent. of his income, as indicated by his house rent. According to the consideration just mentioned, the real income of the taxpayers may be considered to increase at a greater rate than do the rentals which they pay. If, for instance, we assume that for the more modest rentals a man spends about a fifth of his income for his house rent, we would have to multiply the yearly rental by five in order to get his presumptive income. In the case of the higher rentals the multiplier would have to be more than five, running up to six, seven, eight, nine, ten, and even more, as in the latter case of rather expensive rentals it is to be assumed that a man's income would be at least ten times and more the amount of rent that he pays. The tax, therefore, will have to be based upon a progressively graduated scale, so that the higher the house rent the progressively higher would be the amount of tax.

In order, however, to prevent miscarriages of justice and to obviate the criticism that the presumptive income may be far from being the real income, and that two men living in precisely similar houses may yet have very different real incomes, it should be provided that if anyone finds that the tax which he is called upon to pay amounts to more than one per cent. of his actual income, he shall have the right to declare and to prove his actual income and to have his tax reduced to one per cent. of his income. This would happen in only a comparatively few cases, but would effectually dispose of the criticism. This provision is not found in the draft bill herewith appended, but should be, and could easily be, added thereto.

It is further provided that if a man lives in his own house, the rental value shall be calculated at 7 per cent. of the assessed value of the property. Provision is also made for people who live in hotels or apartments, and the tax should be applicable to those who have occupied apartments continuously for at least three or four months.

Several criticisms, which, however, are not valid, might be urged against the Habitation Tax. In the first place, it might be alleged that the tax is a tax on the poor man. In reality, however, the opposite is the case. Under the project of your Committee, all rentals below $50 a month, that is, $600 a year, are entirely exempt from taxation. This corresponds to a total expenditure of from $2,500 to $3,000. Every one, therefore, with a presumptive income under this amount will pay no tax at all. Moreover, the amount of tax on slightly higher rentals is exceedingly moderate, because of the fact that, according to our recommendation, $2,000 should be exempted in every case from the presumptive income in order to reach the taxable income. On the very high rentals, however, this exemption is of no importance, and the tax will be very much greater. From the scale, which is worked out in detail in the bill appended hereto, we make the following extracts to show the operation of the law:

Rental.	Multiplier.	Presumptive Income.	Taxable Income.	Tax.
$600- $700	5	$3,500-2,000	$1,500	5
700- 800	5	4,000-2,000	2,000	10
1,000- 1,100	5	5,500-2,000	3,500	30
2,000- 2,100	5.1	10,710-2,000	8,710	87
2,900- 3,000	5.5	16,500-2,000	14,500	145
4,000- 4,100	6	24,600-2,000	22,600	226
10,000- 10,200	8	81,600-2,000	79,600	796
25,000- 26,000	17	442,000-2,000	440,000	4,400
90,000- 100.000	17	1,700,000-2,000	1,688,000	16,880

From the above table, therefore, it will be seen that the Habitation Tax entirely exempts all these with incomes under $2,500 or $3,000; that it imposes an insignificant burden on those with an income between $3,000 and $6,000 or $7,000 a year, and that it considerably increases the burden as the income augments. The Habitation Tax is thus not a tax upon the poor man and not an appreciable burden upon those in moderate circumstances.

In the second place, it might be alleged that the Habitation Tax falls upon the real estate owner for the reason that a prospective tenant of, let us say, a $650 apartment, would insist upon having his rent reduced to $600 in order to escape the tax. This argument, however, is to a great extent fallacious.

As a matter of fact, the $650 tenant will never secure the owner's consent to a reduction of $50 in rent in order to enable the tenant to save $5 in taxes. The same would be true even more of higher rentals, because, according to the scale proposed, a reduction of every $100 in rental would involve the saving of only $5 in each case. So that even at the very worst it would only be at the margin of each class of tenants that there would be any pressure at all to demand a reduction of rent. But even this is open to considerable doubt. The only way in which a landlord could be induced to grant a reduction of rent would be through the fear of having his apartments vacated. If, however, the tenants of a particular grade of apartments would actually be induced to move to a lower-priced apartment because of the tax, the place vacated by them would be filled by the influx of tenants from the next higher grade of apartments that would, under the hypothesis, in like manner be induced to seek lower-priced apartments. The fact that there are relatively less higher-priced apartments would only slightly retard this tendency. Therefore, what might possibly be lost in one way would in large measure be gained in the other, and the only apartments which might suffer a possible reduction of rental because of a threatened disappearance of their tenants would be the highest-priced apartments in the city. These, however, are occupied by the wealthiest classes, and the amount of taxes to which they would be subjected would be such a small proportion of their entire income as, in all probability, to lead to no such transfer at all.

Thus it will be seen that the argument that the Habitation Tax falls on the real estate owner is largely fallacious. If it is shifted at all to the real estate owner, only a small part will fall upon him and the rest will still be paid by the tenant, while only the owners of the most expensive apartments could suffer. But even these, as we have seen, will probably not suffer at all, or to any perceptible degree.

Above all, however, it must be remembered that even if it is true that the Habitation Tax would fall to a very slight extent on the real estate owner, it is a question of choice between the Habitation Tax and an increased rate on real estate. If the additional revenue must be raised by a direct tax, which is practically a tax on real estate, the real estate owner will have to pay all of it. If the necessary revenue is derived from a Habitation Tax, the real estate owner will at the very worst pay only a small part of it, and, in all probability, as we have seen, he will pay none of it. As between the Habitation Tax, therefore, and the real estate tax, the Habitation Tax is in the interest of the real estate owner.

The Habitation Tax is, therefore, not a tax on the poor man, nor is it a tax on the real estate owner. It is a tax on the presumptive income of everybody who resides in New York City. Its chief value, as compared with our present system of taxation, is that it reaches the man who is not in business in New York City and also that it reaches the rich man who now escapes taxes entirely by living here and claiming a residence outside of New York. The Habitation Tax does not depend upon legal residence. It must be paid by all with incomes of approximately $2,500 to $3,000 who rent apartments or who live even for a limited time in New York City.

The Habitation Tax, however, will not affect those who earn their living in New York City but who do not live here. These classes also possess an ability which ought to be reached, and in the City of New York they form an exceptionally numerous class. These it is proposed to reach by

II. THE OCCUPATION TAX.

This is a tax on the premises occupied for business or for securing a livelihood. It reaches the non-resident and the resident alike. Your Committee, after considering the various methods employed in different parts of the world, have come to the conclusion that the Occupation Tax should be levied on the basis of the annual rental value of the business premises. In some of the Canadian and European cities where this tax is in force, an attempt has been made to graduate the Occupation Tax according to the character of the business, on the assumption that different businesses will require varying degrees of floor space for their purposes. After a study of the world's experience, your Committee have come to the conclusion that the greater degree of theoretic fairness which would follow from such a system of classification would be more than outweighed by the complexity of the scheme and by the inability after all to secure exact justice. Your Committee, therefore, believe that we should follow the example of the most important cities, and should impose a flat tax on business rentals. We accordingly suggest a tax of 7% of the annual rental value of all business premises, and we propose, in order to lighten the burden on the small man, a deduction of $20 tax in every case, with a complete exemption of all business rentals up to $50 a month.

The Occupation Tax, it will be seen, is, therefore, not a tax upon the small business man. Business premises are liable to be taxed only when the rent exceeds $50 monthly, or $600 a year, and as the tax is levied at the rate of 7% only on the rental exceeding that sum, with the further provision that $20 is deducted in every case, the amount of the tax would be insignificant on even the more moderately successful business man. With business rentals of $1,000 a year, for instance, the tax will be only $50. Where a man occupies his own building for business purposes, or for purposes of a livelihood, the rental value is estimated, as in the case of the Habitation Tax, at 7% of the assessed valuation. Moreover, if a person is subject to both the Habitation Tax and the Occupation Tax, he may deduct the one from the other. Finally, it may be pointed out, that in the Occupation Tax, as in the Habitation Tax, if any one should be held to pay a tax on his personal property, he would be entitled to deduct the amount of the personal property tax from the Occupation Tax or the Habitation Tax as may be.

It may be conceded that the Occupation Tax is not an ideal tax, but it must be remembered that it is far better, even so far as the business man is concerned, than a tax on personal property or a tax on his stock in trade. At the present time, the business man contributes virtually nothing to the expenses of the city. An attempt to tax him on his stock in trade without deduction for debts, which would be a result of levying a tax on his tangible property, would be both more onerous and less equitable than the Occupation Tax.

Neither the Occupation Tax nor the Habitation Tax would, however, reach the salaried classes who secure large incomes in New York City, and who neither live in New York nor themselves pay any rent for business purposes. All these, for instance, who receive large salaries from corporations would be exempt from taxation. Your Committee feel that this would be unjust and they, therefore, recommend an addition to the Habitation Tax and the Occupation Tax of

III. A SALARIES TAX.

This is a tax on all salaries paid or received in the City of New York except salaries paid by the Federal Government. The exemption should be, in all cases, about $2,000, and the tax should be graded from the rate of one per cent. up to the figure of five per cent. on the excess of all salaries over $30,000. Provision is made in our bill for the reporting of salaries by employers and for the withholding by them of the tax at the source.

As before, where the taxpayer, subject to the Salaries Tax, is subject to either the Habitation Tax or the Occupation Tax, he may deduct the one from the other; and, in the same way, he may also deduct any tax that he happens to pay on his personal property.

Here, again, several possible misconceptions ought to be removed. In the first place, it would not be true to state that the Salaries Tax is a tax on the small man. Since all salaries up to $2,000 are exempt, and since the rate is only one per cent. on the excess over that amount, the recipient of even a $3,000 salary would pay only $10 a year as his entire tax to the city. On the other hand, higher salaries, like that of the more successful professional man and of the well-paid corporation officials are taxed at considerably greater figures. The Salaries Tax is, therefore, in reality a tax upon large incomes derived from personal exertion. It is a tax upon the wealthier classes, not upon the poor man.

In the second place, it would be equally fallacious to state that salaries are taxed while other incomes are not taxed. Business incomes are supposed to be reached by the Occupation Tax; other incomes, in general, by the Habitation Tax. Nobody has to pay more than one of these three taxes. The purpose of the Salaries Tax is not to single out for taxation people with salaries, but, on the contrary, to prevent people with large salaries from entirely escaping taxation—especially the recipients of large salaries in this city who live outside of New York City. The Salaries Tax, instead of being an unequal tax on a special class, is an endeavor to secure equality of taxation by reaching those who would otherwise escape.

If we consider the Ability or Presumptive Income Tax in general as to all of these three parts, it will be realized that it has two great advantages. In the first place, it will be exceedingly easy, as well as inexpensive, to administer. Moreover, it can be readily executed by the city officials without any necessity of depending upon the State administration. As regards its practicability, its certainty, and its inexpensiveness, it satisfies three of the cardinal rules of taxation.

In the second place, the revenue will be large. Your Committee estimate, on the basis of figures furnished to them by the Internal Revenue Department at Washington, that in the City of New York alone, at the rate suggested, the revenue would be from $20,000,000 to $25,000,000.

In the face of these great advantages, the only possible objection to the scheme is that it is not absolutely equal. We concede this at once, but urge its other advantages. Theoretically, our Personal Property Tax is in many respects unobjectionable, but in actual operation it is open to the gravest criticism. We must remember that a fairly rough approximation to justice which is administratively simple and workable is far better than a more ideal scheme which does not work out in practice. Under our present system vast classes of the population escape and a very small proportion of the population bears the burden. Under the scheme herewith submitted, many classes will be reached who now are not reached, and while ideal justice will not be attained, a step forward will have been taken. As in every question of tax reform, we must consider the proposition not from the point of view of ideal justice, but from that of substantial progress. It is easy to criticise any project for reform, but it is far more difficult to submit a constructive proposal. We ask that the entire scheme be regarded from the point of view not of the ideal but of the practicable.

ALFRED E. MARLING,
EDWIN R. A. SELIGMAN,
FRANK HARVEY FIELD,
JOSEPH N. FRANCOLINI,
JOHN J. HALLERAN,
HAMILTON HOLT,
JEREMIAH W. JENKS,
WALTER LINDNER,
CYRUS C. MILLER,
DAVID RUMSEY,
OSCAR R. SEITZ,
F. S. TOMLIN.
CHARLES T. WHITE.

ABILITY TAX.

Concurring Memorandum By Mr. Simon.

In expressing my opinion as to the Ability or Presumptive Income Tax, I am assuming that the schedule part of the Habitation Tax is merely tentative and for illustrative purposes. These figures, in my opinion, may need revision.

ROBERT E. SIMON.

ABILITY TAX.

Concurring Memorandum By Messrs. Purdy and Kline.

We concur in the recommendation that cities be permitted to levy a presumptive income tax as a substitute for the personal property tax.

LAWSON PURDY,
ARDOLPH L. KLINE.

ABILITY TAX.

Memorandum By Mr. Binkerd.

As a permanent part of the city's revenue system, I am opposed to the proposed ability tax. As a temporary measure to meet the extraordinary demands of the next few years, I would support it, if accompanied at least by an unearned increment tax as a permanent part of the city's revenue system, and eventually supplanting the ability tax.

ROBERT S. BINKERD.

ABILITY TAX.

Dissenting Memorandum By Messrs. Leubuscher and Howe.

The presumptive income taxes are illogical and unjust. The majority designate them *"ability"* taxes. They are only *liability* taxes.

A. THE HABITATION TAX.

The majority aver that the payment of $600 a year rent presupposes an income of $2,500 to $3,000, and say: "Every one, therefore, with a presumptive income under this amount will pay no tax at all." It has escaped the attention of the majority that a large family requires more rooms than a small one and must pay more rent therefor; and the bigger the expenditure for rent, the larger the other necessary expenses for a family. In the case of maried men, the amount paid for rent is therefore usually as evidence of *inability* to pay taxes. In the case of single men, the rent paid may not be any criterion. A bachelor earning $10,000 would not usually pay over $1,500 for rent, or about one-seventh of his income, while a married man with a wife and three children to support on a salary of $5,000 would pay about the same rent, and that is nearly one-third of his income.

The $30 Habitation Tax on the married man is a vastly heavier burden than the $30 Habitation Tax on the bachelor.

The Habitation Tax violates the primary sanction of justice recognized in the provisions of nearly all income tax laws which place the exemption for married men higher than for single men, and the provision of most income tax laws which allow exemptions for minor children.

B. THE OCCUPATION TAX.

The Occupation Tax will hit the industries, and encourage the overcrowding of factories down to the very low standards of the Labor Law, and the crowding of offices, as to which there is no legal limitation. It is proposed to tax rents 7%, with a deduction of $20 tax in every case "in order to lighten the burden on the small man"—the majority state.

A newsdealer in Harlem pays $1,500 for a little 5 x 20 store. The proposed tax on his pernicious industry would be $105 minus $20, or $85 net. This is almost ten per cent. of his income of $900 a year. The majority can find no excuse for using the taxing power of the State for *social* purposes, but they do not hesitate to recommend the use of the taxing power for *anti-social* purposes; to produce room overcrowding among the middle classes, to crowd workers in factories and offices, to increase rents, to drive people into poorer quarters, and to mulct the workers generally—for the benefit of land owners.

C. THE SALARIES TAX.

The proposed Salaries Tax is a frank admission that the high cost of living in New York City, and, particularly, high rents and heavy taxes on homes, are driving many men with small salaries out of the city, and thereby reducing the taxable base of the city. The majority's recommendation is tantamount to the time-honored custom of cutting off one's nose to spite one's face.

It would seem that the real estate members of the majority, on the ground of self-interest alone, should have repudiated this economic mistake. A man with a salary of $3,000, a wife and three children, who comes to the city will increase the assessed value of land by at least $2,000, the assessed value of buildings by at least $4,000, and the taxable value of buildings by at least $6,000. The net ground rent on $2,000 collected by the land owner would be about $100; while with a tax rate of 2% this family living in New York would add $120 directly to the income of the city. Instead of encouraging such a family to come here by reducing their rent or the local taxes on their home, the majority propose to "get even" by imposing a paltry $10 tax on his salary. Obviously, if this **man's** family lived here they would spend most of their $3,000 here.

FREDERIC C. LEUBUSCHER,
FREDERIC C. HOWE.

ABILITY TAX.

Dissenting Memorandum By Mr. Wilcox.

When the Abilities Tax was before the Committee, first as an emergency measure last winter, and again recently as an alternative to a State income tax as a permanent source of additional revenue, I reluctantly voted for it, with the reservation that upon further reflection I might change my mind before the filing of the Committee's final report. While I prefer the Abilities Tax to a State income tax for the reasons given in my dissenting memorandum on the income tax, I am unwilling to recommend it at the present time for the reasons given by Mr. Leubuscher in his dissenting memorandum and also for the following reasons:

(1). The majority states as if it were indisputable that real estate is already carrying more than its share of the tax burden and must in any event be relieved of the additional taxes required to meet the emergency of the next few years. It seems to be forgotten that the best measure of the economic advantages of city life is the annual site value of the land upon which the city is built. The expenses of city government are, for the most part, made necessary by the *disadvantages* of city life. Certain of these disadvantages *must* be overcome; others can be accepted permanently, or for a time. Cities have often neglected to pay for the removal of certain disadvantages on the theory that they could be permanently endured, only to learn later that the judgments of civilization have been piling up against them for their neglect and *must* be paid. This refers primarily to matters pertaining to children and home life, such as sanitation, breathing spaces, play and education. I believe that the cost of removing the disadvantages of city life normally falls upon site values, in which primarily the advantages of city life are reflected. I do not believe that land should be relieved of the payments made necessary by past neglect, even though the assumption of these payments may result in some shrinkage of market values, especially as the policy of saddling public burdens upon the future has resulted in a considerable inflation of land values. There is no doubt that the actual annual rental value of sites in New York is sufficient to pay all the present expenses of the city government and to provide for the large increases which public welfare and good business policy demand. With all or a large portion of the tax taken off buildings and with special assessments and the increment tax properly developed, I am of the opinion that it will be for the best interests of the city to allow the tax rate on land to increase as far as may be necessary to meet the legitimate expenses of the city government. When the tax rate on land has reached the limit of endurability, it is a sign that the city has reached or is closely approaching the economic limit of its growth. This time can be postponed by reasonable economy and efficiency in governmental expenditures, but if it is postponed by the neglect of necessary municipal functions or by the device of new taxes of uncertain incidence and the city is encouraged to grow beyond its normal limit, the penalty will have to be paid later on in economic and social poverty and distress.

It is unfortunate, in some respects, that our real estate taxes are levied on the basis of the capital selling value of the property with the taxes discounted in the price. Of course, taxes on real estate do not diminish its use value or gross rental. But the tax being levied on the selling value, the higher the tax rate the lower will be the selling value and, presumably, the assessed value. An increase in the tax rate should be followed by a decrease in the taxable base. But it is clear on the one hand that the decrease in the base will never be sufficient to offset the additional revenue resulting from a higher tax rate, and, on the other hand, that no matter how high the tax rate may go, it will never take all of the annual rental value of the property. This can be illustrated by the following simple formulae:

Formula No. 1:

$$\text{Selling value (assessed valuation)} = \frac{\text{Annual Use Value}}{\text{Money rate} + \text{Tax Rate.}}$$

Formula No. 2:

$$\text{Tax revenue} = \text{Selling Value} \times \text{Tax Rate.}$$

If we assume that a given piece of real estate has an annual use value of $1,000, over and above operating expenses and depreciation. and that money is worth five per cent., then if there is (a) no tax, the formula will be this:

(a) Selling value (assessed valuation) $= \dfrac{\$1{,}000}{.05} = \$20{,}000.$

If the tax rate is (b) 2%, (c) 5%, (d) 10%, (e) 95%, or (f) 195%, the formula will be as follows:

(b) Selling value (assessed valuation) $= \dfrac{\$1{,}000}{.05 + .02} = \$14{,}286.$

(c) Selling value (assessed valuation) $= \dfrac{\$1{,}000}{.05 + .05} = \$10{,}000.$

(d) Selling value (assessed valuation) $= \dfrac{\$1{,}000}{.05 + .10} = \$6{,}667.$

(e) Selling value (assessed valuation) $= \dfrac{\$1{,}000}{.05 + .95} = \$1{,}000.$

(f) Selling value (assessed valuation) $= \dfrac{\$1{,}000}{.05 + 1.95} = \$500.$

No matter how high we go in the tax rate there will still be some selling value, though this value will be less than one year's use value when the tax rate gets above 95%. But the tax revenue will continue to increase as the rate increases, though it will always be less than the annual use value. This is shown by the following applications of Formula No. 2:

(a) Tax revenue = \$20,000 × .00 = 0.
(b) Tax revenue = \$14,286 × .02 = \$285.
(c) Tax revenue = \$10,000 × .05 = \$500.
(d) Tax revenue = \$6,667 × .10 = \$667.
(e) Tax revenue = \$1,000 × .95 = \$950.
(f) Tax revenue = \$500 × \$1.95 = \$975.

If all land were appropriately improved, or if the entire ground rent were taken for public purposes, it would be more logical to use the actual annual rental value of land rather than the assumed selling value as the basis for taxation. But, under present conditions, the levy of the tax on actual ground rentals would permit the holder of vacant and unused land to escape entirely, unless the increase in the value of his land from year to year were treated as income or ground rent and taxed accordingly, as it should be.

A further complication arises from the fact that the value of improvements paid for by special assessments, although it enters into and becomes a part of the site value, nevertheless does not represent an unearned or community-created increment. If buildings are untaxed, the portion of the site value represented by special assessments heretofore or hereafter paid should also, in strict theory, be untaxed. But the fact that many of these increments of land value, due to improvements other than buildings, are relatively imperishable and readily merge with site value makes it somewhat impracticable to class these improvements with buildings for untaxing purposes. It would be practicable, however, to protect from any increase in the regular tax rate all future improvements, the cost of which is to be subtracted from the increment before the increment tax is levied.

(2). The possible extension of the special assessment principle as a means of securing additional revenue and relieving the tax rate is referred to more fully in my concurring memorandum in favor of the increment tax. But the Committee as a whole has brushed aside too lightly the possible increase in revenues from miscellaneous sources. For example, high-power and high-speed automobiles eat up the roads provided for general use, increase the cost of police protection and subject pedestrians and ordinary vehicular traffic to expensive perils. It would be quite proper to make the new means of locomotion carry the full burden of its cost.

(3). Moreover, the water department, with the assumption of the Catskill development, will have to sustain additional annual carrying charges of $7,000,000 or $8,000,000 without any immediate increase in revenues and with only about $1,000,000 saving in operating expenses. Meanwhile the department is getting more than one-half of its total revenues from the sale by meter measurements of 26.5% of the total amount of water supplied. Obviously, the water revenues of the city could be greatly increased by the extension of the meter system, or else great savings could be made through the reduction of waste and leakage. It is well known, however, that the real estate interests, which are insisting on the necessity of relief in the matter of taxation, are largely opposed to the introduction of water meters into apartment houses and other multiple-family dwellings. The meter system is equitable, efficient and financially sound. There is no good reason for resorting to new forms of taxes for the relief of real estate while the introduction of elementary business principles in the sale of water is strenuously opposed by the realty interests.

(4). The citizens of New York do not seem fully to realize that when the dual rapid transit system, now under construction, is completed and in operation, either the traveling public or the taxpayers will have to supply for local passenger transportation $35,000,000 *or* $40,000,000 *a year in cash more than they supply now.* The benefits of the $350,000,000 of new investment devoted to transit will go primarily to the land owners of the city or to the traveling public, or to both. It follows either that land should be made to bear the cost or that the transit system should be made self-sustaining. Certainly there is no ground for imposing a Habitation Tax or a Salaries Tax to help sustain the subways.

(5). Other special sources of miscellaneous income might be developed on the basis of special privileges enjoyed or special governmental expenses caused. Until a comprehensive effort has been made to meet the emergency along the lines above indicated, I am not prepared to approve either a State income tax or a local Abilities Tax as a means of raising additional revenue for the City of New York.

DELOS F. WILCOX.

ABILITY TAX.

Dissenting Memorandum By Messrs. Mullan, Shipley and Woodward.

We dissent from the recommendation of the proposed Habitation and Occupation Tax for the following reasons:

1. It is wholly improbable that the people of the State would at this time approve of any such novel and untried device. And if the people of the State as a whole do not favor it, neither the present legislature nor any legislature in the near future can be expected to enact it into law, as new ideas of any sort must make their way slowly, if at all, into statutory form, and experience has shown this to be particularly true in respect of taxation measures. It is no answer to say that we ask for it for the City of New York alone, for it is quite unlikely that if a legislature should disapprove of the principle of any form of taxation it would be willing to create an entering wedge for state-wide adoption of it by allowing it to be used in any part of the State.

2. The tax is a "presumed" abilities, or income tax. The presumption is based on what in any given case may be, and in a vast number of cases will be, a very false guide to ability, namely—outward appearances, manifested by the occupation of a particular residence or place of business. A tenant takes a lease of a residence or business place, at a time when, presumably, his circumstances and prospects fully justify him in undertaking such a burden. His condition changes, his income falls, but he is compelled, nevertheless, to perform his lessee obligations, and thus, by continuing in occupancy, to furnish an untrustworthy criterion of his income. This likelihood of deception of outward appearance is equally true of the ownership of property of either a residential or business character, and the degree of injustice to occupying owners is probably greater even than that to lessees. The possible answer to this objection, viz., that the owner may sell his property, or the lessee his lease, is unsatisfactory and unconvincing. Sales at fair prices cannot be forced, and even at a sacrifice they can be made only slowly, and sometimes not at all.

3. Any scheme of multipliers by which the rental value of premises occupied by the owner is derived, is necessarily arbitrary and artificial. It is possible that a fairly accurate average of all such rental values may be properly arrived at by a given scale of multipliers, designed, as it must be, to cover all cases, but a knowledge that the tax averages well would be far from satisfying any particular owners who are taxed on the basis of rental values they could never hope to obtain on a lease. In the case of residential property, the injustice to many owners would be particularly flagrant.

4. As to whether the incidence of a Habitation Tax, in the case of leased premises, would fall on the landlord or on the tenant, it is impossible accurately to state. In point of fact, it is probably true that in some cases it would fall on the tenant and in others on the landlord. The result is bad in either event. If the tax should fall on the landlord, it would be, in effect, a tax on real estate, which is already overtaxed. If it were, in the first instance, shifted to the tenant, its burden inevitably would lead the tenant, in order to lessen his tax, to hire a lower-priced residence, or, worse still, to give up housekeeping. Either of these results would obviously be harmful to the owners of private dwellings and apartment houses, and would, in addition, make for social disservice by putting a premium on inadequacy of housing accommodations, and thus numerically reduce the class most wholesome and valuable to any community, those who make and pride themselves in their homes.

5. It is wholly impracticable to attempt to reach residents in hotels, clubs, furnished rooms and boarding houses, as was shown by the various futile efforts made by the Committee to cover this important ground. Furthermore, rents paid by such residents are, for a very large part, utterly non-indicative of income. A millionaire bachelor may live at a club, or at a hotel, for a very small outlay, which it would be palpably absurd to take as a fair measure of his income.

6. At the last moment a feature has been added to this proposal designed to abate the rigors of the original scheme in the case of persons unduly taxed because of the false criteria of outward appearance. Such persons are to be allowed to present a statement of their true income, and have to pay on it, instead of upon their inaccurately presumed income. Without having been able to give much thought to this eleventh hour modification, which was not made the subject of discussion in the Committee, it seems to us to weaken, rather than strengthen, the original scheme. In the first place, the very existence of such a modification carries with it an implied admission that the basic plan would work injustice. In the second place, under the modification a man too heavily taxed because of false appearances is compelled, in order to reduce his burden, to disclose and pay on his real income, while such persons as are not taxed heavily enough because of the artificiality

of the multiplying system, are allowed to escape payment on what in many cases would be a large part of their real income. The effect is not only to produce inequality of taxation, but, under the guise of a Habitation or Occupation Tax, to force on some, and not on all, a real income tax. In the third place, one of the supposed advantages of a Habitation or Occupation Tax claimed by the advocates of that proposal was that it was as indisputably valid as to non-residents as it was in the case of residents. They certainly can make no such claim in so far as their plan forces a tax on real instead of assumed income, and becomes, in consequence, a direct income measure. We purposely refrain from detailed discussion of what we conceive to be the several legal obstacles erected by the proposed modification, partly because of lack of time and partly because we find it difficult to believe that the proposal in question, either with or without the modification, has any chance of approval on its merits as a tax measure, regardless of purely law defects.

GEO. V. MULLAN,
FREDERIC B. SHIPLEY,
COLLIN H. WOODWARD.

ABILITY TAX.

Dissenting Memorandum By Mr. Pink.

I dissent from the recommendation of an Ability Tax.

LOUIS HEATON PINK.

4. THE INCREMENT TAX ON LAND VALUES.

Majority Report.

In the early part of this report your Committee have called attention to the fact that from forty to fifty millions of dollars would before long be needed in the shape of additional revenue. We have pointed out that a very substantial part of this increase can be derived from either a Direct Income Tax or a Presumptive Income or Ability Tax. There still remains, however, a material sum that must in all probability be raised. This leads your Committee to take up again the question of taxation of land. Some members of your Committee are in favor of this, quite irrespective of the other recommendations.

While it is true, as your Committee have already pointed out, that of all possible times this is the most inopportune to increase the burden on land, because of the great depression of real estate, and while both in view of the particular conditions of New York and of the general principles involved, your Committee have previously stated that they do not believe in the exemption of buildings from taxation or in the imposition of any heavier burden upon existing land values, it remains none the less true that we should regard with open minds the general question of the advisability of raising in the future an additional revenue from land values.

On this point, we agree with the majority of modern economists that land values afford an especially promising and suitable basis for local taxation. We do not indeed believe that land values should form the exclusive basis of taxation. We hold, however, that under certain conditions, to be described in a moment, a larger revenue may in the future be derived from this source than is the case at present. Land values in a growing city tend to increase, notwithstanding periods of temporary regression. Land owners, moreover, as a general class, are in a position to amortise a burden of taxation, and if care be taken not to decrease the capital value of the investment in land in the hands of present owners, since future purchasers may be depended upon to buy themselves free of any increasing tax burden that has accrued in the interval, it is possible to secure additional revenues from land without injustice.

How can this be accomplished? In the first part of the report, your Committee have indicated their reasons as to why they disapprove of the exemption of buildings from taxation. It will be remembered that the chief objection was stated to be that land, especially in the present depressed condition, is already bearing more than its due share of taxation; and that, in the opinion of your Committee, it would be inequitable to frame any scheme of taxation which would reduce the capital value of land in the hands of existing owners. Your Committee, however, have considered whether some scheme of land taxation would not be possible without exposing it to the objection mentioned above.

In the opinion of your Committe, it is still possible to accomplish the desired result by imposing a tax on the future increase or increment of land values. Your Committee recommend that there be levied a flat one per cent. on all future increases of land values, making the basis from which the future increment is to be estimated the value, with the exception noted below, at the time when the law is enacted. Owing, however, to the present depression in real estate, the basis from which the increase is to be calculated should be not the year 1916, but any year between 1910 and 1914 which marks the highest assessed valuation, provided the property has not been sold in the meantime. If, for instance, a plot of land in the year 1912 was assessed for $10,000 and in the year 1916 at only $8,000, then if its value in 1917 or thereafter should rise, it would not be subject to the increment tax until the value would again rise to over $10,000. Moreover, in assessing the Increment Tax allowance should be made for any sums paid for special assessments which would increase the value of the land.

In considering the application of the Increment Tax, attention should be called to a distinction which is of considerable practical importance. There is no doubt in our minds that if the Increment Tax be accepted it should be immediately adopted in the case of all vacant land, as well as in the case of underimproved land. Where, however, there are existing normal improvements on particular plots of land, it is susceptible of proof that unless great care be observed considerable injustice may result. As a matter of strict equity, no increment on land values ought to be figured until the value of an existing normal improvement, properly amortized, merges into the value of the land. There are, for instance, many examples in the City of New York where, at a given time, entirely proper improvements, as, for instance, six-story tenements or apartments, were put upon the land. So rapid, however, is the change in conditions in New York City that after the lapse of ten or fifteen years land values in particular sections may increase so much as to make it profitable to cover an adjoining vacant or underimproved lot with a twelve-story structure or even a skyscraper. This will, of course, relatively depreciate the value of the six-story structure which was an entirely normal improvement and which is as yet by no means worked out or obsolescent. The owner of the six-story structure finds that the value of his land is normally increased considerably, but the total value of his property is now less than before, because the structure is worth practically nothing and his total income is very much less than before because his six-story structure will be more and more deserted for the better accommodations in the neighborhood. Although the selling value of his structure has virtually disappeared, the assessed valuation on the tax books has decreased little, if at all. He is, therefore, paying actually more taxes and is getting less revenue than before, that is, he is hit at both ends and has really suffered a detriment. If, now, in addition he has to pay an Increment Tax because of the increased value of the land, he will suffer a third time.

There is, perhaps, no city in the world where there are such rapid shifts as in New York. It is not unusual for the same plot of land to be successively covered by three or four different kinds of structures within a generation. The situation is far more common than is ordinarily thought. Your Committee, therefore, believe that a perfectly equitable Increment Tax could be applied in such cases only where the value of an originally normal improvement, when properly amortized, merges into, or is overtaken by, the value of the land. It is only from that point on that the increment in land values should be considered taxable. It would be relatively simple, moreover, for the tax authorities to provide a proper amortization rate for each kind of building as they now provide for the factors of assessment.

It need scarcely be pointed out, however, that if a proper zoning system, with reasonable limitations upon the height of buildings, were adopted in the City of New York, the above considerations would not apply. For, in that case, it is not likely that a twelve-story apartment or skyscraper would be erected immediately adjoining a six-story structure until the whole character of the neighborhood had so completely changed as to render existing improvements sub-normal, thus bringing about an alteration in the character of the zone itself. If, accordingly, the above rather complicated considerations are to be avoided, it is in the highest degree desirable that the introduction of a land Increment Tax should be attended by the adoption of a zoning system.

In considering the Increment Tax, it must be borne in mind that the two objections that might be advanced against it are really destitute of foundation. It might be said, in the first place, that the land Incremen Tax is an entering wedge of the single tax. This is an error. The single tax contemplates the taxation in part or in whole of existing land values, thus diminishing or destroying the capital value of land. Entirely different, in our opinion, is the Increment Tax, which affects only future increases of land value, and which is founded on, and recognizes to the full, the existing capital value of land. Increment value taxes, which deal only with the future, should not be confused with taxes on existing land values.

In the second place, it might be objected to that the Increment Tax imposed additional burdens upon real estate as a whole. This, again is, in our opinion, erroneous. The Increment Tax in reality levies a tax where taxation ought to rest, namely, upon those best able to pay. Is it not true that when a land owner secures an appreciable increase in the value of his land, either through the action of the government or through the general growth of the community, he is really making a profit, a part of which might equitably go to the government?

Apart from this general consideration, it may be pointed out that the increment tax must be considered as primarily a burden on the particular owners who are especially benefited. The completion of the vast scheme of rapid transit, costing about $350,000,000, and for which the taxpayers have, in large measure, to pay, will substantially increase land values in some sections of the city and, perhaps, in all the boroughs. The imposition of an Increment Tax diminishes the burden on the land owners who may suffer a decrement or whose property remains stationary; for, if there were no Increment Tax, the ordinary tax rate on real estate would be raised throughout the city. The burden which in this way is removed from the land owners who do not benefit is thus borne by those land owners who are best able to pay, namely, those whose land enjoys an increase in value. The Increment Tax really amounts to a supplementary income tax or Ability Tax.

The revenue to be derived from this Increment Tax would, indeed, not be great at first, but it would substantially increase, from year to year. In proportion as there will probably come within the next few years a restoration of prosperity in the real estate situation, and even on the assumption that the average increase of land values during the next five or ten years will be only $75,000,000 or $100,000,00 a year, the land Increment Tax will, within a very few years, yield a considerable revenue to the city, and not the least claim to our consideration is the fact that it forms a revenue which will be derived without interfering in any degree with the existing property rights of land owners in the City of New York.

EDWIN R. A. SELIGMAN,
FRANK HARVEY FIELD,
JOSEPH N. FRANCOLINI,
HAMILTON HOLT,
JEREMIAH W. JENKS,
WALTER LINDNER,
LOUIS HEATON PINK,
OSCAR R. SEITZ,
FREDERIC B. SHIPLEY,
F. S. TOMLIN.

INCREMENT TAX.

Concurring Memorandum By Messrs. Marling and White.

The undersigned, in considering the whole question of new sources of revenue, cannot withhold their opinion that it is equally important that every economy that can be made in the administration of the City should be practiced, but that if there are no other economies possible than those already realized, and if it shall still be necessary to secure additional revenue, then we reluctantly regard an Increment Tax on land values on the lines submitted as under those circumstances being desirable for a limited period, and not to be adopted as a permanent means of revenue.

ALFRED E. MARLING,
CHARLES T. WHITE.

INCREMENT TAX.

Concurring Memorandum By Mr. Simon.

I am in favor of the suggested Increment Tax, provided, however, that in addition to the other suggestions contained in the report, provision is made whereby no tax is charged on any increment which may be the result of improvements for which a special assessment has been levied.

ROBERT E. SIMON.

INCREMENT TAX.

Concurring Memorandum By Mr. Binkerd.

I believe in raising additional local revenue by an unearned Increment Tax on land.

ROBERT S. BINKERD.

INCREMENT TAX.

Concurring Memorandum By Mr. Wilcox.

I concur in the majority recommendation of a tax on the increment of land values, but dissent in regard to some of the details and, in numerous respects, as to the statement of reasons for the tax. To my mind, the Increment Tax is just because it aims to take a portion of the future increase in land values created by the growth and general prosperity of the community and by public expenditures for improvements not paid for by special assessments. If the Increment Tax is ever to be adopted in New York, the present is a most appropriate time for introducing it. The city's enormous expenditures for rapid transit improvements are in large measure responsible for the present demand for a great increase in revenues. Many citizens believe that rapid transit extensions, especially in the comparatively undeveloped sections, should have been paid for by special assessments. That has not been done, and now it is possible to accomplish the same result in part by the Increment Tax. From the increment is to be deducted the amount of intervening payments on account of special assessments. The two plans dovetail into each other very well.

The Committee was unable to complete its study of possible extensions of the special assessment plan, but the introduction of the Increment Tax will not in any way interfere with the larger use of special assessments in the future. The Increment Tax, if introduced now, will undoubtedly bring a large revenue by the time the full effect of rapid transit development on land values is realized. In the meantime, several classes of improvements, heretofore paid for out of bond issues, most of which are hereafter to be included in the annual tax levy under the pay-as-you-go policy, might, with considerable propriety, be paid for by special assessments. Many of these are improvements that will be required in unusual number during the period of the shifting of population now under way. I refer to such things as the purchase of school and library sites, the construction of school buildings and fire stations, the purchase and improvement of parks and playgrounds, the extension of water mains and the repaving of streets. For these purposes the city spends about $15,000,000 per annum. They all benefit the particular localities where the improvements are made.

It would be particularly appropriate that repaving should be paid for by special assessment wherever original paving is paid for by this plan. The argument sometimes advanced to the effect that repaving should be a general charge because the special benefit to abutting land is exhausted with the original improvement seems to me fallacious. When a property owner pays for a pavement, and secures a corresponding benefit, he buys the benefit for the life of the improvement and no longer. If it be urged that he does not himself wear the improvement out, it may be answered that he gets the benefit of it chiefly because it is used by the general public. He should be required to replace the improvment when it is worn out just the same as he has to replace his buildings when they become useless. Anything that a man buys or pays for, he is bound to replace if he wishes to retain its value. If the pavement on a certain street were allowed to wear out and disappear, abutting lands would suffer. For this reason special assessments paid for repaving ought not to be deducted from the increment in determining the amount against which the Increment Tax shall be levied.

I am of the opinion that the Increment Tax should not be regarded as supplementary to some large new plan for securing additional revenue, but that it should be put forward in connection with a larger use of special assessments, as a just and permanent means of securing revenue, the introduction of which at the present time is particularly expedient.

DELOS F. WILCOX.

INCREMENT TAX.

Dissenting Memorandum By Messrs. Purdy and Others.

We dissent from the recommendation of an Increment Tax on land values.

LAWSON PURDY,
ARDOLPH L. KLINE,
DAVID RUMSEY,
COLLIN H. WOODWARD.

INCREMENT TAX.

Dissenting Memorandum By Messrs. Miller, Halleran and Mullan.

We dissent from the report favoring the Increment Tax.

Our Committee, various other committees who have investigated the subject, as well as most men in the community who have any knowledge on the subject, recognize the growing tendency to levy the increasing expenses for the government on real estate, and have agreed that there is a necessity now not only not to increase the taxes on real estate, but to find other sources of revenue so as to relieve real estate, and yet this committee proposes to suggest another method of increasing the burden on real estate in the form of an Increment Tax.

The Increment Tax seems to be suggested *because* the owner of land makes a profit and, therefore, should give up an extra part of such profit over and above the normal rate which every owner pays. There is no other form of wealth in the community which is treated in this way.

The man who invests the profits of his labor in land and pays taxes on it for a long time in advance of its sale, to support the government, and takes his chances on a profit, is a public benefactor. He must practice far more optimism and self-denial than the merchant who makes quick turns on his goods.

The Increment Tax, which is a special tax used in England and Germany, taxes the increase in value, as the system of taxation there is not a capital tax, i. e., a tax on the value of the land,—but a rental tax or a leasehold tax, or occupation tax, or a poll tax, or an income tax, or whatever it may be, so that an increment tax is necessary to tax the increase in value. In this country we tax the capital value, so that where there is an increase in the value of the property whether by additions through assessments or by improvements or by unearned increment so-called, the increase in the value is taxed. We pay an Increment Tax now. Why pay it twice? It is to be seen, therefore, that systems of taxation which suit conditions in other countries may not fit conditions here.

WHO WILL REFUND THE DECREMENT?

It is claimed that the Increment Tax is just because it is caused by the increase in population and the resulting increase in demand, and is not earned by the owner. If the population moves away, what redress is there for the owner who has expended his money on buildings and improvements, relying on the permanent stay of the population? If there is a tax on the unearned increment where there is an increase in value, should there not be a return for the undeserved detriment where there is a decrease?

It does not seem to impress those who favor the Increment Tax that the more property is taxed the less capital will be invested in it, thereby retarding the development of real estate. The fact seems to be forgotten also that the Increment Tax will bear more heavily upon property in the suburbs than in the center of the city, because in the suburbs the percentage of increase, when there is an increase, is higher than in the center. The injustice of taxing the increment in the suburbs lies in the fact that capital has been invested in the suburbs sometimes many years before there is an increment. In the meantime taxes, assessments and interest have accumulated. These are to be repaid only when the increment begins to grow, but at this point the State steps in and takes what the investor should have had to repay him for his foresight and frugality. The inevitable tendency of the tax will be to retard the development of the suburbs and to increase congestion in the center.

NOT COMPELLED TO INVEST.

Capital is not compelled to invest in real estate. It will go there only when it is assured of a profit. The ultimate benefit to the community requires that all obstacles to the free flow of capital be removed. Increment is the profit coming to the prudent investor in real estate and should belong to him. This is the only way to encourage enterprise. If an Increment Tax is to be imposed because the population makes the value, why not tax the increment in goods manufactured in New Jersey, where there are not enough people to buy them, and transported to New York where there are people enough to buy them? How does real estate differ from any other commodity?

DETERIORATION OF BUILDINGS.

The increase in land values makes up for the decrease in values of buildings which become worn out or out of date. The hope of an increase in the value of the land induces capital to invest in real estate. The building, of course, must decrease in value. If this loss is not made up by increase in land values it must be paid by tenants in the form of higher rents. Any Increment Tax on land values must lessen the compensation for the loss of buildings.

The Commission on New Sources of City Revenue, in its report to the Board of Estimate and Apportionment on January 11, 1913, says:

"The proposed tax should not be levied upon any increment which results from the labor or expenditures of the owner. If land appreciates because of improvements paid for by the owner, such as grading and clearing, or connections for water, light and sewage, or street openings, paving, etc., such an increment, to the extent that it represents capital invested by the owner, would not be subject to the tax. We propose, in short, that the tax shall be levied only upon the unearned 'increment' which results from the growth of the city and from improvements made by the city or by others than the owner himself. If, therefore. the value of a piece of land should rise from $100,000, in 1912, to $110,000, in 1913, and the owner can show that he has expended $4,000 in permanent improvements, either upon his own initiative or in payment of special assessments levied by the municipality, he would be subject to an Increment Tax on only $6,000; and thereafter the base valuation of land from which future increments would be calculated would be $104,000 instead of $100,000."

OWNERS ENTITLED TO INTEREST.

Two very important omissions here should be noted. First, the report does not propose to allow the owner interest on the cost of his improvements. In every other investment of capital interest on the money is computed before a profit is declared. Sometimes the interest exceeds the increment. Second, the report does not subtract from the increment to be taxed, the manufacturer's profit belonging to the owner from having invested his capital and labor in improvements on an unproductive property and converted it into a productive one. This is not an unearned increment. We think also that the base valuation of land from which future increments would be calculated would be $106,000 and not $104,000.

Lastly, if the justice of the principle of an Increment Tax be conceded, what guarantee is there that it will be limited to 1% of the value of the increment? There seems to be nothing to prevent the whole of the increment from being taken, except the whim of the lawmakers.

To recapitulate: An Increment Tax is a foreign idea not fitted to our system of taxation, as we pay an Increment Tax now; it will diminish the amount of capital invested in real estate, thereby retarding real estate development; it will discourage enterprise by taking away the profit from investment in real estate; it does not allow a deduction of interest on investments and the development profit to be taken out before it is imposed; it will bear most heavily on suburban development, where the increment is deferred for a long time while the investment is increasing; while the community may be able by it to collect an extra tax, it will lose as much or more in other ways through the discouragement of capital.

CYRUS C. MILLER,
JOHN J. HALLERAN,
GEO. V. MULLAN.

INCREMENT TAX.

Dissenting Memorandum By Messrs. Leubuscher and Howe.

We oppose the proposed tax upon increases in land values for the following reasons:

1. The yield from an Increment Tax will be small, especially in comparison with the needs of the city. There will be many complexities in administration, particularly when property is subdivided. Such a tax will also lead owners to bring pressure on the Tax Department to keep down the normal increases in assessed valuations, and will invite litigation over assessments.

2. The Increment Tax discriminates against the small home owners in the outlying boroughs for the benefit of the multimillionaire land owners of Manhattan. A large portion, if not most, of the land in Manhattan, has now a capitalized congestion selling price and assessed valuation, and it will not increase greatly in assessed value for many years, while the city needs a large additional revenue at once. The assessed value of land in Manhattan is this year $3,184,445,000. The assessed value per acre of land in the five boroughs of the city this year (1915) is as follows: Manhattan, $226,844; The Bronx, $13,288; Brooklyn, $15,855; Queens, $3,782; Richmond, $1,123.

The State census shows that the population of Manhattan is stationary or decreasing; so that the large increases in the assessed value of land in the future must occur in the outlying boroughs, where there is much wider distribution of land ownership. This will be caused by new subways, etc. Ninety-nine families own nearly one-seventh of the assessed value of land in Manhattan,—$450,000,000; but they own only about one-seventieth of the assessed value of land in The Bronx and Brooklyn—$17,000,000. With a super-tax on land values of 2 mills (20 cents per $100) these ninety-nine families would pay annually about $946,000, while with the proposed land Increment Tax, even assuming an annual increase of land values of 4%, they would pay only $189,000,—while they probably would not pay $75,000. There are only about 30,000 owners of land, most of them well to do, in the Borough of Manhattan, and the land Increment Tax would tax the small home owners in the outlying boroughs for their benefit.

3. The Increment Tax is discriminatory in that it favors the financial beneficiaries of past governmental expenditures against those who will benefit from such future expenditures. The majority say that this tax "affects only future increases of land value and is founded on and recognizes to the full the existing capital value of land."

4. The Increment Tax can be successful only as a revenue measure if there are great and continuing increases in land values, which can occur only if rents are continually forced up by increasing congestion of population and business. Thus the adoption of an Increment Tax

commits the government to a policy contrary to the public welfare that demands relief from congestion and exorbitant rents.

5. The English Parliamentary Land Enquiry Committee after studying both systems (Increment Tax and Super Tax) recommended the uniform super tax upon all land values. It stated: "Every local authority should be required to raise by a rate (tax) on site values the whole amount by which its expenditure out of rates in any future year exceeds its expenditure in the year immediately preceding that in which this proposal comes into force."

6. It is as illogical to levy a tax only on future increases in land values, as it would be to levy an income tax only on increases in incomes.

7. It will render more difficult the adoption of a super tax on land values; for it will be claimed that the imposition of an Increment Tax was tantamount to a declaration that the then existing land values should forever after be held sacrosanct.

CONCLUSION.

The majority say: "The completion of the vast scheme of rapid transit, costing about $350,000,000, and for which the taxpayers have in large measure to pay, will substantially increase land values in some sections of the city, and perhaps in all of the boroughs." This recognition by the majority of the proper source of revenue for municipal purposes,—the land values of the city which they admit are created by municipal expenditures paid for by the people—only the more conclusively shows the futility, as well as the injustice, of their proposals for securing additional revenue.

FREDERIC C. LEUBUSCHER,
FREDERIC C. HOWE,

5. SUPER-TAX ON LAND VALUES.

Memorandum By Messrs. Mullan and Others.

It was suggested as an available means of procuring additional revenue, that a super-tax be imposed on land values. The discussion of this particular device was so meagre as not to elicit much, if anything, in the way of argument for and against, being little more than a consideration of and deliberation upon the form of the vote to be taken upon the proposal. An overwhelming majority of the Committee voted against a super-tax, which action served to check further discussion of the proposal whether regarded either as a temporary expedient or as an expression of principle. It is to be assumed that the majority of the Committee were of the opinion that the adoption of such a measure of relief would be inadvisable for the obvious reason that instead of relieving the already greatly overburdened realty base the imposition of a super-tax would be adding to realty one more load, possibly the last straw. It is difficult to conceive of a form of taxation better calculated to destroy realty values. Its only recommendations are the ease and simplicity of its levy and collection, virtues full of menace to the land owner. Once establish such a precedent, and every owner of realty must be kept in a state of constant terror, realizing that as a budget soars so would soar the tax on his property, regardless of the existence and extent of other forms of wealth available for taxation. A super-tax is one of the various forms into which the single taxers mould their convictions. It fastens itself upon the thing that to them should furnish the sole basis of taxation, land. The adoption of such a device would be a beginning, an entering wedge, a step in the direction of their goal. Every argument against the single tax is an argument against a super-tax; the difference is merely one of degree. The arguments against the exemption of improvements from taxation, stated in the majority report upon that question, make unnecessary any more extended or detailed discussion of this proposal.

GEO. V. MULLAN,
ALFRED E. MARLING,
COLLIN H. WOODWARD,
JOSEPH N. FRANCOLINI,
CYRUS C. MILLER,
DAVID RUMSEY.

SUPER-TAX.

Concurring Memorandum By Messrs. Field and Others.

We concur in the recommendation of the Committee opposing a super-tax on land values.

FRANK HARVEY FIELD,
JOHN J. HALLERAN,
HAMILTON HOLT,
JEREMIAH W. JENKS,
ARDOLPH L. KLINE,
WALTER LINDNER,
LOUIS HEATON PINK.
OSCAR R. SEITZ,
FREDERIC B. SHIPLEY,
CHARLES T. WHITE.

SUPER-TAX.

Concurring Memorandum By Mr. Simon.

I concur in the opinion of the Committee as expressed in the Chairman's report that a super-tax on land is inadvisable and undesirable.

ROBERT E. SIMON.

SUPER-TAX.

Dissenting Memorandum By Professor Seligman.

Although, as a member of the majority of the Committee, I have expressed my conviction that both according to the general principles and in view of the particular situation in New York, the exemption of buildings from taxation is inadvisable, it remains nevertheless true, in my opinion, that we should regard with open minds the advisability of placing in the future an increasing burden upon land values.

While I hold the arguments of the single taxers to be erroneous, I agree with the majority of the modern economists in the belief that land values afford an especially promising and suitable basis for local taxation. I do not believe that land values should form the exclusive basis of taxation, but I do think that, under certain conditions, a larger revenue may be derived from that source than is the case at present. The majority of the Committee are clearly of this opinion, as is evidenced by the fact that they have recommended an increment tax on land values. While I have been glad to sign that recommendation as a member of the Committee, I feel that very much the same argument may be utilized in favor of a carefully devised super-tax on land values. I do not, of course, believe that both an Increment Tax and a super-tax on land values should be levied at the same time; but I desire to set forth the reasons why, in my opinion, a super-tax on land values may, if necessary, be utilized in lieu of an increment tax on land values.

As has been pointed out in the majority report on the untaxing of buildings, I do not agree with many of the stock arguments advanced by the single taxers. I do not think that land is so entirely different from other forms of property as to justify the single tax. I do not believe that an increment tax on land values is needed to force land into use, since under present conditions of taxation in New York City it does not pay to hold land out of use. I do not believe that taxes should be levied on land in order to free products of industry, because this assumes that taxes are generally or must otherwise be levied upon such property; whereas, as was stated in the majority report, the whole trend of modern taxation is to take income and not property as the basis of taxation, and there are many incomes in modern times which are not derived from property at all, but from all kinds of privileges and relations of an economic kind. I do not believe that land values should be taxed for the reason that property in land is unjustifiable. I do not believe that land values should be taxed in any exclusive sense in order to lessen the number of those who get incomes without earning them; for, in my opinion, not alone is land only one of the sources of such unearned incomes, but the revenue from land is sometimes earned in the same sense as the revenue from anything else which is based upon care, attention and good business judgment.

Despite these facts I think that a good case may nevertheless be made out for a greater taxation of land values. Land values, in a growing city, are apt to increase, notwithstanding periods of temporary regression. Land owners, while they do not form the only class of people that benefit from city expenditures and while they are not the sole class of the community that possess an ability to contribute to the communal burdens, are nevertheless in a better position than almost any other class to amortize any increasing burden of taxation.

Furthermore, while land, indeed, does not constitute a monopoly (for the supply of urban land may undoubtedly be augmented by drawing upon outlying districts) land none the less differs, not indeed from all other kinds of wealth, but from many other kinds of wealth, in that the increased supply can be secured only at an increased cost; that is, while the tendency of most manufactured products is to fall in price with the development of science, the price of land like that of most raw products tends to increase in price. The growth of demand, therefore, acts differently in the case of land and natural products from what it does in the case of most manufactured products. It is not a clear distinction between land, on the one hand, and labor products on the other; but it is a distinction between those forms of wealth which respond to an increased demand at the same or a decreasing cost, and those which respond to this demand at an increasing cost. Land differs from other things, in short, not absolutely in kind, but simply in the degree to which increase in demand affects change in price. Moreover, the land value tax is perhaps of all taxes the simplest to assess and the easiest to collect. The land value tax, again, is perhaps, of all taxes, the one to which a community can most readily adjust itself. The land value tax, finally, is one, which if carefully devised and administered, will tend to cause the least interference with economic and social conditions. In short, while land does not differ in essence from all other forms of wealth, it does differ in degree from some other forms of wealth, and it is precisely this difference in degree which justifies, in my opinion, a somewhat higher tax upon land.

The principles, which, in my judgment, should obtain in applying the doctrine of increased land values are as follows:

(1). A portion of the increased revenues that are needed should come from other sources. In the opinion of a majority of this Committee this portion of additional revenues, as we have seen, should come from a tax on the general income of the inhabitants, through either a direct income tax or a presumptive income tax. The remainder may well come from an additional tax on land values either in the shape of an increment tax or in the shape of a super-tax.

(2). Care must be taken not to interfere with existing land values. The chief objection as we have seen, to the untaxing of buildings, is that it may decrease the selling value of the property of entirely innocent holders. Such a glaring infraction of property rights could be justified only by considerations of overwhelming necessity, and such considerations are entirely lacking in this case. It is, therefore, highly desirable that in the assessment of any super-tax on land values a provision be introduced that the additional tax when capitalized should never exceed any intervening increase in land values; for only in this way can the above injustice be prevented.

It will be asked what is the difference between a super-tax and an increment tax. The difference is obvious. It is true that the tax will not be assessed in either case unless there has been an increase in land values; but in the case of an increment tax, the tax is proportionate to the increment, while in the case of the super-tax the tax stands in a definite relation not to the increase in land value but to the capitalized value of the land. The super-tax, in other words, is a more comprehensive tax than the increment tax.

The difference can be illustrated by an arithmetical example. Let us assume, for instance, that a given plot of land has increased in value in a definite period from $10,000 to $12,000. An increment tax of say one per cent. on the $2,000 increase would amount to $20. These $20 capitalized at five per cent. amount to $400, thus making the selling value of the land $11,600 after the tax was imposed. On the other hand, let us assume that a super-tax of as much as three mills on the dollar is needed. A three-mills tax on $12,000 would amount to $36. Thirty-six dollars capitalized at the rate of five per cent. equals $720. The consequence is that the property will advance in price from $10,000 to $11,280 and that the tax will stand because the capitalized tax, or $720, is less than the increase of land values, or $1,280. If, however, the increase in land values had been less than the capitalization of the super-tax, the super-tax would have to be diminished in proportion.

The practical difference between the increment tax and the super-tax is that the super-tax would tend to take a larger share of the increment, and that it might be simpler to levy a low super-tax than a high increment tax.

The advantages of a super-tax as against the untaxing of buildings are, therefore, as follows:

(1). There would be no injustice done to the present owners of land.

(2). There would be no reduction in the assessed valuations of real estate, thus eliminating all possibility of embarrassment in either the debt situation or the tax situation.

(3). There would be only a slight slackening in the increase of land values which may be normally expected in a growing city.

(4). If the super-tax is definitely fixed in advance, it would be so amortized as to create practically no embarrassment to future holders of land.

(5). To the extent that the super-tax is levied, it would tend to prevent that part of the increase of rent which is due to a tax on buildings. It would be a mistake, indeed, as was pointed out in the majority report on the untaxing of buildings, to think that a change in rent is to be measured by the change in the rate of the tax on buildings; for there are many other factors, as we have seen, which affect the relative cost of buildings. While, however, due allowance must be made for these other factors, it is none the less probable that a failure to increase the rate on buildings will tend, on the whole, to prevent any corresponding increase in rents.

I think, then, that the future of municipal revenues, not alone in the United States but throughout the world, has in store for us a reliance on the one hand on increased income taxes, in order to tap the abilities of those who profit by the opportunities of our large cities; and on the other hand, on an increase of revenue from land values in order to reach the abilities of those who derive additional and increased benefits from the special privileges afforded by our growing cities.

I believe, in short, that a super-tax on land values, carefully restricted and equitably enforced, will form a precious source of increased revenue to the cities of the future; that it will tend, on the whole, to secure advantageous social results; and that it will not be attended by injurious consequences either to innocent property owners or to the community at large.

EDWIN R. A. SELIGMAN.

SUPER-TAX.

Dissenting Memorandum By Messrs. Leubuscher and Howe.

This is the proposition that was submitted to the Committee: That a part of the additional revenue required by the city be raised by a super-tax on land values. The majority report is in error in stating that "Every argument against the single tax is an argument against a super-tax." The single tax involves two things: First, the taking by taxation of substantially all the economic rent. Second, the abolition of all other forms of taxation. A super-tax means that the present general tax on both land and improvements, besides a multitude of other taxes, remain undisturbed, but that, in order not to increase the general tax rate, a small additional tax be levied on land alone. If an income or abilities tax were adopted, they might not furnish the necessary additional revenue, so that, if the principle of a super-tax were also adopted, the balance of additional revenue might be secured in that way. For example: If twenty-five million dollars additional revenue were required and it was thought unwise to increase the general tax rate, and the income or abilities tax raised only twenty millions, the additional five million dollars could be procured by a one-mill tax on the five billions of land values. This would be no great hardship, even from the conservative standpoint, on real estate. A typical tenement house, for instance, which was worth $30,000 for the building and $10,000 for the land, now pays about $760 tax, and a super-tax of one mill on the $10,000 lot would add only $10 to the tax.

The majority speak of "the already greatly overburdened realty base." As pointed out in the minority report on the untaxing of buildings, real estate is less burdened with taxes in this year of grace 1915, than it was thirty-five years ago. According to the 1913 report of the Department of Taxes and Assessments, in 1880 real estate paid 87% of the total budget, and in 1913, it paid only 75% thereof.

In view of the very meagre majority report on the question, it would be well to state the reasons, founded on both justice and expediency, why the city should have the power to impose a super-tax on land values for the purpose of raising additional revenue.

The per capita cost of local government and the city's share of the State Direct Tax is, in round figures, $38, or $190 for a family of five.

Mayor Mitchel testified before the Joint Legislative Committee on Taxation that, even if the cost of government can be kept at its present level, the city will, in 1920, have to raise, exclusive of the State Direct Tax, $34,554,000 more than its present budget of nearly $200,000,000.

The local budget will be, in 1920, about $250,000,000. Assuming an average increase of population, this will be about $47 per capita, or $235 for a family of five, in addition to the State and Federal indirect taxes.

The per capita cost of the Federal Government is about $7, of the State government, about $5; so that even if there are no unusual increases in Federal and State expenditures by 1920, the average charge per family in New York City for the privilege of being governed will be around $300.

The term "new sources of revenue" should be discarded, as it is inaccurate. There are only two sources of revenue: Earnings, current or accumulated, and Ground Rents. It is agreed that all taxes, except those on Inheritances, Incomes and Land Values, can be shifted to the user of the article or service taxed. It is agreed that unwise or too high taxes can destroy almost everything except land values.

The city has undertaken public improvements, transit lines, water supply, etc., which will be largely wasted unless the population increases rapidly and is self-sustaining.

The average per capita net debt, in 1912, of all cities having a population of 30,000 or over, was $68.74. That of New York was $156.57; of Chicago, $28.62; of Philadelphia, $60.64; of St. Louis, $33.72, and of Boston, $106.42.

The financial benefit of many of the improvements, for which the city's great debt was incurred, will be realized within the next few years by the land owners of the city in the increased selling price of land,—if population increases.

As was clearly shown at the public hearings, high selling prices of land are a detriment to the producers and workers of any community, because they are the result of large ground rents.

New York cannot afford to make it any more difficult or disadvantageous for manufacturers to locate here; and large increases within the next few years in the selling price of land would operate against the increase of factories and industry.

Judging from the experience of the last ten years, and with the present tax rate on land values, the net increase in the selling price of land would be at least $1,000,000,000, and probably $1,200,000,000, during the next decade. Such an increase in the selling price of land would require $50,000,000 to $60,000,000 more ground rent to be paid the land owners on this increase, in addition to the $250,000,000 net ground rents they now receive, before the real producers of the city are requited for their labor and industry.

It would clearly be to the advantage of every one in New York City, except a few land owners, as such, to have the selling price of land here remain stationary, or increase only very little in the future. This is fully as important for the city's development and prosperity as securing additional revenue.

The two desiderata can be achieved effectively and equitably by recovering annually for the maintenance of our local government a part at least of the increase in the selling price of land, by means of a super-tax on land values.

In a very few cases, this might work a temporary hardship, but, owing to the concentration of the ownership of valuable land in New York City, this would be the fairest way to secure additional revenue for local purposes on the basis of financial benefit received. It would also result in reaching those who do not pay their full share of the cost of local government.

One of the arguments in support of the residence, occupation and salary taxes is that they will reach the non-resident who makes his money in this city and lives elsewhere. It is admitted that they will not reach the real non-residents, like William Waldorf Astor. But it is also admitted that a super-tax on land values **will** reach the real non-resident.

The amount New York City must raise next year is, in round figures, $213,000,000, or about $14,000,000 more than this year. Even if the entire additional revenue were raised by a super-tax on land values, the rate on sites would be increased only three mills, and the rate on buildings and personal property would remain at $1.90.

With this super-tax rate, the one hundred families who are the owners of record of land assessed for $473,808,075, located chiefly in Manhattan, would pay $1,411,424 more than at present. Under a general tax rate of two mills (approximately the increase in the rate required to raise $14,000,000 additional revenue), they would advance only $1,262,646, because the assessed value of the buildings of which they are the owners of record is only $157,515,233. Since they would be able ultimately to shift the tax on their buildings to their tenants,—that is $315,030—their own contribution out of their present ground rent of about $20,000,000, would be only $947,616, or $473,808 less than they would pay with a super-tax of three mills on land values.

These hundred families include most of the wealthiest in the city and those whose wealth is due to the growth of the city's population and industry and its expenditures.

Two thousand families would justly pay approximately half of the $14,000,000 with this super-tax on land values, because these two thousand families have been to this extent the fianancial beneficiaries of the city's growth, industry and expenditures.

The owner of a small home whose site is assessed for $1,000, and building for $3,000 would pay $8 with a general increase of two mills, and only $3 with a super-tax of three mills on land values.

The owner of a $30,000 tenement on a $10,000 lot would ultimately pay $30 more with the super-tax on land values as against the $80 he would pay with a two mills increase in the general tax rate, of which he might collect $60 from his tenants by increased rent or decreasing service. He would pay personally about $10 more with the land values super-tax than with the two mills general increase in the tax rate.

The maintaining of the selling price of land at about its present figure, and the prevention of speculative increases, together with the knowledge that there would not be any increase in the tax rate on buildings or machinery, would encourage manufacturers to locate here, and, therefore, be of direct advantage to the city as a whole.

A far greater advantage would be the exemption of the tools of production.

Even those who are opposed to the untaxing of buildings should not object to the super-tax on land values, because it will not reduce the present selling price of land materially, and will not affect the status quo.

FREDERIC C. LEUBUSCHER,
FREDERIC C. HOWE.

SUPER-TAX.

Dissenting Memorandum By Messrs. Purdy and Wilcox.

The City of New York should have power to levy a super-tax on the value of land. Various reasons for conferring this power upon the city are well presented by Prof. Seligman in his memorandum, and other good reasons are presented in the memorandum signed by Mr. Leubuscher, and others.

One fact should be stated, which is not stated in these opinions, and that is that there is a tendency to over-assess buildings, which it is impossible for the best assessing department to counteract. Assessors must follow the evidence of value. When property rises in value assessments must follow and therefore must always be somewhat lower than full value. When the value of property falls for the same reason assessments must always be somewhat higher than full value. In this city, land generally appreciates in value, whereas buildings always depreciate and decline in value. Not only are buildings subject to depreciation from use but more important in this city is the depreciation due to obsolescence. Good buildings frequently lose all their value because of change of character of neighborhood. A super-tax on land values may be used to counteract this tendency.

LAWSON PURDY,
DELOS F. WILCOX,

SUPER-TAX.

Dissenting Memorandum By Mr. Tomlin.

I dissent from the recommendation of the Committee opposing a super-tax on land values for the reasons stated in my memorandum of dissent from the majority report opposing the untaxing of buildings.

FRANKLIN S. TOMLIN.

SUPER-TAX.

Dissenting Memorandum By Mr. Binkerd.

For the reasons stated in my dissenting memorandum on the untaxing of buildings, I believe in raising additional local revenue by a super-tax, or an unearned increment tax, on land.

ROBERT S. BINKERD.

PART THREE.

MEMORANDUM OF BILLS FOR ADMINISTRATIVE CHANGES UNANIMOUSLY RECOMMENDED BY THE COMMITTEE

BILL NO. 1.

Tax Law, Section 4, Subdivision 7.

Amend by omitting the words "or is in good faith contemplated" so that real property shall not be exempt when vacant though owned by a charitable or other such corporation.

This subdivision provides for the exemption of the property of various corporations organized exclusively for religious, charitable, benevolent and other like purposes. One clause of this subdivision, which was inserted in 1891, makes exemption depend upon the state of mind of the officers of the corporation when the land is not in use for the purpose of the corporation by reason of the absence of suitable buildings. As the property may still be exempted if the erection of suitable buildings "is in good faith contemplated by such corporation or association," this amendment provides for the omission of the words above quoted. If this omission is made exemption will depend on the actual facts and not upon what the officers of the corporation may at the time contemplate.

BILL NO. 2.

Tax Law, Section 12.

This is the section which provides for the taxation of the personal estate of domestic corporations. Amend by omitting the provision for the deduction of surplus and the provision for the deduction of the assessed value instead of the actual value of real estate. The change will increase the revenue from domestic corporations to some extent, perhaps $100,000.

BILL NO. 3.

Tax Law, Section 45-a.

Add new subdivision to Section 45-a in which provision shall be made for the State Board of Tax Commissioners to report to the local assessors throughout the State an identifying description of real property of public service corporations exclusive of their special franchise. In tax districts which have tax maps such description shall be by lot and block numbers. The State Board shall report the value of the land as reported to them by the owner of the special franchise, the reproduction value and present value of buildings, the reproduction value and present value of the plant, also the valuation placed by the State Board upon land, buildings and plant for the purpose of determining the amount by which the gross earnings shall be reduced on account of the ownership of such property.

Increase in revenue expected on account of the receipt of such information, either in respect of the assessment of special franchises or other property of public service corporations, at least $500,000.

BILL NO. 4.

Tax Law, Section 48.

This section provides for the deduction from a special franchise tax of the amount paid by the owner of the special franchise as rental for the franchise and any sums paid which are in the nature of taxes, such as car licenses, etc. The operation of this section was in many cases to decrease the actual tax payments made by the owners of special franchises to a sum less than they were required to pay before the amendment of 1899, known as the Special Franchise Tax Law. This section should be repealed. The increased revenue will amount to about $800,000.

BILL NO. 5.

Tax Law, Section 204.

By this section the Secretary of State is required to report to the State Comptroller certain details concerning all certificates of incorporation and amendments to such certificates filed with him. Add to this section the requirement that the Secretary of State shall send a duplicate report to the assessors of each town, city and village named in a certificate of incorporation as the principal place of business of the corporation.

This procedure will tend to increase the assessment of domestic corporations at least throughout the State, will check the tendency to have the principal place of business at Esopus or Painted Post when the principal place of business, in fact, is in New York, and will thus increase the number of corporations taxable in New York; further, it will supply information to the New York Tax Department without cost that now costs at least $600 a year to obtain.

BILL NO. 6 (Became Law, Chapter 600, Laws of 1915).

Greater New York Charter, Section 926.

When the charter was amended to provide for semi-annual tax payments the time for sending unpaid personal taxes to the marshal was not changed. The date for paying personal taxes was made May first, instead of October first. This bill changes the date for sending personal taxes to the marshal from January to the preceding August. This will give more time for the collection of personal taxes and commence the proceeding earlier.

EXHIBITS ACCOMPANYING REPORT.

UNTAXING OF BUILDINGS.

QUESTIONS PREPARED BY THE COMMITTEE TO BE CONSIDERED IN CONNECTION WITH PUBLIC HEARINGS, AND ANSWERS THERETO SUBMITTED BY VARIOUS ORGANIZATIONS AND INDIVIDUALS.

COMMITTEE ON TAXATION.

QUESTIONS TO BE CONSIDERED IN CONNECTION WITH PUBLIC HEARINGS.

Question Series 1.

ON THE EFFECT OF THE UNTAXING OF BUILDINGS UPON LAND VALUES AND UPON SPECULATION IN LAND.

1. To what extent has the development of land values in different parts of the city been irregular? To what extent, at different times and in different portions of the city, have the land values decreased, and what have been the causes of such decreases?

2. To what extent may we expect in the near future a more normal increase in land values than during the past few years? What will be the probable effect of the new subway system upon land values? To what extent has the prospective increase been discounted?

3. What proportion in the amount and value of the land in the several boroughs of Greater New York may be classed as appropriately improved? What proportion is inappropriately improved? What proportion is unimproved?

4. Can the transfer of the tax from buildings to land ever increase the value of improved land? For instance, if there are two parcels of land, each worth $100,000, Parcel A having land worth $70,000, and a building worth $30,000 and Parcel B having land worth $30,000, and a house worth $70,000, if buildings are exempted from taxation, and assuming that the value of Parcel A will decrease, will the capital value of Parcel B increase? If so, why?

5. How frequently, under typical conditions in New York, does the nature of the "appropriate improvement" of a parcel of land change?

6. What are the standards now employed in fixing land values? What part is played by the prospective use value in the future?

7. To what extent are so-called "taxpayers" erected in New York City? i. e., to what extent are cheap, temporary improvements made for the purpose of carrying the land until the time is ripe for appropriate permanent improvement?

8. Are increased land values the result of the increase of population alone, or to the increase of the community's wealth?

9. What would be the effect on the aggregate land values in New York City, and separately upon improved and unimproved land, if it were known that the population of the city, as a whole, would remain stationary?

10. How closely is the estimated future growth of population reflected in present land values, i. e., how far do present values include a

capitalization of the additional rental values which are expected from an increase of population for an indefinite period in the future?

11. What is better for a great city, high land values or low land values?

12. To what extent is land acquired in New York for speculative purposes? In other words, is land purchased, not for the purpose of investment or use by improvement, but for the purpose of resale at a profit?

13. If all taxes upon buildings were transferred to the land, would the effect be the discouraging of land speculation, and if so, would this result in the general depreciation of land values?

14. Assuming that these results would follow, would the social and economic effects of this change be wholesome or otherwise?

15. What are the relative advantages and disadvantages of land speculation? In what respect does land speculation differ from the speculation carried on in the stock and produce exchanges?

16. To what extent is unimproved land in New York City ripe for improvement? In other words, to what extent is land held out of use which ought to be improved immediately?

17. Assuming that the transfer of the tax from buildings to land would tend to stabilize values and check speculation, could these results be obtained as well or better by means of the "land increment tax?"

18. To what extent, if any, would the transfer of the tax from buildings to land tend to accentuate the depreciation of land, when for other reasons its value is shrinking?

19. What would be the effect upon loans in a case where the transfer of the tax from buildings to land will neither increase nor decrease the amount of the tax levied upon a particular parcel of real estate? Will the value of the land be in any way affected by the transfer? In other words, does the tax on a building have the same effect upon the value of the land as a tax levied directly upon the land itself?

20. To what extent is the land of New York owned by a small number of owners or in small parcels by a large number of owners?

21. To what extent are real estate mortgages in New York City owned in large lots by a small number of owners or in small lots by a large number of owners?

22. Would the untaxing of buildings increase or decrease the taxes paid by the owners of skyscrapers, who, at the same time, owned the land?

23. What effect would the untaxing of buildings have upon the small home owners in the various boroughs in New York? Would it affect small house owners in Manhattan like those in Brooklyn?

24. What effect would the untaxing of buildings have upon house owners where the value of the real estate is from ten to fifty thousand dollars? Would the effect be the same in Manhattan as in the other boroughs?

25. What effect would the untaxing of buildings have upon the relatively small and more modest owners in each class of owners of buildings, as compared with the relatively weathier members in each class?

26. To what extent can the effect of the untaxing of buildings upon land values be predicted with accuracy in the different parts of the city?

Question Series 2.

ON THE EFFECT OF THE UNTAXING OF BUILDINGS UPON BUILDING OPERATIONS, HOUSING CONDITIONS, AND CONGESTION.

1. Would the untaxing of buildings stimulate the erection of buildings? If so, why?

2. Would the untaxing of buildings encourage the preparation of vacant land for use? For example, low lands that need to be filled in and high lands that need to be graded down?

3. Would the untaxing of buildings hasten the replacement of old and inappropriate buildings by new and appropriate buildings?

4. In general, would the untaxing of buildings lead to a more intensive use of the land?

5. Assuming that the untaxing of buildings would tend to stimulate the improvement of vacant land, would this effect be most noticeable and most immediate in the case of lands nearest the business centers, or land, which for other reasons is the most valuable of the lands still unimproved? When would the new equilibrium be reached and what would be the final result?

6. Would the untaxing of buildings tend to bring about the over-development of the most valuable lands? For example, would it tend to cause the erection of buildings higher than would normally be appropriate for the location?

7. Will the untaxing of buildings tend to greater compactness in the development of the city? In other words, would it tend to cause the chief center and all the subcenters to be built up solidly rather than in a straggling and irregular manner?

8. Assuming that the untaxing of buildings would tend to promote compact development, to what extent would this result in the encroachment upon public places, or in the occupation for building purposes of private spaces which are now held open, either intentionally or otherwise, for the public good?

9. To what extent would the untaxing of buildings tend to the subdivision of parcels of land or to the covering up of larger proportions of each parcel with buildings, or with unduly high buildings?

10. To what extent would the untaxing of buildings necessitate the acquisition by the city of additional land to be reserved for open spaces, particularly in the central part of the city?

11. To what extent would this increased expenditure still further augment taxes?

12. To what extent, if any, would the untaxing of buildings increase the necessity for building restrictions, such as limitation of the height of buildings, limitation of proportion of lot space covered, etc.? If the untaxing of buildings is desirable, would it be better to untax buildings before or after the additional legislation referred to above had been attained?

13. To what extent, if any, would the untaxing of buildings tend to discourage the acquiring and holding of large lots and grounds for lawn or garden purposes in the suburban districts? Would this be a good or a bad thing?

14. Would the untaxing of buildings tend to change in any respect the internal design of the buildings, for example, would it increase the size of the rooms and suites?

15. Assuming that the untaxing of buildings would promote the construction of larger and better buildings, with more commodious rooms, would this have the effect of destroying the value of existing buildings by rendering them obsolete?

16. Would the untaxing of buildings tend to encourage temporary or ad interim improvements pending the final determination of the character of the appropriate improvement for a given location and pending the arrival of the time when such appropriate improvements can be profitably made?

17. Would the effect upon vacant lands suitable for truck farms be to continue them in use for this purpose longer than would be the case under the present system of taxation?

18. If the untaxing of buildings would decrease the value of lands in the outlying districts, would this cheapening somewhat offset the tendency to economize in the use of land for lawn and garden purposes which might result from the higher rate of taxation of land values? If so, how long would this continue, and what would be the final result?

19. What are the criteria for determining at a given time whether or not a city is overbuilt with respect to any particular class of building? What is the influence of the loan market in this respect? Is it important?

20. To what extent are the different classes of buildings now in existence in New York vacant?

21. To what extent are the buildings now vacant really suitable for occupation? In other words, to what extent are the vacancies ascribable to the buildings having been inappropriately constructed in the first place or having become obsolete?

22. Are the modern and better types of buildings of the different classes more fully occupied than the older and inferior types? Does the erection of new buildings of a better type and more suitable for the purposes for which they are designed have any tendency to force the destruction of older and less suitable buildings?

23. If so, would this be likely to result in a material increase in the cost of building, by reason of the cost of labor and materials; and if so, at what point would the tendency to stimulate building operations check itself?

24. What effect would the untaxing of buildings have upon such developments as the Sage Foundation Homes Company?

25. What effect would the untaxing of buildings have upon the necessity for, and the practicability of, city planning schemes for outlying districts?

26. To what extent would the larger supply of buildings tend to attract population to New York City or to cause a shifting of population from one section to another in New York City? How far might this tendency go to offset or to accentuate the effect of transit facilities in any particular locality?

27. If the untaxing of buildings tended to greater compactness in the development of the city, to what extent would this render the problem of street transportation, such as rapid transit, trolley, and vehicular traffic, location of pipes, wires, conduits, etc., more or less difficult than they now are?

Question Series 3.

ON THE EFFECT OF THE UNTAXING OF BUILDINGS UPON RENT.

1. To what extent is land leased in New York City on the basis of pure ground rents with the lessee making the improvements?

2. To what extent are parcels of improved real estate in New York City leased or rented as a whole?

3. What are the usual terms of building leases as to duration, renewal, liability to pay rent, improvements and maintenance, payment of taxes, and special assessments?

4. To what extent are buildings in New York City leased or rented piecemeal?

5. Where different tenants occupy as lessees separate portions of a building in New York City, what are the usual terms of the leases as to improvements and maintenance?

6. Where different tenants occupy as lessees different portions of a building in New York City, what are the usual terms of the leases with reference to free services rendered by the landlord, such as janitor service, elevator service, lighting, heating, etc.?

7. What are the elements that go to make up rent for the various types of buildings, and under the various types of leases in use in New York City?

8. Does the landlord normally collect in ground rent all that he can get or, in other words, all that anybody is willing to pay for the privilege of occupying the particular location?

9. If the landlord now collects in ground rent all that the location is worth, and if taxes now levied on buildings were transferred to the land, would the landlord, by reason of the increased tax on the land, be unable to increase the ground rent?

10. Are the taxes now levied on the building properly regarded as a part of the operating expense of the building separate from the land, or do they come out of the landlord as a deduction from ground rent? In other words, do taxes levied upon the value of buildings have any different effect upon rents than do taxes levied upon the value of land? Do tenants pay any higher rents on account of a high tax rate on land and buildings, or either of them, than they otherwise would?

11. To what extent, under present conditions, do owners of improved property count upon the appreciation in land values to offset depreciation in building values? To what extent are rents kept down by the elimination of building depreciation?

12. If the transfer of the present tax on buildings to land values had the effect of checking the increase in land values, to what extent would property owners be compelled to increase their depreciation reserve on account of their buildings, and would such increase in depreciation charge be added to rents?

13. If the untaxing of buildings should result in the construction of more buildings and larger and more commodious ones, would the effect be through competition to reduce rents in all buildings or only in the older, smaller, and less commodious ones?

14. To what extent would lower rents due to a larger supply of buildings in New York City tend to attract population from outside the city, particularly from suburbs in New York and New Jersey to which

people doing business in the city have heretofore gone in search of lower rents? To what extent, by this increase in the demand for buildings, would the tendency toward lower rents be checked?

15. If the effect of untaxing buildings would be to stimulate the construction of buildings, and thereby through competition to reduce the rental per unit of space occupied, to what extent would the renters take larger accommodations for the same money rather than occupy the same accommodations for less money?

16. If the untaxing of buildings would lead to a reduction in rents, could the reduction in rents ever be greater than the amount of the tax so transferred? If so, why?

17. Would the assumed tendency to shift to the tenant the benefit of the lower tax on buildings meet, under the actual conditions in New York City, with friction? i. e., are there any peculiar conditions connected with the mobility of the population which would interfere with this assumed reduction of rents?

18. What is the connection between rents and wages in New York City? Are wages higher in New York than in other cities? If so, why? If one of the causes of high wages in New York is higher rents, would a decrease in rents mean a fall in wages? If not, why not?

19. In general, are high rents in New York due more largely to high land values or to other causes? What is the relative influence of taxes upon rents as compared with other factors that cause high rents?

20. To the extent that taxes form an element in rents do tenants, at the present time, in New York City, feel that they are interested in the city budget, that is, in the city expenditures which result in city taxes? If it be assumed that the benefit of the untaxing of buildings would accrue to the tenants, would this not mean a lessening of interest in the budget of the great mass of tenants? Would this fact accentuate the tendency to have all the taxes paid by one class of the population and to have the expenditures voted by another? Is this a healthy tendency in a Democracy?

Question Series 4.

ON THE EFFECT OF THE UNTAXING OF BUILDINGS UPON PUBLIC REVENUE AND PUBLIC CREDIT.

1. Would the transfer of the tax now levied upon improvements to land values so increase the tax rate as to make the taxes levied uncollectible?

2. Would the revenue from the land tax be reduced by the reduction in the value of the land and the resultant reduction in the assessment or tax base?

3. Would the transfer of the building tax to land result practically in the over-assessment of land, either through the reduction of existing land values or through the increase of assessments for the purpose of keeping down the tax rate?

4. What is the proportion of true value of both land and buildings carried on the assessment rolls for New York City, as a whole, and for different portions of the city?

5. To what extent do assessments necessarily or actually lag behind the increase or decrease of values?

6. To what extent are buildings in New York City depreciated below the cost of reproduction now in the assessments?

7. To what extent do the assessments in New York City reach speculative values?

8. If the increase in the tax rate on land should result in the curtailment of speculation and the partial or complete elimination of speculative values, would this necessarily result in lower assessments? What distinction, if any, is there between assessed valuation and selling valuation for speculative purposes?

9. What proportion of taxes levied on real estate in New York City remains uncollected at the close of the tax year? At the close of the second year? At the close of the third year? At the close of the fourth year? At the close of the fifth year?

10. Assuming that the untaxing of buildings would lead to over-assessment of old values, what effect, if any, would such over-assessment have upon the sale of city bonds within a debt limit?

11. Assuming that buildings continue to be taxed on an assessment representing 1% of their real value, would, in your opinion, the courts hold that it was proper to include the other 99% within the valuation of real estate, or would the courts hold that only 1% should be so included; and what would be the effect, both upon the constitutional tax rate and upon the constitutional debt limit?

12. If buildings were untaxed, would this tend in any way to remove the objections that now lie against the taxing of exempt property such as churches, etc.?

13. If it be assumed that the untaxing of buildings would result in a more compact development of the city, to what extent would this affect the cost of government functions and thereby increase or decrease the amount of credit or current revenue necessary for city government?

14. If it be assumed that the untaxing of buildings would result in a more intensive use of the land and in the consequent necessity of more parks, open spaces, wider streets, etc., to what extent would this increase or decrease the amount of credit or of current revenue necessary for the city government?

15. In general, would the more compact development of the city mean more expenditure or less, that is, higher taxes or lower taxes?

16. In case the untaxing of buildings resulted in a shifting of real estate development accompanied by a shifting of population and business, to what extent would these changes render existing municipal buildings obsolete?

17. If the untaxing of buildings resulted in a shrinking and partial confiscation of land values, to what extent, if any, would the deliberate adoption of this policy by the City of New York tend to affect the city's business relations and actual borrowing ability?

18. If all existing taxes on buildings were transferred to land values, would this tend to diminish or to accentuate the evil effects and unpopularity of an increasing tax rate?

19. If all taxes on buildings were transferred to land values would this remove a practical obstacle in the way of a full development of the single tax theory which would result in the gradual diminution and ultimate absorption of a larger and larger proportion of ground rent in the form of taxes?

Question Series 5.

ON THE EFFECT OF THE UNTAXING OF BUILDINGS UPON MORTGAGE LOANS.

1. To what extent, if any, would the untaxing of buildings reduce the security value of a parcel of land appropriately improved?

2. To what extent, if any, would the untaxing of buildings reduce the security value of a parcel of land partially or inappropriately improved?

3. To what extent, if any, would the untaxing of buildings reduce the security value of unimproved land?

4. What proportion of improved land in New York City is covered by first mortgages? What proportion by second mortgages? What proportion by third mortgages?

5. Up to what proportion of full market value will money be loaned on the security of first mortgages in the case of fully improved land in New York City?

6. Up to what proportion of full market value will money be loaned on the security of first mortgages in the case of partially or inappropriately improved land in New York City?

7. Up to what proportion of full market value will money be loaned on the security of first mortgages in the case of unimproved land in New York City.

8. Up to what proportion of full market value will money be loaned on the security of second mortgages in the case of fully improved land in New York City?

9. Up to what proportion of full market value will money be loaned on the security of second mortgages in the case of partially or inappropriately improved land in New York City?

10. Up to what proportion of full market value will money be loaned on the security of second mortgages in the case of unimproved land in New York City?

11. As to what proportion of lands in New York City subject to mortgage do the owners hold an equity of less than ten per cent. of full market value? Of less than twenty per cent.? Of less than thirty per cent.? Of less than forty per cent.? Of less than fifty per cent.?

12. In case the untaxing of buildings resulted in reducing the relative proportion of land value to total value of real estate, to what extent would this tend to reduce the borrowing power of the property?

13. In case the untaxing of buildings should result in a decrease of ten per cent. in the total value of real estate, to what extent would equities be wiped out and existing mortgages have to be foreclosed?

14. If the untaxing of buildings resulted in a readjustment of relative values as between land and buildings, and if this resulted in a reduction of the security value of improved real estate, would the ultimate effect be to decrease the size of loans obtainable on mortgage, or to increase the rate of interest demanded and paid?

ANSWERS TO QUESTIONS SUBMITTED BY THE SOCIETY TO LOWER RENTS AND REDUCE TAXES ON HOMES; BENJAMIN C. MARSH, EXECUTIVE SECRETARY.*

SERIES 1.

On the Effect of the Untaxing of Buildings Upon Land Values and Upon Speculation In Land.

1. (a). The development of the selling price of land has been irregular in New York City to the extent that it has been affected by the following influences:

1. Construction of large office buildings and overcrowding of tenements.
2. Projection or construction of transit lines.
3. Construction of public improvements, docks, piers, etc.
4. Construction of arterial lines of communication and to a lesser extent of smaller roads.
5. Location of settlements, such as of negroes.
6. Location of nuisances, such as gas plants and slaughter houses.
7. Shifting of business and mercantile interests.
8. Heavy discounting of the demand for land and consequent high ground rents.
9. Reduction of local demand for land by construction of bridges and transit lines.

(b). There have been decreases in land values frequently, due to the reasons enumerated above, in many sections of the city, particularly where the land has attained a capitalized congestion selling price. The decrease in one section of the city, however, has usually resulted in an increase in another,—so that it has really meant merely a shifting or transfer in the selling price of land.

NOTE.—It is essential to differentiate between "selling price of land" and "land values." Were government to take all the ground rent of the city for public purposes—which we do not advocate—the use value of the land would not be reduced at all, although it would not have any selling price.

2. This question must be considered from two points of view; the selling price of all the land of the city, and the selling price of individual parcels of land.

(a). The increase in the selling price of land of the city will depend chiefly upon the tax rate on land values. The increase of land values in the city will depend solely upon the increase in the demand

---

*In these and the other sets of answers the numbers refer to the numbers of the questions in the preceding questionnaire to which the answers are directed.

for land and expenditures for public improvements, regardless of the system of taxation.

(b). The increase in the selling price of parcels of land in the City will depend upon the conditions enumerated in answers to question 1 (a).

The new subway will probably increase the selling price of land affected in the outlying Boroughs and the lower west side; it will probably reduce slightly the selling price of land in some sections of the City, as along Lexington Avenue, by enabling people to reach pleasanter surroundings in less time.

The increase in selling price of most land which will be affected by the new subway system does not seem to have been materially discounted, though much of this land is held at a very high figure.

3. The answer to this question depends upon the definition of "an appropriate improvement." If that definition is an improvement worth two or three times as much as the value of the land, then only a very small proportion of the parcels in any Borough of the City are adequately improved.

There were in Manhattan, in 1914, 7,202 absolutely vacant parcels of land assessed for $158,681,830, and comprising approximately 9,000 vacant lots, while in 1912, there were about 19,000 parcels which had one, two or at most three-story improvements.

In 1910, fifty per cent. of the population of The Bronx lived on five per cent. of the area.

In the Borough of Brooklyn, only about one-half of the area is adequately improved with buildings; while Queens and Richmond are practically agricultural boroughs, less than a quarter of either being improved with buildings. Whether buildings be untaxed or not, large areas in both these boroughs, whose combined acreage is nearly 111,000 acres, could profitably be used for many years to come for intensive gardening, which is now being carried on profitably in both boroughs. A large proportion of both boroughs is assessed as acreage. The result of heavy taxation of land values would not be to compel construction of tenements or even of single family houses on every lot in the greater city before 1926; but to compel owners to sell at reasonable prices, to use their land productively for intensive gardening or small homes, and to return to the community a larger part of the ground rent, due to public expenditures.

The "appropriateness" of an improvement does not depend upon its size. The City Investing Building, Woolworth and Equitable Buildings are monstrosities, due to greed to corner the office market and the craze for advertising, but primarily to the moral anarchy of land speculators, and their control over the Board of Estimate and Apportionment, and the Board of Aldermen, as these bodies could, at any time, have put reasonable limits upon the height or size of all buildings, except possible tenements. Many of the larger office buildings of the city rob the neighboring properties of light. This is legal in the United States, but prevented by the "law of ancient lights" in England.

4. No. The selling price of land is its clear net rental capitalized, regardless of the value of improvements thereon.

5. The life of an ordinary brick tenement or house is twenty to forty years, but there are thousands of such buildings in the city which have been "dead" for many years. Many office buildings outlive their usefulness in twenty to thirty years.

6. The law requires land to be assessed for what it will bring in the open market at a free, not a forced sale. For many years the Tax Department has sought legislation to compel the true price paid to be recorded to facilitate the very difficult task of assessment, but land speculators, fearing a just assessment, have defeated the effort. The net ground rental is the usual determinant of the selling price, and prospective use plays a part in fixing the net ground rental.

7. No statistics available, probably several thousand in the city.

8. The value of movable property is relative with respect to time and place. A railroad bond, payable at a remote date, changes in value as the prevailing rate of interest changes and its value changes on account of its location, because of the rate of exchange between two places, such as London and New York, and because of particular burdens, such as taxes to which its ownership may subject its owner in a particular place.

A parcel of land cannot be moved away, and, therefore, it does not change its value because of its location, but it does change from time to time because of a change in the circumstances affecting its value. One reason for increase in value is because of the parcel's peculiar adaptability for a particular use. For instance on the upper east side, at the intersection of a cross street with an avenue, three of the corners are owned by an estate which will not lease its property for the sale of liquor. The fourth corner is said to rent for twice as much as any one of the three corners. There can be only one saloon at the intersection and this gives a certain limited monopoly to the corner that can be leased for liquor selling.

Another reason for an enhanced value is the hope that there will be an increased demand for it at some later period. All of the circumstances which indicate an increased demand for a particular parcel of land have a tendency to increase its value.

A rule in the Department of Taxes assessing unimproved land at a third of its value and improved land at two-thirds of its value tends to increase the value of unimproved land, to encourage speculation by owning unimproved land and holding it out of use. This used to be the rule in New York City. A rule which assesses all land—improved and unimproved—at full value tends to decrease the value of unimproved land relatively to what it was before the law was observed. A change in the law placing all taxes on land, without regard to improvements, would tend to decrease the value of unimproved land, and would encourage improvement—just the contrary of the situation as it existed under the old rule of the Department of Taxes to discriminate in favor of unimproved land and against improved land. It is difficult to see how there could be a great increase of population without an increase of the community's wealth.

All increase of population comes from increased business facilities and business opportunities, which imply an increase in the capital invested. It is difficult to see how the private income of a particular tenant would increase the rent of the parcel of land which he occupied.

Public improvements for which the people pay are an important factor in increasing land values.

9. If it were known that the population of the city, as a whole, would remain stationary, it might slightly depress the aggregate selling price of land in the city, if other factors remain constant. When values

are going up, or when the prevailing rate of interest is declining, the price at which a security sells includes an allowance for expectation of a rise.

10. Probably the estimated immediate future growth of population for a year or two is reflected pretty accurately in present land values.

11. We assume that in the question, "what is better for a great city, high land values or how land values?" selling price is meant, and *high* means above the real value, and *low* means below the real value. It is not good for a community to put an exaggerated value on anything. We refer the Committee to the statement of Mr. Richard M. Hurd, that low land values are good for a community because then their ground rents are low. The value of land is not the important point, but the selling price.

12. The Real Estate Record and Builders' Guide stated editorially a few years ago: "New York City, probably more than any other city in the world, has been the paradise of the real estate speculators and operators, of the man who buys real estate, not for the purpose of improving it, but for the purpose of appropriating a probable increase in value."

The question is misleading since it differentiates between purchasing land "for the purpose of investment" and "for the purpose of resale at a profit." Most of the large land-holding companies and estates buy land for speculation,—probably, at least, a quarter to a third of the value of land is so held, and a third to half of the area in the outlying boroughs.

13. Yes. Land speculation would be discouraged, but not stopped till all the ground rent is taken by taxation. Transferring taxes now levied on buildings to land values, during a period of five to ten years, would depreciate the selling price of land (the present assessed value) but would retard the rate of increase.

If all taxes upon buildings were transferred to the land, it would discourage the holding of land out of use, because of the increased carrying charges. Untaxing buildings would encourage the erection of buildings by decreasing the carrying charges of the investment in the building. In a growing community, untaxing buildings should have the effect of lowering rents, through the operation of the law of supply and demand.

The average annual increase in the tax rate on both land and buildings in 1908, 1909-1910 was nine cents on $100, but during these three years the increase in the selling price of land was about $400,000,000; the increase in the assessed value was much larger.

Transferring taxes now levied on buildings to land values, gradually, through a period of ten years, would involve an increase in the tax rate on land alone of only about eleven cents on $100, while the stimulus to manufacturing would tend to keep the selling price of land stable.

14. The social and economic effect would be to decrease the cost of living, to improve the housing and working conditions, to increase the purchasing value of wages, and to provide more employment and better wages. Whether this would be considered more employment or otherwise, depends upon whether it is good for the laboring man to be well paid, to live and work under safe and healthy surroundings, or in dangerous, unhealthy surroundings. Some people think it is bad for the laboring man to have high wages. We do not so believe.

The city would also acquire land cheaper for public purposes.

15. The advantages and disadvantages of land speculation are no different from the advantages and disadvantages of speculation in general, so far as the speculator is concerned. The effect on the community, however, is different. In so far as land speculaton holds land out of use, it gives an artificial value to land in use, increases rents and the cost of living—to the disadvantage of all of the community except the land owner. The users of land have to pay ground rent on land speculators' profits—users of other commodities speculated in do not.

16. When population is so congested as to increase illness and to create immoral and indecent conditions, we may be sure that some unimproved land is ripe for improvement, although increased transportation facilities, sewers, streets, fire houses, sidewalks, pavings, police stations and many other requirements may be necessary as a part of the improvement. From the point of view of the owner of a lot, his lot is not ripe for improvement until the city has spent a great deal of money in its neighborhood. From the point of view of the public, a tract of land is ripe for improvement when there is a reasonable demand for the land. This calls for the necessary money to be spent by the public and the owner in fitting it for the uses of which the population has need. No one can say, statistically, to what extent unimproved land in New York is ripe for improvement, but obviously a good deal is—the amount will be determined when taxes now levied on buildings to prevent their construction is transferred to land values.

17. A land increment tax which would take *all* of the increment would have considerable effect in stabilizing values and checking speculation, but it would be a gross discrimination in favor of those who have profited by land speculation to date, and would not be either a sound fiscal nor economic policy. By reducing the general tax rate, it would also add to the acquired profits of land speculation. A very low land increment tax would have negligible economic results and would yield little revenue.

18. The transfer of the tax from buildings to land, while at once depreciating land values, ought to tend to counteract some of the factors tending to make its value shrink. The lowering of rents ought to temporarily attract an increased population. If business can be sure of not being taxed business should be attracted.

Land in New York City has borne heavier burdens than almost anywhere else, and still the selling price of land has increased enormously.

19. Untaxing buildings and putting an increased tax burden on land values ought to help loans on real estate, because such a policy would tend to increase the population, assuming, of course, that the money raised from taxes was spent with reasonable efficiency for the benefit of the land.

The tax upon buildings has exactly the opposite effect upon land values from a tax upon land values. Assuming a stationary population and no other factors tending to increase land values (an assumption always hitherto contrary to fact in New York City) a higher tax rate upon land values would depreciate the selling price of land, regardless of the value of the improvement thereon.

20. Exact figures cannot be obtained because so much land is held by dummies, and because the true owners of all property are not re-

corded. Property owners are averse to having the ownership of property here known. This society will shortly submit a list of the largest owners of property and the amounts, showing that about one thousand families are the owners of record or control corporations owning between a fourth and a fifth of the total value of land in the city. The ownership of land should have been obtained by the Tax Committee itself. To fail to do so would be proof that the Committee had no intention of ascertaining facts essential to determine the results of transferring of taxes now levied on buildings to land values. There may be as many as 150,000 owners of property in New York City.

Much property is owned by absent landlords. The study of this Society indicates that about two thousand families, and a few real estate corporations which they control, own more than half of the value of land in the city. The vast majority of the property owners of the city do not own more than $800 to $1,500 worth of land.

21. Most mortgages are owned by small investors through life insurance companies, savings banks and other financial institutions, which loan on real estate. Unless these institutions have loaned much more than the law allows on property the savings would not be affected by the transfer of taxes on buildings to land values in one year. These savings are perfectly safe if the transfer is made in not less than five years, as the average loan is for three years and very few exceed five, while the change would not reduce the selling price of land so would not impair the value of the security.

22. It would decrease the taxes paid by the owners of skyscrapers, but not an owner of a skyscraper wants the change because he knows he would be obliged through the competition of new buildings to reduce his rents by at least as much as the reduction in his taxes. The change would increase the total taxes paid by the "skyscraper" district below Chambers Street in Manhattan nearly a million and a half.

23. There are practically no small house owners in Manhattan like those in Brooklyn. The land of the small house owners in Brooklyn is assessed for $1,000 and $2,000, of the "small" house owners in Manhattan from $5,000 to $10,000. Most "small" house owners in Manhattan would realize from $2,000 to $5,000 unearned land increment on the sale of their property if they have held it for any length of time. A large proportion of them would pay about the same taxes, under the proposed change, or slightly more because of their unearned increment; while the small house owner in Brooklyn would save on the average $40 to $75 a year in taxes.

24. The effect depends upon the relative assessed value of land and improvements of each parcel in every borough.

25. The effect depends upon the relative assessed value of land and improvements, but, in general, and with practically no exceptions, the relatively modest owners of each class of owners of buildings, whose buildings are buildings and not taxpayers, fire-traps nor consumption factories, would save taxes, while the wealthier members in each class would pay more taxes.

The Tax Committee must be aware of the fact that nearly three million people live in firetrap tenements, and hundreds of thousands in consumption factories.

26. To the extent that the relative assessed values of land and improvements are known, and the development of the city and the influ-

ence of countless forces can be predetermined. The tendencies are known, and will be beneficial to all except land speculators, and financial interests because speculative selling prices of land increase interest rates.

SERIES 2.

On the Effect of the Untaxing of Buildings Upon Building Operations, Housing Conditions and Congestion.

1. Yes, as admitted by most who oppose the change and whose opposition would otherwise be largely illogical. It will enable builders to secure land for a lower price than with the present tax rate on land values and reduce the fixed charges on adequately improved property also, by reducing the total taxes. People construct buildings for the profit they can get, and not for their health. The owners of unimproved and underimproved property will be obliged to choose between a larger net loss and a smaller net profit. The change would also tend to lower interest rates.

2. Yes. For the same reasons as given in 1, above.

3. Yes. For the same reasons as given above.

4. No, because land is now used as intensively as possible by a few under our present uniform tax rate on land and buildings.

By putting heavier carrying charges on vacant or underimproved land it would force the owners thereof in self-preservation to favor rational limitations on the volume of buildings so a few land hogs couldn't corner the office space market. The realty interests have, for years, prevented any limitation upon the volume or size of office buildings and prevented the Board of Estimate and Apportionment and the Board of Aldermen from limiting the same. Realty owners, by their own action, have, to quote Hon. Lawson Purdy, "shot land values to pieces." Except for the opposition of realty owners, a districting system for the city would doubtless have been in force for all buildings.

5. Partly answered in 4, above. It would make people use their brains, instead of privilege, to get a living everywhere and encourage consecutive improvements.

6. Most land speculators say in the same breath that no loans can be secured for constructing buildings, and that every owner of land will construct immediately a huge building. Neither statement is true. Owners of land will improve rationally more quickly. (See 4, above.)

7. It will tend to cause logical and consecutive improvement from the center out, with better provision for light and ventilation, and open spaces, because with a good supply of buildings tenants will take only the better ones, just as the owners of the new office buildings are taking the tenants of the old and darker ones away from them. It will tend to prevent straggling development.

8. It will have the reverse tendency. The higher tax rate on the land values would enable the city to acquire land for open spaces cheaper, and to protect the need of the workers, instead of as to date, encouraging the greed of land speculators.

9. Not at all. New York City could accommodate five times its present population, with a density of less than 250 to the acre, while we have many blocks with a density of 750 to the acre now.

10. New York City never acquires public necessities on the basis of need, but with the kind permission of the real rulers of the city—the land speculators and the financial interests. The proposed change will open the way for earlier and more adequate provision of public needs, by breaking the grip of these two classes of exploiters upon the conduct of the city's affairs.

11. Probably only slightly, but to the extent it did, most of the revenue would be secured from land owners for whose financial benefit the expenditures are made, instead of as now, chiefly out of the wages of the workers.

12. Not at all, as experience has conclusively shown. It would, as pointed out above, merely make such police regulation easier of accomplishment. It would be better to begin untaxing buildings first and then to put on restrictions. The land speculators will fight both in the future, as hitherto and now.

13. Within a score of years, there will probably be 2,000,000 families in the city. Within the five boroughs, there are not much over 100,000 acres available for residential purposes or counting 16 net lots to the acre, 1,600,000 lots. Obviously, few families need expect permanently to have over two or three lots apiece, without paying a little more for the privilege, which cannot be enjoyed by many. For the immediate future, however, the proposed change would make the acquisition of a single lot or two small lots by families much easier, because the owners of large acreage tracts, in all the boroughs outside of Manhattan, would sell lots much cheaper to would-be small home owners. A 20 x 100-foot lot affords opportunity for a garden.

14. It would make the rents for better apartments and more rooms lower.

15. It would remove the present premium upon every old and unhealthy buildings and not *render* them obsolete, for they are that already, but would make them unprofitable, and many of them ought to be vacated by the authorities because they are unfit for human habitation or occupancy and dangerous to life and health.

16. It would hasten the time when the owners would improve land adequately.

17. No. The Farmers' Association of Queens would not be able to hold acreage tracts so long before they unload them at city lot prices.

18. Yes. Land would come into the market cheaper and quicker.

19. Whether the supply of buildings is restricted by taxes in restraint of their construction. The loan market is of importance. Preventing speculative increases in the selling price of land would improve it.

20. Thousands of buildings that ought to be vacated are largely tenanted at relatively high rentals. We have 20,000 new cases of consumption annually.

21. To a small extent. Vacancies are largely due to the causes ascribed in the question.

22. (a) Yes, in newer district only.

(b). Yes, and the proposed change will accelerate such destruction.

23. Taking ground rents instead of wages, to pay the cost of government, reduces the cost of living and increases the purchasing power of wages. It is real, and not nominal, wages that count. The supply of buildings will not be too great for many years to come, if at all.

24. It would reduce the profits from land speculation they now make under the guise of "philanthropy."

25. It should precede city planning—to make city planning more effective.

26. As soon as results are shown, other cities and states will be obliged to follow this.

27. People, not buildings, create the necessity for transit, etc., and untaxing buildings will not increase the fecundity of women, but will tend to decrease the birth rate by improving economic conditions. Getting revenue from the proper source—ground rents—will make it easier for the city to provide transit and galleries for substructures as will also the control over the city's development be facilitated by land values taxation. Taking the profits of congestion for government will make congestion less sought by land speculators.

SERIES 3.

On the Effect of the Untaxing of Buildings on Rent.

1. Not much. It is the custom of a few families.

2. No figure available. Question plainly irrelevant.

3. On business properties tenants usually make all repairs, on tenement and other residence properties landlords usually do so. The ground lessee usually pays the taxes, but in other leases the landlord pays the taxes, except water rates. Assessments are usually paid by the landlord.

4. Almost entirely.

5. Landlords usually attend to both.

6. Except lighting and frequently heating, all usually rendered by landlord.

7. Landlords try to include interest on mortgage, depreciation, taxes, profits, etc., and then get what they can under the law of supply and demand.

8. He would be a "philanthropist," not a landlord, if he didn't.

9. Yes. That is why he objects to the transfer.

10. (a). Taxes on buildings are properly regarded as part of the operating expenses.

(b). Yes, taxes on rented buildings are paid by tenants; taxes on land values come out of unearned profits of land owners.

(c). Yes, tenants pay higher rents on account of a high tax rate on buildings, because that limits the supply of buildings and gives them a scarcity value. A high tax rate on land values would, as pointed out above, bring land into the market earlier and cheaper to meet increased carrying charges.

11. Owners of most buildings include depreciation in their rent, under the present tax system, and take the appreciation of land values as "velvet." Rents are not kept down by the elimination of depreciation, but by the number of "To Let" signs in desirable quarters competing for tenants.

12. Property owners would be compelled to take what they could get. Depreciation charges would not be affected by the proposed change and couldn't be added to rent.

13. In all buildings.

14. There would be a tendency to attract population, dependent upon rapidity with which change is made in New York and rapidity with which other places show equal common sense.

15. Many of those who live above the line of dependence would be apt to take larger quarters. Those below the line of dependence would probably get rid of the lodgers who prevent the privacy to which the workers are entitled, and spend more for food and clothing or possibly indulge in the luxury of saving a bit.

16. Yes. Rents would be reduced in many old worn-out tenement properties on which the taxes would be increased materially—because these properties would have to compete with a large supply of good tenements.

17. There would be some friction for the landlord to get their rents. Tenants have eyes and can read "To Let" signs.

18. Wages depend upon the margin of production, or upon the produce which labor can obtain at the highest point of natural productiveness open to it without the payment of rent.

Wages fall as rents rise.

Wages are also determined by the law of supply and demand over any period of time. Money wages may be increased temporarily by organization or by strikes, and money wages, in certain industries, are higher in New York City than in most other places, but it is doubtful whether, considering the cost of living, real wages are.

If rents were reduced because factories and other employment moved away taking workers with them so that there were a large sudden excess of accommodations, then money wages would be apt to fall also because of a surplus of labor.

When rents are reduced by increasing the number of buildings, through transferring taxes on buildings to land values, the stimulus to industry and increased employment would increase wages, because of competition to get workers.

19. High rents in New York are due to the high selling price of land and to heavy taxes on buildings.

20. (a). Land speculators claim that tenants want too much from the city now.

(b). Probably tenants would not be any less interested in getting their money's worth when they are freed from double taxation than they are now under double taxation.

(c). Question is irrelevant and misleading. The city would secure more of its revenue from the community-earned ground rents and less from the wages of the workers. The Board of Estimate and Apportionment and the Board of Aldermen vote the expenditures, and they are almost exclusively land owners now, and probably will be.

(d). Such an honest system of taxation seems a healthy tendency in a Democracy.

SERIES 4.

On the Effect of the Untaxing of Buildings Upon Public Revenue and Public Credit.

1. Obviously, it would not.
2. The revenue from the land would be determined by the budget.

3. Not if the city administration is honest and efficient.

4. Probably about 100 per cent., though there does not seem to be any case on record in which the city has acquired property at its assessed value.

5. Cannot be answered definitely. Variation from proper assessment could be largely prevented if property owners would permit the true price paid to be recorded in deeds.

6. Rarely, if ever. The reverse is more apt to be the case, as buildings have three dimensions and impress themselves upon assessors, while a reduced income from buildings is harder to appreciate.

7. Assessments rarely keep up with the claims of real estate brokers and auctioneers—sometimes they may exceed speculative values, more often they lag behind them.

8. (a). As answered repeatedly before, it would result only in retarding the increase in the assessed valuation, i. e., selling price of land in the city, if it were put into operation gradually, and would not result in any reduction of the present assessed value per se.

(b). Assessed valuation should represent what the land would bring in an open free market; selling value for speculative purposes represents a gamble on futures.

9. See the records of the Tax Department for this non-germane question, and consider also the heavy assessments for premature or unwise improvements, to benefit favored land speculators.

10. The assumption is misleading—probably unintentionally. The debt limit of the city has been a curse to it, and the debt service of the city is the greatest burden on the city's prosperity. We should long since, doubtless, have had a decent system of getting revenue, except that the tax rate could be kept fictitiously low by borrowing through long-term bonds. It would be best to adhere rigorously to the pay-as-you-go policy, finally adopted only when it had to be, because of the debt limit.

11. This question is framed to deceive. The Committee was not appointed to investigate or discuss any such proposition.

No change in the method or percentage of assessment is advocated nor considered, but a gradual reduction of the tax rate on buildings to one per cent. of that on land values so that if the tax rate on land values were $3.00 per $100.00, the tax rate on buildings would be 3c. on $100.00.

As long as buildings are taxed at all they are subject to taxation, therefore, the constitutional provision as to the debt limit would not be affected.

The Constitution provides: "The amount to be raised by tax for county or city purposes in any county containing a city of over one hundred thousand inhabitants, or any such city of this State in addition to providing for the principal and interest of existing debt, shall not in the aggregate exceed in any one year two per centum of the assessed valuation of the real and personal estate of such county or city to be ascertained as provided in this section in respect to county or city debt."

In 1914:

The assessed value of ordinary real estate was........	$7,458,784,625
The assessed value of real estate of corporations was..	186,654,976
The assessed value of personalty was................	340,395,560
Total	$7,986,735,161

A tax rate of 2% upon this valuation would have yielded. $159,734,703.22
The debt service was 52,283,178.64

Total amount that could have been raised by tax.. $212,017,881.86

Taxes on Real Estate, Special Franchises of Corporation and Personalty were.... $142,994,191.25
Bank, Excise and Mortgage Taxes were.. 10,318,726.15

Total 153,312,917.40

Additional sum that might have been raised by taxes $58,704,964.46

Obviously, the amount that can be raised by taxation has nothing to do with the relative tax rate on land and buildings in any case, and the interjection of this issue, only to confuse the public mind, is inexcusable.

The important fact is that nearly fifty-nine million dollars more could have been raised last year in the city by taxes however levied, without in any way interfering with the 2% tax rate bugaboo invoked by land speculators in their fight to prevent honest taxation.

Three other factors also should be considered:

(a). The adoption of the "pay-as-you-go" policy for self-sustaining improvements and the payment for self-sustaining improvements by fifteen-year serial bonds instead of by fifty-year bonds, will for several years increase the debt service materially, and so increase the amount that can be raised by taxes.

(b). As admitted by those opposed to the change, it will not, at least, reduce the assessed value of land below present figures, and it will stimulate the construction of many new buildings, so increasing much more rapidly the total assessed value of real estate. The temporary lull in the selling of land, due to the war, will mean a more rapid increase hereafter. The increase in the assessed values of land and buildings will probably be at least $175,000,000 to $200,000,000 annually within a few years. Even assuming that the proposed change would make the increase in assessed land values $8,000,000 a year less than under the present uniform tax rate, while making the increase in the assessed value of buildings $20,000,000 to $30,000,000 a year greater, the net gain will be appreciable, so that the city can raise even more by taxation within the 2 per cent. rate limit.

(c). The revenue the city will receive from assessments, water rates, docks, ferries and subways, rentals, reimbursements, permits, licenses, privileges, tolls, franchises, fines, interest on taxes, etc. sales of city articles and real estate, State School moneys, etc., will be about the same, doubtless, in the future as hitherto, and these revenues amounted last year (1914) to approximately $43,409,000.

12. It would emphasize the justice of permitting the people to recover for public purposes more of the land they create.

13. Compactness and logical, instead of straggling and illogical, development would reduce municipal expenditures.

14. An assumption so contrary to fact is hardly entitled to consideration. Many of the narrowest streets are in the most congested districts. Parks are needed, but not supplied, on basis of population, whether crowded or not.

15. In general, it would mean less taxes.

16. No basis for determination, but it seems improbable.

17. Stupid, deceitful phraseology, such as this, should not be used to beg the question. It is not "confiscation" to recover more of publicly created values for public use. To secure more of these values would encourage industry and improve the city's financial status. As Mr. Richard M. Hurd, President of the Lawyers Mortgage and Trust Co., has put it, "So far as mortgage lenders are concerned, any factor which improves housing conditions and hence the wealth and producing power of the people gives a genuine and underlying strength to real estate values." It does the same to the city's credit.

18. It would distinctly tend to diminish them—except for land speculators.

19. Only if the change would benefit an overwhelming majority of the people, and that it would is admitted by the opponents of the plan.

SERIES 5.

Upon the Effect of the Untaxing of Buildings Upon Mortgage Loans.

1. Not at all per se in a growing section, and probably not in any case. (See Answer to Question 17, Series 3.)
2. Same as 1.
3. Same as 1.
4. No records available.
5. By careful lenders about two-thirds.
6. About half.
7. Not much over a third to two-fifths.
8. Half or a little more.
9. Not much.
10. None.
11. No statistics available.
12. It almost never would, per se, and the active causes of any decrease would have to be known before the question can be answered.
13. It is inconceivable that any such reduction would be brought about by the proposed change. Assuming it, however, as one of the many improbabilities dragged into this question, only inexcusable shoestring equities would be wiped out, and no mortgages would have to be foreclosed.
14. It would not have either effect per se, for the selling price of the land would remain constant or increase very slowly. By reducing the selling price of land below what it would be in ten years hence; with a uniform tax rate on land values and buildings, and hence a lower tax rate on land values; it would release more money for productive investment and reduce interest rates through competition of capital. Speculative loans command a higher rate of insurance which is not really interest, though the distinction is frequently overlooked.

ANSWERS TO QUESTIONS SUBMITTED BY THE ADVISORY COUNCIL OF REAL ESTATE INTERESTS.

SERIES 1.

On the Effect of the Untaxing of Buildings Upon Land Values and Upon Speculation in Land.

1. The development of land values in different parts of the city has been very irregular, depending upon the development of transit facilities, causing appreciation in one section, and sometimes very serious depreciation in another section.

2. The effect of the new subway system will be to equalize values in the outlying boroughs, probably creating a tendency to decrease, to some extent, the land values in the central borough. This, with regard to the central section, may be offset by an increase in the growth of the city. However, the prospective increases in land values have been very largely discounted.

3. See the records of the Tax and Tenement House Departments.

4. The transfer of the tax from buildings to land can never increase the capital value of improved land. For instance, in the case of the two parcels mentioned, assuming that the transfer would operate to diminish the capital value of land by 10%, the diminution for parcel A would be $7,000, making it worth $93,000, while parcel B would be decreased in value by $3,000, and then be worth $97,000. In either case the value of the property would be less than $100,000. There is no reason to suppose that any compensating increase would occur as to the value of the improvements.

5. Under ordinary conditions in Manhattan, the appropriate improvement of land changes on an average in from twenty to thirty years.

6. The value of a piece of vacant land is determined by the estimate formed of the net revenue which may be obtainable from that land when it can be advantageously improved. The capitalization of this revenue, discounted to allow for interest, on the money now invested and taxes, or carrying charges, from the present time until that supposed time of advantageous improvement, is the present value. Expectation of revenue in the meantime and uncertainty of income are elements causing variation.

7. The taxpayer, strictly speaking, occupies but a very small part of the improved area of the city.

8. Increase of land values is due to increase of population, increase of community wealth and many other causes.

9. If there were no other element to be considered, then there would be a decrease.

10. See answer to question 6.

11. High or low land values are to be regarded as an effect and not as a cause. Whatever the system of taxation may be, the rental

value of land is determined by the advantage to be derived from the occupancy of the land. Therefore the desirability of high or low land values is not a practical question.

12. There is no appreciable purchase of property in New York City, with a view of holding it out of use for long periods and then reselling it at a profit, for the simple reason that the carrying charges are so great that such a course would mean that there would be no profit. When one man buys, another sells, and the transaction is quite as likely to hasten the bringing of land into use as to retard it.

13. No; there would be a general depreciation of land values. There would be no diminution in speculation, but speculation would be on a lower level.

14. Unwholesome; because there would be a destruction of land values and a loss of confidence, resulting in discouragement of initiative. No speculation means no pioneering; no pioneering means no growth or development.

15. If land speculation were carried on as stock and produce speculation is carried on, it might be considered injurious; but land speculation cannot be conducted in that way.

16. Very little land is held out which is ripe for improvement and can secure financing. To hold land beyond such a point would invite disaster.

17. Better by a proper land increment tax because this reflects ability to pay.

18. Any additional burden to shrinking values would aggravate the effect of depreciation and tend towards panic.

19. (a). Loans would be called, in order to re-establish margins, because of the loss in capital value.

(b). See answer to question 4.

(c). See answer to question 4.

20. See records of the Tax Department.

21. Nearly all mortgages are owned by small investors because life insurance companies, savings banks and other financial institutions interested in real estate are only intermediaries for policy holders, depositors, and so forth.

22. See the report of Dr. Haig upon "Some Probable Effects of the Exemption of Improvements from Taxation in the City of New York."

23. See the answer to question 22.

24. See the answer to question 22.

25. See the answer to question 22.

26. See the answer to question 22.

SERIES 2.

On the Effect of the Untaxing of Buildings Upon Building Operations, Housing Conditions and Congestion.

1. Land will not be used until it is ripe and financing is available.

2. See answer to question 1.

3. See answer to question 1.

4. In general, any additional impost on land would tend to a more intensive use of the land beyond the point of appropriateness.

5. (a). Yes.
(b). Impossible to answer.
6. See answer to question 4.
7. Yes.
8. Every available inch would be covered in central locations.
9. See answer to question 8.
10. In direct proportion to the increased congestion.
11. See answer to question 10.
12. To a great extent, as illustrated in the reports of Dr. Haig. It would be better to untax buildings after the additional legislation referred to was first obtained.
13. To a considerable extent; and it would be a bad thing.
14. This depends entirely upon whether the policy of untaxing buildings would decrease or increase actual rents to the occupant, and to what extent this would take place.
15. Yes.
16. Yes.
17. No.
18. It would tend somewhat to offset the effect of the higher tax, but the net result is stated in the answer to question 13. Accordingly, the second part of this question lapses.
19. The net return is the best criterion.
20. No source of information.
21. No source of information.
22. Yes.
23. Yes to the first part of this question; at the point of overproduction is the answer to the second part.
24. Same as elsewhere. See the reports of Dr. Haig.
25. The necessity for city planning for outlying districts would be deferred by reason of the intensification of the tendency towards concentration in the older parts of the city.
26. Buildings never attract anyone.
27. Much more difficult.

SERIES 3.

On the Effect of the Untaxing of Buildings Upon Rent.

1. Very little.
2. In regard to business property, slightly. To a greater extent in regard to tenement houses during hard times. When times are good and houses are fully rented, expenses are not so important, but during hard times, many vacancies and loss of rent cause leasing
3. Five to twenty-one years. Renewals usually only in case of ground lease. The other terms mentioned vary with the character of the building, while all these items may be found in some leases.
4. Nearly entirely.
5. Landlord usually attends to improvements and maintenance.
6. Usually all these services, with the exception of lighting, are rendered by the landlord.
7. When contemplating investment in real estate, the rent return is *expected* to cover the standard rate of interest on the investment in land and building, operating and maintenance expenses (including

taxes), and allowance for annual depreciation on the improvement, account being taken furthermore of the expected increase in the value of the land and also of the benefit or burden resulting as regards the building, by reason of the increasing value of the land. Actual rent is purely a question of supply and demand.

8. Yes.

9. Yes.

10. (a). Taxes levied on a building are properly regarded as part of the operating expenses.

(b). Yes.

(c). A high tax rate on buildings theoretically increases rents. A high tax rate on land theoretically has the effect of reducing the value of the land and falls on the landlord, but the only reason why the tax on buildings is declared to be shifted to the tenant, while that on the land is not, is to be found in the competition of builders. A policy of high taxation on land would operate as a great discouragement to real estate investment and building enterprise, thus tending to counteract the supposed stimulus to building.

11. To an extent determined by the amount of that expected appreciation.

12. See answer to question 11.

13. In the case supposed, the effect would be general.

14. An answer here would be mere guess work.

15. See answer to question 14.

16. No.

17. Yes.

18. High rents are one of the causes of high wages and, accordingly, a decrease in rents would tend to lower wages.

19. (a). High rents cause high land values and not the converse.

(b). Relative influence of taxes upon rent is a subordinate one.

20. (a). Some do and some do not.

(b). Yes.

(c). Yes.

(d). No.

SERIES 4.

On the Effect of the Untaxing of Buildings Upon Public Revenue and Public Credit.

1. No.

2. The revenue from the land would be whatever the budget requires, and the rate would be determined accordingly.

3. If the city officials do their work honestly, there should be no over assessment.

4. To a large extent assessment is higher than the true value.

5. Tax officials seize upon increases promptly and are loath and slow to grant decreases.

6. To a very great extent.

7. To a large extent and in some cases exceed them.

8. (a). Yes, depending upon the efficiency of the tax department.

(b). There is no clear distinction.

9. See the records of the Tax Department.

10. If the bankers and bond investors realized that there was an over assessment it would very detrimentally affect the sale of city bonds.

11. We are advised that the courts would be likely to hold that the 99%, which would be excluded from computation, would not be included in the base upon which the constitutional debt limit would be figured. The effect upon the constitutional tax rate would have to be determined by adding the impost on the land to the impost on the building and then finding whether the two together exceeded the constitutional tax rate.

12. No.

13. Congestion of population would increase the cost of governmental functions such as police, health, fire, charities, corrections, etc.

14. The loss of income and the cost of maintenance of parks, open spaces, wider streets, etc., would be in proportion to the value of properties affected by these improvements.

15. Higher taxes.

16. An answer to this question would be mere guess work.

17. Very seriously.

18. See answer to Question 20, Series 3.

19. Yes.

SERIES 5.

On the Effect of Untaxing of Buildings Upon Mortgage Loans.

1. To an extent of the increase of taxation upon land value capitalized at the prevailing rate of interest.

2. To the same extent as stated in the answer to question 1.

3. At least to the same extent as stated in the answer to question 1.

4. Probably 9/10. Unable to state as to second and third mortgages.

5. By intelligent lenders, 66 2/3%.

6. About 50%.

7. From 40% to 50%.

8. From 75% to 80%.

9. Hardly any.

10. None.

11. Unable to state.

12. If such a policy were introduced, much more than in proportion to the loss of capital value.

13. This might bring about a wholesale foreclosure of mortgages, with a resulting real estate panic.

14. Both.

ANSWERS TO QUESTIONS SUBMITTED BY THE REAL ESTATE BOARD OF NEW YORK THROUGH A SUB-COMMITTEE OF ITS COMMITTEE ON LEGISLATION AND TAXATION.

Sub-Committee of Committee on Legislation and Taxation.

DAVID A. CLARKSON, Chairman
E. A. ALEXANDER
CHARLES H. AYRES
JESSE C. BENNETT
JOS. L. BUTTENWIESER
EDWARD C. CAMMANN
RICHARD COLLINS
ROBERT E. DOWLING
JOHN P. LEO
LAURENCE McGUIRE
E. A. TREDWELL

SERIES 1.

On the Effect of the Untaxing of Buildings Upon Land Values and Upon Speculation in Land.

1. So far as we know the development of land values in different parts of the city has always been irregular. We cannot say to what extent. Land values have decreased in some portions while in others they have increased, and the causes have been various, such as removals from established trade centres to new centres, from old residential sections to new, and, markedly, changes in the transportation system, desirability of new buildings over old, etc.

2. There is no way of predicting normal increase. If the experience of the past is repeated, property along the line of the new subway will be generally improved in value. We cannot say as to what extent the prospective increase has been discounted.

3. We cannot answer this question.

4. The transfer of the tax from buildings to land cannot increase the value of improved land. The capital value of parcel B as a whole might be increased, but the land value will not be increased.

5. We are unable to answer this question.

6. Standards employed in fixing land values vary from one district to another.

7. To a very slight extent.

8. Increased land values are the result of increase of wealth as well as population.

9. The effect on the aggregate land values in New York City would be detrimental, if it were known that the population of the city as a whole would remain stationary.

10. We are unable to answer this question.

11. It depends upon what the city government wishes to do. In prosperous cities, land values, generally speaking, are high.

12. To a very slight extent.

13. We are not sure whether, or to what extent, the effect would be to discourage land speculation. Speculation does not permanently create land value.

14. We do not know.

15. We cannot answer the first part of this question except to say that speculation tends to restrain sharp changes in value. Land speculation differs as much from speculation on the stock and produce exchanges as the ordinary mercantile transactions differ from land speculation.

16. To a very slight extent. Most land held in an unimproved state is so held because there is no demand for it. Very often the demand comes too late to result in profit to the owner.

17. We do not assume that the transfer of the tax would stabilize values and check speculation.

18. We cannot say; probably to a considerable extent.

19. The change to a tax system, with which they are unfamiliar and fear, would have a disturbing effect in the minds of lenders. The transfer of the tax from buildings to land which will neither increase nor decrease on a particular parcel of real estate would undoubtedly affect the lender's security, as the value of the land is decreased even though the net tax remains the same.

20. We should say the land of New York is owned by a considerable number of owners—approximately 200,000.

21. The number of owners of real estate mortgages is very large. We should say there are probably as many lenders as there are owners.

22. It depends upon whether the increased tax on the land would be offset by a greater or less decrease in the tax on the building.

23. It depends upon the relative value of the land to the building.

24. It would depend upon the proportion of the value of land to building.

25. We think it would have the effect of increasing the taxes on the owners of small properties.

26. We are unable to answer this question.

SERIES 2.

On the Effect of the Untaxing of Buildings Upon Building Operations, Housing Conditions, and Congestion.

1. Yes, during the first few years of the operation of a law untaxing buildings; because the heavy burden of taxes laid upon the land and the exemption of the improvements from taxation would combine to induce, almost to the point of coercion, the owner of vacant or inadequately improved land to erect new buildings. Of course, the stimulus

would, after a few years, be dissipated by the over-production which would result from the artificial inducement to build.

2. It seems unreasonable to suppose that, except in rare instances, men would make large outlays for unproductive improvements, unless they saw an immediate opportunity for sale to builders. In fact, enactment of the proposed law would operate indirectly as a damper upon any activity in this direction.

3. A law untaxing buildings would operate just as in the case of vacant land, but in inverse ratio to the value of the building, that is to say, if the building and the land were of equal value, the temptation to replace the old building by a new one would be slight. According, however, as the building represents less value and the land more value, the inducement to erect a new building increases during the first years of the operation of the law.

4. Yes.

5. We are inclined to think that the untaxing of buildings would stimulate improvement, first of the most valuable of the lands still unimproved or most inadequately improved, irrespective of their proximity to the business centers. We cannot, however, conceive that there would be land more valuable than that near the centers of business, excepting a very few restricted private residence sections, which may not in all cases respond to the unalterable law of supply and demand. We hardly think that an equilibrium will ever be reached, but rather that the untaxing of buildings would finally result in a serious over-production and a final upheaval of all values, with the result that the experiment would have to be discontinued, but not until irreparable injury would have been done, not alone to owners, but also to the City's credit and to its bonded indebtedness.

6. Most assuredly. It could not fail to have that effect.

7. Absolutely; it follows as a corollary to No. 6.

8. So far as these spaces are under private ownership, they would certainly be promptly built up during the first few years of the operation of the law.

9. This question has practically been answered above. Human nature will always remain the same and naturally every owner would, if the law were enacted, be tempted to improve the largest possible percentage of his land with the highest building he could possibly erect.

10. The congestion that would ensue would result in conditions so serious that no man can foresee what the city could do to provide open spaces, especially in the central part of the city. Besides, we fear the enactment of the law would reduce the city to such straits that it would be powerless to raise the large additional funds required to provide such open spaces.

11. If it were possible further to tax values, which under the operation of the proposed law would rapidly have decreased, it would add heavy items to the City Budget. One need but turn to the prices which had to be paid for the land for the new court house to judge what would be the cost of supplying open spaces in the center of New York. The cost would be prohibitive.

12. Of course, the untaxing of buildings would necessitate limitation of heights of buildings and proportion of lot space covered. Since it is inconceivable that those who have the interests of the city at heart would ever say that the untaxing of buildings is desirable, the question of whether the enactment of the law untaxing buildings should precede

or follow the legislation above referred to, is academic. It would, however, be far wiser to have the limitation of height of buildings and proportion of space covered precede the enactment of the law untaxing buildings, which we trust no legislature will ever be unwise enough to put upon the statute book.

It would discourage it and would be an undesirable result.

14. No, it would have no effect in this regard. Owners and speculators will always adopt the design which rents the best and which will produce the largest returns.

15. Yes, it would depreciate the value of the old buildings.

16. Not to any great extent. Taxpayers will be built on valuable land, irrespective of the exemption of the building.

17. Perhaps not at first, but certainly in the end.

18. It might, after years of operation of the law.

19. The number of vacancies in the particular class of buildings and the comparative rents paid for the occupied portions. The loan market does, at times, tend to discourage speculative builders from erecting any more of the class of buildings for which there is no demand.

20-21. To answer these questions (Nos. 20 and 21) with any satisfactory degree of accuracy would require many months of careful investigation in order to secure the necessary statistics.

22. The modern and better type of buildings, during the first few years of their construction, are more fully occupied than the older and inferior types. It does not, however, tend to force a destruction of the older and less suitable buildings except where the latter are grossly inadequate and dilapidated.

23. In regard to the increased cost of building tending to operate as a check to over-production, it would seem to us that over-production would check itself almost irrespective of a rise in the prices of materials. The labor unions pretty well steady the cost of labor in the building trades.

24.. No other appreciable effect than upon other property similarly situated.

25. It is very hard to foretell, but probably not beneficial to the interests of the community.

26. Population is attracted to New York by profitable employment and the attractions and opportunities offered by a large city rather than by supply of buildings. Either transit facilities would have to be greatly increased or the overcrowding in traffic would be seriously aggravated, if it can be established that large numbers would be shifted to outlying sections of the city.

27. The sewer system would have to be changed and reconstructed, the sidewalks and streets would not be wide enough to accommodate those who want to use them, nor would there be room for vehicular traffic. This is evidenced by the present condition of Nassau Street; even Broadway during rush hours would be congested beyond endurance.

SERIES 3.

On the Effect of the Untaxing of Buildings Upon Rent.

1. Only a small proportion of land in New York City is leased on the basis of pure ground rents—less than one per cent.

2. Parcels of improved real estate are not usually leased as a whole—not three per cent. of all, excepting private dwellings.

3. Building leases are usually made in terms of one, three or five years, sometimes with privilege of renewal. If the tenant takes the entire building, he usually makes interior repairs, sometimes exterior, but except in cases of leases of twenty-one years, it is customary for the owner to pay taxes, assessments, etc.

4. Much the greater number of buildings are leased or rented in part or piecemeal, approximately 97%, except in case of private residences.

5. When a building is leased to several tenants the landlord maintains and repairs it.

6. When a building is leased to several tenants the landlord furnishes elevator and janitor service; sometimes light and heat.

7. All the elements mentioned in Nos. 5 and 6 are included in the rent, in addition to taxes and interest on investment.

8. Ground leases have never been largely taken in New York City in relation to its size. They were more common formerly, when the rate of interest paid on bond and mortgage was higher than the rate the ground rent bore to the value of the land. At present but few new ground leases are made. The owner of the land usually sought for security of income and freedom from care, but not for the highest return.

9. Since under all long-term ground leases, the lessee and not the landlord pays the taxes, there would be no possibility for any change in the ground rent until the expiration of the existing lease. Upon the expiration of existing lease the amount of ground rent would be determined by the valuation of the land at that moment. But, in most cases the ground rent could not be reduced, since most ground leases contain a provision that the renewal shall be at a rental not less than the original lease.

10. It is clear that finally a higher tax rate upon improved property, whether upon land and buildings, or upon either, or upon both, will in the end result in higher rents. Tenants do not take the rate of taxes paid by the landlord into consideration when negotiating for a lease. They only pay as rent the worth of the premises leased as compared with other premises. If, however, taxes were so high as to bring the net return below the interest returned on other forms of capital, no new buildings would be put up until rents increased sufficiently to bring as large a net return on the money invested as would equal the prevailing rate of interest on capital.

11. It has not been the custom among owners of real estate in New York to carry a fund to cover the depreciation of buildings, as the expected increase in the value of land has been relied upon to cover this loss; it may, therefore, be presumed that rents have been less by as much as would have been sufficient to create such a fund.

12. If the present tax on buildings were transferred to land, it would diminish land values and, consequently, owners, to cover the depreciation of their buildings, would have to add such a depreciation charge to rent, in order to obtain a return sufficient to yield the prevailing rate of interest on capital.

13. Accepting the hypothesis that this change of taxation would

result in a fall in rents, it would affect the older and poorer buildings most severely.

14. How greatly such a change would tend to draw population to New York from outside is impossible to estimate. It would depend on the fall in rents and could only be brought about by a large increase in building.

15. If such a fall occurred, the choice of occupancy of larger space at the same rent or the same space at lower rent would depend upon the enterprise of the tenant and the prevailing conditions in the business world at the time of the change.

16. The reduction in rents might conceivably be greater than the amount of tax transferred if it led to such a change in values as would result in a panic in real property.

17. The necessity of certain classes of workers to live near their places of employment; the desire of many to remain in the neighborhoods to which they have been accustomed; and the natural tendency of foreign peoples to concentrate in a district; all would tend to check the mobility of the renting population.

18-19. Higher rents and higher wages in New York than in most other cities come from the greater opportunities offered here; if from any cause these opportunities were diminished both would fall. But it must be remembered that wages and rents do not necessarily move in parallel lines.

20. As long as buildings are taxed and some portion of the city's expenditures fall upon tenants, they have an interest in keeping down the expense of government. If it is true that the proposed untaxing of buildings throws the payment of the greater part of the taxes on the land owners, who form but a small class of the community, and relieves, for the most part, all other classes from taxation, it would certainly diminish care for economical government. It would be most unfortunate in a democracy to have all or practically all expenditures paid for by those who by reason of their small number have but little voice in the government. Would not such a condition afford an almost irresistible temptation for the many, for their own benefit, to exploit the few? Would not the use of taxes for all kinds of extravagance and schemes ensue? If all taxes were placed upon land, would not the taking of all land value by taxation result, as was so forcibly predicted by Henry George in his "Progress and Poverty" in these terse sentences:

"I do not propose either to purchase or to confiscate private property in land. The first would be unjust; the second needless. Let the individuals who now hold it still retain, if they want to, possession of what they are pleased to call *their* land. Let them continue to call it *their* land. Let them buy and sell, and bequeath and devise it. We may safely leave them the shell if we take the kernel. It is not necessary to confiscate land; it is only necessary to confiscate rents. * * * We may put the proposition into practical form by proposing to abolish all taxation save that upon land values. * * * That is the first step upon which the practical struggle must be made. When the hare is once caught and killed, cooking him will follow as a matter of course. When the common right to land is so far appreciated that all taxes are abolished save those which fall upon rent, there is no danger of much more than is necessary to induce them to collect the public revenues being left to individual land holders."

SERIES 4.

On the Effect of the Untaxing of Buildings Upon Public Revenue and Public Credit.

1. It would be introducing the Single Tax and would work a profound change, not only in our revenue system, but fundamentally, as it is designed to do, in our system of land holding. The Single Tax is a method of introducing social reform by using taxation as a lever. All scientific economists declare that taxation, which is "the enforced contribution of society for the support of necessary government," should never be associated with other matters, no matter how desirable. The great and only desideratum is to arrange taxation to bear on all, with as even a pressure as possible.

2. Naturally the tax revenue would suffer severely after a short time. The added taxation charge would produce lower capitalized land values, calling for a higher tax in order to produce the taxation required. It is a vicious circle. At what point, if any, it would stabilize itself or hold steady, no one can tell.

3. The present standard of values would be reduced, making present tax assessed land values practically all over-assessed. Increase of assessment cannot be added beyond to-day's practice, which is over value. While strong-arm methods could be used, unfair practice always reacts and the City would have to pay the price in the end, which would be heavy.

4. The law says 100%. Never in the history of the City were tax valuations higher. It is the general opinion of most professional realty men, that present day assessments throughout the City are 10% over conservative valuations. In other words, real estate is now tax valued at 110%—an over-assessment of 10%. The 1910 assessment roll more nearly represents current value than the 1911-1915 rolls, which were openly padded in 1911 to provide subways, and valuations have been kept fairly rigid since to avoid grave financial trouble.

5. Before 1910 they were usually from one to two years behind. Since 1910 the Tax Assessors have been ahead of values and have generally been unable to see the handwriting on the wall.

6. The architect's rule of depreciation is 2½% per annum. Little account of this is taken in the assessment rolls. Improvements are assessed now at least 25% more than their actual value. Indeed, in this is where the great overcharge in assessment lies to-day. The land value assessment is much nearer real value than the building assessment as a rule.

7. As property is now over-assessed, as a rule, all speculative value is more than anticipated. Speculative possibilities are charged for in advance.

8. Yes, lower assessment values would come in time—gently when you meet the market—with violence when postponed. Water finds its level, so must tax values in time.

No distinction between assessed value and speculative value exists to-day. One who buys an assessed value now, hoping for speculative profit later, will likely perish from over-optimism.

9. The following information, covering a specific period, has been supplied to the Real Estate Board by the Collector of Assessments and Arrears. Taking the tax for 1911, this shows that the Receiver of

Taxes had to collect as of May 1st, 1911, $124,845,015.49. On the following March 1, 1912, he returned as arrears $17,774,489.04. The amount of this return uncollected on December 31st, 1912, was $6,345,481.09. The amount of said tax uncollected on December 31, 1913, was $3,466,885.97, and the amount of said tax uncollected on December 31, 1914, was $2,101,401.49.

10. The City's credit and borrowing power are both impaired. If the bonds could not be sold (which must be considered,) any sale made must be at a discount suitable to the estimated risk involved.

11. Why not introduce Single Tax at once and have done with it? When you palter with the idea, recognize it in part and not entirely, you encourage the effort of the Single Tax enthusiasts to insist on the whole medicine being taken, and rightfully so. Either they are right or wrong. Real estate values, equities, mortgages and taxation have all been built upon the one principle of treating land and buildings both alike as component parts of a complete whole. Separate them and you open a Pandora's box of real trouble, but is it not better to have it all with a huge shock, than linger along awaiting the inevitable? The Court's action can never be predicted in advance. A constitutional debt limit is all right, providing a check is put upon the spenders. The Courts clearly failed to do this in 1910-1911, when it was sorely needed. It is apparently neither the policy nor the duty of the judiciary to check extravagance where no manifest fraud is involved.

12. We fail to see how it will remove the objections that now lie against the taxing of exempt property.

13. This is most difficult to answer. Untaxing buildings promotes intensive building—thereby congestion and the necessity for open spaces, small parks, etc. Consequently, it would apparently increase city expense.

14. Presuming that additional parking or open spaces equal, perhaps, to a 10% greater area than now required, the added expense might be hypothetically determined as about the same relative percentage.

15. Congestion never yet meant less civic expense.

16. According to the percentage of the shift, outlying school houses would have more vacancy or be longer in filling up and additional school houses would be required as present or new congestion districts developed. Municipal buildings of all kinds, school, fire houses and police stations would naturally follow suit. They always have.

17. The City's one and only customer—in a trade sense—is the taxpayer, who pays 96% of the gross yearly revenue. If his assets are depreciated, he suffers, but the City does not escape. It suffers even more, for the underlying basis of its credit and its bonds is being seriously undermined.

As for future borrowing, the City would not be able to borrow without raising the constitutional limit to perhaps more than a 20% margin, instead of the present 10%. With less security to the investor, city bonds are less desirable; naturally they would bring a lower price.

18. The evil effect would be accentuated as to popularity. No tax is ever popular except with those who do not pay. The unpopularity of the Single Tax is determined by the refusal of real economists and the voter heretofore to sanction it. Enough of it is known as a demonstrated fact to make all real estate men disbelievers in its alleged virtues.

19. If all the tax was on the land value, what is that but Single

Tax? There is no "obstacle" then—it is Single Tax. Then all that is needed in the absorption process is to make land a public utility and not a private holding. All of which the increasing expenses of government through socialization earnestly, if unconsciously, tend to do.

SERIES 5.

On the Effect of the Untaxing of Buildings Upon Mortgage Loans.

1. It is impossible to tell to just what extent the security would be reduced. Taxes ultimately would be higher, and it is reasonable to assume that the security would be reduced.

2. To a greater extent than a parcel appropriately improved.

3. It would in a great number of cases practically confiscate the value.

4. It is estimated that about 50% of the assessed value of all land in the City of New York is covered by first mortgages. The proportion covered by second and third mortgages, as far as we know, has never been estimated.

5. It depends largely upon the character of the improvement. Generally speaking, from 50% to 66 2/3%.

6. It depends entirely on the character of the improvement. Such loans are difficult and almost impossible to secure. Savings banks are restricted by law to 40% of their market value.

7. We know of no way to fix the proportion. The result of any attempt to fix the proportion would, at best, be a wild guess.

8. We know of no way to fix the proportion.

9. It depends entirely on the improvement.

10. It is difficult and in many cases impossible to obtain second mortgages on inappropriately or unimproved land.

11. It is impossible to answer this question. To do so intelligently would require an appraisal of each individual parcel in the city. Foreclosure records are, perhaps, the best guide to answering this question.

12. This question is too general to answer intelligently. It would, in any event, reduce the borrowing capacity of real estate far beyond the ratio which the reduction in value bears to the entire value of the property since it would unsettle confidence in real estate as a security.

13. Any untaxing of buildings, without regard to the percentage—the fact that the theory was adopted—would cause general foreclosing.

14. The ultimate effect would be to turn most of the mortgage money, if not all, out of the City, as the consequent hazard would result in a rate in excess of 6 per cent., which would be usurious. If new loans could be obtained at all they would be smaller in amount and at a higher rate of interest.

Respectfully submitted,

REAL ESTATE BOARD OF NEW YORK.

(Signed) DAVID A. CLARKSON,

Chairman Sub-Committee Legislation and Taxation.

ANSWERS TO QUESTIONS SUBMITTED BY MR. STEWART BROWNE, PRESIDENT UNITED REAL ESTATE OWNERS' ASSOCIATION.

SERIES 1.

The Effect of the Untaxing of Buildings Upon Land Values and Upon Speculation in Land.

1. The 1873 panic decreased realty values until 1886; from 1886 to 1892 they increased; the 1893 panic forced a decrease until 1900. These decreases and increases in value were pretty general all over the city. The building of the elevated railroads and their extensions somewhat shifted values by increasing the values of the outlying sections and decreasing values in certain central sections.

The Spanish-American War unduly expanded our credit situation, and its close brought hundreds of millions of European capital into this country for new development purposes, and New York realty received a large benefit from this. Free mortgage lending, large purchase money, second and third mortgages and trades, between 1900 and 1907, brought an era of tremendous realty improvement and expansion throughout Greater New York.

The extension of the subways enormously increased the values of outlying sections, and the use of skeleton steel construction increased values in the center of the city by ability to build skywards, but decreased adjoining values, which latter is not yet fully recognized.

When Europe stopped supplying us with credit in 1907 there was a financial panic, after which came the Wilson Tariff Bill; these curtailed the industries of the country and brought all values and incomes down to hard pan.

The talk of single taxers, of building exempt taxers, increasing municipal taxes and general reduction in values from above causes brought about the calling of mortgage loans, with the final result that the present condition of real estate is worse than it has ever been in its history.

History shows that no matter what declines take place in realty values in any city or country, it is only a question of time when the trend will be upward and beyond any previous average high level. There are, of course, individual values that will never go back, and some sections to-day are lower than they were fifty years ago.

2. (a) As a whole, a decrease rather than an increase may be expected during the next five years; (b) first a speculative increase, then a decrease; (c) as a whole, 100% for the next seven years.

3. (a) For present purposes, as a whole, an excess of improvement; (b) during the past ten years fully 95% is fully improved faster than the demand; hence from demand standpoint practically none is inappropriately improved; (c) in area 60%.

4. (a) My process of reasoning can't differentiate between a separate tax on land and on building of urban fully improved property; both land and buildings are merged in one. If the gross tax is the same, it is immaterial whether it be wholly on land or wholly on building—and if other factors remain constant, the gross value remains the same, irrespective of any division of value the tax department may place upon it. The trouble is the other factors won't remain constant under such a change, but what effect such other factors may have, one man's guess is as bad as another's. (b) Example depends upon the resultant tax on land, whether for own occupancy or rental and, if latter, the resultant effect on rents.

If the gross tax remains the same and rentals the same, there is no change in value; if the gross tax is reduced and rentals remain the same, the value is increased; if the gross tax is reduced and rentals are reduced equal to tax reduction, there's no change in value; if the gross tax is increased and rentals remain the same the value is decreased; if the gross tax is increased and rentals are increased equal to the tax reduction, the value remains the same.

5. Between twenty and thirty years.

6. (a) So-called expert appraisers use different rules; some allow 100% of such results, some 75% and some 50%; the aggregate value depends largely whether 'tis for sale, loan or tax purposes. Traders and speculators have rules of their own that differ from expert appraisers; (b) depends upon whether the appraisal is for sale, loan or tax purposes, and whether made by expert appraiser, trader or speculator.

7. (a) Every building is really a taxpayer, whether it be underimproved, fully improved or overimproved; no improvements are actually permanent, nor will they be unless there is building height limitation; (b) temporary "taxpayers" values don't exceed 5% of the aggregate improvement values.

8. (a) First, population; next, capital borrowed or owned or both taking the speculative chance of supplying prospective demand; lastly, developers speculatively furnishing the supply and actually forcing the demand to come to the supply; (b) increase in a nation's price level increases property values also; (c) increase in wealth (including credit in wealth) is one of the principal factors entering into "price level" and values.

9. (a) Central improved values might decrease or increase, depending upon other factors foreseeable and unforeseeable; (b) central vacant land values would probably decrease 50% and outlying vacant land values would probably decrease 75% to 90%. Outlying improved properties would probably decrease about 50%.

10. (a) There probably will never be an increase in rentals in existing underimproved properties for like occupancy; (b) in existing fully improved property, an increase in rentals can only come from increase in price level or increase in population, or the demand overtaking the supply. Such increase in rentals will not happen for between five and seven years; (c) present assessed values represent a capitalization of 25% excess annual rent.

11. Immaterial as long as values are normal; high values must exist in large progressive cities. Falling values are always detrimental to a state or city.

12. 90% speculative and for resale, whether for improvement or otherwise.

13. (a) Force selling, reduce buying, present vacant land values would fall 50% to 75%; (b) the effect on improved property would depend upon whether the resultant gross tax was increased or decreased and upon the resultant future rentals.

14. (a) Disastrous to the sellers; (b) if all other factors remained constant, which they won't, it would be beneficial to the buyer for im--provement and occupancy in reducing the purchase price; (c) have no effect on the community generally, if all other factors remained constant, which they won't; "by and large" the general effect would be bad, but time would efface them.

15. (a) Man's life and all his activities from the cradle to the grave are speculative; when time emerges, speculation is born; (b) 75% good, 25% bad; (c) stock and produce exchange speculation steadies prices and makes a market, realty speculation builds up a community.

16. Not 5%; supply has always been faster than demand.

17. Nothing in the universe can be stabilized or remain constant; nothing checks speculation in securities or realty so much as inability to borrow or borrow freely. Building exempt taxation or "uncashed property increment tax" would only produce chaos in values; "cashed in increment property tax" would have no such effect, because it would be a tax realized on profit and not a tax on "illusions."

18. One factor acting produces certain results; increase the number of factors and the effects become compound. "'Tis the last straw that breaks the camel's back."

19. (a) Lenders are properly laws unto themselves; capital or credit is the most timid thing in our civilization; 'tis like the wind, it comes from nowhere and disappears nowhere; it would be most disastrous. American value of securities and realty is borrowing value; kill credit and you kill values. (b) With such a radical change the static effects on individual cases has no bearing; the effect is on realty as a whole, which reacts back on individual cases.

20. 80% of owners own one parcel.

21. The principal holders of mortgages are life insurance companies, savings banks, trust companies, estates and title guarantee companies; the ultimate beneficiaries of the first are represented by policyholders averaging $2,000 each per policy and the second by the lower middle and lower classes; the third by estates and the fourth by small holders of their guaranteed mortgages. There are very few indiviual lenders holding a number of mortgages.

22. Would staticly decrease the taxes of some and staticly increase the taxes of others, the percentage depending upon the relative existing assessed values of land and building; on the other hand the land tax might require to be so increased that there might be no decrease but an increase tax on both. Unless some land assessed values were increased, and some decreased, would produce inequalities of taxation between "skyscraper" owners.

23. There are no such small house owners in Manhattan as there are in Brooklyn.

24. (a) Depend upon the relative assessed values of land and building and the resultant gross tax; (b) would vary.

25. Depends entirely upon the relative assessed values of land and building of each such class of owners and the resultant gross tax; in-

dividual cases would require to be investigated and then grouped.

26. The general result can be predicted fairly well from a by and large standpoint, but not minutely.

SERIES 2.

The Effect of the Untaxing of Buildings Upon Building Operations, Housing Conditions and Congestion.

1. (a) As regards vacant land (90% of which is held for rise in values or rental improvement), it would decrease new building erection; it might increase for owner's occupancy, provided the same mortgage loan could be obtained and that the resultant land tax was one-half of the present gross tax; but the resultant land tax might equal or even exceed the present gross tax; (b) improvements are caused by "demand" and in spite of taxation and not because of it.

2. Would discourage.

3. Not of itself; only demand will do that.

4. If it forced "new building," it would increase "building height," unless the latter was limited by law.

5. (a) Closest to the centre of population and then spreading out therefrom; (b) don't understand the last question.

6. (a) Overdevelopment is a matter of opinion and appropriateness is not a static condition; (b) highest values are closest to population congestion, and if new building erection is forced, building height would be increased, commencing with the central location and then spreading out.

7. If it forced new building erection, this would be the inevitable result.

8. It would have a decided tendency to build up existing breathing spaces.

9. If there was a prospective demand for tenants and a full mortgage loan could be secured, the higher the building for rental would go up and, within certain limits, likewise for owner's occupancy.

10. Depends upon the "fads and fancies" of the city administration and the "taxpaying ability" of the people.

11. If bonds issued, to the extent of sinking fund, plus interest on same.

12. (a) Equally good arguments can be made pro and con on height limitation, irrespective of "building exempt taxation"; (b) population congestion increases rents, but increases workers' efficiency, and time; (c) depends on what result is wanted before one can say whether it increases the necessity for "height limitations"; (d) after.

13. (a) Discourage; (b) extremely bad; (c) such owners are heroes, but the mob calls them "hogs."

14. Have no such effect.

15. (a) Assumption is wrong; (b) certainly, for same occupancy.

16. Don't believe would change present practices.

17. Certainly.

18. The land value is decreased, but the tax is increased. Where an existing owner was forced to build, he would economize in lawn and garden; where he was forced to sell, the reduced purchase price would more than offset the increased taxes, and the tendency would be to con-

tinue or even increase lawn and garden; such would continue until population congestion overtook the location.

19. (a) Vacancies; (b) restricts or prevents loans; (c) nothing more so.

20. Few buildings are wholly vacant, but fully one-third of the aggregate floor area is unoccupied.

21. 75% suitable; 25% partially so; all can be made suitable for some occupancy.

22. (a) No; (b) if the occupancy environment has not changed, it forces rebuilding; if the occupancy environment has changed it forces alterations and repairs.

23. (a) No; (b) when loans could not be secured; (c) nothing begins or checks itself.

24. Don't know; they can be a law unto themselves; ask them.

25. City planning may be good or bad depending upon the "final object," and whether those "in favor" can force their views; the possible further effect depends upon the viewpoint. If excessive height be bad, then building exemption, if it forced new building, would make it worse.

26. (a) Would have no effect in attracting population from outside city; (b) so many other factors to consider that I can't answer this.

27. Materially increases these problems, as would intensify location population congestion.

SERIES 3.

The Effect of the Untaxing of Buildings Upon Rent.

1. (a) No ground rents but leaseholds; (b) under 5%.

2. Dwellings 100%; hotels 100%; lofts 15%; factories (not loft buildings) 75%.

3. (a) 1, 3, 5, 7 and 10 years; mostly between 1 and 3 years; (b) 90% assumed by landlord.

4. Apartment houses and hotels 100%; office buildings 100%; tenements 100%; hotels (to guests and tenants) 100%; loft buildings 85%; factories 25%.

5. (a) Improvements, 99% paid by landlord; (b) maintenance, 100% paid by landlord.

6. Landlord assumes all except lighting, which latter is assumed by landlord in a few cases.

7. Only one element—get all you can.

8. The landlord doesn't collect a ground rent for location or for anything else; this is a fiction of theorists; he collects a rent for certain floor area; he receives certain rent and the tenant pays certain rent; a hundred and one different elements may enter into such rent by both parties; but for anybody to try and put a value on any of these elements, let alone be conscious of what they are, is preposterous.

9. (a) He doesn't; (b) if he paid no more gross tax and such tax was shifted, calling it a tax on the building, a tax on the land, a tax on the plant, a tax on the windows or a tax on the owner's body would not change conditions.

10. Theory again; the question is preposterous; you might as well ask what value I put on the constituent parts of a twenty-dollar gold

piece when I take it or pay it out in exchange for another commodity. The tax is considered as a whole and is supposed to be shifted to the tenant; but the increased taxes during the past eight years have not been so shifted as the supply of space exceeds the demand.

11. (a) Until lately so-called land values kept increasing much faster than building depreciation from any cause, but the latter was never considered; now owners are forced to realize that building depreciation (not necessarily physical) is actual and land appreciation is largely illusory; (b) never considered.

12. Neither owners nor tenants keep psychological tabs on their emotional explosions, brain emanations or reflex actions; the landlord gets all the rent he can for any old reason or reasons and the tenant pays as little as he can for like reasons. Rents are not factory products.

13. (a) If there was no "oversupply" there would be no reduction in rents; (b) if there was an oversupply, it would reduce all rents, and older buildings more so than newer ones.

14. (a) It would not bring factories and stores from outside the city; (b) I don't believe dwellings rents could be so reduced in New York as to bring tenants from outside the State or outlying suburbs; contiguousness and "time" to occupations would be the determining factor; (c) strength of supply and strength of demand always react on or check one another.

15. Psychological conundrum.

16. Not from such cause; any result is possible in life if the necessary causes exist.

17. (a) Friction exists everywhere and in everything; (b) landlords reduce rents when compelled to and not otherwise, which is active resistance; (c) If "mobility" means shiftability to secure some advantage financial or otherwise, I can understand it having a retarding effect on increase in rents, but not on a decrease in rents.

18. (a) High wages produce a high price level and a high price level produces high wages; cause and effect seem interwoven; but it takes time for each to overtake the other. Labor unions have discovered this; therefore per diem "union wages" are slightly ahead of rising prices, and behind falling prices.

19. (a) There is no such thing as high rents and high realty values; these terms are relative; (b) rents and realty values follow the "price level" and the latter is composed of a million and one factors acting and reacting on one another; where wages are high rents are high, where wages are low rents are low.

20. (a) Tenants no more pay taxes than they pay wages, salaries, interest and other charges that enter into the cost of producing and selling any product; they have and take no interest in the cost of government; (b) it wouldn't change the present conditions; (c) "Representation without Taxation" is a thousand times more destructive to good government than "Taxation without Representation."

SERIES 4.

The Effect of the Untaxing of Buildings Upon Public Revenue and Public Credit.

1. (a) On fully improved property, no; (b) on partially improved property, sometimes; (c) on vacant land, yes.

2. Certainly.

3. It would, provided owners didn't force a reduction in assessed valuations by court proceedings or otherwise.

4. 120% on the average.

5. Ahead of increase in values and long way behind decrease in values.

6. Has no bearing, as 50% of Manhattan's buildings would not be reproduced.

7. 120%.

8. (a) It would necessarily result in lower actual values, but assessment values would not be lower until forced; (b) assessed values 120% of selling speculative values.

9. (a) 15%; (b) 10%; (c) 5%.

10. It ought to and would seriously interfere with their sale if the realty owners exposed as they would the actual conditions.

11. The courts would hold that such violated the Constitution; but the same result could be obtained by making the tax rate on buildings 1/100th of 1%.

12. Why should it? They would still be exempt

13. Would not reduce and might increase as the city is already committed to public improvements for an area twice the necessary area; would increase the cost of social uplift "fads and fancies."

14. Same answer as to No. 13.

15. Less expenditure if city's area had been limited ten years ago; would have no effect now unless city's area be further extended, which would mean more expenditures; for instance, the aggregate length of improved streets in Queens exceeds those of Manhattan; would increase cost of social uplift fads and fancies.

16. Not any more than at present.

17. Its borrowing ability is limited by its legal debt limit; its ability to borrow would depend entirely upon other sources of revenue; the aggregate realty tax collected would be fully 25% less than now; that would kill the city's credit; but if other sources of revenue raised more than the 25% realty reduction, the city's credit might be improved.

18. Accentuate it, of course.

19. It would mean the start of the so-called Single Tax; but the pure Single Tax has never been adopted anywhere and couldn't be adopted in the United States; the so-called Single Taxers are not Single Taxers and don't know what the Single Tax really is; further, I take entire exception to the theory that a tax on fully improved urban land can't be shifted to the tenant; it can't in theory, but it can in practice, because the other factors are never fixed or constant.

SERIES 5.

The Effect of the Untaxing of Buildings Upon Mortgage Loans.

1. The immediate result would be to reduce loan values by a sum equal to capitalized value of the increased tax, plus an unknown psychological addition; this result would be modified when the increased tax commenced and continued to shift on to the tenant.

2. Same answer as given to No. 1.

3. 75%.

4. (a) 90%; (b) 50%; (c) 15%.

5. Two-thirds of full appraised value.

6. 50% to 60%, depending upon bondsman.

7. Hard to get; 25% to 50%, depending upon bondsman, rate of interest and commission.

8. Depends upon interest rate, commission and bondsman; might go as high as 100%. Purchase money second mortgages up to 100%.

9. Same answer as to No. 8.

10. Practically none, except in cases of purchase money second mortgages, and then up to 95% or higher.

11. (a) 85%-10% and less, under normal conditions; (b) under present conditions have little, if any equity above mortgage; (c) can't give percentages between 20% and 50%, but very small.

12. Depends upon the psychology of the lender; for the first few years until conditions had equilibriumized themselves; should say would reduce it 25% to 50%; at first might be much more than the capitalized value of the increased tax.

13. It would result in reducing loans from 25% to 50% in one payment or spread over, depending upon the equity and the finances of the borrower and whether on bond or not; the lender would force reductions in loans where he could and would foreclose if he thought he could obtain a purchaser for amount of loan, or if not, he might be willing to take a loss; most equities are small, and where so, most owners would give deeds in preference to reducing loans and take chances of suit on bond if on it; it would be a game of "bluff" between borrower and lender, or a complete "lying down" on the part of the "weakling" owners.

14. It would decrease loan amounts and increase interest rates.

INFORMATION SUPPLIED BY HON. JOHN J. HOPPER, REGISTER OF THE COUNTY OF NEW YORK, FROM DATA IN HIS OFFICE, IN ANSWER TO CERTAIN OF THE QUESTIONS CONTAINED IN THE LIST OF QUESTIONS TO BE CONSIDERED IN CONNECTION WITH PUBLIC HEARINGS, PREPARED BY THE COMMITTEE.

QUESTION SERIES 3.

On the Effect of the Untaxing of Buildings Upon Rent.

1. To enumerate each instance in New York County (Manhattan) where the land is owned by one person and leased to another person who owns the improvements would needlessly encumber the record. Trinity Church, Columbia College, Sailors' Snug Harbor, New York Hospital, and families, such as the Astors, Rhinelanders, Stuyvesants, Moores, Lorillards, Lispenards, Spinglers, and others may be mentioned among those owning land leased on a pure ground rent basis. The leases are usually for twenty-one years with provision for one, two or three renewals. As a rule the *lessee pays all the taxes.* The result of this provision is that the land owner under such leases is protected from any change in the land tax laws or increase in the land tax rate. His rent is reserved free and clear above all charges of maintenance, both public and private, since all building charges, as well as all land tax charges for government maintenance, must be found and paid by the lessee.

Following are some specific examples of pure ground rent leases as disclosed in the records of the Register's Office:

(1). LOCATION: Bankers' Trust Building, northwest corner Wall and Nassau Streets—Lots 17, 19, 20—Block 46, Section 1;

OWNER OF LAND: Adele Livingston Sampson;

OWNER OF BUILDING (LESSEE OF LAND): Bankers' Trust Company, July 17, 1909, Liber 125, Page 116, Section 1;

ASSESSED VALUE OF LAND: 1915, $3,200,000; improvement, 31-story steel frame fireproof office building.

ASSESSED VALUE OF BUILDING: 1915, $2,600,000.

ANNUAL GROUND RENT: 1st year, $50,000. 2nd year, $80,000. 3rd year and balance of the term, $90,000;

TERMS OF LEASES AND OTHER INFORMATION: Term, 21 years and two renewals, rent or renewal to be fixed by appraisers, but not less than $90,000;

Building reverts to land owner at end of third term without compensation;

Lessee to pay *all taxes* and similar charges;

(2). LOCATION: Postal Telegraph Building, northwest corner Broadway and Murray Street, Lot 29, Block 134, Section 1;

OWNER OF LAND: Rector, Church Wardens and Vestrymen of Trinity Church;

OWNER OF BUILDING (LESSEE OF LAND): John W. Mackay, March 23, 1892, Liber 8, Page 168, Section 1;

ASSESSED VALUE OF LAND: 1915, $1,025,000;

ASSESSED VALUE OF BUILDING: 1915, $900,000;

ANNUAL GROUND RENT: 1st year, $17,500. 2nd year, $24,000. 3rd year, $52,500. Renewal: 21 years at $52,500;

TERMS OF LEASES AND OTHER INFORMATION: 3 years, from May 1, 1892, with renewal for 21 years, at $52,500 rent.

Second and third renewal, rent not less than immediately preceding period to be fixed by appraisement.

At end of third renewal, lessor may pay lessee value of building or grant further renewal for 21 and 13 years (a total of 100 years), building then reverts to lessor.

(3). LOCATION: Wanamaker Buildings—East side of Broadway, between 8th and 10th Streets and a small plot on Fourth Avenue, north of 10th Street;

OWNER OF LAND: Sailors' Snug Harbor;

OWNER OF BUILDING (LESSEE OF LAND): A. T. Stewart Realty Co. Owned and controlled by John Wanamaker; April 30, 1903; Liber 113, Page 328; Section 2;

ASSESSED VALUE OF LAND: 1915, Parcel 1, $1,830,000; Parcel 2, $1,615,000; Parcel 3, $95,000; Total $3,540,000.

ASSESSED VALUE OF BUILDING: 1915—Parcel 1, $4,625,000; Parcel 2, $2,000,000; Parcel 3, $105,000; Total $6,730,000;

ANNUAL GROUND RENT: 1st 7 years, $83,400; Balance of term, $113,620; Renewal 21 years at 3% upon full value of the land;

TERMS OF LEASES AND OTHER INFORMATION: 91 years from May 1, 1903, with renewal for 21 years at annual ground rent of 3% upon full value of the land to be determined by appraisers, etc.

Lessee to pay *all taxes* and similar charges;

Lessee to erect 14-story building to cover one of the parcels and at expiration of lease, lessor was to have option of paying the lessee the value of building or to grant renewal as above;

(3a). LOCATION: Northeast corner of Ninth Avenue and 22nd Street, 24 ft. 8 in. x 78 ft.

OWNER OF LAND: Clement C. Moore Estate, Katherine T. Moore, an heir;

OWNER OF BUILDING (LESSEE OF LAND): Ella Grace Lamb—January 1, 1914—Liber 192, Page 417, Section 3;

ASSESSED VALUE OF LAND: 1915, $17,000.

ASSESSED VALUE OF BUILDING: 1915, $7,000;

ANNUAL GROUND RENT: $900.

TERMS OF LEASES AND OTHER INFORMATION: 21 years, from January 1, 1914, at $900 yearly, with an option of buying the buildings at the end of the term or giving a renewal of the lease.

(4). LOCATION: Northwest corner of 50th Street and Fifth Avenue; (123 x 35 ft. 5 in.) irregular; Lot 34, Block 1266, Section 5;

North side 50th Street, 123 ft. west of Fifth Avenue 41 x 100 ft. 5 in. irregular—Lot 31, Block 1266, Section 5;

OWNER OF LAND: Trustees of Columbia College;

OWNER OF BUILDING (LESSEE OF LAND): Walter S. Gurnee, October 24, 1888; Liber 111, Page 103, Section 5; Assigned to Benjamin Altman;

William P. Clyde, Assigned to Benjamin Altman;

ASSESSED VALUE OF LAND: 1915, $710,000; 1915, $110,000;

ASSESSED VALUE OF BUILDING: 1915, $60,000; 1915, $20,000;

ANNUAL GROUND RENT: 21 years, at $4,424. See below; $4,042 in 1905, but see below;

TERMS OF LEASES AND OTHER INFORMATION: 21 years, from October 24, 1888; Leased for 13 years 6 months, at ground rent in 1873 of $900.

Ground rent in 1885 was $1,810;

Ground rent in 1905 was 4,042;

(Benjamin Altman, in 1905, combined the above two properties in a single lease from Columbia College for 21 years at $17,500, at end of term lessor may buy buildings or renew for 21 years. At end of third term lessee may remove building or lessor pay 2/3 of value of them.)

(5). LOCATION: North side of 14th Street, next east of corner Fifth Avenue (50 x 129) Lot 5, Block 842, Section 3;

OWNER OF LAND: Heirs of Mary S. Van Beuren (daughter of Eliza M. Fonerdon, a Spingler heir;

OWNER OF BUILDING (LESSEE OF LAND): Metropolitan Safe Deposit Company, October, 1903;

ASSESSED VALUE OF LAND: 1915, $137,500;

ASSESSED VALUE OF BUILDING: 1915, $30,000;

ANNUAL GROUND RENT: $6,000.

TERMS OF LEASES AND OTHER INFORMATION: 21 years, from October, 1903, Option to lessor to renew lease or take buildings at an appraised value;

In 1846 the ground rent was $625 (Thomas Oliver).

In 1867 the ground rent was $3,000 (Lorenzo Delmonico).

In 1888 the ground rent was $5,500 (James R. Boyd).

(6). LOCATION: Northeast corner of Fifth Avenue and 14th Street; 100 ft. on 14th Street and half block along 5th Avenue, Lot 1, Block 842, Section 3;

OWNER OF LAND: Heirs of Mary S. Van Beuren (daughter of Eliza M. Fonerdon, a Spingler heir).

OWNER OF BUILDING (LESSEE OF LAND): Samuel H. Blatchford (et al trustees);

ASSESSED VALUE OF LAND: 1915, $270,000;

ASSESSED VALUE OF BUILDING: $1915, $70,000.

ANNUAL GROUND RENT: $7,250.

TERMS OF LEASES AND OTHER INFORMATION: Ground rent in 1835 was $390 (Samuel H. Tisdale); 1856, was $1,375 (Moses H. Grinnell); 1887, was $3,500 (Moses H. Grinnell).

These are examples only of the Spingler Estate leases which included land west of Union Square, along the north side of 14th Street and covering several of the streets and avenues in that neighborhood.

2. There is a tendency toward a *decrease* in the number of parcels leased on a pure ground rent basis and an *increase* in leases where the land owner owns the building or builds a building to suit a lessee and

leases the entire premises for a long term of years. This tendency is due mainly to two things:

First. As ground leases expire the ownership of the buildings reverts in many cases to the land owner, who then finds a new tenant who leases the entire premises. This is more especially true in some of the older residence neighborhoods such as lower Greenwich Village.

Second. In the newer business localities, such as Fifth Avenue, below 59th Street, a land owner and a lessee will contract for a lease for a new building to suit the special requirements of the lessee. The rental is usually a precentage based on an appraised value of land, plus the cost of the building. This method is growing in favor as it places the lessee practically on the same financial basis as though he found the cash, purchased the land and built the building. The land owner is assured of his income on the land valuation and is also permitted to realize on the future increment in land value as the community prospers and grows. The following is typical of this kind of lease:

LOCATION: Gimbel's Building, westerly side of Sixth Avenue, between 32nd and 33rd Streets—Lots 21-65, inc.—Block 808, Section 3;

OWNER OF LAND: Greeley Square Realty Company (John D. Lockman, Pres.).

OWNER OF BUILDING (LESSEE OF LAND): Gimbel Bros. (Jacob Gimbel, Pres.), April 23, 1909—Liber 148, Page 107, Section 3;

ASSESSED VALUE OF LAND: 1915, $4,100,000;

ASSESSED VALUE OF BUILDING: 1915, $2,750,000;

ANNUAL GROUND RENT: 1911, 1912, 1913, $605,000; 1914, $615,000; 1915, $620,000; 1916-1920, inc., $630,000; remainder of term, $655,000.

TERMS OF LEASES AND OTHER INFORMATION: Leases land and building. Term, 21 years, from August 1, 1910;

Renewals for one, two, three or four successive terms: 1st—not less than $655,000, nor more than $705,000.

The store properties of Arnold Constable & Company, Bonwit, Teller & Company, A. A. Vantine & Co., and others, may be mentioned as illustrating this kind of lease.

A third class of leases of entire improved properties represents practically *management* of improved properties under which the lessee guarantees the owner of the building a certain net return and relieves the owner of all care. The lessee makes what he can above the rental to the owner and presumably his profits are measured by his skill in the detail of management. This is a growing custom.

BRIEF SUBMITTED
ON THE
UNTAXING OF BUILDINGS.

BRIEF SUBMITTED ON BEHALF OF THE SOCIETY TO LOWER RENTS AND REDUCE TAXES ON HOMES.

By Benjamin C. Marsh, Executive Secretary.

I. MORAL REASONS FOR UNTAXING BUILDINGS.
II. ECONOMIC REASONS FOR UNTAXING BUILDINGS.
III. FISCAL REASONS FOR UNTAXING BUILDINGS.
IV. ALLEGED OBJECTIONS TO UNTAXING BUILDINGS.
V. RESULT OF UNTAXING BUILDINGS ELSEWHERE.

I. MORAL REASONS FOR UNTAXING BUILDINGS.

There is no justification for taxing labor or the products of labor unless the revenue to be derived therefrom is needed for the cost of government efficiency and properly administered because adequate revenue for such purpose cannot be secured from any other source.

There are, however, only two sources of revenue for government—taxation of land values and taxation of the products of labor.

The city budget of New York City is (1914)...........$192,995,000
The tax levied upon land value is 82,472,000
The tax levy upon buildings is 51,359,000
The tax levy upon land and buildings is 133,831,000

The ground rent of New York City calculated at only 6% on assessed land values is $276,180,000.

The transfer of $51,359,000 of taxes now secured by taxing buildings to land values would increase the levy on land values to $133,831,000. This would leave the land owners (calculating the ground rent as above at 6% on the assessed value of land), $142,349,000, or 3.1% on the assessed value of land. Recent sales of real estate indicate that the selling value of land is considerably greater than the assessed value taking the city as a whole.

The ground rent of the city, as a whole, is probably nearly $300,000,000, so that even with the transfer of taxes from buildings to land net ground rents would be about $170,000,000 a year—or putting the value of land at $4,800,000,000, the net ground rent would be about 3.6% in addition to the annual increase of land values which average nearly $100,000,000 net exclusive of assessments, which during the past 8 years have averaged only about $8,900,000. Calculating the net increase in land values at $90,000,000 annually, the profits of land ownership in the city are 5.4% net.

There is obviously no justification for taxing buildings on the plea that the city needs this source of revenue since the owners of land would secure larger net revenues with buildings untaxed (including increases in land values) than depositors in saving banks and nearly three times as large as the interest paid by the U. S. postal savings banks.

Were even more of the ground rent of the city taken, however, than the $133,831,000 contemplated by transferring to land values the present levy on buildings so that land owners received only 1% or 2% net revenue, land owners would have no just cause for complaint. Land values and ground rent are peculiarly the product of population and of public improvements paid for by the population.

These values may be shifted from one part of the city to another by migration of population or of business and said fluctuation should be and in this city is recognized by reducing assessed values of land where it has shrunk and increasing it where it has risen.

It should be noted, too, that nearly 6/7 of the value of land in the city has some building improvement, however small, and the owners are securing revenue therefrom.

In 1913, the assessed value of the 191,742 absolutely vacant parcels (not lots) in the city was $644,635,185 out of a total assessed land value of $4,599,892,350. The assessed value of such vacant land was, in Manhattan, $182,598,890; in The Bronx, $150,940,152. The greatest acreage of vacant land is in Queens, Brooklyn and Richmond, but the greater part of such acreage is still in large tracts in these boroughs and at least part of this acreage in The Bronx and a large part of it in Queens and Richmond would yield a fair return if utilized for intensive gardening. Some of the most successful market gardening in the world is now being carried on in Queens and in Richmond, although in both of these boroughs large tracts of land assessed at $1,000 to $2,500 per acre are being devoted to weeds. The owners of much of this land prefer to hold it idle and try to secure transit lines out to their holdings so that they can sell a lot at about the assessed value of an acre rather than to put it to the purpose to which it is adapted until it is ripe for building. This is the direct result of our present system of taxation under which land owners pay only $42,472,000 in taxes for the cost of local government and the city's share of the direct state tax, while the workers pay most of the balance of this budget, $192,995,000 (1914), i. e., $110,520,000.

The present division of the profits of land ownership between the few thousand people who own most of the value of land here and the 5½ million population whose presence is the chief factor in creating and maintaining land values and ground rent is immoral and cannot be justified.

The gross profits of land ownership, including ground rent and the increase in land values, are this year about $400,000,000. Out of this sum land owners pay in taxes $82,472,000 and in assessments on land about $9,000,000, a total of $91,472,000, making the net profits of land ownership approximately $309,000,000. The principle involved can be made clearer if it be imagined that one person owned all of the land of the city and secured this profit of $309,000,000 after paying $91,000,000 for the cost of government here. Probably not a dozen people in the city outside of the family and immediate friends of such "Owner of New York" could be found to justify this division and the consequence. It would be a matter of relatively small importance whether this man had inherited part of the land from ancestors who stole it from the Indians or bought it from them for a trifle or whether he had paid 25%, 50%, 75% or 90% of the present price of the land. His utter inability to earn such an unfair proportion of the profits of land ownership would be appreciated by all and there would be universal demand for a reversal of this division between the people and the "Owner of New York." The plea of "confiscation" would be forgotten. The question would be "What have you done to earn any of the principal or the interest, the land values or the ground rent?"

There is little difference in principle so there may be a fictitious difference in "expediency,"—whether one person or ten thousand people "own" the land of the city.

THE EXISTING LAND MONOPOLY IN NEW YORK CITY.

It is impossible to give the exact figures as to the land monopoly in the city because the real estate interests have succeeded in defeating legislation requiring the name of the true owner to be recorded—a practice obtaining in Germany—and because they have similarly defeated bills requiring the "true price paid" to be recorded in deeds. The following figures are based upon the assessed value of land and the holdings so far as they can be traced without such full investigation as would seem necessary only to those who uphold the present system of taxation.

Five thousand people own over half of the value of land.

8 families, estates and corporations own about 1/23 of the value of land.

The Astor family owns about 1/60 of the value of the land.

Several corporations own 500 lots in Manhattan and from 100 to 1,000 acres in The Bronx, Brooklyn, Queens and Richmond.

Under the present uniform tax rate, a reduction in the tax rate to reduce expenditures would benefit chiefly land owners, and not the people of the city who create and maintain the land values and ground rents of the city.

In 1913, the assessed valuation of the different classes of taxable property in the city was, as follows:

Land	$4,590,892,350
Buildings	2,796,344,754
"Real Estate of Corporations"	180,549,176
"Special Franchises"	438,861,581
Personal Property	325,421,340

With the tax rate to be reduced by 5 mills on the dollar, the saving would be as follows:

On Land	$22,945,461.75
On Buildings	13,981,723.77
On "Real Estate of Corporations"	902,745.88
On "Special Franchises"	2,194,307.90
On Personal Property	1,627,106.70

The total savings to land owners would be $22,954,441.75, and to all other classes of property only $18,705,884.25. Land owners as such would save over $4,000,000 more than all other property owners and land owners would secure the benefit of most of the other reduction as well as in that on land although the tenants (9/10 of the city's population) would get practically no benefit from any of the other reductions.

The reduced tax rate on land values would also mean that the price of land would increase enormously, probably at least $500,000,000, and this would be a net unearned bonus to land owners and land speculators.

II. ECONOMIC REASONS FOR UNTAXING BUILDINGS.

1. Untaxing Buildings Will Lower Rents and Reduce Taxes on Homes.

No economist of repute denies this and a few, if any, land speculators, although they may differ as to the extent of rent reductions.

The following questionnaire was sent to this list of economists regarding the reduction of the tax rate on buildings in New York City to ½ that on land, by five consecutive annual reductions:

QUESTIONS.

1. Would the selling value of land be appreciably reduced?
2. Would the increase in the selling value of land be appreciably less?
3. Would the result of the higher tax on land and lower tax rate on buildings be a greater increase in the number of buildings than with the uniform rate of taxation?
4. Would rentals in tenements and other buildings be reduced more than the total taxes on improvements?
5. Would the possibility of a slight decrease in land values due to the higher tax rate on land cause the calling of loans on improved property?
6. Can the landlord shift the increase in taxes on a property where the land is worth much more than the buildings to the tenant?
7. Is it just to tax land increments (i. e., increases in land values after a given date) at a higher rate than that imposed on all land in the city?
8. Is it "confiscatory" to increase slightly the tax rate on land values?
9. Is it "discrimination" to tax land values at a higher rate than buildings?
10. Is it good fiscal policy to tax land values more heavily than buildings?
11. Would the lower tax rate on buildings encourage home ownership?
12. Would the increased values of buildings under the stimulus of the lower tax rate increase the taxable base of the city?

ECONOMISTS.

Prof. Irving Fisher, Yale University.
Prof. T. N. Carver, Harvard University.
Prof. Walter H. Clark, College of the City of New York.
Prof. E. A. Ross, University of Wisconsin.
Prof. John R. Commons, University of Wisconsin.
Prof. C. Linn Seiler, University of Pennsylvania.
Prof. Franklin L. McVey, University of North Dakota.
Prof. Royal Meeker, Princeton University.

Only one of the eight, Prof. Ross, thinks that the selling value of land would be appreciably reduced. Prof. Carver thinks it is doubtful. Professors Clark, Carver, Meeker, and Ross think the increase in the selling price of land would be appreciably reduced. Prof. Fisher thinks that it would be slightly reduced, and Professors Seiler and McVey that it would not be reduced at all.

All are agreed that more buildings would be constructed with the halved tax rate on buildings than with the uniform tax rate.

The six replying to the question say rents would be reduced to a greater extent than the reduction in taxes.

Only one thinks that loans could be called on improved properties to amount to anything, Prof. Seiler, who thinks this might possibly be done for a short time.

Only Prof. Seiler thinks that where the total tax on an improved property is increased because the land is worth so much more than the building, the owner can shift part of the increased tax to the tenant generally; the rest deny this.

All are agreed that it is just to tax land increments at a higher rate than that imposed on all land in the city.

As to whether it is "confiscatory" to tax land values at a slightly higher rate, Prof. Ross says, "No"; Prof. Seiler, "Difficult to answer"; Prof. Fisher, "All taxation is confiscatory"; Prof. Carver, "Somewhat but not enough to count"; Prof. Clark, "Not unless every tax is confiscatory"; Prof. Meeker, "The definition of 'confiscatory' must be left to the lawyers."

To the question whether it is "discrimination" to tax land values at a higher rate than buildings, Prof. Fisher says, "No more than the difference in any other taxes, e. g., whiskey and matches." Prof. Carver, "Yes." Prof. Clark, "It is valid discrimination." Prof. Ross, "It is proper discrimination based on difference in origin of such values." Professors Seiler, McVey and Meeker, "No."

Every one of them agree that it is good fiscal policy to tax land at a higher rate than buildings.

All but Prof Carver think it would encourage ownership of homes.

Professors Clark, Fisher, McVey and Meeker think that the half tax on buildings would increase the taxable base of the city through stimulating the construction of new buildings; Prof. Carver thinks this doubtful. Prof. Ross omitted to reply. Prof. Seiler says it would not if the city is normally increasing in wealth.

Prof. Commons sent the following statement: "I have long been strongly convinced that a gradual reduction of the tax rate on buildings leading finally to exemption of all improvements would be one of the most important gains that could be accomplished in our system of taxation. This is peculiarly true as a city grows in size and, of course, my judgment would apply to New York more than any other place in the country."

Prof. Henry R. Seager, in his "Principles of Economics" (p. 532), says: "The increase in the rents and price which city lots command as compared with open fields is due chiefly to the growth of the city and to improvements for which the city has paid. It, therefore, seems but just that a large part of the income received from city lots should go to the city treasury.

"On these grounds, and others of a more technical character, a gradual increase in the proportion of municipal taxation that falls on land as distinguished from improvements and different forms of personal property is much to be desired."

Prof. E. R. A. Seligman stated to the New York Commission on Congestion of Population which recommended the reducing the tax rate on buildings in New York City to ½ that on land:

"A tax upon anything produced tends to check the production of that thing. The remission of the taxes tends to encourage the production. The house is produced for what you can get out of it and if you make it worth while for people to put money into houses, of course, they will do so."

The late Mayor Gaynor put the immutable economic law as follows:

"If buildings were no longer taxed that would stimulate people to build buildings; but when you clap a tax on buildings then the people are not in a hurry to build them. They have to calculate it all out and see where they are coming out, where they can get the rents to pay interest and taxes. But if buildings were freed from taxes, there would be more buildings put up; and the more buildings put up, the lower rents would be. I am back to my starting point that rents of buildings depend upon supply and demand; therefore any system of taxation which stimulates the building of buildings multiplies the number of buildings, automatically lowers rents."

An application of the results of untaxing buildings and transferring these taxes to land will illustrate this fact.

The average uniform tax rate in all counties of the city is this year $1.80 per $100 of assessed value. Were buildings untaxed, the tax rate on land values would be $2.91. A tenement house assessed for $40,000, the land for $10,000 and the building for $30,000, pays this year $720—were buildings untaxed, total taxes on the land would be $291, i. e., the owner would save $429. Obviously he could give each of ten tenant families a reduction of $40 a year in rent and still be better off than he is to-day. The taxes on tenement house property assessed for $20,000, the land for $15,000 and the building for $5,000 (ratio not uncommon in some of the worst tenement districts) are this year $360. Were buildings untaxed, the total taxes on the land would be $436.50, an increase of $76.50.

Would the landlord be able to increase his rents in this tenement by $76.50? Would the owner of a tenement house property of which the land is assessed for $10,000, the building for $2,000, be able to charge his tenants the increased taxes with buildings untaxed, amounting to $75? Obviously not, for the following reasons: (a) There are in Manhattan, 1913, 8,211 absolutely vacant parcels, many of them comprising several lots—a total of approximately 10,000 lots. These vacant parcels are scattered throughout the entire borough in about 2/3 of the blocks. There are also approximately 20,000 lots with improvements of 3-stories or less, most of them one or two stories "taxpayers," similarly scattered throughout the borough. All these vacant and under-improved lots in Manhattan are a source of potential competition to the owners of existing tenements which would be sufficient to prevent them from attempting to raise rents even should the taxes on old worn-out tenement properties be doubled. The taxes on vacant land would be increased by about 3/5 (from 1.80% to 2.91% on the assessed value), while on a good many properties with worn-out improvements they would be increased by 1/5 to 1/2.

Naturally the increased tax rate on all land will compel the owners to sell their land at a lower price than they would with the present tax rate.

A vacant lot which would sell for $10,000 at the present tax rate, would probably be sold for at most $9,000 if not for $8,500 with a tax rate of $2.91. A man who wants to construct a $30,000 tenement on such a lot would save at least $1,000 on the original cost, that is, at 5% an annual carrying charge of $50. His total taxes, as shown above, would be about $430 less than at the present uniform tax rate, i. e., he would make a total annual saving of nearly $500 on this property through untaxing buildings.

The purchaser of the vacant lot would have an advantage over the owner of vacant lots, for the owners, in the words of one of the most successful land speculators, would "like to unload their vacant lots" as soon as heavier taxation of land values begins.

As is well known, not 1/3 of the land in the Borough of Brooklyn is improved with buildings, not 1/6 of the Borough of The Bronx where half of the population live on about 1/20 of the area, not 1/20 of the area of Queens, while Richmond is still a borough of "little farms" and big farms. At least 3/5 of the area of Greater New York available for building is still available for some building improvements or for more intensive building improvements than it has at present without any danger of over-intensive use of land or congestion of population per acre or block.

(b). The assessed value of land in Manhattan (1913), is $3,155,389,410, approximately 3/4 of the total assessed value of the city ($4,590,892,350).

The provision of more rapid transit lines to the outlying boroughs and control over the location of factories, with a gradual removal of factories from Manhattan to the other boroughs, will effectually prevent tenement owners in Manhattan from either charging higher rents, if their taxes are increased, or from keeping any advantage of lower taxes on adequate improvements when buildings are untaxed. The tremendous competition of vacant lots in all the other boroughs will be sufficient there to give tenants this advantage, even with the rapid increase in population and factories. The opposition of landlords in all boroughs to the change is proof that they appreciate this fact.

2. Untaxing Buildings Will Lower Interest Rates.

Interest rates are determined primarily by the law of supply and demand. The interest rate on even a risky investment will be less if there is a greater quantity of capital seeking investment than if through extensive government loans, industrial developments, wars, etc., there is a stringency in the money market.

If buildings were untaxed and the levy upon buildings transferred to land values, tenants and small home owners, and business men as such would be saved approximately $50,000,000. Most of this saving would accrue to tenants and small home owners. Part of this saving would be seeking investment, probably at least $10,000,000 to $12,000,000 a year. The small saver accepts a lower rate of interest than a person with large wealth. This is proven by the fact that savings bank depositors accept 3½% to 4%, while the U. S. Postal Savings Banks have been able to secure large and rapidly increasing deposits at 2%.

In February, 1911, there were 48 postal savings bank offices in operation in the country and the balance on deposit was $110,884.38. In June, 1913, the balance on deposits in 12,158 offices was $31,512,333.46.

Even with the small savings through reduced rents and lower taxes of $12,000,000 a year, this would amount to $120,000,000 in a decade.

Moreover, with buildings untaxed, the city will be in a position (as shown more fully in the next section, III) to pay more of its expenses currently and to abolish other sources of revenue, to the advantage of everyone in the community except the land speculator.

Thus, with buildings untaxed, a tax rate on assessed land values (1914), of only 5 mills on the dollar would yield $23,015,000 or over 1/3 of the average annual issue of corporate stock during the past 8 years

A tax rate of a little less than 3 mills on the dollar on land values would enable the city to give free water although it collects this year about $14,000,000 for water. Free water would save the average family in the city $5 to $10 annually. Within 10 or 15 years with buildings untaxed and land values heavily taxed, say, at the rate of 3.5%, 3.75%, hundreds of thousands of families in the city of the class now existing below a safe and sane standard of living would be able to save $20 to $25 for investment; in the aggregate, saving for such purposes in addition to present savings would, doubtless, be $15,000,000 to $20,000,000 a year.

It should be noted, too, that the current payment of current expenses now met by issuing (chiefly) 50-year corporate stock will release $20,000,000 or so a year for investment. The conspicuous and blatant methods in which our multi-millionaire land speculators and their families consume the ground rents we pay them does not add to capital, it reduces and destroys it.

A total increase of even $30,000,000 a year seeking investment would materially reduce interest rates, to the manifest advantage of legitimate business as distinguished from speculative purposes. Untaxing buildings will permit the most effective organization of credit—and for the benefit of workers instead of land speculators.

3. Untaxing Buildings Will Reduce Unemployment.

Nearly half of the men employed in the building trades in the city are, and have been, unemployed for many months, partly due to the fact that the per capita value of buildings being constructed is only about ½ as large as in 1910.

The replacement of the tens of thousands of old, unsanitary fire-trap buildings in this city with modern, safe buildings, which will be stimulated by untaxing buildings, will furnish employment not only to those in the building trades but, as well, to those who manufacture commodities they use. Prof. A. C. Pigou states, in "Wealth and Welfare": "As the rate of interest falls, instrumental goods come to be built more solidly and to be repaired and renewed more readily when need arises." (p. 81, footnote.)

Thus production and consumption will be encouraged and stimulated when taxes on objects produced are reduced as well as when interest rates are reduced. The operation of both forces is identical when land values are taxed heavily.

The heavy and unnecessary burden of taxes on modern healthful tenements is appreciated when it is realized that although the assessed value (1914) of all buildings of every description in the city is only $2,855,932,518, the value of the tenements constructed since the present

Tenement House Law went into effect, July 1, 1901, is $902,947,841. The assessed value of these tenements is this year at least $875,000,000—that is, they are paying about 1/3 of the total taxes on buildings in the city. Although these new law tenements house only about 1/5 of the tenants of the city, they pay approximately half of the taxes on tenements.

III. FISCAL REASONS FOR UNTAXING BUILDINGS.

New York's system of raising revenue is archaic and unjust. The chief object of most administrations has been to keep down the tax rate, by saddling upon future generations the cost of public improvements and current expenses which should have been paid currently by current revenues. These administrations have realized that a higher general tax rate would prejudice their party with the voters who if tenants would see their rent increase and if small home owners their total taxes largely increase while buildings are taxed at the same rate as land values.

The loaning interests of the city which, with the land speculators, have controlled the city government without intermission as they do to-day, have naturally favored this policy of a low tax rate and heavy loans. Through their manipulation they have kept the city going deeper into debt so that the debt limit is now practically reached.

The tax rate on assessed land values has varied from $1.49 per $100 in 1907 to $1.84 in 1912. In 1907, land was assessed at about 90% of its market value, so that the tax rate on full value was only about $1.33.

The ground rent of the city from 1906 to 1913, calculated at 6% on full land values, amounted to $2,051,717,352. The increase in land values was about $1,200,000,000. Total gross profits of land ownership during the past 8 years—$3,251,717,353. The total taxes on land values during the past eight years were only $71,819,659. The total assessment on land values during the past eight years was only $548,181,865.

The total charges on land during the past 8 years were only $620,-001,524.

Net profits of land ownership here during the past 8 years—$2,631,-715,829.

The total current city budget in these 8 years was $1,238,383,455. Since the cost of government not met by taxing land values has been paid by taxes upon labor and the products of labor, this total charge during 8 years past has been approximately $675,000,000. (Since, about $15,000,000 has been received from the school moneys of the state.) During these 8 years, the net funded debt of the city has been increased by over $408,526,642—from $430,556,400 to $839,083,042. Corporate stock was issued during these 8 years in the sum of $519,177,711; while the interest paid on the city debt amounted to $234,118,908, and only $63,992,725 of the city debt was paid off.

TO SUMMARIZE: The profits of land ownership in New York City during the past 8 years have been approximately $3,251,000,000. The current and corporate stock budgets have amounted to only $1,-757,561,166, or about 1/2 of the profits of land ownership. Instead of paying this cost of government currently out of ground rents, land values have paid in taxes and assessments only $620,000,000, the workers of the city have been mulcted out of about $675,000,000 and the city has borrowed about $519,000,000 upon which it will have to pay approximately $1,000,000,000 in interest during the next 50 years. This has been an orgy of frenzied municipal finance, with the tenants and small home owners of the city mulcted wittingly by the two past administrations for the benefit of land speculators and the financial interests.

Comptroller Prendergast has reported to the Mayor that the debt-incurring power of the city on January 2, 1914, was $51,373,749.62. This is practically all mortgaged for schools and other current necessities.

The city should spend at once $100,000,000 to $150,000,000 on the port and dock development. Instead of being in a position to do so, it is acquiring driblets of land in the most expensive and unsatisfactory way for the city, though it is highly satisfactory to land speculators.

The efforts of the financial interests of the city to compel the city to resort to private capital and to insure high dividends to private capital has been successful.

The stupidity of land speculators which is exceeded only by their cupidity has got them into hot water. Had they eight years ago permitted even, not to say urged, that the land values be attached at $2.25 on full value while buildings were taxed at only the actual rates during these past eight years, the city would have secured about $221,000,000 more revenue, or 2/5 of the indebtedness occurred during this period.

The system of taxing labor and the products of labor has increased rents and sickness and delinquency and the cost to the city of caring for the victims of disease and delinquency.

Directly and indirectly, the city is spending about $10,000,000 a year, not to prevent disease and delinquency, but to cure the victims—a stupid and unnecessary expenditure which increases the tax rate.

The city has paid on the average about $18,000,000 a year for land since 1906. Mr. Wm. H. Chesebrough, who was chairman of the Real Estate Owners' Association, said last fall:

"One of the most efficient instruments for mulcting the taxpayers has been the system of acquiring land by condemnation under the methods which have existed for many decades past. As a general rule, it is not, I think, too much to say that land so acquired has cost the city at least twice and, in many cases, three or four times what it was actually worth."

City Chamberlain Bruere stated last fall: "Real estate speculators have tapped the city treasury to their heart's content."

The method of condemnation, however, is not responsible for the high prices paid for land by the city as much as the present system of taxation.

The assessed value of land acquired last year for the Court House was $4,077,500. The Elkus Commission, which condemned this property, did their work very efficiently, relatively. But they awarded a much larger sum than the assessed value of the land.

It is admitted by land speculators themselves that if the tax rate on land were, say $3, instead of $1.80, the owners of the land would sell their land decidedly cheaper. It is most conservative to estimate that the city would save annually on real estate acquisition (since the buildings represent ordinarily only about 1/3 of the total award) at least $2,000,000 to $2,500,000 if buildings were untaxed, even if it continues the present policy of issuing long term corporate stock to pay for real estate, and that it would save about $3,500,000 a year as soon as it begins to pay a just proportion of its expenses currently and stops paying an average of about $40 a year per family for interest on the city debt.

It must be apparent to the densest standpatter that it is very expensive to business men of all sorts, manufacturers, merchants, small storekeepers and all, to have to pay their share of the interest on the city debt incubus, which amounted last year to $45,000,000, nearly ¼ of the total city budget.

New York City is the largest employer of labor in the city. It has about 90,000 persons permanently on the city payroll, and 15,000 per diem or temporary employees (besides numerous Mayoralty secretaries, research experts and accessory specialists).

Their salaries and wages amount to about $98,000,000 a year for those in active service, while the city has not yet begun to pension all its employees. If it does pension them on a 35% basis, the wisdom and justice of which is not properly to be debated here, this would mean a very large additional expense within a few years. It is not claimed by the Board of Estimate and Apportionment that "readjustment of salaries" will reduce total salary and wages budget. It will doubtless, like most "efficiency and economy" measures, increase the total. About $25,000,000 of the city's payroll goes for rent. Nearly all the city's employees (except those with salaries of $7,500 or over) want their salaries or wages increased, and the most common reason is high rents and high taxes on homes. Untaxing buildings would (as demonstrated in Section II) reduce rents by 1/5 to 1/6 and taxes on small homes by 1/2 to 3/5. It would be equivalent to raising the wages and salaries of city employees by $4,500,000 to $5,000,000 or more and IT WOULD BE MORE EQUITABLE AND JUST TO THE TENANTS AND SMALL HOME OWNERS OF THE CITY NOT IN MUNICIPAL EMPLOY TO DO IT IN THIS WAY; but within a short time (probably just before the next municipal election) wages and salaries of city employees will be raised if they do not secure relief from high rents and high taxes on small homes.

Our present system of taxation is stupid from a fiscal point of view because: (a) It compels the city to pay enormously high prices for land; (b) it keeps manufacturers away from the city and so reduces the taxable base of the city; (c) it compels the city to pay high nominal NOT real wages to its employees, for the benefit of land speculators, to the detriment of tenants and small home owners, and with no advantage to the employees themselves; (d) it compels the city to borrow money to pay for improvements by long term corporate stock issues which should be paid for out of current revenues because the working people cannot and will not stand any more taxes, direct or indirect, and no administration will dare to impose such unjustifiable and iniquitous taxes; (e) it causes sickness and delinquency as well as unemployment and involves a huge expense to the city to deal with these results and conditions. The only way to change these evils is to untax buildings and other products of labor and secure more of the ground rent to the cost of government.

IV. ALLEGED OBJECTIONS TO UNTAXING BUILDINGS.

1. "It is 'confiscation' to take away any of the capital invested in land 'without due process of law.' While this system might be fair in a new community it is unjust with present values."

The assumption in this "objection" is that the government has ever impliedly or directly guaranteed to maintain land values at the highest point of speculative prices to which the cupidity of land speculators has been able to boost them and also guarantee any net profit on such speculative prices. This assumption is so ridiculous as to discredit both the intelligence and sincerity of those making it. If this assumption were correct, plungers on the stock exchange would be entitled to receive compensation for their losses and losers would be pensioned for life at public expense.

That it is not unconstitutional nor confiscating to untax buildings would seem adequately determined by court decisions as well as by practice.

A case recently before the U. S. Supreme Court on which they delivered an opinion, April 4, 1910, upheld the right of a state to differentiate in its system of taxation (Southwestern Oil Co. vs. Texas, 217 U. S., 114, 30 Supreme Court, 496, affirming 100 Texas, 647). A Texas statute imposed a 2% tax upon gross receipts from any or all oils, etc., sold at wholesale in the state and a tax amounting to 2% of the cash market value sold or handled or disposed of in any manner in the state. This was upheld by the state court, but appeal was taken to the U. S. Supreme Court, which affirmed the state court in the following opinion:

"The Fourteenth Amendment was not intended to cripple the taxing power of the states or to impose upon them any iron rule of taxation. This court will not speculate as to the motive of a state in adopting taxing laws but assumes—the statute neither upon its face nor by necessary operation suggesting a contrary assumption—that it was adopted in good faith. Except as restricted by its own or the Federal Constitution a state may prescribe any system of taxation it deems best and it may, without violating the 14th Amendment, classify occupations, imposing a tax on some and not on others, so long as it treats equally all in the same class. An occupation tax on all wholesale dealers in certain specified articles does not, on its face, deprive wholesale dealers of their property without due process of law or deny them equal protection of the law because a similar tax is not imposed upon wholesale dealers in other articles, and it was so held as to the Kennedy Act of Texas in 1905, levying an occupation tax on wholesale dealers in coal and mineral oils.

A Federal Court cannot interfere with the enforcement of a state statute merely because it disapproves of the terms of the act, questions the wisdom of its enactment or is not sure as to the precise reason inducing the state to enact it."

The power of the Legislature in matters of taxation is broader than in almost any other field. In the case of Janet vs. City of Brooklyn, 99 N. Y., 300, the Court of Appeals said:

"The power of taxation being legislative, all the incidents are within the control of the Legislature. The purposes for which a tax should be levied; the extent of taxation; the apportionment of the tax; upon what property or classes of persons a tax shall operate; whether the tax shall be general or limited to a particular locality and in the latter case the fixing of a district of assessment; the method of collection and whether a tax shall be a charge upon both person and property or only on the land are matters within the discretion of the Legislature and in respect to which this determination is final."

Discrimination between different classes of property or different kinds of transactions is generally recognized in our present law. Thus in New York, transfers of stock are taxed but not transfers of general merchandise, and inheritances are taxed at various rates according to the value of the property affected and the relationship of the beneficiaries to the deceased owner. Mortgages are taxed differently from personal property, and this mortgage tax law was upheld by the Court of Appeals in a strong decision in the case of People vs. Ronner, reported in 185 N. Y., page 285. Similar differentiations exist in the tax laws of other states.

The tax rate on buildings in Houston, Texas, was in one year reduced to 1/3 of the tax rate on land, and the Legislature of Pennsylvania last year passed a law reducing the tax rate on buildings in Pittsburgh and Scranton to 1/2 that on land, but the courts have not yet declared the law invalid; while land in Kansas City, Mo., benefited by parks is assessed with a large part of the cost of maintenance.

Partly through regulation by the Federal and state governments, the average surpluses earned by all the railroads of the country fell from 6.3% in the years 1905, 1906, 1907, to 4.4% in 1911, 1912, 1913; but this fact did not entitle stockholders to remuneration from either the Federal or state governments.

It should be noted, too, that "due process of law" is contemplated, since the proposed change in the law is to be accomplished by the method provided in the Constitution.

The burden of proof obviously rests upon those who claim that the people want the existing system while opposing the referendum on changing it. They must also disprove the equally obvious fact that the present system has been perpetuated by legislative bodies in fact representative of and controlled by land speculators and other real estate owners, and not representatives of the people as a whole. It is not, in any real sense, the fault of those oppressed by the present system of taxation that buildings have not been taxed at a lower rate than land for a good many years at least. The admission that more or most of the ground rent might properly have been taken for governmental purposes if we had started that way (but we shouldn't start now) is tantamount to claiming that repetition of a wrong transforms such wrong into a virtuous act.

2. "Untaxing buildings will reduce the taxes on the homes of the wealthy."

A fair test of this claim is Fifth Avenue. If buildings had been untaxed this year, the mansions on the east side of Fifth Avenue, from 51st Street north to 77th Street, would have paid in round figures $334,000 more taxes than this year's levy.

3. "Untaxing buildings will wipe out the small home owner."

The taxes on a $3,000 home on a $1,000 lot are, outside of Manhattan and The Bronx, about $73.60. With buildings untaxed, the total taxes would be only $29.10, saving in taxes $44.50. It is also claimed that the selling price of land would be reduced by the increase in tax rate. What is meant is that the increase in the selling price of land will be retarded. The average annual increase in land values (NOT assessed land values) is about 3½%.

The selling price of a lot at $1,000 is a 5% net ground rental. Untaxing buildings would involve an increased tax rate of about 1.1% on assessed land values or slightly over 1/5 of the present net ground rent. The selling price of the $1,000 lot might be reduced by about 1/5 by untaxing buildings, i. e., by about $220, IF land values in the city were stationary. As a matter of fact, they are not stationary but are increasing in most sections of the city. The natural and average increase of 3% in the selling price of a $1,000 lot would mean an increase of $30 a year.

We may put the advantages of untaxing buildings to the home owner, described as follows, for a 20-year period:

Increase in value of lot (uncompounded)	$600
Saving in taxes at $44.50 a year (excluding interest)	890
Total profits	$1,490
Depreciation in capital value of land	220
Net profits	$1,270

The situation might be put instead that the value of the lot of this home owner instead of increasing about $600 in 20 years would increase only about $400, while the outstanding fact is that THE SAVING IN TAXES TO THE AVERAGE HOME OWNER WITH BUILDINGS UNTAXED WOULD BE AT 4% COMPOUND INTEREST OVER $1,000 OR FIVE TIMES AS MUCH AS ANY POSSIBLE DEPRECIATION IN THE SELLING VALUE OF HIS LAND.

Few, if any, small home owners buy land for the increase in land values. They buy it for a home. Two other facts should be considered:

a. Within 25 or 30 years, the growth of the city will require the use of much land now occupied by small homes for tenements or business purposes so that the owners will secure much higher prices than they otherwise would. This movement will be accelerated by regulations limiting the height and size of buildings and the proportion of the lot area which they may occupy by the distribution of factories.

b. There are not over 100,000 acres outside of the Borough of Manhattan available for resident purposes. Allowing 16 lots to an acre, this means only 1,600,000 lots. The population of these boroughs is at present over 3,000,000. Within a quarter of a century the population of these boroughs will be probably at least 6,000,000, and within half a century 10,000,000, even at the present rate of increase for the next 25 years.

Probably at least 3/4 of the city's population will live in tenements and within relatively few years more of the lots of the city used for resident purposes will provide shelter for at least three families.

It is manifestly unfair that one man should secure the increase in land values due to the necessities of two other families—just as unfair in principle as that the Astors should secure the increase in land values due to the necessity of tens of thousands of families. Justice is qualitative, not quantitative.

4. "It will reduce taxes in the skyscraper district."

It is true that taxes on 7 or 8 of the large skyscrapers of the city would be reduced by a few thousand dollars if buildings were untaxed. The owners of these buildings are bitterly opposing the untaxing of buildings because they know it will stimulate the construction of more office buildings or loft buildings in their vicinity, and reduce rents so that they will not get any of the advantage of the reduction of the taxes on skyscrapers.

The district below Chambers Street, in Manhattan, would, however, have paid about $1,600,000 more taxes.

5. "New York City is overbuilt now."

Tenement House Commissioner Murphy states:

"A careful census of the city, made recently, indicates not more than 5% of vacancies, and the unanimous testimony of agents is that renting is good."

10% of vacancies is not unusual. It takes longer to construct tenements than for babies to be born, or immigrants to arrive by thousands.

"Good renting" for agents means high rents for tenants.

In 1910, Mr. Lawrence Veiller, housing expert, stated:

"We have 80,000 buildings, housing nearly 3,000,000 people, so constructed as to be a standing menace to the community in the event of fire.

"In no other city is there so great congestion and overcrowding. In no other city do the poor so suffer from excessive rents."

The Tenement House Committee of the Charity Organization Society and the Tenement House Department of the City have recently prepared a pamphlet on housing conditions for distribution among tenants, and in a chapter entitled, "Don't rent dark rooms," they state: "Fresh air and light in every room are better than medicine. Plants cannot grow in the dark, neither can children. How often have you gone to the doctor or dispensary during the last year? Ask him about dark rooms. A dark room is a consumption factory. Gas bills and medicine bills soon equal the difference in rent between good, light rooms and dark, unhealthy ones."

They frankly admit the fact that New York City is oversupplied with tuberculosis factories, but no one, except the beneficiaries of the present high rents prevalent in New York City, will claim that the city is overbuilt with either tenements or homes.

6. "Money will not be loaned if there is any danger that the selling price of land will be reduced."

As has been proven above, the selling price of land will not be reduced below the present figures by the gradual increase in the tax rate on land, and the depreciation in buildings will not be any more rapid under the proposed untaxing of buildings.

Most of the water has already been squeezed out of the land values of New York City. Any loaning institution, therefore, in making a loan under the proposed change will know that their security will be unimpaired, and that the higher tax rate on land will not affect the security of investment.

The proposed change would increase the tax rate on land only about 10 points a year, while during the three years, 1908, 1909 and 1910, the average increase in the tax rate on all clases of property was about 9 points yearly. There was no panic then nor any unusual number of foreclosures of mortgages. The borrower of money to construct buildings hereafter will be able to make just as good a profit on his investment in buildings as to-day, although the profits on his investment in land will be reduced by the extent to which the heavier tax rate retards the increase of land values. Improved real estate will still be as safe an investment as to-day, since the change goes into effect so slowly, and the result will be discounted a year or two in advance of the beginning of the operation of the bill.

As pointed out in Section III, the competition of additional capital will work to lower interest rates and encourage capital to take a smaller return.

7. "Savings bank depositors will lose their deposits."

Most mortgages are made for a period of only 3 to 5 years, probably an average of 3½ years. Since the measure goes into operation so gradually there will be time for an adjustment of gradual reduction in the amount of the loan, if such should be necessary. Loans are limited to 60% of the appraised value of property. If the loan exceeds this, the responsibility rests upon the loaning company, not upon the tax system.

As pointed out, there is practically no danger of reduction of the value of property due to the tax system within less than five years. However, any mortgage hereafter given by savings banks could protect the interests of depositors by a clause providing for the gradual scaling down of the mortgage if the value of property should be depreciated. Savings bank depositors would thereby be entirely protected. It is worthy of note, moreover, that where the untaxing of buildings has been tried, in part or in whole, there has been no calling of mortgages or loans.

8. "Equities will be wiped out."

The preceding paragraphs of this section show that, where the equity is not a shoestring equity, as is often the case, or the property has been overloaned, the equity will not be wiped out by the gradual reduction.

If a man has speculated in vacant or under-improved land he is not entitled to any sympathy except from the classes who are speculating themselves.

9. "The borrowing capacity of the city will be reduced."

The opponents of this measure claim that there will be an enormous increase in the number and size of buildings and, therefore, frankly admit that money will be loaned, while also admitting that the assessed value of buildings will be tremendously increased, and, as has already been pointed out, there will be only a slight reduction in the assessed value of land.

This will *not* reduce the assessed valuation or borrowing ability of the city. The experience of all cities where the tax rate on buildings has been reduced or abolished proves this, as well as our own experience.

The tax levy upon land values here was greater by $33,451,834 in 1913 than in 1906. During these years:

The assessed value of land was increased by............	$1,223,658,604
The assessed value of buildings was increased by	837,165,390
Total increase in assessed values was..............	$2,060,823,994

All this, in spite of the increased levy on land values, which is about 2/3 of the increase in the levy on land if the tax rate on buildings were reduced to 1% of that on land.

It is thoughly understood, however, as pointed out in Section III, that the city should not be so heavily in debt; and one of the primal advantages of the heavy taxation of land values and untaxing buildings will be that it will enable the city to pay its current expenses in the most equitable way, currently, instead of running into debt so heavily. The Constitution states that the indebtedness of any county or city shall not exceed "10 per centum of the assessed valuation of the real estate of such county or city, subject to taxation."

The RATE of taxation is not mentioned. Both land and buildings in New York City have been taxed as low as $1.41 per $100 of assessed value; and they were just as much subject to taxation as when taxed

$2.48 (in 1909); and when the buildings were taxed $2.48, they were no more subject to taxation than they would be if taxed $1.03 or $1.04 per $100 or even less. Therefore, the claim that to reduce the tax rate on buildings to 1% of the tax rate on land would mean to exempt buildings and, therefore, would ipso facto eliminate the assessed value of buildings, in calculating the debt-incurring capacity of the city, is utterly illogical.

10. "Rents will be increased."

This astounding discovery has been made by Mr. Allan Robinson, President of the Allied Real Estate interests of New York, and is based upon the primary discovery that the depreciation in the value of buildings will have to be paid by the tenants. Of course, the tenant has been paying this constantly, and the argument further adduced that interest will be increased, so increasing the cost of building, has already been met in Section II, on Economic Advantages.

11. "There will be an intensive use of land, and none but large buildings put up."

That this is illogical is proven by the fact that under the present uniform tax rate on land and buildings, as enormous structures as possible have been erected. The same landed interests that have fought for years the effort to secure reasonable regulation of building construction and limitations upon the height, size and volume of buildings, are opposing the untaxing of buildings. Lessening the height of tenements is essential, but that will not lessen rents, and the heavier penalty imposed upon the vacant land speculators by untaxing buildings will lead them to support a movement to prevent the construction of a few enormous buildings so as to corner the office, factory or tenement market.

12. "Untaxing buildings will increase congestion."

This is merely the confounding of more floor space and more people, a mistake so stupid as to be unworthy of any intelligent mind. Congestion involves people per acre, and also per room. If there were no tenants in the Woolworth Building, there would be no congestion of population on this site.

13. "The market is bad."

It may be freely admitted that the profits of land speculation are not quite so large to-day as they have been in recent years.

If the moral principle, however, is right, that portion of the community is entitled to more of the ground rent than they are receiving to-day. This is not altered by the fact that land speculators are not making ordinary speculative profits, while the water is being squeezed out of land values.

Moreover, this would improve the real estate market, particularly in brokerage, through stimulating the locating of factories in New York City. It is true that much of the labor and factory legislation recently enacted in this State will increase the cost of doing business here; but most of this cost can be shifted, and has been shifted by the manufacturers wherever possible, on to the consumers.

14. "Untaxing buildings will impoverish widows and orphans."

This charming illustration of widows and orphans is the perennial spectre of privilege. The City of New York is admitting the right of every resident, not subject to deportation or to removal to the place in this country where he has his legal residence, to be supported at public expense. This recognized right justifies the city, if any such justification were required, in adopting an equitable policy of taxation.

It is highly improbable that any widows or orphans would be seriously affected by this change going into effect so gradually as is proposed. The present system hurts widows and orphans tenfold as much as any possible reduction in the income of these classes through the proposed change in the system of taxation.

15. "To exceed the 2% tax limit would be unconstitutional."

The State Constitution (Art. VIII, Sec. 10) says:

"The amount hereafter to be raised by tax for county or city purposes, in any city, or county containing a city, of over 100,000 inhabitants, or any such city of this State, in addition to providing for the principal and interest of existing debt, shall not in the aggregate exceed in any one year 2 per centum of the assessed valuation of the real and personal estate of such county or city, to be ascertained as prescribed in this section in respect to county or city debt."

The assessed value of real estate (1913) was $7,567,786,280. The assessed value of personal estate (1913) was $325,421.340. Total, $7,893,207,620. Two per centum of this assessed value of real and personal estate is $157,864,152. The debt limit (interest and principal) is about $70,000,000. Total revenue that may be raised by tax, $207,864,152.

Out of the city's budget this year of nearly $193,000,000, only about $170,000,000 was raised by tax; the balance by water rates, school money from the State, rentals, license fees, etc. In other words, the City of New York could have raised at least $38,000,000 more revenue this year by tax.

As has been demonstrated earlier, there will be no reduction in the total assessed value of real estate in the city, but a decided increase, with buildings untaxed, so that even were the debt service reduced, the city could raise probably $40,000,000 annually more revenue by tax without affecting the constitutional provision cited. The only result, since no substitute for a tax is suggested, will be to enlarge the taxable base of the city so it can secure more revenue without exceeding 2 per centum of the assessed value of real and personal estate.

V. RESULTS OF UNTAXING BUILDINGS ELSEWHERE.

Prof. E. R. A. Seligman stated to Mayor Gaynor's Congestion Commission:

"It must be stated, however, in defense of the claim that the exemption of improvements is desirable, in so far as I know, no town or city which has gone over to the exemption of improvements has receded from that position."

(1) VANCOUVER, B. C.

It is true, as claimed by the opponents of untaxing buildings and increasing the tax rate on land values, that the value of buildings constructed in Vancouver in 1913 was not so large as in 1912. Prof. Chas. S. Bullock, of Harvard University, states that the value of buildings for which plans were filed from January to May, inclusive (1914), "is $1,820,000, indicating total operations of between four and five million dollars for the year 1914." Prof. Bullock adds, "If the single tax rather than the previous period of flush times accounts for the increase in building operations from 1909 to 1912, it must accept the responsibility for the slump of 1913, 1914."

As Prof. Bullock admits elsewhere, however, nothing approximating the "single tax" has been in operation in Vancouver, nor has it in any other city where buildings have been untaxed. The tax on land values in Vancouver takes only about 20% of the ground rent, while in New York City it takes nearly 30%, and under the "single tax" it would take approximately 100%. There has naturally been land speculation, and wild land speculation, for Vancouver, instead of taxing land values has plunged heavily into debt, besides taxing many things in addition to land, just as New York City has done for the same reason: it is profitable to land speculators and money lenders.

Prof. Bullock fails to observe that although the total value of buildings constructed in Vancouver was only $10,423,000 in 1913, instead of $19,388,000 as in 1912, the per capita value of new building construction was still in 1913 $91.30, as against $92 in 1912, i. e., practically the same, and the per capita construction both years was larger than it was in 1906, with buildings taxed at half the rate on land—$82.85.

There has been a land boom in Vancouver during the past 10 years. Ordinarily, under such circumstances, rents increase very rapidly. Not only have rents NOT increased in Vancouver but they have decreased materially, and this reduction is deplored by some of the people who most loudly assert that untaxing buildings has been a failure in Vancouver. That rents would have been reduced still more had land values been taxed twice as heavily is self-evident. A comparison of the per capita value of buildings constructed in New York City and in Vancouver is illuminating.

The per capita constructing of buildings in the two cities for given years was as follows:

	New York.
1910	$45.47
1913	27.63
	Vancouver.
1909	$92.00
1913	91.30
1914	43.86 (estimating construction at $5,000,000 and taking 1913 population).

The population of Vancouver is stated to be only about the same this year, 1914, as in 1913. The per capita construction of buildings was also nearly three times as large in 1913 as in 1902, with buildings taxed at ½ the tax rate on land.

It will be seen that the impetus to the construction of buildings through untaxing them, even with land values decidedly undertaxed so as to stimulate land speculation, is nearly twice as effective in Vancouver in its terrible "slump" year as in New York City in 1913, and more than twice as great in a banner year, 1913, in Vancouver, as in a banner year in New York City, 1910.

It is manifestly unfair, however, to take any one year as a "slump" or "banner" year since the operation of economic law through a series of years is necessary to test it effectively, and to learn what its workings are.

The result in Vancouver of untaxing buildings has been to stimulate the construction of enough buildings to reduce rents, and it has encouraged home ownership, about ¾ of the wage earners owning their homes.

Vancouver's experience proves that the results of untaxing buildings are good, and, at least inferentially, that the results of taxing land values heavily would be better.

There are doubtless land speculators in Vancouver who would like to return to taxing buildings, which merely proves that human nature is not extinct in Vancouver.

(2). EDMONTON, ALBERTA.

In 1901, the population of Edmonton was only 2,500; this year it is 72,500. Buildings have not been taxed at all in Edmonton. There was a rental tax which has recently been abolished. The value of the permits for the construction of buildings issued in 1912 was $15,000,000, as against one and a half millions in 1906.

(3). VICTORIA, B. C.

Victoria, B. C., 40,000 population, having also exempted improvements, reports that the building permits for 1912 were eight millions, against only four millions in 1911.

(4). WINNIPEG.

Winnipeg in 1909 exempted 2/3 of the value of buildings. In a municipal election in 1911, 24 out of 28 candidates declared in favor exempting buildings altogether.

(5). Perhaps the best proof of the advantages of untaxing buildings to tenants and small home owners and legitimate business men, NOT to land speculators and the financial interests, is the fact that despite a recession in Vancouver, which is probably temporary, all northwestern Canada is following suit and untaxing buildings.

The third biennial report of the Minnesota Tax Commission (p. 154), states:

"The most striking feature in a study of tax reform in western Canada is the strong trend throughout the country in the direction of the Single Tax principle. That so far it is working satisfactorily wherever tried is generally admitted, even by opponents of the principle. In no district in which the principle has been applied is there any noticeable desire to return to the old system. From present indications it is safe to predict that within the next 10 or 20 years the Single Tax principle will be adopted by every taxing district in western Canada."

Hon. George Langley, Minister of Municipal Affairs in Saskatchewan, in his report for 1912, says:

"That scheme of taxation whereby buildings and improvements are not assessed is ever increasing in popularity throughout the province. In our rural municipalities and local improvement districts, the land alone has always borne the rates of taxation and there is not the slightest tendency to change the system."

In Ontario, 300 municipalities have petitioned for power to reduce the tax rate on buildings.

(6). Throughout the province of Saskatchewan, all buildings are, by law, exempt 40%, but by law of 1911, cities and towns were authorized to increase this exemption and about 20 of them have done so.

(7). TORONTO.

Under date of February 10, 1914, Silas C. Thompson, Secretary of the Tax Reform League of Eastern Canada, wrote:

"The City of Toronto, by vote of 25,773 against 6,440, decided to ask for privilege from the Legislature to reduce the tax rate on buildings, incomes and business assessments and to increase the rate on land values."

(8). The Legislature of Pennsylvania last year passed a law gradually reducing the tax rate on buildings in Pittsburgh and Scranton to

½ that on land values. It is naturally too early to determine any definite results, although it may be noted that Pittsburgh manufacturers, and real estate operators as well, are advertising the change in the tax system as an advantage to prospective manufacturers.

(9). The experience of Houston, where, in 1912, the tax rate on buildings was reduced to about 1/3 of the tax rate on land, is shown in the attached copy of "The Tenants' Weekly," Vol. 1, No. 15, in a letter from Tax Commissioner Pastoriza, of Houston.

SUPPLEMENTARY BRIEF, SUBMITTED BY THE SOCIETY TO LOWER RENTS AND REDUCE TAXES ON HOMES, BENJAMIN C. MARSH, EXECUTIVE SECRETARY.

Why Construction of Buildings of Large Volume or Size Will Not Be Encouraged By Transferring Taxes Now Levied On Buildings to Land Values.

It has been claimed that the untaxing of buildings and heavier taxation of land values will cause many enormous buildings to be constructed. The Heights of Buildings Commission investigated this question fully, in 1913, and reported that buildings of enormous volume are not commercially profitable. We quote from their report (pp. 19-21):

> "Few skyscrapers pay large net returns. Most of them pay only moderate returns. The cost per cubic foot of tall buildings is greater than that for low buildings. The exact difference can only be approximated because there are so many factors which affect the problem. However, the very tall buildings demand many things out of proportion to their increased bulk. All piping has to be made disproportionately heavier; special pumps and relays of tanks have to be provided. Foundations often call for special construction, wind-bracing assumes an importance, long-run elevators are more costly than short-run elevators, the extra space taken up by express run of the elevators is an additional cost. Thus in the aggregate the total cost per cubic foot of a very tall building may be 60 to 75 cents per cubic foot where a low building of the same class would cost only 40 to 50 cents per cubic foot.
>
> "The net rentable space on the ground floor is worth on the average as much as that of the third to the eighth floors, inclusive. Loss of rentable ground floor space is always serious and must be compensated for in other ways if the building is going to pay. The exceptional size of the columns and the exceptional space taken by pipes and ducts on the lower floors alone, have a serious effect on the net rentable area. However, the great item of waste, in the high buildings, is the big loss of valuable renting space on the lower floors due to the dead run of the express elevators to the upper floors. This amounts to from 50 to 65 square feet per elevator per floor. In a 30-story building, with 30 elevators, this means on the ground floor 1,800 square feet given up to elevators and at least as much again given up to the lobby, so that about 4,000 square feet are loss. As this ground floor space in such buildings

often rents at $20 per square foot, the loss of the building is $80,-000 on this floor alone. A 10-story building would save two-thirds of this. The loss on the floors above, due to the dead run of the elevators, also amounts to a surprising total, all of which would be saved in a 10- to 12-story building. This space on the lower floors more than counterbalances the profit on the upper floors. Every building, according to its shape, size, location, and use, has its economic limit.

"But even though a high building may pay a moderate net return as long as it is isolated and surrounded by low buildings, so that all its floors and offices are light and attractive, the result may be very different after it is surrounded by similar buildings, shutting off light and reducing rentals on the lower floors. As a rule, in an area in which high buildings predominate, the rentals are lowest and the percentages of vacancies greatest on the lower floors above the second. If, before the high buildings development, the owners in such districts could have covenanted among themselves to limit heights and enlarge courts, it would undoubtedly have been to the advantage of all concerned.

"The real estate interests which a decade ago were most active in opposing the adoption of a height limit in Boston are to-day among its staunchest supporters. The consensus of opinion among real estate men in Boston is that the height limit instead of depreciating land values or retarding the improvement of property, has been an unqualified success."

MR. CLARENCE H. KELSEY, who has appeared before your Committee, stated to the Heights of Building Commission, September 24, 1913 (pp. 238-239):

"High buildings will make present streets and sidewalks inadequate for traffic.

"The present sewer system was not constructed to serve high buildings. If the city is to be developed with 12- and 14-story buildings, its entire subsurface will have to be rebuilt.

"High buildings make it impossible to forecast real estate values. They have brought the business section into the residence section." Mr. Kelsey didn't know where a high-class retail section could be developed.

"It is becoming increasingly more difficult to borrow money with which to erect high buildings. There has been a decided change in the attitude of the insurance companies and the savings banks in granting mortgages on skyscrapers.

"High buildings encourage the wrong kind of speculation." Mr. Kelsey thought it better to have 12 low buildings owned by 12 men than 4 high buildings owned by 4 men. It is not well to force land into large ownerships.

"High buildings depreciate other land values. The land values south of 23rd Street have lost every bit as much as those north of 23rd Street have gained by the erection of high buildings. The sweatshops have destroyed the Fifth Avenue section. A height limit will make real estate values more stable by diffusing them.

"High buildings rob their neighbors of light."

MR. WILLIAM E. HARMON, President of Wood, Harmon & Co., stated (p. 233):

"Throughout the country the so-called skyscraper probably does not, on the average, produce a net income of over 3½% after a provision for depreciation has been made." He further stated that the space above the third floor in such buildings rarely brings in a net return over the current interest rate on the cost of the building alone, without giving any consideration to the site value. He doubted if 1 per cent. of the skyscrapers in America pay 7 per cent. over a series of years when a proper charge has been made for depreciation and repairs.

MR. REGINALD P. BOLTON, Consulting Engineer, September 22, 1913, stated (p. 181):

"Increased height involves increased cost of construction *per cubic foot of building.*

"Increase of height involves increase of cost of operation and maintenance of all *tentable space.*

"Excessive height injures neighboring properties and reduces local rentals by creating excessive rentable space.

"Rentals must be raised in proportion to height of a building.

"Less rentable space per floor is available as height increases."

MR. CHARLES S. BROWN, of Douglas Robinson & Co., October 17, 1913 (pp. 192-194), stated:

"The net return on real estate does not increase with the height of buildings. The depreciation is larger in the case of a high building than in the case of a low building." He knew of only one building where the owners maintained an exact and elaborate sinking fund of the structural loss. In his opinion, the loft buildings of, say 9 and 10 stories, produce the best return. "None of the very high buildings in New York pay a good return, when structural depreciation, etc., is considered; they are also extremely difficult to sell.

"High buildings do not pay. Almost every one who is familiar with them realizes this fact and knows that the net return is very small, and, in addition, no one knows what deterioration a high structure suffers, but every one does know that every year the amount of the upkeep increases; and, now that real estate values have fallen in New York, those who have invested in these high buildings have made serious losses, much greater than if they had improved their land with comparatively low buildings. It is also known that in the case of tall buildings the structural depreciation is large, owing to the great amount of machinery and metal in them, and owing to the possible changes of style in construction and arrangement which are continually being made."

"High buildings lower values of land near them. In theory they should not; practically they do, partly because they cause an oversupply of renting space which, to be filled, must be let at such low prices that it takes tenants from other buildings near by. If the supply of tenants kept pace with the supply of space, this would not occur, but, in the case of New York, the growth of the city has in no sense been equal to the increase of high buildings."

The claim that transferring taxes now levied on buildings to land values will compel the construction of large buildings is without foundation in fact, as real estate owners and builders will not, as a body, throw their money away.

Although enormous skyscrapers are earning only small returns, even when fully tenanted, they take tenants away from smaller buildings, and so deprive the owners of smaller buildings of a fair return on their investments.

Financial considerations, as well as justice, will prevent multiplication of skyscrapers under the proposed change in the tax system.

MEMORANDUM SUBMITTED BY THE SOCIETY TO LOWER RENTS AND REDUCE TAXES ON HOMES ON SOME FOREIGN PRECEDENTS FOR EXEMPTING BUILDINGS FROM TAXATION AND HEAVIER TAXATION OF LAND VALUES.

(Information Secured From Bulletin of U. S. Department of Labor 158, "Government Aid to Home Owning and Housing of the Working People in Foreign Countries.")

EXEMPTION OF BUILDINGS FROM TAXATION IN PART OR WHOLE.

AUSTRIA.

In Vienna and the provincial capitals, newly-erected buildings pay from one-fourth to one-third less than the usual state rent taxes, the lower rate applying to dwellings with exclusively small apartments, erected by public welfare building associations.

Communes are also authorized to levy a land increment tax, and many of them have recently done so.

BELGIUM.

Societies whose sole object is to provide dwellings for the working classes, and who comply with the building laws, are exempted from certain stamp duties, registration fees, etc. For the eighteen-year period, 1895 to 1912, the average tax exemption for 165,455 houses was $2,047. Workmen's dwellings are also exempted from the provincial and communal share of the land, the window and the door taxes.

CHILE.

Owners of all buildings constructed thereafter in conformity with the law and declared by proper authority to be sanitary were, by a law of 1906, exempted from municipal and fiscal taxes for a period of twenty-five years.

A reasonable amount of drinking water is supplied the owners of such houses at ten per cent. of the ordinary price, and other similar concessions are made to them.

FRANCE.

By an act of 1912, a "cheap dwelling" which conforms to the law is exempted from the land tax upon as much of the ground as is actually covered by the building, as well as from the door and window taxes, for a period of twelve years. Building and loan associations for cheap dwellings are also exempted from registration and stamp fees.

GERMANY.

By a law of 1861, a reduction of the general house tax is granted on dwellings of artisans, factory workers, etc., in rural communities in which the tax is not assessed on the basis of actual rents.

By the Law of 1891, building associations whose business activity is limited to their membership are exempt from the income tax, and such associations whose object is stated in their by-laws to be exclusively the provision of sanitary low rent buildings are exempted from the occupation tax.

These and similar associations are also exempt from the stamp tax.

Twenty-four cities, each with a population of over 50,000, have granted exemption or respite from payment of street construction costs, or of ground or house taxes.

"The activity of the modern land reformers is, to-day, concentrated in a vigorous agitation for the adoption of a ground tax, according to the actual value of the ground, and of an unearned increment tax."

A rapidly progressive tax is levied upon increments of land values with certain exemptions for small holders. Fifty per cent. of this tax goes to the Empire, ten per cent. to the Federal States for administration and collection, and forty per cent. to the communes. Several hundred cities levy this tax, and the total yield was about $9,500,000 in 1912.

GREAT BRITAIN.

The following recommendation of the English Parliamentary Land Enquiry Committee is given in the Department of Labor bulletin:

> "That an official inquiry shall be undertaken to ascertain how such transit facilities [as are needed] can best be provided and financed, especially how the increment in land values due to new transit schemes can be secured by the authority providing them."

The following recommendations of this Committee are *not* given in the bulletin:

> "All future increases in local expenditure that are chargeable on the rates should be met by a rate upon site values."
>
> "Assuming that the subventions paid out of Imperial taxation in aid of rates are substantially increased, existing expenditure should be met in part by a penny rate on capital site value."
>
> "On the same assumption, local authorities should be given the option of raising, by a rate upon site values, such further rates as they think fit."
>
> "We should emphasize the fact that in alterations of the present rating system, in the direction of placing a larger proportion of the burden upon the site and a lower proportion on the building, is to be found one of the most hopeful methods of substantially reducing the cost at which satisfactory housing accommodations can be provided for the workingman."

HUNGARY.

Nearly all the larger cities have, for many years, granted exemptions from local taxes on newly-erected buildings for fifteen or even eighteen years.

In 1870 permanent exemption from state taxes was granted to dwellings allotted without charge to industrial and agricultural laborers by their employers.

In 1907 permanent exemption from state taxes was granted on all company houses complying with the sanitary laws and built to be rented or sold on easy instalments to workmen; also a provisional exemption for twenty years from state, municipal and certain communal taxes was granted to new houses to be sold or rented to workmen either by employers or others engaged in housing work.

ITALY.

Communes are empowered to construct people's dwellings exclusively to be rented, and people's lodging houses, whenever the supply of such dwellings is inadequate, and the former are exempted from taxes for ten years, the latter for twenty years, as are also similar buildings constructed by co-operative societies. Communes that find it necessary to encourage the construction of dwellings are empowered to impose a tax of three per cent. on the value of unused building sites. In Rome, half of this tax is paid to the Association for Low Cost Dwellings in Rome.

ROUMANIA.

Houses constructed by societies or individuals (particularly employers) interested in housing work are exempted from taxation, permanently or temporarily.

SWITZERLAND.

In Geneva, workmen's dwellings are exempted from public taxes.

MEMORANDUM SUBMITTED BY THE ADVISORY COUNCIL OF REAL ESTATE INTERESTS, OCT. 24, 1914, ON UNTAXING IMPROVEMENTS ON LAND.

A new Herrick-Schaap bill (named after its last sponsors) will be submitted to the Legislature of the State of New York. It contains the same provisions as its predecessor, the Sullivan-Shortt Bill, which was defeated in 1911. These bills are known as the "half-tax" bills because they aim to divide the tax on buildings and other improvements into two parts, one to be levied on the improvements, and the other to be added to the present tax on land. This will result in a "half-tax" on buildings and an extra tax on land.

The bill sets forth that 10% of the tax on buildings shall be taken off each year for five years and added to the land tax. It should be understood that the plan is a half-way station to the Henry George single tax, by which all taxes (instead of half) are to be taken from buildings and placed on land. The principles applying to both half tax and single tax are the same. The single tax theory is that land and air and water are natural products and belong to mankind in general so no individual should have exclusive ownership of them; while buildings and other improvements are the products of labor and should be exclusive property of the persons who create them. To carry out this theory the single taxers propose to leave the land in possession of its owners but to levy upon it a tax equal to its producing power, or rents, so that the possessors of the land cannot have its income, which will be divided among the community to meet the burdens of the government. This is a fair statement of their plans.

A HENRY GEORGE THEORY.

Perhaps some quotations from "The Conditions of Labor," by Henry George, will not be amiss.

> "Being created individuals with individual wants and powers, men are individually entitled (subject, of course, to moral obligations that arise from such relations as that of the family) to the use of their own powers, and the enjoyment of the results. There thus arises, anterior to human law, and deriving its validity from the law of God, a right of private ownership in things produced by labor, a right that the possessor may transfer, but of which to deprive him without his will is theft. This right of property originating in the right of the individual to himself, is the only full and complete right of property. It attaches to things produced by labor, but cannot attach to things created by God. * * * We propose leaving land in the private possession of individuals, with full liberty on their part to give, sell, or bequeath it, simply to levy on it for public use a tax that shall equal the annual value of the land itself, irrespective of the use made of it, or the improvements on it."

LAND AS A LABOR PRODUCT.

It is to be seen that the whole theory is based upon the idea that land is not the product of labor. If it be shown that in a civilized community land is a product of labor, the theory falls to the ground.

Let us examine this idea in detail. No one will question that land, air, and water in a new community are natural products common to everyone, but like every other natural product, they are converted easily into products of labor. Our friend, the fruit grower, buys compressed air in cylinders from a concern which takes this natural product and compresses it. He uses it as a motive power to spray his trees. In my offices we use bottled water which we buy from someone who collects this natural product and sells it to us. Miners take gold and precious stones and coal, and oil, out of the earth, and after they have treated them by various forms of human labor, either in manufacture or transportation, exchange them for other products of human labor.

When our forefathers stepped upon Plymouth Rock, they found before them an unbroken forest, a natural product. It had no selling value. They chopped down trees, pulled the stumps, blasted or picked off the rocks and stones, filled the ravines, built roads, and converted the land into a product of human labor. Anyone could do so who would. Now it is proposed to lay a tax on that land which shall be equal to its producing power, because, they say, the community is entitled to the income and not the individual who expended his labor on it, or his successor. Perhaps it will be said that land in the cities is not farming land, and the same reasoning will not apply.

In the beginning of the city, land was free to all. Some men worked on the land and converted it into farms, others invested their capital in merchandise, all helped to build up the city. The man who made bricks, which were the product of his labor, sold some and bought land with his profits. He wanted the land, others wanted the bricks. Out of his savings, he paid the taxes on the land to carry on the government and assessments to build streets and sewers and lay pavements and prepare the land for the time it would be needed for buildings. The bricks were the primary product of his labor, but the land no less represented his labor, and was the product of it in the wider sense. While he held the land, he had to go without interest on his original capital, the taxes and assessments.

LAND AS A SAVINGS BANK.

All of these items went into the land as they would into a savings bank, some day to be returned, he hoped. Finally, a demand came for his land, as it had for his bricks, and he sold it, sometimes with a profit, sometimes without. The community encouraged him to put his savings into land. What can be said of an attempt to take it away? It may be said again that it is not the intention to take away the land from his possession. This is true, but it is also true that the plan is to take away its selling value by taking away its income or its potential power to produce income.

A lot is worth a sum upon which it will produce a fair return after the taxes have been paid. A fair return is, let us say, 5%. It is worth $1,000 if it will produce $50 (5%) and the taxes, say 2%, or $20, which is $70 in all. If the taxes are raised to 3%, the income will be reduced to $40 and the lot will be worth only $800 to sell. If the taxes are increased to 4%, the income will be $30, and the selling value $600 and, finally, if the tax is increased to 7%, the entire income will be taken and the lot will have no selling value at all.

Who will pay $1,000 for a lot if he cannot sell it again for the same amount, or if he cannot gain an income from it on that sum? If the income is taken away, the selling value of the lot is lost. This means that thousands and thousands of small owners who now have their savings in a home or tenement upon which there is a mortgage, and whose equity only equals the selling value of the land, will see their mortgage get the property and their investments wiped out.

FALSITY OF THE CHEAP RENT THEORY.

It is thought that taking away the selling value of the land will make it possible for men to build homes on it and have cheap rents, and escape the congestion of the cities. Let us examine that theory. Undoubtedly, the first effect would be to make vacant land cheap in localities where improvements such as regulating and grading, sewering, and paving, have been paid for, because these investments as well as the original capital invested in the land would be lost; but as soon as these lands were occupied, who would invest in other lands, years before they were needed for dwellings, and pay the taxes and assessments necessary to convert these lands into building lots suitable for a city?

FALLACY OF THE RELIEF OF CONGESTION THEORY.

Now they are ready to relieve congestion in the city long before there is any demand for it. On what would the assessments be levied if the lands had no selling value? Who would advance the money for these improvements? Again, if the tax on the building is half that on the land, the tendency would be to build upon as much of the land as possible and have most of the investment in the building. If we exempt the buildings, the owners of skyscrapers will get more benefit than the owners of the small private houses. It is to be seen that a worse congestion would occur than any we now have, and rents would rise as the demand increased. In a few years they would be bigger than they are now. If inducements were not made to investors to go out into the suburbs and prepare them for buildings when congestion in the city shall demand it, there would be no development of the suburbs. The building of a Chinese wall around the present city would be no more effective to prevent further expansion than a law which forbids profits from investments on land.

It is hard to understand the argument that buildings and improvements should be exempted from taxes. The object of taxes is to support the government in the discharge of its functions, such as the operation of the Fire Department and the Police Department, and the Courts, and all its other activities. What are these for more than for the preservation of buildings, and other improvements? Vacant property does not need the Fire Department, or the Police Department, or the Courts, yet it is proposed to relieve buildings and improvements which are the direct beneficiaries of the tax, and place the burden on land, which gets little or no direct benefit from it.

The larger the ratio which the value of a building bears to the whole investment, the greater the need of governmental functions supported by the tax; but the single tax would exempt the building and charge the land.

Another fact which appears to be forgotten is that the building is bound to wear out or become out of date, and the only chance the owner has to offset the diminishing value of his building lies in the increase in the value of his land. If he is denied the increase in the value of his land, he must charge higher rents so as to provide a sinking fund for his building. This necessary consequence explodes the lower rent theory.

Present investments on bond and mortgage are made on the security of the land as well as the building. The fact that the increase of the land is likely to offset the decrease of the building value is an item which the loaner takes into account. Naturally, a higher rate must be charged for the money loaned where the perishable building is the only security. This will make it more difficult to obtain a loan for a man who wants to build a home, and will make the rents of the building higher.

PRACTICAL DIFFICULTIES.

Let me call attention to the practical difficulty of levying the single tax. To quote again from "The Condition of Labor":

"The value we propose to tax, the value of land, irrespective of improvements, does not come from any exertion of labor or investment of capital on it or in it; the value produced in this way being values of improvement which we would exempt."

If the capital invested in a piece of land is to be exempted from taxation, we shall find that many lots which now are not worth the capital invested in them, plus interest, will have no tax levied upon them. This will create a heavier burden for other lots to bear. Suppose we exempt the natural value of land, and tax the so-called "social value"? How can we determine what part of the present value to tax? If, on the other hand, we exempt the capital invested and interest, we find often that the sum invested will be far greater than the present value. Every lot would have a different amount of exemption from its neighbor, according to the capital invested in it for its development.

History tells us that Peter Minuit, the first director-general of the Dutch East India Company, paid to the Indians, in 1626, the sum of 60 guilders or about $24 for the land on Manhattan Island. In 1913, the assessed value of this land was $3,155,389,410, but when we figure that this same $24 if put out at the prevailing rates of interest since 1626, would amount to $12,884,901,824 in round numbers, we conclude that the unearned increment or "social value" was not so much after all.

CAPITAL JOINED WITH THE LABOR.

In a settled community, where capital has been invested in land, it is practically impossible to find out what part of the land represents capital or labor and what part unearned increment, so called. By unearned increment is meant the increase in value by reason of the increased demands of a growing population, for which the owner does not pay. When was there a time when both capital and labor were not spent on it? In a new community when everyone starts off on an even basis, and it is agreed that land shall have no selling value at all, the single tax may be as good as any other, but not so where all the land values in the community are based on investments from the proceeds of labor. In fact, in such cases as the New England farms before mentioned, their entire value is the result of labor. In the case of unimproved city lots, although the original capital invested was small, the taxes, interest, and investment, assessments, and interest on them, sometimes exceeded by a large sum the present value of the lots. Only a short time ago an article in the newspaper called attention to a lot in Tremont Avenue, The Bronx, which the owner bought, in 1872, for $5,000. In 1912 it was sold, and now it is worth $30,000. At the time of the sale, the unpaid taxes and assessments amounted to $14,000. What other sums he paid for taxes, assessments and repairs is unknown, but let us consider, for the sake of argument, only $14,000. On the face of it, the owner made a large profit, but upon analysis it appeared that his original investment of $5,000, with interest for the 40 years, amounted to $35,000. He paid out taxes and assessments of $14,000. His investment amounted to $49,200, while his property was worth only $30,000. What part of this should be taxed? Will the city repay to him the sum he has spent for investments, taxes, assessments, and interest over the selling value of the property?

It may be seen, therefore, that land in the city is not a natural product but a product of labor. In this it differs in no respect from merchandise in whose exclusive ownership the investor is entitled to all the protection of the laws, and that a tax designed to take away the selling value of his property is only a confiscation under the form of the law.

UNEARNED INCREMENT.

Much is said of the unearned increment of land, caused by the increased demand for it, due to increase in population. The hope of this increase is what induces persons to invest the proceeds of their labor in the development of vacant property, long before it is needed for building. After such investment, if the population moves away, does the community pay the owner for the loss? Assuredly not. Why should it have the increase? The increased tax on increased values pays to the community a share of the increase.

SHRINKAGE OF OUR CITY BONDS.

I need not go far into the question of the effect which the shrinkage of land values, due to the single tax, would have on New York City securities, sold to people all over the world. A community which would confiscate the property of its own citizens would not be very considerate of the owners of its securities. The assessed value of the land in New York City is $5,000,000,000. By law our bonds may not exceed 10% of their assessed valuation. The assessed valuation must conform to the selling value. If we take away the selling value of $5,000,000,000 worth of land, out of the total of $8,000,000,000 of land and buildings, a shrinkage in the value of our present outstanding securities must result, and we have no security for future issues to carry on the needs of the government.

MORTGAGES.

Millions of dollars of the savings of our people are deposited in savings banks and invested in mortgages. What will become of them, if the value of the land on which they are based is taken away? Five-eighths of their security will have vanished. The same result will be experienced by all mortgages. Can it be supposed that such wholesale disaster will be of benefit to the laboring classes or any other class? It is a well known principle that no law which is unjust to one class is of any lasting benefit to any other class.

Let us take two instances, to see how the proposed plan would work. A lot is worth $10,000, the house on it $20,000. At 2%, the tax on the lot would be $200, and on the house, $400, or $600 in all. If the tax were taken off the building and the land taxed for the rental value, of 5% (the Henry George plan), the tax would be $500, a difference of $100. Here is an apparent saving but what is the truth? In the first place, the owners would lose $10,000, the selling value of the lot, and in the next place, when the building was worn out he would have nothing but the right to build again on the lot. Next case, a lot worth $1,000, and a house worth $4,000. Take 2% tax on lot, $20, tax on house, $80, or $100 in all. If the house is exempted and lot taxed 5%, the tax will be $50. Again, an apparent saving of $50 a year, but the $1,000 selling value of the lot will have gone, which he might receive in 20 years at $50 a year; but in the meantime, his house will have worn out or become out of date, and he will have nothing except the right to build again. Who is to gain by all this?

(Signed) CYRUS C. MILLER, Chairman,
Advisory Council of Real Estate Interests.

MEMORANDUM SUBMITTED BY THE REAL ESTATE BOARD OF NEW YORK, OCTOBER 19, 1914, ON UNTAXING IMPROVEMENTS ON LAND.

To the Mayor's Committee on Taxation,

Gentlemen:

The Real Estate Board of the City of New York begs to present its views on the question of the untaxing of buildings.

The partial or total removal of taxes on improvements on land, would logically lead to the removal of all taxes, except those on land, for what good reason could be given to tax any other form of property if taxes on improvements be removed. The proposal is based on the theory that all taxes should be put on land alone, that is the single tax, as advocated by Henry George. This is directly opposed to our present system of taxation and to our law, which regards all improvements on lands as real property. It would lead ultimately to the absorption by taxation of all income derived from land and the abolition of private ownership of land.

Henry George's opinion of the effect of placing all taxes on land is shown by the following quotation from his "Progress and Poverty":

> "I do not propose either to purchase or to confiscate property in land. The first would be unjust; the second, needless. Let the individuals who now hold it still retain, if they want to, possession of what they are pleased to call their land. Let them continue to call it their land. Let them buy and sell, and bequeath and devise it. We may safely leave them the shell, if we take the kernel. It is not necessary to confiscate land; it is only necessary to confiscate rent.
>
> "We may put the proposition into practical form by proposing to abolish all taxation save that upon land values. That is the first step, upon which the practical struggle must be made. When the hare is once caught and killed, cooking him will follow as a matter of course. When the common right to land is so far appreciated that all taxes are abolished save those which fall upon rent, there is no danger of much more than is necessary to induce them to collect the public revenues being left to the individual land owners."

Thus the judgment of the chief advocate of the single tax is that the adoption of the principle of the removal of taxation from improvements would result in the abolition of private ownership of land.

The theory of the single tax has not been accepted by most students of political economy, see Prof. Johnson's article in the Atlantic Monthly for March, 1914, which also presents a statement of the advantages of private ownership of land.

That the untaxing of improvements has not diminished congestion, increased building permanently, nor lowered rents, in Australasia was shown in Prof. Seligman's article in the Political Science Quarterly for March, 1913.

The trial of the exemption of improvements from taxation in Vancouver showed that, while the rate of building was at first stimulated, it later fell below that existing before the change.

The Real Estate Board opposes the untaxing of improvements because:

First. It would be unjust to the owners of land as it would take value from them without compensation.

Second. Its partial adoption would completely disarrange and greatly diminish the revenue of the city.

Third. Where it has been tried, notably in Vancouver, it has increased congestion.

Fourth. It will not cause a steady increase in building; if it should do so at first, there will be a great falling off after a year or two, for the amount of building is governed, like the satisfaction of any human need, by the law of supply and demand.

Respectfully submitted,

THE REAL ESTATE BOARD OF NEW YORK,

Per DAVID A. CLARKSON,
Chairman Sub-Committee, Committee on Taxation and Legislation.

BRIEF SUBMITTED BY STEWART BROWNE, PRESIDENT UNITED REAL ESTATE OWNERS ASSOCIATION, ON EXEMPTING BUILDINGS FROM MUNICIPAL TAXATION.

I see no objection, per se, to exempting **all buildings** from taxation; I equally see no objection, per se, to exempting **all land** from taxation; if either had been in force for the past 100 years New York City would be exactly as it is to-day; there would be no more and no fewer buildings because of the one or the other; "gradual tax evolution" (irrespective of tax) injures no one, because it disappears in the "price level," but "tax revolution" is chaos, because it destroys. History shows that all old taxes are good taxes, and all new taxes bad taxes.

In considering this subject let me state a few economic truths which should be, but are not generally understood, and all of which have a bearing on the above question.

The only real value known to finance and commerce is "exchange value"; cost of production is only "cost value"; such does not enter into "exchange value"; the "cost value" of a thing may be little, but its "exchange value" great, and vice versa.

"Exchange value" does not emerge or come into being until the moment of exchange; before and after exchange the value is only potential.

The "price level" of a town, city or country is based upon the average annual income (expressed in money) of labor; where annual income expressed in money is low, the "price level" will be low; where annual income expressed in money is high, the "price level" will be high; one is not exchanging his share of the products of his labor for money, but for a share of the products of others' labor; money wages are only the assumed par of exchange value placed on one's share of the product of one's labor expressed in the money denominator, to be subsequently exchanged for the share of the product of others' labor.

All wealth is stored or saved labor; taxes of all kinds always have and always must be paid by labor; to say you tax realty and tax personalty is as untrue as to say realty and personalty pay taxes; it is the owner that is taxed based on their assumed or assessed value, just as man is taxed on his income; the fact that the municipality or state may have a tax lien on realty does not change the nature of the act; the owner of realty or personalty pays his taxes out of the product of his saved or daily labor and he often is compelled to pay such tax when the net income of his realty or personalty falls short of the tax; it is this misuse of words that is responsible for the belief that it is all wrong to tax the product of labor, and that labor and the product of labor should be "untaxed"; it is impossible to pay one dollar in taxes except from the product of labor.

All taxes, irrespective of their kind, are shifted on the entire community, just as wages are; new taxes or a sudden large increase in old taxes are not automatically shifted; it requires a number of years; but when shifted they finally disappear in the general "price level"; man and nations adapt themselves and their business affairs to their ever-changing environment, taxed and otherwise; cities and nations grow and flourish not because of taxation but in spite of taxation; the highest taxed cities generally flourish, while the lowest taxed generally remain stagnant or decay, but neither effect is produced by reason of taxation.

Exemption from taxation has never in the history of the world been adopted by flourishing communities; but always by "one horse," new and relatively small municipalities, which have offered to proposed new industries cash bonuses, loans, free land sites and freedom from all taxation for from 10 to 20 years; proposed industries have put themselves up to the highest municipal bidder; in some cases such bonuses, etc., etc., have been municipally beneficial but in others disastrous; municipal cash bonuses and freedom from taxation have reached such an insane craze in the Canadian Northwest that the Provincial Governments in 1914 legislated against such in future.

Up to a few years ago no municipality (even picayune ones) ever conceived of offering perpetual tax exemption on all new buildings, residences included, as an inducement to build; if such be economically sound, land tax exemption for 10 to 20 years as an additional inducement to build is equally so.

EFFECT ON MANUFACTURING INDUSTRIES.

The City of New York is to-day the greatest manufacturing city in the world and has become so without "building tax exemption"; factories are located where there are superior shipping facilities, superior labor markets, and a hundred and one elements that appeal differently to each factory owner; to have exempted factory buildings from taxation during the past ten years would not have built a single factory that New York has not now; to exempt factory buildings from taxation in the future would not add a single new factory building to New York. If a bank found that it could get all of its deposits free from interest it would be foolish to offer interest; so likewise when New York has found, and still finds, that it has all the factories it now has without tax exemption it would be foolish to offer such. A certain section of the community think that New York has too many factories; that it could conveniently, and to its benefit, reduce their number. The city, by the existing building and occupancy restrictions, and the state, by its excessive labor compensation laws, as compared with other states, unless modified, will drive many existing factories away and will prevent the establishment of new ones.

EFFECT ON UNDER-IMPROVED PROPERTY.

There can be no doubt that if an owner thought the existing tax on land would not be increased and that a new building would be "tax exempt" he would seriously consider the question of improving, and he might take greater chances against possible "future tenancy" than he would take to-day; but that improvement, if undertaken, would mean "increased height"; on the other hand, exemption from building taxation on his present building might so increase his net income, as to deter him from improvement; what the net aggregate results of rebuilding might be, 'tis impossible to say. If "underimproved buildings" were taxed and new buildings tax exempt, the net aggregate results would be very different. Is underimprovement or overimprovement the better for New York City? We spend large sums for parks as open spaces; does not underimproved property retain the "breathing spaces" and overimprovement kill them? What guarantee, however, is there that the net results of building tax exemption would not increase the land tax on "underimproved" property to such an extent as to equal, if not exceed, the existing gross tax? My view is that the advantages and the disadvantages would be about equal, and that the only thing that would force building erection is, as now, the belief in "demand" or increased concentration of population.

EFFECT ON FULLY IMPROVED PROPERTY.

The only effect would be to put a penalty on buildings having a much less value than the land and put a premium on buildings having a much greater value than the land; the City would be deliberately injuring the former and benefiting the latter; the former would have a right of action against the City for damages, and I would not hesitate to bring injunction proceedings against the City to prevent it putting such a tax law into effect.

EFFECT ON VACANT LOTS.

These are principally in the outlying sections; ninety per cent. of them are held for future increase in value; the owners are willing to sustain present losses for future profits in the hope that the latter will largely exceed the former. Just as soon as owners believe that the future gains will be less than present losses *they'll sell;* if they could sell and *pocket their losses;* double their taxes and they would try and sell, but the buyers would be few and far between, as the future possibilities would be too uncertain; where sold, prices would be from 25 per cent. to 50 per cent. of existing values, and if not sold, the City would "hold the bag." In this connection it must be remembered that vacant lots are at present assessed at future potential values, which possibly may be reached in between five and ten years from now.

As for forcing improvement; I doubt if it would force any improvements; it might "cheap shacks"; improvements are forced by demand for occupancy or belief in demand; increasing land taxes doesn't increase that demand or that belief.

EFFECT ON EXISTING MORTGAGES.

When the Federal and State agitation against railroads became acute some few years ago, three of the largest financial corporations in the United States stopped buying their securities, and, instead, decided to lend principally on mortgages throughout the United States and started large mortgage departments for such purpose; some four years ago these companies, and since then, nearly all New York City corporate mortgage lenders, in view of the Single Tax and Building Exempt Tax agitation and the increasing municipal taxes on realty, decided to either call or reduce all mortgage loans as they matured and they have been doing so to-day, and they are perfectly justified in so doing; I suppose that 50 per cent. of due mortgages are carried on sufferance because the lenders are afraid to foreclose.

EFFECT ON NEW MORTGAGES.

It is extremely difficult to get new mortgages to-day and when obtained, they are not for over 60 per cent. of what would have been obtainable five years ago; with "building tax exempt" in force, the conditions would be far worse; how much, no one could even guess at; if lenders actually believe that such would become law, I don't believe they would lend at all and those who are now lending are generally buying guaranteed mortgages so as to have "a buffer" between them and harm.

RENT REDUCTION.

The advocates of "building tax exemption" say it will reduce all rents; there are only five ways to reduce rent: (1) to reduce price of labor and material used in construction of buildings (the labor unions will oblige in the first and builders will oblige in the second); (2) to increase the value basis of mortgage loans from, say, two-thirds to ninety per cent., or to reduce the interest rates to 3 per cent. (of course, mortgage lenders will prefer to make and increase loans and reduce interest to reduce rents; this has not been their past or present habit; they will, however, do so to prove the theories of Single Taxers and Building Exempt Taxers correct); (3) to reduce taxes; (the City Administration will do so to oblige); (4) to build in excess of "the demand" (speculators and investors will do this to oblige); (5) to reduce "the demand" (the public will leave New York City to oblige).

PRESENT REALTY VALUES.

Speaking generally, the American people are not investors but speculators; this applies to realty as well as to corporate securities; income value is the least of the elements that enter into the basis of our "exchange value"; ability to borrow is 90 per cent. of the elements that constitute "exchange value"; on the Stock Exchange "no borrowing" means a reduction of 50 per cent. in all values; eliminate all borrowing on realty and buying and selling is reduced 90 per cent. in volume; when realty is sold under mortgage foreclosure, it seldom brings the mortgage debt unless the purchaser can obtain a liberal loan.

Up to fifteen years ago New York City realty values were stable; values could be relied upon; there was a fairly even annual increase in the older sections, and the new sections increased in value, but not at the "value expense" of the former.

During the past fifteen years there has been a tremendous activity in realty; one-half of Manhattan has been rebuilt, and The Bronx, Kings and Queens have become large cities. Certain values have doubled, trebled and quadrupled in a few years, while other values have decreased. Certain values have doubled in three or four years in certain sections and lost one-half of their increase in two or three years; the high and low fluctuations of realty values in New York have almost been as great and as erratic, although not as frequent, as Stock Exchange securities; all this has been due to dreams of building promoters, "trades," credit for material, ability to borrow freely at low interest rates, large purchase money mortgages, first, seconds and even thirds, improved transit on elevated, surface and subway lines.

We have also had increasing wealth of the population and consequent increased extravagance in living; change of habits and fashions;

"keeping up with Lizzie"; changing racial population environment; change even overnight; potential values assumed to be actual, until it was found that the potential was a dream; corporate lenders making new loans which killed their old loans.

The result of all the above has been that to-day the aggregate actual cash value of New York realty, taking it by and large, isn't 25 per cent. of what it was a few years ago; that values will go back and beyond what they were is unquestioned; but when- depends upon the length of the existing war and whether such end means immigration from or emigration to Europe, liberality of mortgage loans, future rate of interest and freedom from increased taxation and unwise municipal regulations.

SUPPLY NOW EXCEEDS DEMAND.

The thinking public now complains about the multiplicity of retail stores; that these hordes of middlemen increase the cost of everything to the consumer; all this is true; notwithstanding this, the proposal is seriously made to exempt retail store buildings from taxation so as to increase their number; the city is even conducting free markets, which means reduction in the number of existing stores.

We have had too many department stores; a number have closed up, and a few others are hanging on the financial "ragged edge"; yet it is proposed to exempt department store buildings from taxation so as to increase their number.

One-third of the aggregate space in loft and office buildings between 59th Street and the Battery is now vacant and yet it is proposed to exempt loft and office buildings from taxation so as to increase their number.

One-half of New York's hotels are making no money and many are losing, yet it is proposed to exempt hotel buildings from taxation so as to increase their number.

The newer apartment hotels are only holding their own; some are losing money; the older ones are losing money; private dwellings in Manhattan, except in a few streets, are "down and out"; yet it is proposed to exempt such buildings from taxation so as to increase their number.

PRESENT ASSESSED VALUATIONS.

Taking the entire city, the assessed valuation of New York Realty is 25 per cent. in excess of its true actual cash valuation from an income producing or a selling standpoint.

Under the Seth Low administration in 1903, the city changed from an assumed two-thirds valuation to an assumed 100 per cent. valuation. When this change took place it was stated that no increase in taxes would take place; that the only object of the change was to increase the city's borrowing capacity; since then, taxes on the same specific properties have been increased every year, until to-day they are from 50 to 100 per cent. higher, with an average of 25 per cent. decrease in rents.

In a city like New York, with its ever "now you see it, and now you don't" changing realty values, almost overnight, 100 per cent. assessed valuation is a crime; one gets the increase but seldom the decrease; in fact, the increase has been in many cases imaginary and due largely to the new theoretical and so-called scientific basis of assessed valuation.

In the old days we had a crude but "horse sense" basis of assessed valuation, which produced many inequalities between owners, but none of these were other than favorable to the owner; under the new theoretical and so-called scientific basis of assessed valuation, we have the same inequalities between owners but most of them are against the owner.

Our land assessed valuations are based upon assumed potentialities of value; we don't call it that, however; we call it the unit system; it is not a fact that two adjoining inside lots of equal width and depth have the same value, whether on a residence, a retail, a wholesale, or office building street; they may not even have the same potentialities of value; in fact, they often do not; what would be thought of necessarily assessing two 100-acre farms adjoining, and with the same frontage, at the same value? One may be worth only 25 per cent. of the other; yet such is no more ridiculous than what we are now doing. If the city had a maximum building height limit of six stories, the inconsistency of potentialities of value assessment and the unit rule would not be so glaring; but with no height limitation, no more unjust basis could be conceived of; one must "skyscrape" to reach these value potentialities, and if all or a majority did, which they don't and can't, these potentialities would be proven, as they actually now are, an iridescent dream, except for the tax assessor and collector; where a few have competingly "skyscraped," the potentialities of value of all have been reduced, but the assessed valuations have not. Another injustice of the present system is the unbusinesslike method provided to get quick relief from over-valuation; its theory is all right, but its practice is bad. The Tax Department's new so-called scientific basic values are based on "skyscraping" congestion; Brother McAneny's height of building committee is engaged in destroying the very values that the former is so industriously creating as a basis for increased bond issues; Brother McAneny, with his height of building committee, is also doing his best to reduce the values that produce the taxes that he is so desirous of spending on his "fads and fancies."

To place separate values on the land and building of improved property originated as the entering wedge for the Single Tax; Lawson Purdy is responsible for this and he is a Single Taxer; only a theorist or a man with an obsession could so value improved property; when urban land is built on, the values are merged into one; they have ceased to have separate values; the basis of such value is the usage or income value. Our tax department will take a 50-foot frontage and value it at $200,000 and value the building thereon at its cost of, say, $200,000, and value the adjoining 50-foot frontage at $200,000 and value the building thereon at its cost of, say, $200,000; each pays the same taxes, but one may not and never will be worth 75 per cent. of the other; such enequalities exist in every part of the city.

EFFECT ON BUILDING TAX EXEMPTION ELSEWHERE.

Vancouver, Edmonton and other towns in Northwest Canada, and certain picayune towns in Australia and New Zealand are held up as the great examples of what building tax exemption has done.

The Australian and New Zealand Government reports are the very reverse of what is claimed; up to 1913, Vancouver, Edmonton and other Northwest Canadian towns showed wonderful increase in population and in new building erection per capita, but less than in Seattle, Los Angeles and other cities, even including New York. Since 1913 the bottom has dropped out of Vancouver, Edmonton and other Northwestern towns. If building tax exemption was responsible for the "boom," then it must be held responsible for the "collapse"; the truth is that it had no more to do with either than the phases of the moon. Winnipeg in the 1880's, with a tax on buildings, had a greater boom than any Canadian Northwest town has ever had; but its collapse was as great and more sudden than its boom.

I personally have known the Canadian Northwest from the days when Winnipeg was Fort Gary and there wasn't a village between there and Victoria, B. C.; I have been all through these boom towns and twice have seen lots increased from $1,000 to $100,000 in a year, when such increase in values was only represented by purchase money mortgages. The whole Canadian Northwest, farm land, villages, towns and cities, has been boomed by new railroad construction, rushing in of immigrants with money from the States and Middle Canada to populate the farms, villages and towns; municipalities borrowing unchecked and beyond their means; everybody in the land business, buying and selling like madmen; everybody making money on paper; then a collapse. Net result—50 per cent. good, 50 per cent. bad; many values will come back in from ten to fifteen years from now and many values will never come back.

PEOPLE BENEFITED.

The only people benefited will be the owners of the Woolworth and other large office buildings and large property owners where the building value is twice and thrice the land value; their taxes will be reduced at the expense of the majority of the small property owners.

PEOPLE INJURED.

There are 170,000 vacant lots in the Boroughs outside of Manhattan; their owners' taxes will be increased and, if they build a private house on each of these lots, nearly every owner will pay higher taxes than he will under the present law. The vacant lot owner, to pay relatively less taxes, must build tenements and not dwellings

EFFECT ON CITY BOND ISSUE.

For bond purposes the aggregate 1914 assessed valuation of New York realty is $8,049,859,912, of which $4,602,852,107 is ordinary land values, $2,855,932,518 is building values, $404,420,311 is special franchises, and $186,654,976 is property not segregated. The city is, by the State Constitution, limited to an outstanding bond issue in aggregate not exceeding ten per cent. of its aggregate assessed valuation. The city has now $757,705,833 outstanding bonds or within $47,000,000 of its maximum legal limit, and it is questionable if such $47,000,000 is not also exceeded. Eliminate the building values of $2,855,932,518 from the aggregate assessed valuation and deduct 10 per cent. (a very low percentage) from the aggregate land value of $460,385,107 for reduction in value due to doubling the tax on land; and the aggregate assessed valuation for city bond purposes would be $4,733,642,287; 10 per cent. bond limit upon the latter would be $473,364,228, while the existing bond issue is $757,705,833.

EFFECT ON PUBLIC IMPROVEMENTS.

The city needs tens of millions more for necessary public improvements; where is the money to come from? No more bonds could be issued until the aggregate assessed valuation of the land exceeded the existing bond issue. The assessed land value of New York has only increased $1,235,000,000 in the last nine years and only $39,000,000 in the last three years; assuming an increase equal to the first period it would take two and one-half years for the land values to equal the existing combined land and building values; but no such like increase is possible; on the basis of the last three years' increase, it would take ten years for the land values to equal the existing combined land and building values.

LEGALITY OF ELIMINATING BUILDINGS FROM ASSESSED VALUATION.

While no one could prevent the Legislature from passing a building exempt tax statute, the courts would, I believe, declare it unconstitutional; any city bondholder could get an injunction against the city from putting such law into effect as such would be an impairment of the contract rights between the city and its bondholders. An injunction would also lie against the city by an owner of property where the land value was, say, two or three times the building value, because of the rent competition by properties where the building value was two or three times the land value, the net income of the first would be reduced.

CONCLUSION.

Building tax exemption in New York City would be ruinous to everyone, because it would revolutionize everything; it is the craziest of all crazy propositions that are now running amuck; 'tis said "fools rush in where angels fear to tread."

NOTE.

This article is written from the standpoint of 100 per cent. building tax exemption; if it be 25 per cent. or 50 per cent. the static effects would be correspondingly reduced, but the psychological effects would be exactly the same 100 per cent.

New York City, October 25th, 1914.

BRIEF SUBMITTED BY STEWART BROWNE, PRESIDENT UNITED REAL ESTATE OWNERS' ASSOCIATION, ON SHIFTING A TAX ON LAND.

Probably the majority of political economists believe that, while a general realty or building tax can be shifted, a tax on land cannot be shifted. This view has been swallowed, "holus bolus," by the Single Taxers and Building Exempt Taxers and is the foundation upon which they build their entire structure.

Practical experience has shown that many of the theories of political economists are wrong. Their theories on shifting and incidence of taxation might all be put in a hat, one picked out at random, and it would be as true as any of them. Many of them deal with words, theories and abstractions and not with the happenings of every-day life.

WHAT IS THE MEANING OF SHIFT A TAX?

Does it mean that concurrently with the imposition of a new or increased tax the original owner of the commodity taxed can increase the selling price of the commodity taxed to the first purchaser in amount equal to the tax, irrespective of outstanding agreements, the size of tax, the supply and demand of the commodity taxed and one hundred and one other factors? It cannot mean this, because such shifting could never be done. It can only mean that the original owner can raise his price to the first purchaser, provided, and as and when the supply decreases or the demand increases, and there is no term contract between the parties as to the continuance of price. Shifting takes different periods of time, dependent upon the nature of the commodity, whether usable or unusable, consumable or non-consumable, and luxurious or necessitous. (The word "commodity" used above includes land, building, realty, rent.)

HOW AND WHEN CAN A TAX BE SHIFTED?

The owner of the commodity taxed can shift such tax wholly or partially only when and to the extent that he can increase to the first purchaser the price of the commodity taxed, irrespective of how the result is accomplished; this is a question of fact and not of abstract theory. This applies to all commodities, including land under separate ownership, building under separate ownership or land and building under one ownership.

If the price, rent or net income is increased the tax is shifted in amount equal to such increase; if it is not so increased or is reduced, then the tax is not shifted.

If there be a law or a term agreement between the original taxed owner and the first purchaser, that during the term of such agreement the owner pays the tax or any increased tax, or if not, and the price cannot be increased, then such tax cannot be shifted until the expiration of the agreement or till an increase in price.

If there be a law or a term agreement between said parties, that in addition to an agreed upon price, the first purchaser shall pay the tax or any increase thereof, then such tax is shifted for the full remainder term of such agreement.

The only question in dispute therefore is the shiftability of tax at the expiration of the old agreement, and such depends entirely upon the terms and conditions of the new agreement; this is again a question of fact and not of theory.

WHAT IS THE MEANING OF INCIDENCE OF TAXATION?

This means upon what person or persons and in what proportion, how and when does any tax finally rest after it has been once shifted.

I liken this to the billions of drops of water going over Niagara Falls and billions of drops of water finally entering the ocean. Who can identify the drops going over the Falls with the drops entering the ocean? What drops and percentage of drops evaporate on their course to the ocean and where and when do they evaporate? What drops and percentage of drops are taken up by the sun and reach mother earth, respectively, in the shape of rain, hail and snow; where and when in this country, in Europe or in Asia?

The logically thinking man who examines the subject thoroughly will answer "goodness knows,"—which answer is condemned by some Political Economists.

I claim that all taxation, direct or indirect, Federal, State or Municipal in all countries is included in and increases the "Price Level" of a country. The "Price Level" is like the ocean, into which all streams flow. The "Price Level" is the net result of the people bartering the products of their individual labor with one another through the medium of exchange,—"Credit," expressed in the money denominator or symbol ($—£—&c) of the different countries.

WHAT IS THE MEANING OF CAPITAL VALUE?

Capital value, except exchange value, is a mental concept used for convenience in bookkeeping; such as cost value, book value, market value, usage value, intrinsic value, income value, par value, face value, potential value. The only value known to commerce is exchange value, the price that any commodity is bought and sold for. Exchange value emerges only at the time of sale and then it disappears. All commodities, however, have potentialities of exchange value. The law can't make value. Desire of possession only gives exchange value and desire of possession can only be for use or income purposes and with investments or realty, generally for income purposes.

CAPITAL VALUE GAIN AND LOSS.

There is no capital value gain or loss on securities or realty until a sale actually takes place and the gain or loss actually happens.

The income from securities or realty may decrease or cease entirely for a time, but this of itself does not mean a loss of capital value.

Experience shows how difficult it is for owners of securities or realty to take an actual loss by selling; the lower selling values go, the more they hold tight; even when they could make money by selling they won't. Take realty in 1915. Values have gone down temporarily, but even when mortgage loans are called and there are reduced rents, increased interest rates and taxes, owners beg, borrow and steal to hold their property in the certain hope that in a year or two conditions will change for the better.

PRICE LEVEL FOR LAND AND IMPROVED PROPERTY.

Investigation shows that in all countries and in all cities thereof the realty price level on the whole always keeps increasing. As a country emerges from primitive conditions to civilization values rise higher and higher,—there are, of course, temporary "dips," but the next high level is always higher than the last. New York City realty values and rents in seven or ten years from now will be higher than they have ever been. Nothing can prevent such. All history proves this as a certainty.

ECONOMISTS' MENTAL CAPITAL VALUE GAIN AND LOSS.

Political Economists and their imitators, whenever a realty tax is increased, go through the mental arithmetical gymnastics of capitalizing such tax and saying that all realty has sustained such capital loss.

They don't even wait to see whether the tax has been offset by other gains or savings and the tax so shifted; *instanter it becomes a loss.* This is rank nonsense, because it is not a fact.

Their next step is to say that a lower capital value price level has been created. That by reason of this the increased tax can't be shifted. because it has been psychologically wiped off by the reduced capital value and the assumed new owner won't consider it when fixing rent.

Many Political Economists make the error of supposing that cost fixes prices; it doesn't; prices are fixed by demand and supply; cost being, in course of time, a restraining element on supply; but less with urban improved realty, than with other commodities, as buildings are a necessity and nonconsumable.

Let me assume that the New York City realty tax was 2 per cent. for 1915 and will be 2½ per cent. for 1916 and that all realty is sold to new owners in 1916 at an aggregated reduced value of 25 per cent.; the demand for rents keeps increasing. Would the new owners accept the old rents instead of the new increasing rents because they bought the property cheap? Would the new owners not try to get as much increased rent as the old owners would have done if they hadn't sold? If the new owners can get the rents up to equal or to exceed the increased taxes, I claim the increased taxes have been shifted even although all the old owners suffered an actual loss in capital value.

We are dealing with realty irrespective of the inividual. The unit or individual doesn't count in nature.

This is a plain every-day commercial transaction,—it isn't a theory, an abstraction or a Political Economy question at all.

FACTORY PRODUCTS.

The cost of raw material, wages, taxes, interest, overhead charges, plus profit, etc., are all, in the by and large, paid for by the consumer. There are, of course, many exceptions where for many reasons the consumer pays less than cost price. Being movable, they are interchangeable in the markets of the world. There is, therefore, a world-wide and continuous conflict between supply and demand. Supply and demand never synchronize; now supply is ahead, now demand is. In the long run, however, the cost is shifted to the consumer.

AGRICULTURAL LAND PRODUCTS.

They are like factory products, movable to and fro around the world; and the same world-wide fight between supply and demand takes place.

URBAN LAND PRODUCTS.

Are rents or self-occupancy the equivalent thereof? Urban rents are not movable property. The product can't be taken to the people, but the people must be taken to the product; the fight between supply and demand is not world-wide; it is not even between cities except in a few isolated cases; the competition is confined to within the city itself and for the great majority of classes of buildings to a number of small localized districts thereof. The rise and fall of rents is due entirely to the supply and demand within each district; the supply being the number of competing buildings of each class, and the demand the number of people for each class of building, plus such people's income earning power.

Given a normal supply and a normal demand, plus population and greater earnings,—and rents can be increased. Given a normal supply and an increasing demand, plus greater population and greater earnings, and rents can be still further increased. Any increase in taxes, like any increase in expenses or interest, can be shifted to the tenant,—not because of such increase in taxes, but because of the demand for rents exceeding supply. Such increase in rent would happen even were there no taxes.

Conversely, if the supply of rents exceeds the demand, rents will fall and an increase in taxes, etc., can't be shifted to the tenant.

BRITISH HISTORICAL; LAND (PRIOR TO 1911).

National Land Tax. Paid by the landowner.

Land Tax Rate. Varied back and forward for 300 years between one and five shillings in the £ of assessed valuation.

Assessed Valuation. Varying percentages of actual value; assessed valuations only changed in long periods of years.

Borough and County Rates (Taxes). In England, paid by the occupier. In Scotland, paid about 40 per cent. by the land owner and about 60 per cent. by the occupier.

English Agricultural Land. Nearly all leased by the land owner to tenant farmers under long leases; improvements reverting to land owner; no agreement for tenant paying national land tax.

Land owners in originally making these leases always considered the land tax they paid; therefore the land tax was then and there shifted. If there was a reduction in the tax during the term of the lease, the landlord received the benefit; if there was an increase, he pocketed the loss.

Political Economists say that if the land tax were entirely abolished during the term of the lease, the land value would be increased by the capitalized value of the abolished tax. This is pure assumption; it may be true or it may be equally false.

If the land tax had been increased before the termination of the lease, then the increased tax could not be shifted until its expiration, and whether it could or could not be shifted then depended on the renewal rent the land owner could obtain from a tenant. If the new rent was increased, the tax was shifted to the extent of such increase. If the new rent was the same or reduced, then the increased tax was not shifted,—the net income would be reduced but the capital value of the land had not changed until it was sold.

The price for British agricultural products was steadily falling, owing to competition with foreign countries, and when leases fell in, the renewal rents were reduced, thereby reducing the net income of the land owner,—so that no increased land tax could have been or was, in fact, shifted.

Had, however, the prices for British agricultural products increased, renewal rents would have been increased, and any increased land tax would have been shifted proportionately to the rent increase. Where these lands were not sold, there was no decrease or increase in capital value,—but where and when sold, a decrease or increase would take place about equal to the capitalized value of the net income decrease or increase.

County and Borough rates (taxes) were paid by the tenant in England and about 60 per cent, thereof in Scotland; a decrease in the net income of the farm fell on the tenant until the expiration of the lease; any increase in the tax during the term of the lease fell wholly on the tenant in England and 60 per cent. in Scotland. At the expiration of the lease, as agricultural product prices were falling, the tenant's taxes were in whole or part shifted back to the land owner to the extent of the production in rent.

Had, however, agricultural product prices increased instead of decreased, then such increased local rates (taxes) would have been, as before, paid by the tenant.

English Urban Land. (1) A few freehold properties—land owner and building owner being one; (2) Chief rents in England and feus in Scotland; perpetual and for 999 years; (3) Sub-feus in Scotland; (4) Leaseholds (building) 99 years and shorter terms with reversion of buildings to land owner.

All of the above, except the first, contemplate erection of certain classes of building by other than the land owner for a stipulated single payment or annual rent.

Next come (5) Tenancies for years; (6) Life tenancies—for one or more lives; (7) Yearly tenancies; (8) Tenancies at will. Under Nos. 5 and 6, buildings reverted to land owner, who also had right of prior re-entry if rent not paid within a stipulated number of days or months.

The urban land owner paid the national land tax. In England the urban occupier paid the Borough, County and Municipal rates (taxes) and in Scotland the land owner paid about 40 per cent. and the occupier about 60 per cent. of such municipal rates (taxes). I am not certain whether in Scotland it is the original land owner under the Crown or the feu owner that pays the 40 per cent. municipal tax. I know, however, that the feu owner pays a municipal property tax.

The land owner under the Crown, granting perpetual Chief rents (England) or Feus (Scotland), considered the land tax (whatever it was) at the fixing of the original chief rent or feu duty—if the land tax was subsequently increased he could not have shifted the increased tax; if the land tax was reduced, the land owner received the benefit; he got no benefit from increasing urban land values—the owner of chief rent or feu or perpetual ground rent received the entire benefit.

The British land owner, granting limited term ground rents, or limited term leaseholds, tenancies for years or for life of urban land, has received at the expiration of such agreements, enormous increased rents due to the great increase in British urban values. Agricultural lands have been turned into urban lands. So that any increase in the national land tax and in Scotland in the land owner's percentage of the municipal tax, has been shifted ten, a hundred, a thousand times, first to the building owner and from him down the entire line to the occupier by reason of the ever-increasing rent.

Limited term leaseholds came largely into being from 1800 onwards —when the tremendous increase in values of urban land commenced. Land owners saw how their perpetual grants had resulted—in loss of net income on agricultural land and loss of increment values in urban land, and they hedged themselves for the future by making limited term leases, shorter in term as urban increment values grew.

As the English occupier by law paid the municipal rates (taxes) and the Scottish occupier paid 60 per cent. thereof, and as the urban occupier's rent is continually increasing as a whole, the occupier can't shift his increasing municipal rates (taxes) on to the building owner, and by the latter on to the land owner, as is the case with agricultural land. In Scotland, the urban feu owner's proportion of municipal taxes can be shifted to the building owner on the expiration of his leasehold and then to the occupier by reason of the ever-increasing rents.

ORIGIN OF THEORY OF NON-SHIFTABILITY OF LAND TAX.

When, how and with whom did the above theory originate? There was probably someone before Adam Smith and his contemporary Political Economists; Locke in 1692 appears to have had the same theory. I believe it first originated because English Chief rents and Scottish Feus (both perpetual) were principally in vogue in their time and prior thereto,—under which the building owner's superior landlord under the Crown had to pay the entire national land tax; under these circumstances the land tax could not be shifted even had it been increased tenfold. Another reason was that the owner of agricultural land, owing to decreased prices for agricultural products and consequent decreased net rental, was unable to shift the land tax to the tenant; still another reason was the peculiar tendency of Political Economists to forthwith mentally capitalize any increased tax and reduce all land values in amount equal to such capitalized tax and then claim that the tax was not shifted, as it had been charged off to or deducted from capital value (see remarks under Actual Capital Gain and Loss Values and Assumed Capital Loss Values).

Succeeding economists followed in the wake of the earlier; treating with abstract theories instead of actualities, and the result has been the fetich—a land tax can't be shifted.

Let anyone read (as I have done) the speeches, the parliamentary reports of the leading British statesmen from 1600 onwards and the divergent views of leading Political Economists on every kind of taxation, its shifting and incidence, and one's faith in the logical deductions of the majority of Britain's greatest men is forever shattered.

NEW YORK CITY REALTY.

Ownership. We have no such complex conditions here as exist in Britain; our realty holding and taxing are very simple.

Our Single Taxers love to mouth the phrases "Ground Rents," "Economic Rent" and other euphonious and political economy phrases

We haven't a single (British) Ground Rent in New York City, yet the term appears a dozen times in the Mayor's Taxation Committee's Questionnaire, when Leasehold Rents are meant. "Ground rent" is even used as an assumed rent of land, when there is no rent in actual existence.

We have a few leaseholds for limited terms of years, subject to renewal on rent appraisement and under which the lessee or building owner pays the realty tax. Will any Single Taxer have the foolhardiness to say that the tax assessed on such leased land is not shifted by the land owner on to the building owner? I believe they have. I believe they will say so, because if they don't, their entire contention (not argument, because they have none) is gone to smithereens.

With a few leasehold exceptions all our realty is owned as "freehold" by one person—the owner owning the land and the building thereon.

For anyone to say a tax, whether the tax be 1 per cent. or 10 per cent., on New York City land, where the land and building thereon is owned as freehold by the same person, can't be shifted,—is simply rank nonsense.

If the feu owners and sub-feu owners in the large cities of Scotland can shift their increased municipal taxes on to their building owners and the latter reshift to the occupiers, as they are doing continuously at the end of their short term leases, by raising their rents far in excess of their increased taxes—what is to prevent the New York City realty owner doing likewise?

If the New York owner can raise his rents at the expiration of his leases, he shifts any tax or increased tax to the extent that he can raise his rents. If he can't raise his rents he can't shift the tax—that's the answer to the whole question at issue.

If rents could be raised annually prior to 1907, and subsequently in the case of stores, as they were, what is to prevent a further increase in all rents when demand equals and overtakes supply as it will before long? Will the Single Tax idea of the Tax Department, dividing the actual payable tax into a mental land tax and into a mental building tax in equal or unequal proportions or calling it all mentally a land tax, prevent rents from ever rising again?

Will these Single Taxers tell me the difference between the Scottish feu owner (municipally taxed), the building owner and the occupier;—the New York City land owner-lessor, the building owner-lessee and the tenant—the New York City land owner and building owner (as one person) and the tenant. If it is possible, as it is, for the two first land owners to shift increased land tax to the tenant, it is more easily possible for the latter, because the land owner has a lease, terminable from second to second, with himself as the building owner. If such building owner can increase his rents, the land owners' (Tax Department) assumed land tax has been shifted as and when and to the exact extent that the building owner has been able to increase his rents.

PRICE LEVEL.

The rise and fall in interest rates is one factor of the price level—also credit,—new inventions,—intensity of production and a thousand and one other factors. If a realty owner's or an investor's income be reduced, and he can buy as much or more with the reduced income than he could before, he is not hurt, in fact he may be benefited.

Nominal decreases or increases in income or capital value may not be actual; the actual is to be found only in the Price Level.

TAX DEPARTMENT'S ASSESSED VALUATIONS.

Urban land has no income value except as it is built upon; it is the building that produces the income and gives a capital value to the whole; the actual value of the land and building is merged in one and in fact is one; before being built on the land had potentialities of value; when built upon the potential becomes actual.

Vacant lots should be assessed and taxed on some varying bases of potential value. There are many cases where the potential value is heavily over-assessed-valued and many other cases vice-versa. Nothing is more difficult to treat equitably.

Prior to 1904 the Tax Department showed assessed values of land and building thereon in one amount; since then an assumed assessed land and building value separately is shown. Single Taxers claim that they produced this change.

Capital value of producing realty should be based upon income value; for taxation purposes a reduction from such income value should be made for shrinkage and contingencies. Fully improved realty's assessed valuation should be made by capitalizing the net income. I can take any downtown office building, wreck it, rebuild it with the same floor area at less cost, less running expenses and produce increased rates. Is the value in the land or building? I can compare two buildings within a block of one another; ground area the same, aggregate floor space the same,—building of one cost about one-third more than the other—net income of the latter one-third more than the former; what's the land value? What's the actual land value of No. 60 Fifth Avenue,—building taken down to save taxes? It is true that a building could not be built but for the land. It is equally true that urban land has no value but for the building. How can the land and building thereon of fully-improved realty have separate distinct actual values? It can't be sold, mortgaged or foreclosed separately. Even the City won't accept the land and building tax separately.

For statistical purposes, to know the value of buildings individually and in the aggregate is a necessary thing, but it ought not to be in the tax list and for taxation purposes.

LAST EXAMPLE.

Prior to 1903 assessed valuations were shown on land and building as one; since then they have been subdivided into land and building. How did such separation change the tax payable as a whole? The landlord had to pay it, irrespective of whether it was called a tax on realty or a separate tax on land and a separate tax on building. If such a tax on land couldn't be shifted, why was it possible for rents to be increased subsequent to 1903? There is no doubt in my mind that rentals in a few years will be higher than ever in New York. How can the realty tax, by calling it a tax on land, prevent such increase in rents? If it doesn't prevent such increase, why then is the tax not shifted?

A LAST THOUGHT.

It may be that the divergent views on the shifting of taxes is due to the lack of consensus of agreement as to the meaning of the term "shifting a tax." A large number of Political Economists and prominent men in England have held that no tax on any subject matter taxed can be shifted—that it must rest where first placed. Do those mean that a tax can't be shifted because the price fixed by demand and supply for any commodity is fixed irrespective of any tax? If this is the contention, *then it is true*. Do those who claim that a tax on land can't be shifted, while admitting it can on all other subject matters taxed, mean that because land (except in exceptional cases) can't be increased or decreased in square foot area quantity, such facts puts land in a different category from buildings and other products because man can put a physical limitation on the quantity of the latter that can be produced? If this is the basis for their contention, then their basis is wrong because, while their contention may be true as regards agricultural land, it is wholly untrue as regards urban land, as man can put a physical limitation on the number of buildings that can be erected, this puts a like physical limitation on the quantity of land that is used for building purposes; hence urban land in this respect must be regarded in the same category as buildings and as all other commodities.

Conclusion.

I say without fear of logical contradiction that if factory costs can be shifted, if a combined building and land tax can be shifted, and if a building tax can be shifted, a tax on the land upon which buildings are built can be shifted as outlined above.

It may be properly asked if I believe that a land tax can be shifted; why do I oppose it? My answers are that the belief in anything is greater than the reality; things are only real as we believe them to be so; the great mass of people feel and don't think. Nothing is so timid as capital. Financial institutions get as easily panic-stricken as do Italian laborers. Even although the proposed tax was distributed over twenty years, its evil effects would be greater at once,—because disastrous—than ten years from now. Further, the proposed change means increased taxation on all properties and it would take ten years to shift such a tax, but finally it would be shifted.

December 7th, 1915.

LETTER OF JAMES W. SULLIVAN,

Designated By Samuel Gompers, President of the American Federation of Labor, to Represent the American Federation of Labor in Connection With the Hearings of the Committee on Taxation On the Proposal to Differentiate Between the Direct Taxation of Land and of Buildings By Reducing in Whole or in Part the Tax Rate on Buildings as Compared With That On Land.

Samuel Gompers,
President.

Frank Morrison,
Secretary.

AMERICAN FEDERATION OF LABOR
Main Office
801-809 G St., N. W.
Washington, D. C.

Hugh Frayne, General Organizer,
Bartholdi Building
Corner Broadway and 23d St.
Suite 710
Telephone Gramercy 3373

New York, November 3, 1915.

Mr. Laurence A. Tanzer, Executive Secretary,
City of New York Committee on Taxation,
Room 914, Municipal Building, New York City.

Dear Sir:

In reply to your letter of October 27th, and in response to the request of President Gompers, I herewith give you information regarding the attitude of the American Federation of Labor to taxation as brought out at its conventions.

The records of the proceedings of the Federation conventions for the decade 1905-1914 show that consideration was given in that period to three resolutions relating to taxation.

In 1905, in Pittsburgh, this resolution (No. 147) was introduced by Delegate Frank P. Shalvoy, of the United Hatters:

"Whereas, The question of equal taxation and the municipal ownership of public utilities having become a factor politically in some of our most thriving and industrial centers it is fitting and proper for the representatives of organized labor under the banner of the American Federation of Labor to go on record and express in unmistakable words our attitude in the solving of these problems, which means so much for civilization if they are solved rightly; and,

"Whereas, That the present system of taxation now in vogue is but a copy of the laws governing taxation which have existed under every monarchical form of government in ages gone by and which were instituted to favor the few, the many being subservient to every form of law made. After a fair trial under a free government we find the same identical conditions to prevail—extreme wealth on the one side and extreme poverty on the other.

"Resolved, That in our humble opinion such a system of taxation never should have been adopted for our beloved country to go hand in hand with that immortal Declaration of Independence.

"We favor the gradual abolition of every form of tax upon the products of labor.

"We hold that land itself never had a value until the people created that value and that land is and should by right be held as sacred to the people as the air we breathe.

"We favor the enforcement of tax laws which shall eliminate entirely the products of labor and return to the people for the necessary expenses of our government that value that the whole people create.

"We hold that any other form of taxation is barbarous and unjust and not in keeping with a free and enlightened people. The wealth created by a single individual by every law, human or divine, belongs to the whole people."

The Committee reported as follows on Resolution No. 147:

"In the opinion of this committee the subject matter contained herein is not in proper form to be acted upon by the committee, as it is a declaration of principles instead of a set of resolutions. We recommend that no action be taken thereon."

On motion the report of the committee was adopted.

In 1907, at Norfolk, this resolution (No. 145) was introduced by Delegate George Finger, Brotherhood of Painters and Decorators:

"Whereas, Indirect taxation puts the burden upon the workmen of America, who, like proletarians of other countries, have large families, and therefore are taxed entirely out of proportion whenever they buy any necessities of life; first, because they are poor, and whenever they buy they pay as much tax as the rich; second, by reason of usually having large families they multiply the indirect taxes they pay, and

"Whereas, It ought to be the duty of wise and just legislators to put the burden where it properly belongs—upon the shoulders of those able to pay; and

"Whereas, The present mode of taxation, which is absolutely plutocratic and inhuman, has materially aided our big capitalists in accumulating huge fortunes; therefore be it

"Resolved, That the twenty-seventh annual convention of the American Federation of Labor hereby protests against a system of taxation which is entirely in favor of the small class of exploiters and against the wage class of producers. We demand the abolition of all indirect taxes, and only the small properties of the producers ought to be exempt. We declare in favor of an income tax gradually increasing with the income and are also in favor of an inheritance tax which is to increase in percentage with the size of the inheritance."

The Committee on Resolutions amended as follows:

"Resolved, That we declare in favor of an income tax gradually increasing with the income tax and we are also in favor of an inheritance tax which is to increase in percentage with the size of the inheritance."

The report of the committee was concurred in.

In 1912, at Rochester, this resolution (No. 71), introduced by Delegate Frank H. McCarthy, of the Boston Central Labor Union, was, on recommendation of the Committee on Resolutions, adopted:

"Resolved, That we favor the imposition of a small tax on land values in place of some of the more burdensome tariff taxes."

In the list of questions sent by the Committee on Taxation to the representatives of the American Federation of Labor to be considered in connection with public hearings, is one, Question 18—Series 3, relating to wages:

What is the connection between the rents and wages in New York City?

Are wages higher in New York than in other cities? If so, why?

If one of the causes of higher wages in New York City is higher rents, would a decrease in rents mean a fall in wages? If not, why not?

The members of organized labor hold it as a fact that the level of wages depends mainly on effective trade unionism. The wage scale of a trade union is uniform whatever the variation in the rents paid by its members. A union which controls the supply of the labor of its occupation fixes the scale with far more regard to the profits of the employers than of the rental of habitations. In New York nearly all organizable occupations are organized in unions. In the non-organized, wages are directly influenced by the union scale of nearly related occupations. Within any one occupation also, the union scale fixes, in a general way, the scale of the non-unionists.

The beneficial financial results of trade unionism are a matter of proof year by year. Occupations or areas of the country on being organized almost invariably enjoy higher wages, shorter hours and better working conditions than previously. The advance in dollars and cents, the shortened work day and better conditions are in many occupations to be clearly indicated by statistical presentation. Wage advance due wholly to trade unionism (the production necessary to pay the scale being taken for granted) is a matter of record in each of the one hundred and ten International Unions affiliated with the Federation. At present the membership of the American Federation of Labor is more than two millions. The average weekly increase in wages, if placed at one dollar, would show a volume passing from the employer class to the employed class greater than in the absence of unionism by more than one hundred million dollars annually, but in many unions the increase has been ten, twenty, and even twenty-five per cent. in the last ten years. An increase of three dollars a week per member of the American Federation of Labor would bring the volume of increase to three hundred million dollars a year. Since there are from one-half million to one million organized wage workers not in the Federation, the volume of advance in wages may thereby be increased to one hundred million dollars more, not to mention the betterment in non-union wages as influenced by the union scales.

I make this statement in this form in a letter, inasmuch as the list of questions is almost wholly unadapted to the records of the American Federation of Labor. Politically, all phases of opinion on taxation are represented in the membership of the Federation. All members are at liberty to form their own convictions on the subject. In the capacity of a representative of the American Federation of Labor, I am not, of course, on this occasion free to obtrude my own conclusions on the question.

Very truly yours,
(Signed) J. W. SULLIVAN.

BRIEF SUBMITTED BY J. P. COUGHLIN, VICE-PRESIDENT, THE CENTRAL LABOR UNION OF BROOKLYN,

For Transferring Taxes Levied on Buildings to Land Values.

Organized Labor appreciate that no single measure will secure to the workers of the country the value of what they produce, and to that value they are entitled.

Organized Labor endorses, however, the recommendations of the United States Commission on Industrial Relations made by the three representatives of organized labor on that Commission and the Chairman, to wit:

"The forcing of all land into use by making the tax on unproductive land the same as on productive land of the same kind, and exempting all improvemnets."

We endorse the transfer of taxes from buildings here to land values for the following reasons:

1st. *The worst land monopoly in the world exists in New York City.*

Most of the value of land in New York City is owned by a few thousand people—a thousand families own an average of nearly a million dollars worth of land, while several families own from five to twenty millions worth of land. Taxing land values more heavily will compel these families to pay more nearly a fair share of the governmental expenditures, which, together with the presence of the population, have given the land they hold its value.

2nd. *It will give better housing at lower rents.*

Taxes levied on buildings limit the supply of buildings, and so keep rents high.

Rents, like wages, are determined chiefly by the law of supply and demand. A large proportion of the workers of the city are obliged to live in crowded quarters, unsanitary and unsafe, because the present tax system makes this sort of building, paying very little taxes, more profitable than healthy, safe tenements. No civilized city would permit its population to be housed as are the majority of the people of New York City, and at very high rentals.

3rd. *It will increase home ownership.*

Taxing buildings at the same rate as land values permits the holding of large acreage tracts out of use in all boroughs of the city, except Manhattan, until they can be sold to would-be small home owners at speculative prices. The present system also compels the owner of a small home to pay, on the average, nearly four times as much taxes as the owner of a vacant lot adjoining, although the construction of such a home increases the selling price of vacant lots nearby.

Transferring taxes from buildings to land values will compel land speculators to sell cheaper to prospective small home owners, and will save small home owners at least half to three-fifths of the taxes they pay under the present tax system, without reducing the selling price of their lots.

4th. *It will make more employment.*

Transferring taxes on buildings to land values will, as stated by the United States Industrial Relations Commission, force much unused land into use, and stimulate the construction of buildings, thereby giving more employment directly. By reducing rents and taxes on small homes it will permit nine-tenths of the population of New York—at least a million families—to buy more manufactured goods and produce, and so give more employment indirectly, but just as certainly.

By retarding the speculative increase in the selling price of land, and reducing the total taxes or rent for manufacturers, it will encourage the location of more factories here, through reducing the fixed charges on production, while keeping wages up, through the increased demand for workers.

5th. *It will make working conditions safer.*

Untaxing buildings will stop premium upon old firetrap factories, and the penalty upon constructing safe ones. Fire prevention and labor laws should be enforced, but government should stop taxing owners of buildings heavily for complying with requirements of safety and health.

6th. *It will reduce the unearned profits of land speculators.*

The condition of the workers of the city, organized or unorganized, can be materially improved only by eliminating the various privileged classes, who become wealthy without producing anything, merely by taking the produce of the workers.

This involves several measures and changes, beside taking more of the ground rent for governmental purposes. The fundamental unearned income is ground rents. We favor a rapidly progressive income tax on large incomes for the Federal Government—but taking ground rents for local public expenditures.

LETTER OF CHARLES F. NOYES ON THE PROPOSAL TO UNTAX BUILDINGS.

CHARLES F. NOYES COMPANY,
Real Estate,
92 William Street,
New York.

November 12, 1915.

Laurence Arnold Tanzer, Esq., Executive Secretary,
Committee on Taxation,
Municipal Building, City.

Dear Sir:

Thanks for your recent letter, and the two reports prepared for your Committee by Dr. Haig, in the matter of halving or reducing the tax on buildings.

I appreciate your thoughtfulness, but regret that I have not made a sufficient study of taxation to appear to advantage before your Committee. It may be, however, that you would like to have my ideas regarding the problem, which we know is receiving the best thought of your Committee.

My experience of 17 years in the real estate business has been an active one, dealing almost exclusively in Manhattan properties. We have several hundred buildings under our control, including office buildings, loft buildings and some apartments. We deal directly in a business capacity with about 1,500 tenants. The result of this business experience leads me to state that the high points of real estate value (intensified holdings as you call them) are caused by the following conditions:

First: *Natural advantages,*—such as Riverside Drive for apartments.

Second: *Permanent anchors,*—such as the Grand Central and Pennsylvania Stations, with their network of transit facilities, creating a naturally desirable location between 30th and 50th streets, Fourth to Seventh avenues.

Third: *An established Financial District,* in which is located the New York Stock and Consolidated Stock Exchanges, the Coffee, Cotton and Maritime Exchanges, the Custom House and buildings owned by insurance companies, banks and other financial interests.

Fourth: *The Fifth Avenue District,* famous as a high-class shopping center the world over, and maintained as such because of its proximity to the railroad terminals and fashionable hotels, etc.

These and a half a dozen other examples which could be cited are logical reasons why ground has increased in value so rapidly at certain points, while other property has remained stationary, and in some instances has decreased in value.

And, it should be remembered that as ground value has increased so have the taxes increased. Halving or removing the tax on buildings will not make these high spots of real estate less valuable except in isolated cases. Neither will it, generally speaking, add materially to property values elsewhere. People *live, eat, play or transact business* in these districts of high property value because there are some strong business or personal reasons for their doing so. This has been going on for years until to-day the large proportion of all valuable property on lower Broadway, south of City Hall; the most desirable locations in the Financial District and on Fifth Avenue (from 30th to 50th streets), and practically all of Riverside Drive, is improved with permanent and expensive structures, representing huge investments, and good for many years to come. At a few points, particularly lower Broadway, an over-development has occurred, and for this reason we now have accommodations for the next ten years' growth.

In other sections (not those mentioned above) a large amount of vacant space exists because of trade shifts, which, until ten years ago, were considered impossible.

To me it seems the height of folly to remove the tax on buildings, many of great value, worth from $1,000,000 to $10,000,000, and place it on ground entirely. In the "high spots" of value referred to above, which will change little in character or desirability, little, if any, more can be secured from the ground itself, and the taxable value of the ground would not be greatly increased by removing a part or all of the tax on the buildings. Also as practically all of the desirable ground in these sections is now permanently improved there would be no stimulation of building construction here.

The objections I have to the plan are, briefly:

(a). It would unfairly partially relieve from taxation the owners of our finest buildings in locations which cannot be duplicated, which are the finest investments possible.

(b). The taxes thus shifted from buildings of high value representing many millions of dollars, which would not be profitable elsewhere and which generally speaking cannot be duplicated elsewhere, because practically all the desirable ground has been absorbed, would be placed on the shoulders of owners of ground less valuable, which will not be made more valuable by reason of the tax shift.

(c). It would lead to a period of reckless construction in certain neighborhoods where there is no economic need of new buildings.

Whether or not the people and the government should take over our real property is a debatable question. I do **not** so believe. Many regard real estate as a commodity, the same as the ownership of a business or an investment. The present owners of real estate when purchasing same,—and in the aggregate very little of our property has come down through inheritance,—invested their money in the belief that they would have the right to do with their real estate as they saw fit, provided the laws of the community as to health and order were obeyed. The greater part of real estate is mortgaged, and the statements made to your Committee regarding the difficulty owners are having to pay their interest, tax and governmental charges, are not overdrawn.

My impression is that this agitation to halve the tax on buildings and shift the taxation to the ground has the ring of "single tax" and "government ownership." It does seem to me that this issue should be settled, and the quicker it is disposed of the better it will be for the community, because these continued attacks on real estate, and agitation to "do this and do that," are driving buyers out of the market, and in many cases stampeding owners to sell at demoralized prices, who have heretofore considered real estate as good an asset as they could have. Without willing buyers and a ready market, real estate, which I believe is our best asset, depreciates in value.

Personally I feel that the strong should look out for the deserving weak, and I believe that this country and this city should give all an equal right to own and develop their property, and that the investor in New York real estate is entitled to develop his land as he sees fit, subject to legal community regulation and the proper police power of the State. To this end the community and government should not attack and pull down, but instead encourage real estate investment, and it should not attempt to artificially force industry in construction or create by "theory" new centers, using methods not successfully employed elsewhere. I firmly believe that each citizen is entitled to, and has the right to demand the privilege of employing his own intellect to decide what he shall do with that which he has gained by toil and industry, if in his efforts he complies with the laws of the community.

Hoping that this proposal will be definitely and firmly disposed of by your Committee, and that the agitation to change our tax methods will cease, I am

Very truly yours,

C. F. NOYES.

BRIEF SUBMITTED BY THE SOCIETY TO LOWER RENTS AND REDUCE TAXES ON HOMES,

For a Supertax On Land Values to Meet Increases in the City Budget and the City's Share of the State Direct Tax.

The per capita cost of local government and the city's share of the State Direct Tax is, in round figures, $38.00, or $190.00 for a family of five.

Mayor Mitchel testified before the Joint Legislative Committee on Taxation that, even if the cost of government can be kept at its present level, the city will, in 1920, have to raise, exclusive of the State Direct Tax, $34,554,000 more than its present budget of nearly $200,000,000.

The local budget will be in 1920 about $250,000,000, that is assuming an average increase of population, about $47.00 per capita, or $235.00 for a family of five, in addition to the State and Federal indirect taxes.

The per capita cost of the Federal Government is about $7.00, of the State government, about $5.00; so that even if there are no unusual increases in Federal and State expenditures by 1920, the average charge per family in New York City for the privilege of being governed will be around $300.

How New York City is to secure additional revenue is a matter of concern to every family in the city, and the poorer or larger the family the more vital the concern. The city cannot in its quest for additional revenue ignore the similar need of the Federal and State Governments.

The term "new sources of revenue" should be discarded, as it is inaccurate. There are only two sources of revenue: Earnings, current or accumulated; and Ground Rents. It is agreed that all taxes, except those on Inheritances, Incomes and Land Values, can be shifted to the user of the article or service taxed. It is agreed that unwise or too high taxes can destroy almost everything except land values.

The method by which New York City is to derive additional revenue should be determined in the light of the fact that the poorer families in the city (wage earners and small salaried people) pay a much larger proportion of their earnings in indirect taxes than the wealthier families, and that if the city or state imposes a direct income tax on individuals or on the gross or net incomes of corporations, or an indirect income tax under the title "presumptive ability tax," the Federal Government can collect that much less by the Federal Income Tax and will have to tax the poorer classes more heavily, and even more disproportionately, than at present. This is recognized by Senator Ogden L. Mills, Chairman of the Joint Legislative Committee on Taxation, who urges that states and cities adopt the income tax before the Federal Government dries that up as a source of revenue.

The most radical advocate of the income tax would not claim that more than $300,000,000 to $350,000,000 could be raised by this tax, and to raise this sum would require rates similar to those in the warring European nations.

If there be any justification for the ability to pay theory of taxation it implies the necessity for a much more rapidly progressive rate on large incomes than those of the present law.

The Federal expenditures will probably increase by at least $100,000,000 to $150,000,000 within a year or two. The Federal Government needs every dollar that can be raised by the Income Tax, and that is preeminently the proper source for the Federal Government, because practically all incomes and fortunes in the country, not secured from land, are derived from country-wide and even world-wide opportunity.

Principle of the Income Tax for Local Purposes Most Inapplicable in New York City.

The time and place, as well as the tax, must be considered in determining methods of securing additional revenue.

The city has undertaken public improvements, transit lines, water supply, etc., which will be largely wasted unless the population increases rapidly and is self-sustaining.

The average per capita net debt, in 1912, of all cities having a population of 30,000 or over was $68.74. That of New York was $156.57; of Chicago, $28.62; of Philadelphia, $60.64; of St. Louis, $33.72; and of Boston, $106.42.

The financial benefit of many of the improvements for which the city's great debt was incurred, will be realized within the next few years by the land owners of the city in the increased selling price of land,—if population increases.

As was clearly shown your Committee at its public hearings, high selling prices of land are a detriment to the producers and workers of any community, because they compel the payment of large ground rents.

New York cannot afford to make it any more difficult or disadvantageous for manufacturers to locate here, and large increases within the next few years in the selling price of land would militate against the increase of factories and industry.

With the present tax rate on land values, the net increase in the selling price of land would be at least $1,000,000,000 and probably $1,200,000,000 during the next decade. Such an increase in the selling price of land would require $50,000,000 to $60,00,000 more ground rent to be paid owners of land here on this increase, than the nearly $250,000,000 net ground rents they now receive—before the real producers of the city are requited for their labor and industry. Interest on the probable increase in selling price of land here at 6 per cent. amounts to $60,000,000 to $72,000,000 annually, a dead waste and useless burden on industry, due to unearned profits of land speculators.

It would clearly be to the advantage of every one in New York City, except a few land speculators, to have the selling price of land here remain stationary, or increase only very little in the future. This is fully as important for the city's development and prosperity as securing additional revenue.

The two desiderata can be achieved effectively and equitably by recovering annually for maintenance of government approximately the increase in the selling price of land by a super tax on land values.

In a very few cases, this might work temporary hardship, but, owing to the concentration of the ownership of valuable land here, this would be the fairest way to secure additional revenue for local purposes on the basis of financial benefit received. It would also result in reaching those who do not pay their fair share of the cost of local government, and would reduce the amount collectible here by the Federal Government, through the income tax.

We, therefore, recommend that all increases in the cost of local government and the city's share of the State Direct Tax be met by such a super tax on land values.

The amount New York City must raise next year is, in round figures, $213,000,000 or about $14,000,000 more than this year. To raise this additional revenue by a super tax on land values, would require a rate of only three mills.

With this super tax rate, the one hundred families who are the owners of record of land assessed for $473,808,075, located chiefly in Manhattan, would pay $1,421,424 more than at present. Under a general tax rate of two mills, approximately the increase in the rate required to raise $14,000,000 additional revenue, they would advance only $1,262,646, because the assessed value of the buildings of which they are the owners of record is only $157,515,235. Since they would be able to shift practically all the tax on their rented buildings to the tenants, however—that is $315,030—their own contribution, out of their present ground rent of about $20,000,000, would be only $947,616, or $473,808 less than they would pay with a super tax of three mills on land values.

These hundred families include most of the wealthiest in the city and those whose wealth is due to the growth of the city's population and industry, and its expenditures.

Two thousand families would pay approximately half of the $14,000,000 with this super tax on land values, because those two thousand families have been to this extent the financial beneficiaries of the city's growth, industry and expenditures.

The small home owner whose site is assessed for $1,000 and building for $3,000, would pay $8.00 with a general increase of two mills, and only $3.00 with a super tax of three mills on land values.

The owner of a $30,000 tenement on a $10,000 lot would pay $30.00 more with the super tax on land values, as against the $80.00 he would pay with a two mills increase in the general tax rate, of which he might collect $60.00 from his tenants, by increased rent, or decreasing service now rendered. He would pay personally about $10.00 more with the land values super tax than with the two mills general increase in the tax rate.

The maintaining of the selling price of land at about its present figure, and the prevention of speculative increases together with the knowledge that there would not be any increase in the tax rate on buildings or machinery would encourage manufacturers to locate here, and, therefore, be of direct advantage to the city as a whole.

A far greater advantage would be the exemption of the tools of production.

No fair-minded person can object to the super tax on land values, because it does not seek to affect the present selling price of land materially, but merely to recover for the community the future increases in value of land attributable directly to community activity and expenditure. The specious, selfish and unfounded objections raised to transferring taxes from buildings to land values cannot be urged against such a super tax on land values which does not affect the status quo but merely acts for the future.

TESTIMONY

GIVEN AT THE

PUBLIC HEARINGS

November 8-24, 1915

NOTE.

The material presented herewith does not comprise an exact and complete record of the hearings. In several cases the oral statements of individuals were found to be duplicated in briefs printed in this volume and were therefore eliminated. Exigencies of space made necessary the reduction of the remaining testimony by approximately one-half. To accomplish this each individual's testimony was first submitted to him for correction and then edited, such portions as were considered least likely to be of permanent value being omitted.

FIRST HEARING.

November 8, 1915, 2.30 P. M., Room 16, City Hall.
Professor Edwin R. A. Seligman, presiding.

TESTIMONY OF MR. BENJAMIN C. MARSH,

Secretary, The New York Congestion Committee, The Society to Lower Rents and Reduce Taxes on Homes, and The Business Men's Association to Untax Industry.

MR. MARSH: Mr. Chairman and Gentlemen of the Committee: We advocate the transfer of the tax now levied on buildings to land values within a period of from ten to five years, with a referendum on this question to the people.

The public should know that this Committee was appointed by Mayor Mitchel, in repudiation of a pledge before his nomination not to interfere with the referendum on reducing taxes on buildings in 1914, as was recommended by Mayor Gaynor's Commission on Congestion of Population, in 1911, after a careful investigation. It is to the personal financial interest of a majority of your committee not to have the taxes now levied on buildings transferred to land values. A report against this proposal will be the recommendation of a prejudiced, if not to say, a packed jury.

The Society to Lower Rents and Reduce Taxes on Homes urges a referendum on this question, because the people of the City have a right to decide it, and the action of the voters on last Tuesday on the constitution of Elihu Root indicates that the voters will act on their own judgment and not on the judgment of alleged experts seeking their own selfish ends.

We urge this transfer of tax now levied on buildings here to land values regardless of the adverse effects upon a few individual property owners in the city, for the following, among many other reasons:

1. Ground rents are the proper revenue for local purposes, since all wise municipal expenditures benefit financially only the land owners, and the people, and not the land owners, create and maintain ground rents.

2. It will reduce rents and taxes on small homes.

Now I have been very much interested in the report of Professor Seligman's speech at the National Housing Conference, on this subject. I do not know whether it is accurate or not. It seems to me that the point is rather clearly made there that untaxing buildings would lower rent.

I am sorry to say that my friend, Mr. Miller, the former President of the Borough of the Bronx, has overlooked, in his very lucid recent brief on the subject, the fact that the transfer of the tax to land would lower rent. While President of the Bronx, he warned land owners and landlords in the Bronx as to the effect of our proposed change, and had it written on the official letter head of the borough president of the

Bronx. I will quote very briefly from Mr. Miller's statement. I will read the part that refers to this proposed change:

> The second effect is that the amount of tax taken from present buildings and imposed on vacant and other land causes an unnatural increase of buildings on vacant property, which will be built upon so as to escape heavy taxation. The effect on property having old buildings on it will be to decrease its value, because, the tax on land being increased, the old buildings must be torn down and new ones erected.
>
> By stimulating building so that more buildings are erected than would be the case under normal conditions, both new and old buildings must compete for the same number of tenants, thereby causing a fall in rent, in both new and old buildings.

3. It will cause the substitution of healthful and safe tenements in place of the fire-trap or disease-breading tenements, in which millions of the city's population live, actually millions—Mr. Lawrence Veiller put the figure a little over three million. It will make them more profitable and attractive.

It is because the cheapest thing in New York City is human life that we have the present system of taxation. I could wish nothing better than that every one of you gentlemen on this Committee who does not favor untaxing buildings might be obliged to live in one of those traps—they are strictly legal—live there until you get the first touch of consumption. I do not want you to follow the sad fate of the ten thousand people who die there from consumption every year, because I do not believe in fitting the penalty to the crime. You should at least have a little touch of consumption, just so as to realize that we have twenty-eight thousand new cases of consumption every year. The only thing this so-called reform administration seeks is the conservation of property rights at the expense of human rights.

4. By removing part of the tax on production, industry will be encouraged and the unemployment situation will thereby be helped.

5. Thus it will reduce the high cost of living.

6. It will make those best able to pay, and those benefited financially by municipal expenditures, pay a fairer share of the cost of local government, and relieve those least able to pay, who receive no financial benefit from governmental expenditures, from part of the burden of taxes that they now pay.

The poorer families of New York City are the heaviest taxpayers to-day. They pay probably through indirect taxation anywhere from twelve to fifteen per cent. of their income for taxes, while I am unable to see how you can figure out that the members of the wealthiest class pay anywhere near that percentage of their total income. Of course on that we all agree. I believe that the taxes on buildings are shifted to the tenants, and the best proof from practical experience that untaxing buildings will lower rent and will reduce the profits of the land speculator is their own opposition to this. All the theory I or anybody else can give you is not one-half as substantial or one-half as weighty as the opposition of the landlords and the land speculators to this proposition. If they did not have to reduce rents, and if they did not know and admit they would have to reduce rents, they would not have gotten Mayor Mitchel to break his pre-election pledge by appointing a tax committee when the people could have decided the question on facts already in their possession.

7. It would encourage the construction of small homes.

8. It will prevent land speculation, the speculative increase in land value, and so release more money for productive enterprises.

It seems to me that the fact should be emphasized that if we can prevent the sinking of money unproductively in speculative prices for land that much money will be released for productive enterprises. Mayor Gaynor's Commission on New Sources of City Revenue, in January, 1913, I believe, reported that the average annual increase in land values in New York City for a decade had been one hundred and fifty million dollars. Now, assume their figures are accurate. I presume the increase is not as much to-day, because immigration has been partially shut off by the war in Europe, which of course again proves the fact that the people make land value. But assuming they are correct to even one hundred million dollars a year, in order to do business in New York City, if the land is to be used within the next decade, a billion dollars has got to be sunk in profits to the land speculator, or land-owner, if you prefer the less harsh but inaccurate term, and the interest paid by them, before the workingman or the manufacturer can get any profit. Perhaps it would be clearer if we illustrate by a national situation. Farm lands in this country increased from 1900 to 1910 by 118 per cent., in round figures, fifteen and one-half billion dollars.

9. It will expedite the breaking up of the land monopoly in this city.

A few thousand people own most of the value and a large part of the acreage of the land in New York City. From the only record of land ownership available in this City, the Society to Lower Rents has made a study which we will submit to you as soon as it is completed. The fact is brought out that 99 families own about one-ninth of the value of the land in greater New York.

Most of the cost of national, state and local governments is now borne by the workers, through indirect taxation, including consumption taxes. Of the federal expenditures, amounting to about seven hundred million dollars, only forty-one million, one hundred and sixty thousand was secured last year from the income tax on individuals and nearly six hundred and sixty million from the workers. Of the state budget, in round figures, of fifty million dollars in 1914, three-quarters was secured from the workers through taxes upon industry and the products of labor. Of the local budget of one-hundred and ninety-nine million dollars this year, about one-hundred million dollars is secured from the workers by indirect taxes. Taxes on land values cannot be shifted. but come out of the unearned profits of land owners. If this transfer of the tax on buildings to land values does not take place, the land speculators in New York City who are now making a net, annual profit of nearly one-quarter of a billion dollars, although some may be losing, will continue to do so while the productive workers of the city are legally robbed of so much of their wages or incomes under the guise of taxation. Now that is my brief preliminary statement, Mr. Chairman.

MR. TANZER: If the untaxing of buildings should result in the construction of more buildings, and presumably larger and more commodious ones, would the effect be through competition to reduce rents in all buildings or only in the older and smaller and less commodious ones?

MR. MARSH: I believe it would have the tendency, as admitted by our friend Mr. Miller, to reduce rents in all buildings which are within the zone of competition.

MR. TANZER: To what extent would lower rents, due to larger supply of buildings in New York City, tend to attract population from outside the city, particularly from the suburbs in New York and New Jersey, to which people doing business in the city have heretofore gone in search of lower rents? To what exent, by this increase in the demand for buildings, would the tendency for lower rents be checked?

MR. MARSH: That is a problematical question which no one can answer definitely or statistically. The tendency would be unquestionably to reduce rents here, since the people of New York City now go to the other side of the Hudson because they see no sense in being taxed to pay the cost of the government of New York City while land speculators here make their present profits. New Jersey would, also, doubtless follow our tax policy.

MR. TANZER: But assuming that they did not do so, do you think that that would be an influence that would tend to counteract the tendency toward lower rents resulting from the untaxing of buildings?

MR. MARSH: It might very slightly. There again another factor would be whether or not we put an income tax upon all the workers of New York City, so that what we would save in rent we would be robbed of in the guise of an income tax. That would tend to keep people out of New York City. Another fact is that the rate of taxes on land values is very heavy. If we had a super-tax on land values to meet the increase in the city budget, as recommended by the English Parliamentary Committee on Taxes—and they recommend also, local option in the tax rate—there would be a tendency to much lower rent. Now, of course, in Canada they have not had the single tax. They have not had a heavy land-values tax where improvements in the cities are exempted, with few exceptions. This is because they have run in debt the same way as we have done here. We are spending fifty-five millions in interest alone next year on the city debt, nearly the levy on buildings. If they transfer the tax to the land and raise in that way the additional revenue (about fifty million dollars by 1918), the tendency would be to reduce rents very much more than if they simply transfer the tax now levied on buildings to land values.

I look for permanent appreciable reduction in rents in New York City under our proposal, but not of course in the first year. If we make the change in a period of nine equal reductions or ten equal reductions, by the time it is in effect there will be a much greater reduction. If the change is made in five years it will be still more rapid.

Dr. Haig's conclusions are in substance that this proposed change will be of great benefit to tenants and to many small home owners. That is based not only on the study of the situation in New York City, but is based upon his knowledge of conditions in Canadian cities, where you must remember there was a very rapid increase in population, much more rapid than New York City ever had. When you discuss that question of whether rents were reduced by this change, you must consider what the rents would have been in that Canadian city with an increase of ten or fifteen per cent. in population a year, had it not had this added stimulus of land-value taxation and exemption of improvements.

A VOICE: Dr. Haig points out, does he not, that there are various factors which would introduce friction into the transfer to tenants of benefit?

MR. MARSH: He makes substantially, as was printed in the New York papers, the statement which I gave, that there may be some friction for the time being, because tenants would not know the facts. We will try to show them to the tenants so they will be quite alert to their interests.

PROFESSOR SELIGMAN: Do you think that the inevitable result of this change will be to reduce the value of existing properties in land in New York?

MR. MARSH: I do not. I think it would be quite the reverse. I think that the probable result of this change in the system of taxation will be not to reduce the present selling price. You cannot reduce the value of the land by changing the tax. The land is just as valuable whether the ground rents go into the pockets of the city or into the pockets of the land owners. But it would tend to retard the increase in the selling price of land. Instead of increasing about one hundred million dollars a year, it would increase but a very small amount. If you suddenly untax buildings, I think there would be a great difference. We do not propose any sudden change in transferring taxes on buildings to land value. We expect to do it in a period of from five to ten years. In that case, I rather think there would probably be only a small increase for a few years in the selling price of land in New York City. This would be the greatest boon to the city that we could ever conceive of.

PROFESSOR SELIGMAN: Do you think, Mr. Marsh, that there are any parcels of land in New York City at present which have not increased in value in the last year or two, or which may not increase in the next year or two?

MR. MARSH: Unquestionably there are some parcels of land in New York City, for instance, in 14th Street and 23rd Street, which are less valuable to-day than two or three years ago.

PROFESSOR SELIGMAN: Assuming that there are pieces of land in this city which are not increasing in value, would the supposed transfer of taxes from buildings to land increase or decrease that selling value?

MR. MARSH: It would depend upon a number of factors.

PROFESSOR SELIGMAN: Your advocacy of this change is not affected, is it, by the fact that property rights of individuals will be interfered with?

MR. MARSH: When the rights of property, as was clearly shown in this city, kill off twenty-seven thousand people every year from preventable diseases, when the rights of property conflict with the rights of people, I say that property should make the first concession. Hitherto the people have made all concessions, in my judgment. (Applause)

PROFESSOR SELIGMAN: Are there, in your opinion, any movements on foot, at the present time, making for an improvement of the social conditions of which you speak, or would you say that this contemplated change in taxation is far more important than these other movements?

MR. MARSH: There are some very cheerful experiments going on in New York. They are doing everything except choking off privilege. The Rockefeller foundation is doing things. I believe all those things are very good in their place, but until you can knock out privilege there is no use of trying to solve a problem of poverty. You cannot do it. Long before we advocated this taxation of land values, we urged the Congestion Committee. We favored the bills controlling the height, size and arrangement of buildings. I am going to be frank. In New York the case is practically that the land speculators have absolutely knocked out all efforts to make zones for buildings or to limit their size or height. They have killed every effort to amend the tenement house law so as to permit the Tenement House Department to vacate tenement houses or apartments so defective in light as to be unsafe for occupancy and dangerous to life and health. I doubt if you are going to succeed in doing anything at all until you break down this control of the land speculators in this city which has manifested itself in many different ways. I agree with Justice Hughes, that all of these things are merely an extension of the police power of the state. Over in barbarian Germany, as we here call it, they have adopted this principle of taxation and they have absolute control over city development, as they have in Paris and in Vienna. In England they have the town-planning act. Even in this country the belief is growing that the land values are for the benefit of the entire people. You must give land values to the people who make them.

MR. LINDNER: Are you not aware of the fact that the limitation of the height of buildings and the zoning system has been supported by real estate owners?

MR. MARSH: After some time, by a few. Land owners found out that they had been shooting their land values all to pieces by their methods of construction. They found they were hurting their own land values, so they came around to see us, and said, "Let us pull together to protect land values." Not that they cared for the dear people!

MR. LINDNER: Outside of the question of motives, is it not a fact that the movement to limit the height of buildings by increasing the amount of vacant space required and to create zones is now being supported by real estate owners? The fact is that not only recently but for quite a long time the commission which has been studying this subject has had the support and advice of the responsible organizations and they have whole-heartedly worked for this reform. They believe that better housing can be accomplished by that means.

MR. MARSH: Better housing at higher rent; yes. That is just exactly what all restrictive legislation does.

MR. LINDNER: Will it bring about higher rents of necessity? It only requires that there shall be accommodation for the people who must be accommodated. There may be a more competitive use of the land.

MR. MARSH: Precisely. As long as you have the present system of taxation, it means taxes in restraint of trade in buildings. If you remove that tax you cannot tell what will take place. You do not try to enforce the tenement house law as to overcrowding because it cannot be done. How can you say that the tax on land, with buildings free, will reduce rents while the tenement house law increases rents?

MR. LEUBUSCHER: Does the fact that immigration has practically ceased account, at least in part, for the fact that land values are stagnant?

MR. MARSH: I think that is so. The real estate people admit it and are praying for a cessation of the war, so that land values would go up again here.

MR. LEUBUSCHER: Is it true that the tendency to decrease selling values by the transfer of taxes from structures to land would bring about a lesser capital loss than the annual increase by reason oi the ordinary natural increase of land value? Do you think they balance each other, or do you think that the ordinary increase is greater than the amount of capital loss which would be caused by the transfer?

MR. MARSH: The assessed value of land to-day in New York City is, in round figures, four billion, six hundred and sixty million dollars. Now that is with a tax rate on the average of nearly two per cent. In other words, that is supposed to be the capitalized ground rent at about five per cent., net. Now, suppose in order to untax buildings by the transfer of the tax on buildings to land values, we raise the tax rate on land values to three per cent. That would tend, of course, to decrease the selling price of the land. If you did it in one year the decrease would be one-fifth, or nine hundred million dollars virtually. But there would be other factors operating. Take it on a ten-year basis. The land values increase one hundred million dollars a year. Then the depreciation of nine hundred million dollars in the selling price of land, through the increase of taxes on lands, is offset by the normal rate of increase in land values which would be approximately nine hundred and fifty million dollars, due to immigration and the greater demand for land space, during the ten years. Now that is it, roughly. There are many other circumstances coming in.

MR. LEUBUSCHER: The ordinary increase is fifty million?

MR. MARSH: I said one hundred million dollars.

PROFESSOR SELIGMAN: How much was it last year?

MR. MARSH: Last year I think it was thirty million dollars.

PROFESSOR SELIGMAN: How much was it the year before?

MR. MARSH: About seventeen million. As a matter of fact for the last decade up to last year, it averaged about one hundred and fifty million dollars. That is the reason I did not claim one hundred and fifty million for the period of ten years in the future.

MR. LEUBUSCHER: That one hundred and fifty million dollars, or whatever it is, is land value?

MR. MARSH: I beg your pardon. No. Of course we all recognize that Mayor Gaynor had the land assessment jumped up so that the city could borrow a hundred million dollars. Formerly the assessed valuation on an average approximated eighty-five per cent.

It was ninety per cent. at that time. It has risen very fast. Part of the increase was what you call an assessment increase, but not a real increase. I do not think it is fair to call all of the increase in the assessed value of land during those years a real increase.

MR. LINDNER: What do you think is the ordinary increase in ground values in normal times?

MR. MARSH: If you could believe the people who are selling land, it is two hundred million dollars. Have you any reason to think that the statement of Mayor Gaynor's Commission on New Sources of City Revenue, which was worked to death, that it was one hundred and fifty million dollars a year, was inaccurate?

MR. LINDNER: No.

MR. MARSH: Of course, that is a very hard thing to fix, as the tax rate varies, but I think that one hundred and twenty-five million is a fair average.

PROFESSOR SELIGMAN: You have referred several times in your picturesque language to the land speculator. Would you say as a fact that most of the land of this city is owned by what you call land speculators?

MR. MARSH: My impression is that the major part, both value and acreage, is held by people who bought for speculative purposes.

PROFESSOR SELIGMAN: The small men or the big men?

MR. MARSH: Largely, the big men. Now, there are only about —well, Mr. Allan Robinson put the figures at from one hundred and twenty thousand to one hundred and thirty thousand property owners in all New York City.

MR. STEWART BROWNE: There are over two hundred thousand property owners in New York City.

MR. MARSH: Have you the figures? If you have, you are the only man in New York City who has them.

MR. BROWNE: I say that there are over two hundred thousand.

MR. MARSH: My knowledge is that eight hundred families here own almost exactly eight hundred million dollars' worth of land. I refer to owners of record.

PROFESSOR SELIGMAN: How much land value is there in New York?

MR. MARSH: Four billion, six hundred and fifty million dollars worth.

PROFESSOR SELIGMAN: Are the remaining three and one-half billions owned by small people or large people?

MR. MARSH: The man who has got a little home does not own land worth much over a thousand or fifteen hundred dollars. Is that correct? Mr. Leubuscher is connected with several loan associations, and he knows approximately how many small home owners there are. I should say forty or fifty thousand, and their land holdings make a very small total of the whole land value in this city. Take the great acreage tracts of the Astors, the Wood-Harmon Company and others. The Wood-Harmon Company has about twenty thousand lots in Brooklyn. They have, in Prince's Bay, Heaven knows how many thousands of acres, down on Staten Island. Of course those are cold facts of land ownership which seem to me of prime importance for your Committee to have ascertained. It seems to me those were things very valuable to ascertain definitely. There are a great many small property owners, no doubt, but there is also enormous and unprecedented concentration of land values ownership. I do not consider the man who owns property worth forty thousand dollars really a very small property owner. In the small owning class I will put the man whose total holding amounts, with a home standing on it, to about five thousand dollars. There are nothing like one hundred and fifty thousand like those. Let me add here that this proposal of transferring the tax to land value would benefit these little men materially, that is, assuming that there is retardation, decided retardation, in the rate of increase in the value of their lands, because of the reduction of their tax under this proposed system. Of course, it is Manhattan Island that is going to pay the brunt of it.

PROFESSOR SELIGMAN: Are there any small land owners on Manhattan Island?

MR. MARSH: Small, is a relative term; small as compared with Carnegie, and large as compared with the poor man who is trying to live on what he owes.

PROFESSOR SELIGMAN: You think that the interests of the small owners on Manhattan Island would suffer but that their suffering would be compensated by the advantage to the city as a whole?

MR. MARSH: I don't admit that they would suffer particularly. I thought I made that clear.

PROFESSOR SELIGMAN: I thought you told us that Manhattan Island would suffer?

MR. MARSH: I said it would pay the larger proportion. I did not say it would suffer.

PROFESSOR SELIGMAN: It would not suffer then?

MR. MARSH: Nobody suffers when they pay for what they have. There are people who get things they don't have to pay for. Some of them inherit valuable land. I would suggest, however, of these so-called small home owners who have, say twenty thousand dollars or less, that their land has gone up in land value. I know, for instance, a relative of mine in this city whose land has gone up remarkably, but his building has depreciated. He did not make the land value. He admits that. None of the other small owners have made land values. As they receive the financial benefit of municipal expenditures, I don't see why they should not be willing to pay for it.

PROFESSOR SELIGMAN: You do not think that those who bought land at market values, in recent years, would be a sufficiently large number to be a factor of any importance? I mean people who have invested their money in real estate on Manhattan Island, at market rates, on the assumption that their property was a fairly secure and reasonable investment. You think what would happen to them should be of no concern to the committee, in view of the great social results that you think would follow?

MR. MARSH: I have been unable to see why government should be a sort of dry nurse for property owners and merely a cruel step-father to non-property owners. Government has no business to guarantee a profit on any socially-created value. Of course, all restrictive legislation—whether it is on land or upon what—affirmatively tends to decrease the profits. I consider that in this country we have to-day a conflict of property rights. I do not think the change we suggest should be made suddenly. If you or anybody else can suggest how the people in this country can break up the land monopoly existing here to-day in every section of our country, without curbing privilege, I should be glad to learn. You are up against it all the time. You have a conflict between privilege and the working-people. We can call it by a more euphonious name if we want to. The people who do not own property, and nearly nine-tenths of these in New York City do not, have certain rights which are in conflict with those of the property owners. Whenever a child labor law was passed there was the same old howl raised against it.—"You are robbing us of our property rights." When we passed the tenement house law, the same howl went up. Every effort you make to improve economic conditions in this country is always met with that same howl and cry, "You are interfering with our property rights"—when in fact you are interfering with property wrongs.

TESTIMONY OF MR. STEWART BROWNE,

President, The United Real Estate Owners' Association.

(NOTE.—Since the substance of Mr. Browne's direct statement is included in his brief (cf. supra, pp. 162, 208), it is not repeated here.)

PROFESSOR SELIGMAN: Do you consider the common opinion as to the land speculator to be a fallacious one?

MR. BROWNE: Absolutely.

PROFESSOR SELIGMAN: You think that speculation sometimes does good and that it is does not always harm?

MR. BROWNE: I think that ninety per cent. of speculation is good.

PROFESSOR SELIGMAN: Would you make any distinction between land speculation and speculation on the stock and produce exchanges, which everyone believes is normally useful? Would you say that land speculation, although not organized in the way in which speculation on the stock or produce exchange is organized, also has its uses?

MR. BROWNE: I think it is more beneficial to the community.

PROFESSOR SELIGMAN: You think that the land speculator is a useful member of society?

MR. BROWNE: Absolutely. He takes chances that no other man takes. Most of them are sweating blood by reason of the chances that they have taken. The speculator puts in drains and sewers and fixes up the street and builds houses for the purpose of renting them or selling them. They "hock" everything they have. They don't own a cent. Afterwards they often find that the loan is called in and they are wiped out.

PROFESSOR SELIGMAN: Would you deny, however, that, in so far as the land speculator keeps building land out of use, he may also be doing something anti-social?

MR. BROWNE: I do not think that the land speculator keeps land out of use when he sees a profit. He only keeps the land out of use when it doesn't offer a profit. He carries it along very often at a loss. I have known people living in Germany and in England who bought land along Jerome Avenue away back thirty years ago, and to-day you could not get for it what has been paid in taxes and special assessments.

PROFESSOR SELIGMAN: Would this be a fair statement of your point of view? The preceding speaker maintained that the result of this change would be great social advantages to the community as a whole, especially to the poorer classes or submerged tenth and that there would be in all probability no very great injury to the land owner, and he added that even if there were an injury, it ought to be borne for the sake of the greater good. You, on the contrary, take a diametrically opposite position.

MR. BROWNE: Absolutely.

PROFESSOR SELIGMAN: You say, in the first place, that the alleged social advantages are chimerical and that the disadvantages are very real.

MR. BROWNE: Yes.

MR. LEUBUSCHER: Mr. Browne, during the course of your remarks you frequently used the word "single taxer." Are you aware of the fact that this committee is not considering the single tax proposition?

MR. BROWNE: I understand that thoroughly.

MR. LEUBUSCHER: You said you didn't know of any man who wants to keep land out of use when he sees a profit?

MR. BROWNE: I said speculator. I did not say anybody.

MR. LEUBUSCHER: Well, then, any speculator?

MR. BROWNE: If he can make a profit.

MR. LEUBUSCHER: If he can unload at a profit he will unload?

MR. BROWNE: As a rule he does.

MR. LEUBUSCHER: Does that include the Astors?

MR. BROWNE: They are not speculators in the sense of the term.

MR. LEUBUSCHER: Are you aware of the fact that the land values of the Astors exceed their improved values about four to one?

MR. BROWNE: Suppose they do, what then? That may be beneficial to the city.

MR. LEUBUSCHER: You say it is a benefit?

MR. BROWNE: I said it may be. I do not know as a fact.

MR. LEUBUSCHER: If you, instead of having that elegant Broadway and Maiden Lane Building, should own that corner, and put up a hut on it, it is a good thing for the community?

MR. BROWNE: It may be.

MR. LEUBUSCHER: For the City of New York?

MR. BROWNE: If limiting the height of buildings is a good thing for the City of New York, if having parks and open space and breathing-spaces for the people is a good thing, then under-improvement is a very good thing for New York City.

MR. SIMON: Was it not your thought that men's speculation of the past, that is, every one of men's speculations in the past up to the present time, has been to the benefit of the city, as compound interest is to capital?

MR. BROWNE: Unquestionably so. If it had not been for those men, you would not have the City of New York to-day. You would not have any population. You would not have any enterprises. You would not have any factories, but for the so-called land speculator. And I want to say, that when I use "land" I mean "real estate" speculator.

MR. SIMON: If, as pointed out by Mr. Leubuscher, all of the vacant land now held by such people as the Astors, the Goelets, and others, all unimproved land, were improved to the limits of what we now consider intensive improvement, would the result be that the City of New York would be confined to a very small area or would it be spread out as it is at the present time?

MR. BROWNE: Well, I think it would be more compact than if it were overimproved.

MR. SIMON: Would it be a detriment or a benefit?

MR. BROWNE: It depends upon what you are trying to arrive at. As I said before, my views on that subject are entirely different from those of President McAneny, who believes that there ought to be city planning, that there ought to be distribution of area and that there ought to be height limit to buildings.

MR. SIMON: Would the cost of government be greater or less?

MR. BROWNE: It would be less if you had a more compact city. Now, you take Queens as an illustration. There is more mileage of improved streets in Queens than there is in New York City. Look at the small real estate tax in Queens as compared to Manhattan. They have more mileage there, and more improved streets in Queens than they have in New York City. That shows you how the more compact a city is the less the cost of government.

MR. SHIPLEY: Mr. Browne, you are President of the United Real Estate Owners' Association?

MR. BROWNE: I am.

MR. SHIPLEY: How many members has that association?

MR. BROWNE: Nine thousand.

MR. SHIPLEY: Are they all real estate owners?

MR. BROWNE: Yes, sir.

MR. SHIPLEY: Do you know the aggregate value of their holdings?

MR. BROWNE: I would place it roughly at approximately three hundred million dollars. It is possibly more than that.

TESTIMONY OF MR. HERBERT E. JACKSON,

Vice-President, Lawyers' Title and Trust Company.

MR. JACKSON: Mr. Chairman, in my opinion, the basis of taxation in a city is rent. It is impossible to separate the ground and the improvement upon the ground in the matter of rent. When you come to base taxation on rental values, the separation of the two items is not possible.

For the present and for a number of years past in New York City there is a very large amount of vacant land seeking improvement. The only reason it has not been improved is that people have not been found who are willing to invest or put money in it. Now, as soon as tenants are forthcoming buildings will be forthcoming also. The city is not ready for it.

PROFESSOR SELIGMAN: You think then that the inclusion of the improvements is a necessary thing, and that the exemption of improvements cannot be accomplished by any system of taxation?

MR. JACKSON: No; but I think it is dangerous to try it out, because it would be attempting by artificial means to promote what is a natural routine course of development. If you force an improvement and should put up a hundred thousand dollar building on a plot which to-day only carries a twenty thousand one, it is an economic waste of the difference for the period until conditions have grown up to it.

PROFESSOR SELIGMAN: Is there any such thing in the city, to any practical extent, I mean, as holding of land out of use?

MR. JACKSON: I think not. Of course, you may find an individual here and there if you go around and look.

PROFESSOR SELIGMAN: Would it be wise to untax buildings and to put the burden on the land?

MR. JACKSON: No, sir; I think it would be very unwise.

PROFESSOR SELIGMAN: If there were two adjoining vacant lots, each worth one hundred thousand dollars, and if you were confronted with the question—shall I put a low house on the one and a higher house on the other?—do you think that you would not be affected at all by the question as to whether that structure was going to be taxed?

MR. JACKSON: I should be affected by the knowledge of what the tax would be, of course.

MR. TANZER: That is to say, the tax is only one of the elements entering into the probable income.

MR. LEUBUSCHER: You say that the basis of taxation is rent. Then a vacant lot, for instance, at the corner of Broad and Wall Street, would not be taxed at all—should not be taxed—because it was not producing any rent?

MR. JACKSON: In those cases there would have to be an estimated rent, I presume.

MR. LEUBUSCHER: A very small rate? If a tract of land on Wall Street were sold to-day for, let us say, five million dollars, but was vacant, would you simply tax it as agricultural land?

MR. JACKSON: Yes.

MR. LEUBUSCHER: You say that you do not know of any land held out of use?

MR. JACKSON: Generally speaking none, except in isolated cases.

MR. LEUBUSCHER: Did you ever travel in The Bronx?

MR. JACKSON: Very often, yes sir.

MR. LEUBUSCHER: Did you ever see any big signs on the big Astor estate there reading, "Not for sale"?

MR. JACKSON: I have, I think so.

MR. LEUBUSCHER: Was that land held out of use?

MR. JACKSON: I have no information about it.

TESTIMONY OF MR. RICHARD M. HURD,

President, Lawyers' Mortgage Company.

MR. HURD: As a citizen, I am in favor of anything which will benefit the masses as against the classes. I think that a reduction of the rate of taxes on buildings would have a desirable social consequence, but I think it should be operated with a broader plan, to include town planning, laying out of zones, limiting the height of buildings, and, if the thing is done thoroughly, a constructive plan laid out for the entire city. I think there would be very decided advantages in the long run.

From the standpoint of a lender I think the important effects of any change which would affect values would be temporarily unfortunate, perhaps chiefly from a sentimental standpoint. But I also believe that the value of land would probably diminish, or hold stationary. As far as local conditions are concerned, we all know that we have gone through a period of severe liquidation due to local causes and outside causes, and I think we have pretty nearly reached the end of them. I hope so, at least. When the tide has turned and New York real estate becomes more active, it may be a better time to put this change into effect than when values are tending downward.

I take it for granted the Committee will consider ultimately going to the full extent of freeing buildings entirely from taxes. I should lean towards a movement in the direction of lightening the load on buildings and charging it somewhat more heavily against land. I am not a single taxer. I do not sympathize with the viewpoint that those who operate in land are all speculators and ought to be criticized. There are several classes of speculators. There is the man who will buy a few acres and not touch them until he can make a sale. Then there is the man who buys a few or many acres and who will do something to them—lay out roads, build sewers, lay sidewalks, etc. Also there is the man who buys land to build on. He is in a business. Do not class him as a speculator. He is a producer. Like all business men the speculator's work is sometimes of advantage to the city and sometimes of disadvantage. If he will go ahead in a normal way producing what the people want, can use and pay for, and with the knowledge that they want it, he is of decided service, despite his intelligent selfishness. But if he over-builds, he temporarily hurts the city.

I, as a lender, am not in favor of exceedingly high land values. I cannot see any advantage to the city as a whole or to the mass of the people in having land values very high. It is of interest or benefit only to the people who own the land, I do not care whether there are few or many. As far as the mass of the five or six million people in New York City go, the lower the land values the better off they are because it means they pay less rent.

I think the most effective method of reducing rent is by erecting new buildings. I think it is of great social advantage to spread the city over a larger area, which can be done by better transit and by laying out zones so that a builder will know just what type of building would be permitted. This would be of great advantage to lenders also. If a loan is made upon what proves to be the wrong type of improvement, do we get any benefit from having high land values? We run the risk of having them dropped the same as happened on Sixth Avenue.

As a lender, I would not be afraid, but I think most lenders would be, if the rate of taxes on buildings were less as compared with land. If this were introduced very gradually and on a rising land market, which, I think, we will have here as soon as the war in Europe is over, and probably sooner, I would not be afraid of the effects.

MR. TANZER: Do you think, Mr. Hurd, that, in order to obtain the beneficial effect of a gradual reduction in the rate on buildings, it would be necessary to accompany it by some restriction?

MR. HURD: Limit the height of buildings. I think it would be dangerous to concentrate too many buildings on one plot. It might be well to spread them over the city. I would not be afraid of a tremendous amount of new building. That is influenced by other forces. It is governed by the amount of capital available, the amount that will be loaned on it, the opinion of the builders as to whether or not they can rent or sell their buildings and the judgment of the lending forces as to whether the time is right to lend money—whether it will pay, in other words, to loan money on new buildings. If the city became overbuilt, we would stop loans. That would choke off the speculator and builder. I should say that ninety per cent. of the building in New York City is done on borrowed money.

PROFESSOR SELIGMAN: You say that you think high land values would not be good for a community. Is there any way, in your opinion, in which, in a growing community, you can prevent land values from increasing?

MR. HURD: No, sir; I do not know of any.

PROFESSOR SELIGMAN: Are not high land values the result of population and prosperity?

MR. HURD: Population heavily concentrated causes high land values. I think that can be modified somewhat. If you have good transportation, and could limit the height of buildings, the city would spread out and you would avoid to a great extent this concentration of population.

PROFESSOR SELIGMAN: What influence would you ascribe to the forces of taxation as compared with those other influences of which you speak?

MR. HURD: Quite small.

PROFESSOR SELIGMAN: You are quite sure, in your own mind, that this whole matter of taxation is of relative unimportance?

MR. HURD: Yes, unless buildings were entirely exempted from taxation. Then I think it would be of considerable importance.

PROFESSOR SELIGMAN: I understand you to say, sir, that you would not be averse, on general economic reasons, from a slight reduction in the rate of tax, but that you would be opposed to a total exemption of the tax on buildings?

MR. HURD: I would not be afraid of it. I do not know what would happen.

PROFESSOR SELIGMAN: Then, with regard to a slight reduction in the rate of tax you would be in favor of that only in case it was accompanied by these other things?

MR. HURD: I think it should be part of a complete plan.

PROFESSOR SELIGMAN: Your general conclusion would be that it is well worth considering if it were accompanied by other schemes and especially if we waited for a rising market, but that otherwise you would think it dangerous?

MR. HURD: Yes, in a falling market I do not feel sure.

MR. LEUBUSCHER: I understood you to say that there is no way of preventing land values increasing in a growing community?

MR. HURD: I know of none.

MR. LEUBUSCHER: Would not some of the speculative value on the land, water as it were, be wrung out of land values, that is, of the market value, if the tax on land values were increased?

MR. HURD: I think so, yes.

MR. LEUBUSCHER: It appears that between the years 1906 and 1914 the City of New York increased its net debt about five hundred and fifty million dollars by such things as water works, subways, schoolhouses and the like, which, of course, increased the value of the land necessarily, did they not, Mr. Hurd?

MR. HURD: By bringing population in, not otherwise.

MR. LEUBUSCHER: Land value then is population value?

MR. HURD: Multiplied by wealth—affected by wealth.

MR. LEUBUSCHER: If there were no population here, there would be no value?

MR. HURD: No.

MR. LEUBUSCHER: Then land value is substantially population value?

MR. HURD: Yes.

MR. LEUBUSCHER: Therefore these five hundred and fifty million dollars of improvements were reflected in land values, or land values during that period were increased one billion two hundred and fifty million dollars by reason of these improvements?

MR. HURD: Yes.

MR. LEUBUSCHER: Would it, or would it not be just and ethical to make those people who got the increase because of the improvement pay for that increase? In other words, pay for the debt service of the city?

MR. HURD: But they were not the only ones who benefited. The entire community benefited by them.

MR. LEUBUSCHER: The land owners—were they not the only ones who received the financial benefit?

MR. HURD: No, I don't think so.

MR. LEUBUSCHER: Will you please point out others in the community that received a financial benefit?

MR. HURD: Everybody who uses the subway gets a benefit. He can do more business by being more rapidly transported from one place to another. As to the water works, everybody gets better water, purer water, and on the whole he is a better man.

MR. LEUBUSCHER: I say financially?

MR. HURD: That is financially. Keep your health, and you get more pay.

MR. LEUBUSCHER: Is it not because of additional transit facilities that the land owner puts more rent on?

MR. HURD: In some cases, but not all.

MR. LEUBUSCHER: Where did the people who got the increase of land value profit, except by increasing the rent?

MR. HURD: They put some of the tax value on. Some of it is not there. Mr. Purdy put it there, but it is not there, I am sorry to say. (Laughter.) May I say that the effects of the subway's benefit are very complex. The land at each end of the subway has been benefited. You can get out to the end in forty minutes. The man who has an interest at the lower end is benefited. He can have his offices in a convenient location. Each end has been benefited, at the expense of the middle.

DR. WILCOX: If it be true, for the sake of argument, that the financial benefit of this last amount of improvement has gone to the land owners as such, does it not seem reasonable—debt was incurred therefor, you know—does it not seem reasonable that they should pay that debt service of one hundred and fifty million dollars a year?

MR. HURD: I do not think so.

DR. WILCOX: Why not?

MR. HURD: They should not be the only ones to pay.

DR. WILCOX: Who else got a financial benefit?

MR. HURD: Every person in the city.

DR. WILCOX: Financially?

MR. HURD: Yes.

DR. WILCOX: Has he not paid for it in rent?

MR. HURD: Yes, probably he is getting more benefit for it.

DR. WILCOX: How?

MR. HURD: The new tenement law gives him more benefit.

DR. WILCOX: He gets that from the state.

MR. HURD: Then he lives in a better house, and he gets better social service.

DR. WILCOX: Is he not paying taxes for those improvements in the shape of increased rent? If the land goes up in value the land owner is going to exact a larger return for it.

MR. HURD: No. You get better houses. The value of the land, to my mind, depends entirely on the net rent, that is to say, the rent after the payment of all expenses, capitalized by the current rates of interest. In a city of this kind, New York City, property is capitalized at two and one-half per cent. in zones of concentration, three and one-half in the higher grade of apartment houses, up to five and six per cent. in the poorer but less attractive, and seven and eight per cent. in the tenement house district; and disreputable property brings ten to eighteen per cent. It is all graded up and down. All capitalized rates change when we have a change in the money rates of the world. The European war has diminished the value of every piece of property in New York City. Interest rates are higher now than before. As soon as it is over and financed, and not until then, will we be in any better shape. There are two elements—chief elements in the value of real estate: one is rent, and the other is the capitalization rate. Rents are lower to-day than three years ago.

MR. LEUBUSCHER: The owner has attempted, has he not, to fasten on his tenant the additional tax he was obliged to pay because of debt service?

MR. HURD: I don't think he consciously did. I don't think that enters into it at all. He tried to get all he could. It all depends upon supply and demand.

MR. LEUBUSCHER: Just one final question. This plan that is now being considered of gradually reducing the tax rate on improvements during a period of ten years—would that, if it were adopted, affect the mortgage market appreciably?

MR. HURD: I would qualify my view by saying that if it were put into effect as part of a larger plan with the separation of the city into zones, which I think is very scientific and sound, with the limitation of those enormously high buildings, I should think the economic situation would improve. There are other factors to be considered. But, putting it all down together, I think the total result would be good. It would ease off the burden on the man who builds a building. It would be a slight encouragement towards improving the city and it would be a discouragement to the people who hold land out of use. My personal view of those who hold land out of use is that they lose money by it. I do not consider them a wicked lot. I think they are misguided.

MR. SIMON: With the exception of the time when the new tenement house act was being contested in the court, and no building was going on in the city at all, do you remember any other time when there was no building going on?

MR. HURD: No. Operators got a little ahead of the market at that time. They had a little over-supply, which perhaps made rents go down.

MR. SIMON: Where would the benefit come from in encouraging building, if, at the present time, the building is slightly in excess of the demand for it?

MR. HURD: I don't think it is.

MR. SIMON: It is usually in excess of the demand slightly.

MR. HURD: Yes.

MR. SIMON: And if the reducing of taxes on buildings would have a tendency to increase the amount of building, would not the lender or mortgagee think that his security was melting away by every project?

MR. HURD: I do not think it would go that far.

MR. SIMON: Then there would be no benefit if it did not go that far?

MR. HURD: It would encourage building, but I don't think it would go far enough greatly to lower values. I think there would be some lowering of land values. Of all our loans out, I hate to say how many millions were put in land values which were perhaps higher, but which are certainly lower now. They were high in boom times but are low now. It takes an unnecessarily large amount of capital to carry those buildings, and, as a lender, I do not favor these very high values. I think it would be much better to have the city spread over a large area. I don't think it can be done in that direction nearly as much as the proponent of this plan anticipates. I would, therefore, move slowly. There are many other factors more powerful than taxation.

MR. SIMON: Would, in your opinion, the first effect of commencing any such plan be a shock to the real estate itself?

MR. HURD: Yes, sir.

MR. SIMON: Until people should find themselves, there would be danger of a panic?

MR. HURD: I don't think there would be any panic.

MR. MARLING: Did I understand you to say that New York is not built up to-day, as a whole?

MR. HURD: Yes. There are different classes of property. I think some classes of property are overbuilt and cause concentration.

MR. MARLING: What classes are underbuilt?

MR. HURD: I think some of the medium class of apartments—the five-story walk-up. We have had very little building of them in the last few years. I think this is the time to go ahead on some of those. On the other kind I think the operators have got a little ahead of the time.

MR. MARLING: Do you think the underbuilt kind is in demand?

MR. HURD: Yes, sir.

PROFESSOR SELIGMAN: Have you given any thought to the effect this would have upon rentals in different parts of the city? Suppose we take off ten per cent. of the tax on buildings and put it on the land. Would there be an appreciable reduction in the rental of tenements?

MR. HURD: I doubt very much if there would be any.

PROFESSOR SELIGMAN: Suppose we took off fifty per cent.?

MR. HURD: I think it would bite then. I think the only way that would work, to my mind, would be by competition with other buildings. Of course, there are other reasons, social reasons. A lot of the people like to be close together. They must have excellent transportation before you can tempt them to go so far away. That is one item only.

PROFESSOR SELIGMAN: Would the reduction of rentals be so great as some of the gentlemen imagine?

MR. HURD: I don't think so; no.

PROFESSOR SELIGMAN: How much less?

MR. HURD: Very much less than contemplated.

PROFESSOR SELIGMAN: In regard to all these alleged social results, namely, the very great diminution in rent, which would do away with congestion, tuberculosis, etc., may I inquire whether, in your opinion, even if the scheme went through in the way proposed, these great beneficial social results would show themselves quickly or not?

MR. HURD: If it were done gradually, I think they would not show themselves.

PROFESSOR SELIGMAN: They would not show themselves at all?

MR. HURD: Very little. That would be due to the creation of other buildings in competition with the old ones.

PROFESSOR SELIGMAN: On the other hand, if, in your opinion, the alleged social benefits would not ensue, do you also believe that the alleged economic disadvantages to the owners of land would not ensue?

MR. HURD: By degrees, only as regards the value of the land. I think the value of the land would not go up, though it might slightly tend upward.

PROFESSOR SELIGMAN: As regards these great consequences, you think that if this were done gradually the social benefits would not come?

MR. HURD: Slowly.

PROFESSOR SELIGMAN: You think they would come slowly?

MR. HURD: That is, the whole result would be slow.

PROFESSOR SELIGMAN: In other words, you think that the whole influence of this is very much exaggerated, both so far as congestion is concerned, and as to land values generally. You consider this whole matter of comparative unimportance?

MR. HURD: Everything that affects a large number of people, if the results are in the right direction, I consider of great importance. I think a gradual movement in the direction of land taxation, which would not seriously injure and cripple the present owners of land who bought land in good faith at market prices, would be a change in the right direction.

PROFESSOR SELIGMAN: If you had to choose among these three plans, viz., of transferring the tax on buildings to land, of leaving things as they are, or of gradually imposing a tax on unearned increment, which would you prefer?

MR. HURD: I would prefer gradually untaxing buildings.

PROFESSOR SELIGMAN: Why?

MR. HURD: I think if the unearned increment were taxed, it would to a greater extent discourage the speculator. I have gone on record as being against speculation and I am against booming obviously high values. From the point of view of the lender, that is very dangerous. The owner wants to have some faith that sooner or later he will make a profit out of land and that it won't all be taken away. I think a gradual reduction in the building tax would be discounted, figured on as a firm amount and he would know what to count on. With a tax on unearned increment we would always be in doubt. I think results would work out better in the former case.

PROFESSOR SELIGMAN: We understand that in the main you are not favorable to this scheme unless it were conservatively and gradually carried out and provided that it would be accompanied by these other measures?

MR. HURD: Yes.

PROFESSOR SELIGMAN: Otherwise you would be opposed to it?

MR. HURD: Yes.

DR. WILCOX: Mr. Hurd, do you understand that the value of a parcel of land would be decreased by the taking of the tax off the building and putting it upon the land, if the total amount of taxes on the parcel, land and buildings, were less? Take a case like this: A parcel of real estate is worth one hundred thousand dollars, of which sixty thousand dollars is buildings and forty thousand dollars is land. Assuming that the tax on buildings is entirely transferred to the land, in this particular case the total tax on the parcel of real estate would be less, while the tax on the forty thousand dollars of land value would be much greater. What would be the direct effect upon the value of that parcel of real estate? Assume also that the total valuation of buildings that are affected is equal to the total value of land. What would be the direct effect upon the value of the parcel?

MR. HURD: That would be hard to say. The net return would be larger. The point is that the owner or the loaner would feel that the tax is levied against the land and he would figure out the tax on the land separately. He would say that the building is worth so much and the land is so much. I think he would feel the increase. The selling price would be less.

DR. WILCOX: Is it not true that, if he built another building there, the expenses of maintaining that other building would be less, and the gross return upon it or the net return upon the parcel, both land and building, would be greater?

MR. HURD: You are arguing if the actual tax was diminished the land value would increase?

DR. WILCOX: Would it increase?

MR. HURD: That is very hard to say. I think that the taxes levied against his ground value would be discounted in the price of the land. I think it would tend to make all prices of land, that is, the selling value, somewhat less, although possibly they might remain the same. What a thing is going to be worth in the future is a question of estimate. It is entirely what we think it is going to be worth. From the selling price we get the valuation on which the tax is based.

DR. WILCOX: It is alleged by both sides that this proposition, the taking of the tax off the building and putting it on the land, will tend to depreciate the value of the land.

MR. HURD: That is hard to say.

DR. WILCOX: Will the transfer of the tax from buildings to land decrease the total selling value of the real estate of the city?

MR. HURD: It may do that.

DR. WILCOX: If that is so, would it not be true that the taking of the tax off from the land and putting it on the buildings would greatly increase the selling price of real estate in the city?

MR. HURD: No, because buildings are part of the land they cover.

MR. MILLER: If it is true that the transfer of taxes to the land would not affect the value of the buildings but would greatly decrease the value of the land and there would be a decrease of the total selling value of real estate, is it conversely true that if the tax now levied on the land was transferred to the building, you would have a resultant increase in the value of the land, and not a decrease in the value of the building, and consequently a great increase in the total value of real estate?

MR. HURD: No, for the reason stated above that buildings are part of the land and hence a tax on a building is also a tax on the land it covers.

MR. MILLER: If the value of the building is decreased by an increase of the tax, then the value of the building must increase with a decrease in the tax?

MR. HURD: It only can never go above its structural value.

MR. LINDNER: You cannot go above that, of course.

MR. HURD: But they are replacing materials all the time. Land is limited. There is no monopoly in buildings, but there could be a limited monopoly in land.

MR. LEUBUSCHER: As between an increment tax and a super-tax on land values in order to take care of the increase in the budget, which would you favor?

MR. HURD: A super-tax on land only, do you mean?

MR. LEUBUSCHER: Not an increase in the general land tax, but merely a slight increase, ten per cent. or so, on the increased value of the land, merely to take care of the increase in the budget. What do you think of it? A super-tax instead of an increment tax, as has been suggested?

MR. HURD: I should favor a super-tax.

NOTE.—See the correspondence between Mr. Hurd and Dr. Wilcox, printed as an Appendix following the testimony.

TESTIMONY OF MR. ALFRED BISHOP MASON,

Representing the Manhattan Single Tax Club.

MR. MASON: I would like to suggest to the Committee a forgotten old fact and also a comparatively new plan about the increase in taxes on land values which would follow a reduction in taxes on buildings.

The forgotten old fact is that the present owners of land in this city really pay very low taxes instead of high taxes on their lands. As their complaints about increased taxes are based wholly upon their contention that present taxes are high, if this contention can be shown to be untrue, the complaints may properly be disregarded.

The real estate owners of New York have either inherited or bought their land. Take a case of inheritance, Mr. Vincent Astor's. I name him in no invidious way. It is believed that he means to be and will be a good citizen. But a great point has been made before you of the taxes now levied upon his property. Now Mr. Astor inherited all his property when it was subject to a civic rent charge for the benefit of the community of about 1⅞%. The whole capitalized value of this civic rent charge was deducted from the the value of the property to find the value upon which he paid an inheritance tax. Do not forget that pregnant fact. If a specific piece of land inherited by him was paying $6,875 per annum, which at 5% would mean a gross value of $137,500, he paid an inheritance tax on but $100,000, because the existing civic rent charge took $1,875 and the net return was therefore $5,000 which justified an inheritance tax valuation of but $100,000. If the tax had not been increased beyond 1⅞%, Mr. Astor would to-day be paying no taxes whatever. This year his specific property is to pay $2,120, an increase of $245 or a shade less than one-quarter of one per cent. on the value of the inherited property. That quarter of one per cent. is all Mr. Astor has to pay. You can justly add a good deal to ¼ of 1% before he can justly complain.

Now take a case of purchased land. The same thing is true of this. If a man to-day buys land with a potential yield of $7,000 he pays for it, not the $140,000 upon which $7,000 would pay 5% but only $100,000, because it is subject to a civic rent charge of about $2,000. The entire capitalized value of the existing civic rent charge has been subtracted from the price he pays. If taxes are not increased, he pays no taxes whatever. If they are now increased to 2.12, he pays only ⅛ of 1% in taxes. Is he entitled to complain of an increase? So much for the forgotten fact.

Now for the plan as to increment taxation. Here, as I appear as one of the witnesses for the Manhattan Single Tax Club, I am bound to explain that while the club agrees with me as to the forgotten fact, it does not altogether agree with me as to the plan. The majority of the members think my plan is too conservative. Here it is:

Let every real estate owner fix his own valuation upon his land, subject to official revision if need be. For reasons into which I will not now enter, there will be slight need of revision. Let him continue to pay the present rate of taxation upon this valuation. Let the community take annually 5 per cent. upon the increase in the value of the land above the assessed value the owner has fixed. You have left him all he owns now. You have confiscated nothing. You have even left him part of the unearned increment of the future. But you have assured an ever-increasing income to the community from the ever-increasing value which the community will give to his land in the future.

PROFESSOR SELIGMAN: We are given to understand that your testimony is to the effect that you would prefer to the scheme which we are considering the proposition for a so-called unearned increment tax. Do you not wish to express a preference in the matter?

MR. MASON: I would strongly prefer both of them.

PROFESSOR SELIGMAN: You would like to have them both?

MR. MASON: Yes, sir.

TESTIMONY OF MR. WILLIAM J. SCHIEFFELIN,

Chairman of the Citizens Union.

MR. SCHIEFFELIN: In January, 1913, the Commission on New Sources of City Revenue made its report, and, among other recommendations, suggested the advisability of having an unearned increment tax imposed. We had studied quite fully this question of reducing the tax rate on buildings and improvements. We had several hearings, and we came to the conclusion that the argument that appealed to most of the people who advocated that change was the injustice, as they believed, of having land values increased without any efforts on the part of the owner. It so happened that in foreign countries, Germany and England, an unearned increment tax had been put into effect. Only there they imposed a tax on the transfer of the land, and the Commission on New Sources of Revenue thought that would be more or less a penalty on real estate transactions. We thought it would be better, if possible, to have a uniform tax law that would apply to all properties, whether they changed hands or not. Now, the measure that was worked out was practical. We suggested that in a given year the assessed value of all property be taken as a basis of valuation and that in the following year, if the assessment increased by any other reason than by expenditures of the owner of the land, the increased value should be subject to a tax. The rate was to be one per cent., so that if there were a plot valued at one hundred thousand dollars when the basis was taken and the following year, or later, it was assessed at one hundred and ten thousand dollars, the increase of ten thousand dollars should pay a tax of one per cent. over and above the regular tax. And the justice of that appeared to be that, if this increase was not due to any effort on the part of the owner but was due to the community value, he ought to be willing to give up permanently from twelve and one-half to twenty per cent. of that increased value. Now, if the land should depreciate in value automatically the tax would come off. That, in brief, is the suggestion that was made. Prior to that date, the increase of values in New York City had been such that it was easy to point to a large increase in revenue from this measure, besides satisfying the craving, or feeling of jealousy, on the part of the people who were not land owners. I would like to suggest that this be considered as a half-way concession towards those who are advocating the measure for the reduction of the tax on buildings. That measure might be very just in my opinion, if we were going to build the city all over again. At the present time I think it would not be just at all.

PROFESSOR SELIGMAN: Do I understand, Mr. Schieffelin, that the Commission on New Sources of Revenue, considering this very proposition, finally came to the conclusion that it would not be wise to adopt it?

MR. SCHIEFFELIN: That was the unanimous opinion.

PROFESSOR SELIGMAN: What was the chief reason that led you to negative the proposal?

MR. SCHIEFFELIN: There were three reasons. You may remember that this suggestion was based on the report of the Commission on Congestion. Some of the members of that commission appeared and argued that the measure would reduce congestion. We could not get them to make clear what they meant by congestion. They agreed, as far as I can remember, that it would have to be accompanied by measures limiting the height of buildings. The second reason was that it would be very unjust. We did not have a report like that of Dr. Haig but we had enough statistics to show that the gift to the people who owned the skyscrapers along the middle of the city would be at the expense of the old buildings in the other part of the city. The third reason was that we had a good deal of testimony from men interested in real estate and lending money on real estate to the effect that, if it did not create a panic in the mortgage market, it would depreciate the values of mortgages very much. Those, sir, are the three reasons which influenced the commission. Of course, if the value of real estate was increasing rapidly all the time it might be a little different, but that is not so in this city. We thought the experiment was rather dangerous and that the increment tax would be a long step in the direction of satisfying those who plead with a great deal of earnestness, and with possibly a good deal of justice, that the community value ought to be in part returned to the community.

PROFESSOR SELIGMAN: Were the members of your commission convinced from the testimony that the effects would not bear out the contention of the advocates of this scheme, although you yourselves were very heartily in favor of accomplishing the beneficial social results which these gentlemen desired?

MR. SCHIEFFELIN: We are in favor of the results they were seeking. As a proof of that, I will say that this measure had been introduced in the Legislature in the year before, before our hearings were held. Several organizations of which I was chairman at that time, among which was the Citizens Union, voted that first year to go to Albany and support the measure, and the succeeding year they did not, on account of the arguments that had been advanced against it.

SECOND HEARING.

November 10, 1915, 2.30 P. M., Mayor's Reception Room, City Hall, Professor Edwin R. A. Seligman, Presiding.

TESTIMONY OF MR. CLARENCE H. KELSEY,

President, Title Guarantee and Trust Company, Representing the Chamber of Commerce of the State of New York.

MR. KELSEY: I thought it best to take the five major questions in this questionnaire that has been circulated, and state briefly my views as to each one of these questions.

First, as to the effect of the untaxing of buildings upon land values and upon speculation in land: It will decrease the value of land and decrease most what is least improved. It will ultimately kill speculation in land, because it aims to take away its value.

Second, as to the effect of the untaxing of buildings upon building operations, housing conditions and congestion: If there were too few buildings it would lead to erecting some, and would better housing conditions and reduce rents. But if there were too many buildings, it would not, for there can be no profit in erecting them. Under the present conditions of competition, the cities always run to an over-production of buildings and nothing should be done to foster this tendency. New York is suffering to-day from too many, with the inevitable result that they produce a poor return and are falling in value.

Third, as to the effect of the untaxing of buildings upon rent: It will not reduce rent where there are too many houses, as is now the case in New York. Rents are too low now and the landlord is not getting a fair return on his money, and no such reduction of taxation will be sufficient to induce more men to become landlords, or if it does, it will only add to the ruin.

I might state that I happen to be a director in a real estate corporation, an operating company, which owns over six hundred plots of real estate of various kinds. It has from sixty to seventy tenements, which is the lowest renting property that it has. The statistics for that whole group of buildings for the past five years show a net return on the cost of 4.15 per cent. Most of the property is carried subject to mortgage. The mortgages are for sixty per cent. of the value, and the mortgage interest is five per cent. or more. The result is that this company has been working largely for the mortgagee, and has received for all its efforts 2.86 per cent. on its investment, or about one-half of what it would if it had put its money into mortgages. That would indicate that the tenant is getting his rent for less than he should.

Fourth, as to the effect of the untaxing of buildings upon public revenue and upon public credit: It will inevitably reduce the revenue and injure the credit. Every step toward confiscating, by taxation, the value of the land lessens the desire to own it and the value gradually disappears. It is probably true that there is an over-assessment in the city at large to-day of at least five hundred millions of dollars. If the half-tax on buildings would, as its advocates declare, add still more to the supply of buildings and reduce still more the rents, the ruin of the landlords would be still greater, the over-assessment still greater, and the public credit still further impaired.

Fifth, as to the effect of the untaxing of buildings on mortgage loans: If the untaxing of buildings resulted in the single tax or the taking of all the value from land by taxation, soon there would not be any mortgage loan business. It may be the shortest cut, after all, to higher rents and to a permanent quietus on over-building. We would get down to the leasehold basis; a man would build a small building with his own money instead of a large one with borrowed money, and there would be no more trouble about the too rapid growth of the city.

In my judgment, there is no such thing as the unearned increment in land operations, except in the sense that the owner who carries it unimproved long enough generally fails to earn any increment at all. Whatever profit he does get he earns as surely and as fairly as the man who puts his money into any other raw material and carries it with his capital locked up until a demand for it arises. In fact, he is the more entitled to it for he has paid taxes on it to the state, and the man who stacks up pig iron or bricks, woolen cloth or other personal property generally escapes the tax gatherer.

The advocates of the measure say ground rents are proper revenue for local purposes since all wise municipal expenditures benefit financially only land owners. They say the people and not the land owners create ground rents. Not any more than the people create brick values, or clothing values, or flour values, or any other values. Demand creates value for everything, and there is just as much sense in taking away the bricks from the man who has made them, or the clothing from the man who has made it, or the flour from the man who has made it, and giving it to the people, as to take the land which the man has invested in away from him.

They say it will cause the substitution of healthy and safe tenements for the other kind. It will do nothing of the kind. With conditions such as exist to-day, it will have little effect in stimulating additional construction.

They say that, by removing part of the taxes on products of labor, it will encourage industry and help the unemployment situation. In the long run it will cause unemployment instead of removing it.

They say it will make those best able to pay and those benefited by municipal expenditures pay a fairer share. It is not true that the tenant and the laboring man receive no financial benefit from governmental expenditures or that they bear an unfair burden of taxes. They receive just as much protection and benefit as the landlord, and under present conditions the tenant is not bearing a fair share of the burden of taxes, and the landlord is bearing an unfair share.

They say it will encourage the construction of small homes. But if the small houses are not needed to supply the demand, the encouragement is a mistake and the man who builds will find his property worth less than it has cost.

They say it will prevent most of the speculative increases in land values and so release more money for investment in productive enterprises. That is true, and it is about the worst thing that could happen to the city. If there were no speculators in land there would be no development of the city. As a matter of fact speculation in land has produced fewer fortunes and is less profitable than most other lines of speculation or production.

PROFESSOR SELIGMAN: What would you say to the criticism that speculation in land in a city like New York holds land out of use?

MR. KELSEY: I should say it did not do anything of the kind. People are not carrying vacant land for the fun of it. They would like to get rid of it.

PROFESSOR SELIGMAN: Our attention was called at the last meeting to a sign that used to exist on an estate uptown on a large tract of land, "Not for sale." Would you say, from your point of view, that was an exceptional rather than a typical thing?

MR. KELSEY: My experience is that all land is for sale. That must be a unique instance.

PROFESSOR SELIGMAN: Your view then, Mr. Kelsey, is that the untaxing of buildings would not lead to any very great increase of building operations, because the city is now overbuilt. Is that your belief?

MR. KELSEY: Yes, if capital is prudent.

PROFESSOR SELIGMAN: You do not believe then that if buildings were untaxed we should have lower rents, much larger rooms in each building, less social evil, less over-crowding, less tuberculosis, etc.?

MR. KELSEY: On the contrary, if you take the tax off buildings and load it on to the land the tendency will be to put as much as possible on to the land to get this back.

PROFESSOR SELIGMAN: Your idea is that the untaxing of buildings would lead to more intensive use of the land?

MR. KELSEY: The owner will load it up as much as he possibly can so as to recover the increased cost.

PROFESSOR SELIGMAN: We were told at the last hearing that a more intensive use of the land might be prevented by legislation, such as limiting the height of buildings, limiting the space or area they may occupy, limiting the zones, city planning, etc. What do you think of that suggestion?

MR. KELSEY: That is a good deal like getting a man intoxicated and then giving him something to sober him up. I think you had better not intoxicate him in the first instance.

PROFESSOR SELIGMAN: On the opposite side of the question, it was intimated to us at the last hearing that the fears that have been expressed as to the bad results were exaggerated, the fears, viz., as to the calling in of mortgage loans. What do you think about that?

MR. KELSEY: I do not think they are exaggerated. The owner would be precisely in the same position as if he had hired land of Sailors' Snug Harbor and paid ground rent to them. He will not build on that because in this city people are not ready to build on leasehold land. It is impossible to get a loan on leaseholds. The lenders would feel that the first step taken towards appropriating the value of the land by the city was a warning to them to get out of the mortgage investment business. They would call in their mortgages and put their money somewhere else. They would have to.

PROFESSOR SELIGMAN: From practical experience as a money lender, how far would you say that the small man who builds his own home in the suburbs, borrowing a large part of the money, counts upon the gradually increasing value of that land in order to enable him to pay it off?

MR. KELSEY: You have seen Joseph P. Day's advertisement inviting people to buy land. It is entirely on the theory that buying now for $1,000, in three years it will be worth $2,000, in ten years $5,000 and so on; and the small owner or savings bank depositor is very much attracted by that. The skillful salesman convinces the small saver that he can become a small Astor by buying some New York City land, and thousands of them rely on and yield to those blandishments.

PROFESSOR SELIGMAN: Would you say that if the tax were put wholly upon land it would tend to induce the building of more houses?

MR. KELSEY: It will force them to build houses that are not needed or carry the land and pay a heavier tax than ever.

PROFESSOR SELIGMAN: Would this untaxing of buildings, in your opinion, tend to greater home building by the small man?

MR. KELSEY: If he does not have to borrow money and he is content to live in an untaxed house with no increase from the land, it will work.

PROFESSOR SELIGMAN: As a matter of fact, are most of the houses of the small men built that way, on borrowed money?

MR. KELSEY: Borrowed money, and with the expectation that the city will grow up to it and that the investment will prove good to him.

MR. LEUBUSCHER: You stated if it came to that pass, that the entire rental value of the land was taken, there would be practically nothing but leaseholds?

MR. KELSEY: Correct.

MR. LEUBUSCHER: And that, therefore, no one would want to build a costly structure on a leasehold?

MR. KELSEY: That is correct.

MR. LEUBUSCHER: Are you familiar with the Bankers' Trust Company Building?

MR. KELSEY: Yes.

MR. LEUBUSCHER: Do you know that the Bankers' Trust Company erected that very expensive building on ground leased at $95,000 a year from a lady in Paris?

MR. LINDNER: You have not got the facts right. It is only part of the site that is leased ground. The fact is, they would have paid very much more than the funded value of the rent for a deed to that property at the time they started to erect their building. I am speaking now from exact knowledge of the facts. I had personal charge of the transaction. The larger part of that tract is fee. It is only the extreme corner that is leased from the lady in Paris. As I said, they would have paid more than the funded value of the land for a deed.

MR. LEUBUSCHER: But they are actually paying $95,000 to a lady in Paris for a portion of the site?

MR. KELSEY: Very likely.

MR. LEUBUSCHER: They are doing it notwithstanding and they put up an elegant building on it despite the fact that they had to pay ground rent to some other person?

MR. KELSEY: Yes.

MR. LEUBUSCHER: And, as a matter of fact, John Wanamaker has quite an establishment erected on Sailors' Snug Harbor property?

MR. KELSEY: Yes. The Sailors' Snug Harbor property is a blight on the whole neighborhood and that is what would be on all property all over the city. You would find small buildings and no speculation in land. If that is what you want you will get it.

MR. LEUBUSCHER: How many land owners are there in New York City?

MR. KELSEY: There are said to be about 200,000.

MR. LEUBUSCHER: Where do you get those figures from, Mr. Kelsey?

MR. KELSEY: Well, it is just by computation of the figures.

MR. LEUBUSCHER: I understood from the Tax Department the estimate is about 95,000 to 100,000?

MR. BROWNE: The records show 200,000.

MR. LEUBUSCHER: Assuming that there are 200,000, and the population of the city is 5,200,000, do you think that the lack of prosperity of the few would adversely affect the others?

MR. KELSEY: Those particular 200,000 have been bearing all the burdens of the city.

MR. LEUBUSCHER: Are you aware of the fact that between 1906 and 1914, the net increase in the funded debt of New York City was $437,000,000?

MR. KELSEY: I can quite believe it.

MR. LEUBUSCHER: And the net increase of the land values in that same period was $1,235,000,000?

MR. KELSEY: I don't believe that it was three times the debt.

MR. LEUBUSCHER: Those figures I obtained from the Tax Department.

MR. KELSEY: They may have assessed it at that, but it has not increased that much.

MR. LEUBUSCHER: I am taking the assessed value.

MR. KELSEY: That is a mistake.

MR. LEUBUSCHER: If these figures be true, assuming for the sake of argument that the assessed valuation of the land is the real value, does this not show that the increase in the land value during those eight years was about three times the increase in the funded debt?

MR. KELSEY: Is not a great deal of that an increase in the assessment on construction?

MR. LEUBUSCHER: I am taking only land values. Now, this increase in the funded debt arose from the building of subways, increasing the water supply, school-houses, etc. All of these have a tendency to add to the value of the land.

MR. KELSEY: I suppose they have. Is there any reason why the land owner should not have a profit on his investment? What do you think most of the merchants have done in that time?

MR. LEUBUSCHER: I am not addressing myself to that. Most of the merchants would have been better off if it were not for the increased rentals they have been obliged to pay on account of the increased land values.

MR. KELSEY: There has been no increase in rentals, but a decrease.

MR. LEUBUSCHER: In the aggregate?

MR. KELSEY: By everybody—a very great decrease.

MR. LEUBUSCHER: There has been less return on the four billion in 1914, than there was on the $3,367,000,000 in 1908?

MR. KELSEY: Absolutely.

MR. SIMON: You say that there has been less actual return?

MR. KELSEY: I mean absolutely.

MR. LEUBUSCHER: In dollars and cents?

MR. KELSEY: I do. That is the trouble with real estate owners and the reason there is a blight on real estate.

MR. LEUBUSCHER: Have you any data to enlighten us?

MR. KELSEY: I am trustee of a single estate whose rents went down more than $100,000; expenses have gone up $80,000, and that is typical all over this city.

MR. LEUBUSCHER: Have you any data as to the whole city?

MR. KELSEY: Of course, I have not. I don't know everybody's business.

MR. SIMON: Do you attribute that to anything special?

MR. KELSEY: Over-production—the very thing you are trying to produce by this proposition. From 23rd Street clear down to Leonard Street you can find buildings vacated and ruined by the over-production of buildings above 23rd Street, and up there, one-half of them not paying a return to the investor. They have beggared not only themselves but others. You don't do anything to correct the tendency, but you do something to increase it. It is bad enough, and here you propose to do something to make it worse.

MR. LEUBUSCHER: You argue that this new system would lead to more intensive use of the land?

MR. KELSEY: Yes.

MR. LEUBUSCHER: Before that, you stated that we had over-production of buildings. Nobody is going to build more if we have an over-production now?

MR. KELSEY: They ought not to but they may try because they hope to get out at the expense of their neighbors. If they have land that does not pay they are going to jump in. They don't care what happens to their neighbor.

MR. LEUBUSCHER: If it did continue, what would be the result; would the result not be what you say, lower rents?

MR. KELSEY: It will, ultimately. Everything goes around in a circle. It is like unrestricted competition.

MR. LEUBUSCHER: Do you think that the increased burden of taxes is responsible for the lessening of rental values?

MR. KELSEY: Certainly.

MR. LEUBUSCHER: Are you aware that, according to the Tax Department, in 1888 real estate paid 87% of the taxes—of the budget—while in 1913 it paid 75% of the budget?

MR. KELSEY: That might be true. That is because the budget has gone up. There has been no let-up on real estate owners.

TESTIMONY OF MR. CHARLES T. ROOT,

Vice-President, Business Men's Association to Untax Industry.

MR. ROOT: Buildings, just as much as machinery or merchandise, involve business of some kind. Taxes are naturally repressive. I suppose that "no tax on industry" would be the strongest advertisement that New York could put out. It follows that, if we wish to encourage business and industry in this town we should tax them as little as possible. We have a certain amount of money to raise but we should get the money elsewhere. I think that everybody will admit that taxes are repressive of anything they are put on. If a community does not want saloons it naturally taxes saloons; if it wants to diminish the supply of dogs it loads a tax on dogs. If a community wants less buildings or obsolete buildings all it has to do is to tax them in accordance with their physical value. A common way to tax is according to value, and it is the logical way to secure a supply of old buildings. Now, if a town wants less business transacted within its limits it only has to lay a stiff tax on business to drive away so much of it as can be carried on where conditions are less severe.

Taking up the question of how far New York is justified in unburdening its building and other industries, I have this to say: Any private investment, if wisely made, it is expected will return to the investor in some form of measurable value with a profit. I think there is no public expenditure that is not governed by exactly the same rule. I don't want to say that all public money is wisely expended; but the part prudently invested does come back with profit in measurable value. New York City invests in streets, sidewalks, sewers, light, police, and education every year, and every year it comes back in rent for the land on which the city is located. That is the way it is done. A continuous closed circuit of its vital fluid is necessary to any healthy organism. If anybody is continually losing blood, he is going out of business entirely, or else must get a transfusion of somebody else's blood to keep him going. If a city permits a large part of the income which it gets very obviously from its own investment—if it allows it to go into the hands of others than into the purse of the city, it breaks the circuit and it does not come back to where it started from. There must be a transfusion of some other kind of blood, the blood of labor, of construction, or whatever it may be, to make up the deficit. I think it is quite clear, that, as the average city investment comes back in the form of ground rent, enough of it ought to go back into the public treasury to replace the amount invested.

Now, Mr. Kelsey seemed to assume that we propose to take the long jump from the proposition now before the city to complete single tax, which he claims would take away every cent of the land and confiscate it, as the opponents say, to the public purpose. I anticipate no such result at any time. I think anything that would defeat private ownership in land would be a great mistake and a great misfortune. I think it is impossible for any community to administer its land as economically and effectively as is done by private owners. At present twenty-five to thirty per cent. of the ground rent goes to the public treasury, and the rest of it stays in the hands of those people who have bought the right to collect it. Of course, the amount demanded for that right is what the price of land is. But that is not land value. The only value that land has is for use. And that value for use capitalized is the basis of the price of land.

It is unaccountable to me why people should consider a town rich because of the high price of its land. I mean in any community you will find men boasting that its land is worth five billion dollars, therefore, it is a rich city. They don't seem to recognize that is the biggest debt that the people owe. We have five billions of land prices owned by 200,000 persons. I assume that if the value is five billion it is because it will earn 5%. That means that somebody must earn $250,000,000 each year to pay for it. The rest of the people swell up with pride and say it is a fabulously rich city; it has got so much worth of land. Now the acknowledged debt of the city is about one billion of dollars, but here is a debt owed by five million people to 200,000. I see no reason why the five million should be proud of it.

On the price of land have been built up two great structures, which, in the public interest, should be lowered. One is this tremendous card-house of mortgages, built up on the right to collect and pocket the economic rent, and the other is the enormous city debt caused by the ease of borrowing ten per cent. on this enormous price of land.

If anything could bring down the price of land it seems to me the advantages would be very considerable. If it is done gradually by transferring industrial taxes little by little, it can be accomplished without serious disturbance of any legitimate business. It ought to take twenty-five years to go from the present false basis to the true basis, the rents created by the expenditure of the city's money. This latter is the normal plan of obtaining public revenue.

The ground rent is always more than sufficient for the support of the government. In New York City, it costs $200,000,000 for us to run the city and pay its enormous debt service; but the ground rents are very much larger, sufficient to pay this levy and leave ample compensation to the land owners for administering the stewardship of the land.

Moreover, this plan of obtaining public revenue would make for greater symmetry in the development of this city. I heard a very striking statement by a man the other night. He said that one-half of the mileage, the lineal mileage of the streets of this city goes by vacant land.

I called up the Department of Street Cleaning and found out officially that the mileage of the streets of the three Boroughs of Manhattan, Brooklyn and The Bronx is 1,433 miles. Now, one-half may be an exaggeration, but suppose it is approximately true, then the city has built, and must maintain at the expense of the people, 700 miles of streets, which are not yet needed. That enormous gridiron of streets is unnecessary. Think of our having to maintain this enormous mileage of streets and roads in order to have people pass land they cannot buy. Think of the waste of time and money by the people who must travel to and from their work over 700 miles of unused, unnecessary streets which lead past the vacant lands. Think of the saving of time, strength and cash, if people lived within walking distance or a short ride of their work instead of five or ten miles away in order to find land within the limit of their purse. All of these things would have resulted had New York grown up under the normal revenue system.

PROFESSOR SELIGMAN: As regards your last point, about a compact city, it has been brought out before us by some that one of the objections to the scheme of untaxing buildings is that it would cause too intensive a use of the land; do away with the gardens of the small man, and cause skyscrapers and immense buildings all over the slums. What is your opinion as to the tendency of this untaxing of buildings to bring about that unsocial result?

MR. ROOT: It does not seem to me likely to bring about that result. If it had the desired effect of reducing the cost of land, and if, therefore, instead of having to pay $500 per front foot for the land, which, perhaps, he could not afford to put a garden on, the price of it was reduced by a different form of raising revenue, to $75 a front foot, it would not tend necessarily to restriction of the land to be used; rather the reverse. In speaking of a compact city, I do not, of course, advocate a solidly built-up city. We must have a system of parks. I think that our present park system is damaged by the fact that there is so much temporarily vacant land that the needs for breathing-spaces are not sufficiently foreseen and provided for.

PROFESSOR SELIGMAN: Your interesting rejoinder then, rests on the assumption that the selling price of land will be considerably reduced? I want your opinion on that point because it has been rather emphatically proclaimed to us by some of the other witnesses that the result would not be to reduce the selling value of the land. You think the result of this scheme would be throughout the city to reduce the selling value of the land?

MR. ROOT: That would be the tendency.

PROFESSOR SELIGMAN: I understand you to say that you believe that the working out of the scheme of untaxing buildings ought to take about 25 years?

MR. ROOT: It ought to take that, at least. But I think that if we took off only half the tax on buildings it ought not to take such a length of time as that.

PROFESSOR SELIGMAN: You would not be in favor of immediate total exemption of all buildings from taxation?

MR. ROOT: I think that the present time would be an unfavorable one to make such a severe change.

TESTIMONY OF MR. ADOLPH BLOCH,

Member of the Board of Counsel of the United Real Estate Owners' Association; Member of the Advisory Council of Real Estate Interests.

MR. BLOCH: My experience of twenty years has brought me into contact with a great many people of the middle class, who, by dint of hard work and industry, have accumulated something to invest and have invested that in real estate. I have a great deal of concern for those people.

The profits from ownership of real estate have been very much exaggerated, both as to income and increment. I am most familiar with houses of the smaller type, the five-story double-flat house in Yorkville and the Bronx, averaging $25,000 in value, upon which there may be a savings bank mortgage of two-thirds of that amount. The owner of that house really owns one-third and the other two-thirds is owned by the mortgagee. The income from the ordinary, well-rented house, to which the owner gives a great deal of personal attention—ofttimes acting in the capacity of housekeeper or janitor—is not much more than the income he would have received if he deposited his money in the ordinary savings bank. The difference is scarcely more than one or two per cent. There are, of course, cases where it is slightly higher. There are more cases where it is less. That one, two or three per cent. is a mere pittance for the amount of work, labor and time expended on the house, the risk and worry of being at some time deprived of the savings of a lifetime by the enactment of such laws as that now under consideration by your Committee.

There seems to be no question that the proponents of this measure are on the road to the pure single tax theory. I can scarcely repress a feeling of indignation when I hear the statement made at this hearing about the city appropriating the land and administering it itself, or about some measure that is ostensibly a tax measure but is not really intended as an income producer at all. Those in favor of the plan deliberately say, "Let us adopt some measure for the benefit of the whole community, regardless of property rights. Let us depress values, make land cheap, and it will be freer and all people will be able to use it freely." I speak for myself as well as others, as nearly all of my earnings are invested in real estate. I am talking about real estate of which I am proud. The real estate that I own is managed so that the tenants may live decently, properly and respectably; I can conscientiously point with pride to the houses. I am talking about the conservative man, who, when he bought a house, transferred his savings account for a deed to that property. All that represents labor, and the hardest kind of sacrifice and work. So that, therefore, I say that is my property. I paid for it. I have earned the money in order to buy it. I have a right to rely upon the fact that I will be protected in the ownership of that property. I cannot bear to think that anybody would confiscate that which I own, because that would be spoliation under the guise of law.

I think it will be conceded that imposing a burden upon land will tend to depress the value of land. If you artificially depress the value of that land and make it cheaper, you are depriving the man that I represent and me of that which I have honestly acquired. You have taken it away from us. I have invested, say, $10,000 in real estate. You arbitrarily make it worth only $6,000 or $7,000. If it is going to be reduced to that extent, you are wiping out the equity of the owner, who had but one-third. You also wipe out a substantial part of the mortgagee's interest. If the deliberate purpose is to make that land cheaper, you take away something that belongs to somebody and that means confiscation. You do something which, to my mind, is an immoral thing. If you say that the public need is superior to the need of the individual, then you may as well say, we will take your savings in the savings bank because the city's needs are such that we must have more money. It is absolutely unjustifiable, absolutely unwarranted, and an immoral proposition.

One question you are considering is: Does it lead to intensive use of property? Yes, of course, it does. I have in mind a seven-story apartment house on Park Avenue in the eighties. It is on a corner. The building is about ten years old. It has the improvements of a house of that age. The land is assessed at $265,000, the land and building together for $365,000, so that means $100,000 is the value of the building and $265,000 is the value of the land. Now, immediately adjacent to that building is another building similarly situated. It is on a slightly better street. The land is assessed for $300,000. It is built on. It has the highest building of that type that is permitted to be built—17 stories high. Now, that is taking advantage of every inch of building that is permitted by law upon that plot of land. There you have the intensive use of that land for apartment house purposes. The land and building are assessed at $1,000,000. The building is assessed at $700,000 and the land for $300,000. The lady that owns the first house thought she was going to get an income for the rest of her life. The savings and earnings of her husband have been invested in that property. I do not know what the equity is. I imagine that it is not more than $100,000. She thought, I suppose, that the income on $100,000 ought to be fairly sufficient for her to live decently and respectably. What is the effect of the building of the adjoining house? What would the effect be if you untaxed buildings? She discovers that the taxes are gradually going up so high on Park Avenue that the interest or income from that property is very much diminished. For seven years the rent has not gone up. Now, suppose you had a law such as you propose to enact, wherein you provide for the ultimate untaxing of that building, what would the effect be on a building worth $100,000? It means that the burden will be placed upon the land. It means that the taxes will be still higher. It means that the next house will be taxed very much less. There you have the proportion of seven to three—a building worth $700,000 on land worth $300,000. The first house cannot be profitably maintained as it is to-day. What will be experienced after you put more taxes on that land? Now, if she pulls down that house and erects a building of the same type as the one adjoining, she would first lose the value of the building altogether, that is, the $100,000. The land and building would be depreciated to $260,000, or so, and her equity would be wiped out. That does not take into consideration the depreciation of the land itself. It would involve the loss of all the money she had invested.

Another point: Does it lead to congestion? Of course, it does. The first building that went up on Park Avenue paid very well. It was high and modern. The land was cheap and rental conditions were good. The next house that went up was profitable and paid a fair return. All along Park Avenue you will find block after block from Fiftieth Street up to the nineties where they are putting up large buildings. Soon you will get to a point where over-production exists. There is over-production there, to my mind, already. Soon the mortgage market will tighten for loans on Park Avenue apartments. We have had precedent for that. A few years ago the heads of lending institutions said they would not lend another dollar on any loft building in the city. You are in the hands of the loan institutions. When they say stop, they stop, and all avenues are closed. They merely will not lend you any more money. That is all there is to it.

In talking about the city debt and about the constitutional limit of ten per cent. of the assessed valuation of property, you must bear in mind that real estate has borne and paid nearly 87 per cent. of the entire sum collected in taxes by this city. In my judgment, real estate is assessed at its full value and a little bit more. The debt margin of the city is very small. I think the Comptroller recently estimated it at about $11,000,000. It may be twice or three times that, but it is not five times that. The city owes a thousand million dollars. The assessed valuation is approximately ten billion dollars. You are dangerously near the point of impairing the obligation of the city's bonds. If you depress the value of the real estate, it means that the bonded indebtedness of the city will be impaired and you will have exceeded the constitutional limits.

I do not believe that there are many cases where people deliberately retain or refuse to sell their land simply in the hope of getting very large returns by reason of any unearned increment. There may be some rare instances of it. If land gets to a point where the owner can see a fair profit he generally wants to sell. If he does not sell then, he may lose his chance and never get it again. That experience has been had by people on Fifth Avenue south of Thirty-fourth Street, where there has been a great depreciation in value.

I don't know personally of any great increase in value of land. I rarely hear of it except in auctioneers' advertisements. I bought some land at an auction which was widely advertised—the Joel Wolff Estate at Bronx Park East, near White Plains Avenue and 201st Street. I was told and the advertisement stated that that boulevard was going to be the Fifth Avenue of The Bronx. I went out to the lots that I had picked out on the map and found that they were opposite the entrance to Bronx Park. I referred to the advertisement, and I found that was about the same location relatively as the Plaza Hotel. (Laughter). That piece of property nearly proved my undoing. I paid $1,100 for the corner lot and $900 for the inside lots. I bought four and I paid about $3,500 for them. According to the terms of sale I was offered an opportunity to pay one-third in cash and the balance on mortgage. I did that. I thought in three years the land would be worth more. I had to pay taxes on that property every year, and also tremendous assessments. I had to pay $500 on property worth $3,000 for the laying and paving of a street. There are no houses there. Some of the flagging of the pavement has been taken up and is now used for neighborhood door steps. At the end of three years the mortgage became due. Fortunately I had the money and paid it off. I am quite sure I cannot get now what I paid for the property. I do not think I will ever get what I paid for it originally, figuring taxes and assessments and compound interest on the money. If I had put my money in a savings bank I would be much better off. But, how about the poor purchasers who did not have the experience I had, or that I thought I had, in real estate matters? How about the workingmen who were lured into buying this land? They brought their savings bank-book with them and handed it over, and that is the value of the land. It is not what the community made it, but it represents that man's earnings. To me that is his labor. When the three years were over I do not know what happened to these purchasers but I think a great many of them lost their property.

PROFESSOR SELIGMAN: As a matter of fact, do the increases in assessed land values in the city represent profits to the land owners?

MR. BLOCH: No; they do not.

I have a friend who lives on One Hundred and Fifty-third Street, near Riverside Drive. He has lived there for many years. He told me that one must be almost a millionaire to keep a home there; that his taxes have gone up enormously, and he has to keep on paying and paying more all the time. Now, that does not represent any unearned increment. He has been adding money all the time. He could not sell now if he wanted to. He is losing money on it.

MR. LEUBUSCHER: Mr. Bloch, do you believe in an excise tax?

MR. BLOCH: Yes, I do.

MR. LEUBUSCHER: Is that a tax imposed primarily for the purpose of revenue or for the purpose of regulation?

MR. BLOCH: I think both. I think it is a good means of raising revenue, but it regulates at the same time.

MR. LEUBUSCHER: If you believe, therefore, in that sort of a tax for both purposes, why do you object to a tax imposed as this is proposed to be imposed for both purposes?

MR. BLOCH: Why, I would say that when you talk about a tax measure you have in mind the revenue produced by it. When you refer to a liquor tax you are considering a different problem. When you talk about deliberately depressing values and depriving me of that which I own and have honestly acquired under existing conditions you talk of robbing me.

MR. LEUBUSCHER: Do you think that liquor store keepers who pay a larger tax now under the existing conditions of the liquor tax than they did last year, are being robbed by an increase of that liquor tax?

MR. BLOCH: I think that is a relative term. I would not say they are being robbed. I think the imposition of such a tax may be a fair and reasonable tax, considering the commodity sold, but when you go beyond the province of reasonableness you go towards confiscation.

MR. LEUBUSCHER: Who is to be the judge of the reasonableness? You, Mr. Bloch?

MR. BLOCH: We will leave that to the community.

MR. LEUBUSCHER: How about this proposition?

MR. BLOCH: I only say, leave it to fair-minded men.

MR. LEUBUSCHER: Who is to select the fair-minded, honest men?

MR. BLOCH: Any proposition like this can be determined by any fair-minded man, capable of understanding the subject.

MR. LEUBUSCHER: You have no objection to a referendum on it?

MR. BLOCH: Yes, I have. It took me five years to understand something about this complex subject. The question should not be referred to people who have no opportunity for investigation.

MR. LEUBUSCHER: This poor widow. What did you say the assessed value of her land is?

MR. BLOCH: $265,000.

MR. LEUBUSCHER: What was it assessed at ten years ago?

MR. BLOCH: I do not know.

MR. LEUBUSCHER: Probably it was $100,000, would you say?

MR. BLOCH: I don't know; I would be speculating.

MR. LEUBUSCHER: Is it not a fact that that section of Park Avenue has increased very largely?

MR. BLOCH: There has been a large increase. I do not believe there has been an increase of $100,000 in that one place.

MR. LEUBUSCHER: If this poor widow sold out now she might get not $100,000, but perhaps about $90,000, or even $50,000?

MR. BLOCH: If she sells now, she would probably be wiped out. The character of that building is obsolete compared with the buildings surrounding it.

MR. LEUBUSCHER: That happens under the present taxing system?

MR. BLOCH: Yes.

MR. LEUBUSCHER: You cannot blame the proposed tax system for that building becoming obsolete.

MR. BLOCH: I think things are bad enough without making them much worse.

MR. SHIPLEY: Do you think that the general well-being of the real estate situation is necessary to the welfare of the city?

MR. BLOCH: I think so.

MR. SHIPLEY: Do you regard the lending of money and the placing of mortgages as necessary to the well-being of real estate?

MR. BLOCH: I think, under conditions as they exist to-day, it is absolutely essential.

MR. SHIPLEY: Do I understand you to say that there is a money-lending ring in New York City, which could issue an edict under which money would not be loaned in a given section?

MR. BLOCH: I think conditions are such that appraisers in New York agree as to what should be done and what should not be done.

MR. SHIPLEY: That is tantamount to a mortgage trust?

MR. BLOCH: I am perfectly willing to call it that, for that is what it amounts to in the end. It is a ring. I do not want to imply anything improper. It is a combination which is cohesive. It sticks together.

DR. WILCOX: You spoke of the fact that there had been a great change in values in different parts of the city, and you look with abhorrence upon any individual who would advocate a scheme which would, with knowledge of the individual in advance, result in a re-shifting of values. Do you think that the subway system which is now under construction will result in a destruction of a great many values in different portions of the city and the transfer of such values to other portions?

MR. BLOCH: The effect of so extensive a scheme of subway construction is to bring about the destruction of values in Manhattan in a great many cases.

DR. WILCOX: Do you look with horror upon the individual who advocates that plan or that scheme?

MR. BLOCH: Not with horror; but I think it is unwise in making it as extensive as it is. We lack transportation facilities in the Borough of Manhattan, yet we are going to get them in abundance in Queens, Pelham Manor, and Richmond.

TESTIMONY OF FREDERICK L. CRANFORD,

Vice-President, The Business Men's Association to Untax Industry.

MR. CRANFORD: Without regard to the ethical or moral standpoint, I would like to make an argument urging you to make a report favoring the gradual reduction of the tax rate on buildings for practical and business reasons.

If you will attend the public hearings on the important questions affecting the vital interests of New York at the Board of Estimate, you will find those meetings dominated by a very intelligent group of real estate men, and if you will listen to their talk, you will be convinced that the growth of New York City is dependent upon their efforts. It is not an exaggeration to say that their influence politically is more potent at the present time than the commercial and business interests of this community. They are convinced that they create the land values.

The foundation upon which rests the growth of New York City consists of, first, the unrivalled facilities of the port of New York as the principal gate of commerce of the United States, and, second, the growth and development of the manufacturing and commercial interests which find in this community a favorable economic opportunity. The factors looking toward the improvement of the facilities of the port of New York at the present time are the construction of the Panama Canal, the Erie Canal and the dock facilities of the city.

You must agree that the commercial and manufacturing industries of Greater New York create the values of real estate and afterwards maintain those values. Your Committee has an opportunity to promote this interest, or you have an opportunity to promote the growth of values independent of and at the expense of those industries. There is only one alternative, as I see it. You must either increase the tax on land, or advocate the placing of an increased tax on the industries of this community, because the tax bill is going to be greater. An increasing tax upon land and a decreasing tax upon personal property and buildings would tend to diminish the fixed charges of business enterprises and would show an appreciation by the government of the city of the fact that a manufacturing establishment giving regular employment is a valuable asset to a community. It would tend to stop the continued movement out of New York City of manufacturing plants, particularly those which need a large area of land for their successful operation, and it would tend to make it more easy for them to extend the area of their plant. It would also tend to stop the movement to northern New Jersey of manufacturing establishments formerly located in New York City—in response to the inducement those communities offer of long periods of tax rebates and of cheap locations.

It is a fair statement to make that, in building the public works of New York, in developing the business opportunities, and in constructing the necessary facilities of a great city, you thereby create land values more than equivalent to their cost; and this community must, in the future, take of these values a revenue sufficient to maintain the commercial and manufacturing position of the city and to encourage its growth. No message, as I take it, is more plainly written on the wall as we look at the revolution now in progress in Europe than that we must promote our industrial efficiency. It is inefficiency and wastefulness to permit industrial opportunities of the city to be capitalized into land values for the benefit and enjoyment of those who are not engaged in production.

PROFESSOR SELIGMAN: I take it that your argument means this: We should be very careful to look after the business interests of the community in this matter rather than the real estate interests, and that this contemplated change will be a good thing, first, because it will increase the business of building houses; and, second, because it will decrease the rentals of business premises. Am I correct in my statement?

MR. CRANFORD: My argument, as I tried to give it, was to urge that you report in favor of decreasing taxation on the personal property engaged in business. When I talk about that, I mean buildings, machinery, etc. The building operations of the city are entirely dependent, as I understand it, upon, first, providing for a man the means of making a living in some useful industry; after he has got his living, it is time enough to look after building a home for him.

TESTIMONY OF MR. LOUIS V. BRIGHT,

President, Lawyers' Title and Trust Company.

PROFESSOR SELIGMAN: Is it your opinion, Mr. Bright, that the speculator's activities in land in the City of New York have been a good thing or a bad thing?

MR. BRIGHT: On the whole I don't think speculation has been detrimental. It has led to the building up of sections which would not have been built up otherwise.

PROFESSOR SELIGMAN: Has it led to the withholding of land on a large scale out of use and thus decreased the supply of houses and increased the rentals to the people who live in the houses we now have?

MR. BRIGHT: I do not think it has. As far as I can remember land has been freely dealt in.

PROFESSOR SELIGMAN: Do you think that the untaxing of buildings would normally lead to an increase in the quantity of buildings offered?

MR. BRIGHT: I think that would be the tendency. Of course, one must answer that question within limitations; that is, the number would increase to the extent that you could get capital to go into such improvements.

PROFESSOR SELIGMAN: When we come to the new equilibrium and have a larger supply of buildings, do you think rents would be lower than to-day? If so, to what extent?

MR. BRIGHT: This is a very difficult question to answer. If capital could be obtained, improvements would increase and rents might remain stationary or decline slightly. If capital could not be obtained rents would not go down but would probably rise.

PROFESSSOR SELIGMAN: Why do you think that capital could not be obtained?

MR. BRIGHT: I think that a change in the tax methods would make real estate mortgages less inviting for investment purposes. I think the natural tendency of capital would be to avoid these investments if equities could be destroyed by the taking away by the state of the value of real estate outside of the use value.

PROFESSOR SELIGMAN: Do you think that these alleged advantages of the system, such as lower rents, more spacious buildings, etc., would be attended by this friction to which you refer?

MR. BRIGHT: That is my judgment. I also think the so-called advantages of the change in method are exaggerated.

PROFESSOR SELIGMAN: On the other hand, would you maintain that the fears of real estate owners and of the mortgage holders are also exaggerated?

MR. BRIGHT: What exactly do you mean by exaggerated?

PROFESSOR SELIGMAN: I mean this: You have just stated, that, in your opinion, the anticipated benefits of the scheme are exaggerated.

MR. BRIGHT: Yes.

PROFESSOR SELIGMAN: Now, I ask you, Mr. Bright, whether you think that the anticipated injuries from the system are also exaggerated. By injuries I mean, first, a possible panic due to the calling in of mortgages; secondly, a decrease in land values and the consequent concentration of property; and third, a more intensive use of the land, which would mean greater congestion. Those are the three points I refer to.

MR. BRIGHT: I am inclined to think that those results would happen.

PROFESSOR SELIGMAN: Suppose you take them up in turn, and give us a fuller opinion.

MR. BRIGHT: I think that the tendency would be to more intensive improvement of land. I think there is no question about that. I think that there would be a very large calling in of mortgages. Under the conditions, I do not know whether they could be replaced. The equities would be seriously impaired, if not wiped out. Now, as to the decrease of land values, the effect would be very serious in the case of those who had invested money in small properties.

PROFESSOR SELIGMAN: In case this new scheme was to be adopted would there be, in your opinion, a decrease in the selling value of real estate?

MR. BRIGHT: I think there would be.

PROFESSOR SELIGMAN: What do you say about such a proposition as this: To leave the taxes just as they are now on buildings and lands, but to provide that any future additional revenue that might be needed should be raised in part at all events, if that were sufficient, by taking a small percentage of the increase of value of the land?

MR. BRIGHT: I think that is a much fairer scheme. It is open to some objection, principally this: Who is going to make good the loss on the land when the land depreciates?

PROFESSOR SELIGMAN: Do you believe that the so-called increase in land values, as a whole, represent nothing more than the purchase price plus compound interest thereon, plus taxes and assessments? Or would you say that there has been over and above that amount a distinct profit to the holder of the land in the course of the last generation or two?

MR. BRIGHT: I think there is some profit, but I think the amount is grossly exaggerated.

PROFESSOR SELIGMAN: Do you think that it is entirely unfair to give figures of increases in land values as representing a profit to land owners?

MR. BRIGHT: That is not just.

DR. WILCOX: What is congestion and do you think that congestion would be increased?

MR. BRIGHT: I think the effect if you untax buildings would mean the more intensive development and occupation of the land. The tendency now is for a builder to put up the largest building he can, provided capital can be obtained to erect the structure. This tendency if you untax buildings would be increased, because it would create a form of wealth from which revenue would be derived and which would not be subject to taxes.

DR. WILCOX: Your idea is that it would create more buildings on the land?

MR. BRIGHT: More in height.

DR. WILCOX: There would be more of them?

MR. BRIGHT: Possibly more of them.

DR. WILCOX: That would not result in congestion of business or population?

MR. BRIGHT: Not necessarily.

DR. WILCOX: It is a congestion of improvements?

MR. BRIGHT: Yes. We are keeping down the height of buildings now for reasons of health and safety.

DR. WILCOX: Would not the natural effect of congestion of improvements be the lessening of the congestion of population and business which are now considered great social evils and have been so for generations in New York?

MR. BRIGHT: I do not think you would get that.

DR. WILCOX: How could you otherwise if you have more buildings and have the same number of people?

MR. BRIGHT: Because they go to the points or centers of activity to live a social life. I do not think the tendency would be to spread the people out in the remoter sections.

DR. WILCOX: What would become of the land in the remoter sections?

MR. BRIGHT: It would go down, and there would be less tendency to develop it.

MR. LEUBUSCHER: You say that speculation has not led to holding lands out of use?

MR. BRIGHT: I don't think there is any large holding of land to-day that cannot be bought and sold at a fair price, except that held for individual use.

MR. LEUBUSCHER: You are aware of the value of the holdings of the Astors?

MR. BRIGHT: I know that they are very large.

MR. LEUBUSCHER: Is it not a fact that at least twenty-five per cent. of the value of their land is held out of use?

MR. BRIGHT: I do not think so.

MR. LEUBUSCHER: I just want to get the facts. Is it not a fact that they own one hundred acres in The Bronx that are not developed, that are fenced in and with a sign there—at least it was there within a couple of years ago, saying "Not for sale." Is that not a fact?

MR. BRIGHT: I do not know.

MR. LEUBUSCHER: I know it personally, because I saw it.

MR. BRIGHT: Well, if you know it, the fact must be so. Nevertheless I would like to undertake to buy it just now if I were authorized to do so.

MR. LEUBUSCHER: Have you known of the Astor family selling property?

MR. BRIGHT: Yes.

MR. LEUBUSCHER: Have you known of the Astor family selling land within the last fifteen years?

MR. BRIGHT: A great deal of it. I could furnish you with a large number of conveyances.

MR. LEUBUSCHER: When was that?

MR. BRIGHT: There are a great number of them.

MR. LEUBUSCHER: For a great many years, from the time of Jacob Astor, until a couple of years ago, they did not have any sales at all.

MR. BRIGHT: I would not say about that. I think they held land—

MR. LEUBUSCHER: Do you think the fact that land values have been more heavily taxed recently has anything to do with the Astors beginning to sell?

MR. BRIGHT: I do not think that is the reason.

MR. LEUBUSCHER: You said to Professor Seligman that you thought an increment tax would be fairer than the one proposed?

MR. BRIGHT: I think it has objections.

MR. LEUBUSCHER: How would that compare with a super-tax on land values?

MR. BRIGHT: What do you mean by that?

MR. LEUBUSCHER: What I mean is this: This next year we will have to raise, owing to the direct state tax of about thirteen million dollars, more than we raised in 1915. Would it be fair to raise that by adding an extra tax—just a little tax of twenty mills on to land values—that is a super-tax?

MR. BRIGHT: To put it on both would be fairer. I don't see any difference between this tax and any other.

MR. FIELD: We hear some discussion now about the attractiveness of security investment, bank investment, etc.

MR. BRIGHT: Yes.

MR. FIELD: Is that having any tendency to withdraw investment from real estate because of the fact that people can get larger returns from good, sound securities to-day, than they can get from real estate?

MR. BRIGHT: I think that is true.

MR. FIELD: To what extent does that effect real estate?

MR. BRIGHT: I cannot estimate the exact extent.

MR. FIELD: In your loans you figure as security both the land and building?

MR. BRIGHT: Yes.

MR. FIELD: Assuming that the selling value of the land is taken away for any reason from the man who made a loan for the erection of a building, would you increase or decrease the rate of interest that you charge now?

MR. BRIGHT: It would have to be increased. Then we would be lending almost entirely on the security of the building.

MR. FIELD: You would charge a certain sum for the deterioration of the building, so that it would cost the builder more for money?

MR. BRIGHT: Yes.

MR. FIELD: Would that increase the price of the building?

MR. BRIGHT: I think the operating cost would be increased.

MR. FIELD: Other things being equal, the tenant would have to pay rent based on the increased operating cost in order to give the builder back his money?

MR. BRIGHT: Yes.

MR. FIELD: He would have to pay a higher rent.

MR. BRIGHT: Yes.

MR. FIELD: Then the tendency would be to raise rents instead of lowering them?

MR. BRIGHT: Yes.

MR. FIELD: Could you make them pay that?

MR. BRIGHT: You could, assuming you have a situation where a man must either have the place or do without.

MR. MARLING: Do you consider it unfair to impose an increment tax?

MR. BRIGHT: That is the opinion I mean to give. It is fairer, however, in my judgment, than the single tax.

MR. SIMON: This supposed sign marked "Not for Sale," put up by a large holder for the purpose of withholding property, the fact is, it was put there at the request of an auctioneer who had a large auction sale of 300 lots adjoining this land. He wanted to show that this property was not in the market. But that large number of lots sold did come into the market notwithstanding the sign and in the course of several years no buildings have been put up on the land that was sold. They did not put that sign on the property to withhold it from sale, did they?

MR. BRIGHT: I think it is a joke.

TESTIMONY OF MR. ROBERT D. KOHN,

Architect.

MR. KOHN: I am neither an expert on this subject nor have I formed any opinion as to the results of this measure. I want to apply myself to one phase of it—the importance of certain other regulations which must come if any such proposed scheme is to be seriously considered. I refer particularly to the necessity of districting the city.

I do not know how familiar it is to you what great damage is done in New York City by the wrong sort of improvements; how the threat of the wrong sort of improvement on some piece of property can be used for blackmail to depreciate the value of property in order to force a sale. Most of us know what has happened in the central section of this city. I will recite one venture. A client of mine purchased, between 14th and 23rd Streets, a so-called loft building, badly built, and found that his income from the building was very must less than he had any idea it would be—in fact he said it didn't pay a decent percentage on the investment, owing to the bad character of the building, which was built for speculative purposes and to sell. He decided that in the future he would put his money into better buildings. He went further uptown and purchased three private houses which were not rentable at the time because of the gradual invasion of business—but still it was in general a district of private houses. He purchased those three private houses at a high price, which price had been caused, to be sure, by the gradual approach of business. The buildings were torn down and a twelve story loft building erected. He immediately rented every inch of space at such a price for five year terms that the building paid a very excellent return on his investment. Within two years thereafter the street was solidly built up in Sinclair loft buildings. Within tne five years almost every tenant moved out and went ten blocks further up into another district with exactly the same relation as to light and air and to the shopping district then as his building had had five years before. At the present time the building is only nine years old, and the rents have come down until I do not believe it is paying 3 per cent. on the investment, simply from the fact that it was crowded in by similarly mistaken improvements in that locality. Now the city is just as much interested, from the point of view of taxation in the right sort of improvements, as is the property owner himself, because that particular block of loft buildings does not bring into the city, in the way of taxes, or to the owners, in the way of income, anything like it would have brought in had the improvement there been wisely planned. Had the city limited the size or area of land that the building may occupy—that particular type of improvement, which proved to be a mistaken improvement would not have been made. And, of course, the effect of this unwise loft or factory building construction on the neighboring retail district is too well known to need detailing here. It is for that reason that I believe districting and zoning the city is most important. Now it seems to me here—I know I am getting on dangerous ground,—that, by the same token, if the tax on land is increased and that on a building lowered the dangers from that sort of thing would be greatly increased. It seems to me particularly so—in the residential sections where people are waiting to see what will happen before any important improvements are made. A single owner could erect a stable or a garage (this could be done in the finest residential section of the city), and immediately force down the price of all the neighboring property. Now, under this proposed plan he could easily build that stable at very small expense upon his property and there would be little or no tax on the "improvement". He would be risking very little, but the effect would be to depreciate the value of all neighboring property, and destroy a part of the city's taxable assets. That is my particular point. On one block in which I am interested there have been filed two sets of plans for what I call nuisances, for buildings which are probably never to be built. On the one filed two years ago there has been no move to build. In both cases there was an attempt to secure a neighbor's property which he had been unwilling to sell. I think it would increase the danger of such threats or of actual mistaken improvements, if you decrease the tax on buildings, unless the city is first provided with a scheme of development of districts or zones.

TESTIMONY OF DR. ROBERT MURRAY HAIG,

Instructor in Economics, Columbia University, Investigator for the Committee on Taxation.

PROFESSOR SELIGMAN: I believe you were to speak to us on two points:

First, on the latest developments of the single tax experiment in Canada and in this country, and second, on the probable effects of the reduction in rents in the tenement house district in case the tax was taken off entirely from buildings. Will you say a few words about each point?

DR. HAIG: The first point is disposed of very quickly. The tendency, as indicated in the report which I filed with the Committee some time ago, seems to be working out along substantially the same lines. With the hard times in Western Canada in connection with the war, the pressure upon holders of vacant property was so great, and the amount of unpaid taxes increased so considerably, as to cause some apprehension. In Edmonton the pressure, due to unpaid taxes, was so great as to prompt the mayor to make an attack upon the single tax system in an open meeting of the citizens of the town.

Of interest also is the announcement made by Honorable Wilfred Garrepy, who is minister of municipalities, to the effect that it is the intention of the Liberal Government of Alberta in the winter session of the Legislature to introduce a modification of the plan which is now in force in the towns of Alberta and which has involved some financial difficulty—

PROFESSOR SELIGMAN: Modification of what plan?

DR. HAIG: In the towns of Alberta a few years ago all of the taxes were placed upon the land. The result was, in many cases, over-assessment and very high rates. The problem was so acute that in the last few months an announcement has been made that the Government this winter will make some modification of the plan.

Last Tuesday, I am informed, the electorate of Pueblo, by a small majority, repealed their measure providing for the reduction of the tax on buildings in two installments—one of which had already been made. I made a supplementary note in my report about Houston's situation. On March 3rd, after my report proper was written, a Court order was issued directing the city officials to assess land at the same per cent. of full value as they do buildings. So far as I know that is all that has happened since the report came out.

The other point is really an addendum to my second report, that is the one dealing with conditions in New York City. Since last summer there has been made available information from the records of the tenement house department with regard to the number of apartments in the various tenement houses and the rentals paid. I understand that the rental data is not entirely trustworthy—but, in the first of my statements, I do not depend upon the accuracy of the rental data, but merely upon the accuracy of the data as to the number of apartments in the various buildings. In the report there were five districts selected made up of buildings which are classified as tenements under the law. They were, the uptown east side section, the Rivington Street section, the Houston Street section, the Washington Heights walk-up apartment section, and the elevator apartment section. By using the information in the report in connection with the new information obtained from the tenement house department, I find that the maximum reduction of rents. that is the amount of taxes on buildings which would be removed under this assumption, in the uptown tenement house section on the upper east side, for the first year, to be almost exactly ten cents. To put it in another way, the maximum that the renter of an apartment in this section on the upper east side might receive in the way of reduction in the first year under this plan for reducing the taxes on buildings ten per cent. annually would be 10 cents.

PROFESSOR SELIGMAN: On the total rent for the year?

DR. HAIG: No, sir. Ten cents per month. The figure for the Rivington Street section is eight cents per month, the residents downtown using a smaller amount of building value. In the Houston Street section it is 9½ cents; in the walk-up apartment section, 17 cents; and in the elevator apartment section 35 cents.

At the end of five years,—if the plan which is most seriously considered should be carried into effect, that is to reduce the taxes by one-half by five annual reductions—the maximum available from this source for reduction in rent for the uptown section would be 50 cents. The tenants might possibly pay 50 cents less on their rents. In the Rivington Street section it would be 39 cents, in the Houston Street section 48 cents, in the walk-up section 83 cents, and in the elevator section $1.87.

At the end of the five-year period, if the tenants got the maximum benefit of the reduction in the tax on buildings, the renter of one of the apartments, in the uptown, east side districts may expect to pay $10.82 per apartment per month, instead of $11.32, as now paid. The other figures are, for Rivington Street, $12.89, instead of $13.28; for the Houston Street section, $16.38, instead of $16.76; in the walk-up section, $30.95, instead of $31.78; and in the elevator apartment section, it would be $50.63, instead of $52.50.

The percentages of these decreases are as follows:

Uptown tenements	4.4%
Rivington Street tenements	2.9%
Houston Street tenements	2.9%
Walk-up apartment section	2.9%
Elevator apartment section	3.6%

The data indicates that it may be true that the larger the amount of the rent paid the greater the reduction proportionately, but the basis is entirely too narrow for safe generalization.

May I also say that in the tenement house district the rentals are fixed by 50-cent units, so that the reduction of 50 cents, 39 cents, 48 cents., etc., might possibly be passed on if the pressure became acute.

I want to qualify somewhat the statements made above. As I pointed out, if in discounting the added burdens on land, the value of the land depreciates, buildings would carry a higher share of the burden than indicated. Because of this the reduction will be less than the figures given, but how much less would depend upon the discounting of the future burden.

PROFESSOR SELIGMAN: I understand you to say that if this scheme went into effect, whereby at the end of five years one-half of the tax on buildings would be put upon land, the utmost possible benefit that could come to the tenants of our tenement houses is represented by the figures that you have just mentioned?

DR. HAIG: With the further assumption, of course, that the only benefit we could get would be the decrease in the tax on buildings. If that is granted, your statement is correct.

PROFESSOR SELIGMAN: Do I understand you also to believe that, in your opinion, it is not certain, as an economic proposition, that under actual conditions in New York a decrease in the taxes of buildings would mean a decrease in rentals or proportionately larger accommodation at the same rentals? In your opinion, is there any condition of friction which may militate against this result?

DR. HAIG: There is a serious element of friction in passing on the amount of the decrease. There would be the ignorance as to just what the amount is and the pressure under which the landlord would be to get the last cent out of the tenant because of the increased land tax. The landlord would use the argument for raising the rent that it is due to the pressure put on him because of the increased tax on land. In the long run, I think that the tenants would get the reductions.

PROFESSOR SELIGMAN: Is your general conclusion—on the basis of your investigation—that the statement as to the alleged benefits that would ensue to the working classes of this city through a great reduction of rents or through very much better accommodations at the same rents, appears to be grossly exaggerated?

DR. HAIG: A good many of the statements that I have read have been grossly exaggerated. The whole thing appears to have been grossly exaggerated on both sides. On the basis of the figures the reductions in rents would probably not be more than five per cent.

I believe personally we should collect a larger and larger share of the ground rent, but it should be so arranged as not to confiscate the values of to-day. I think this scheme of reducing the tax on buildings, if carefully imposed, could be introduced without a great deal of danger. The present time is not the time to do it. Moreover, the plan of a stated yearly decrease is not a wise one. I think there should be a flexible plan. I should allow decreases in the good years, and a suspension ot decreases in bad ones. That is also qualified by the financial exigencies of the situation. It seems to me a tax on buildings is not a bad tax compared with some of the alternatives, if we must have money. I do not believe a tax on buildings is the worst alternative.

MR. LEUBUSCHER: In other words, you believe in local option in taxes, that is, if this were a good year you would decrease taxes and if it were a bad year you would not?

DR. HAIG: I believe in elasticity. I don't think that necessarily involves local option. In general, I fight shy of local option in taxes. It is likely to have some very undesirable effects. It seems to me that the Canadian experiment shows that with a proper degree of elasticity the thing could be done gradually without trouble.

MR. LEUBUSCHER: Your figures are given on a five-year basis. The poor tenant on the east side would save only 50 cents a month if the plan was adopted—this five year plan—that is one-half of the taxes on buildings taken off?

DR. HAIG: Yes, that is it.

MR. LEUBUSCHER: That means if the full plan were adopted and all taxes taken off, it would be double that, one dollar a month, so that for a man earning two dollars a day it would mean one dollar a month decrease?

DR. HAIG: That is a substantial item.

MR. LEUBUSCHER: Then, too, you predicate your statement on the reduction of rents merely on the amount of the reduction of the taxes, do you not?

DR. HAIG: I do.

MR. LEUBUSCHER: So, therefore, you did not take into consideration the fact that if we relieve buildings from taxation it may lead to the erection of competing tenements?

DR. HAIG: I don't see how you can possibly get even this amount of reduction without some alternative offered to the tenant in the nature of some other building to which he can go.

MR. LEUBUSCHER: So that if that were a fact and if there were more buildings erected by reason of the increase in land values and a decrease in the taxes on buildings—if the tendency of that was to cause the erection of more buildings then the rents in those tenements at least would be still further reduced?

DR. HAIG: I don't think so.

MR. LEUBUSCHER: Not by competition?

DR. HAIG: No. I think the cost of furnishing those accommodations will be reduced by the amount of fifty cents. If the tenant is very, very lucky, he may get it.

MR. LEUBUSCHER: If we adopted the other scheme it would be a dollar a month?

DR. HAIG: Yes.

MR. LEUBUSCHER: And in the case of the elevator apartments they would save four dollars a month?

DR. HAIG: Yes.

MR. LEUBUSCHER: That would mean $50 a year?

DR. HAIG: Yes, sir.

MR. LEUBUSCHER: You spoke about this benefit to the working classes in answer to the Professor's question. He asked whether this benefit would accrue to the working class, namely, a saving at the end of ten years to the poor tenement house dweller of one dollar a month—would that be the only benefit coming to the working classes upon the adoption of this policy?

DR. HAIG: I think any other benefits that he might get would be very slight. Of course, they are entirely impossible of calculation.

MR. LEUBUSCHER: The probable benefit would be this, would it not? You have just stated that the decrease of taxes on buildings and the increase of taxes on land values would result in the erection of more buildings, at least in the beginning, and that was the case in Vancouver and Edmonton in Canada, was it not?

DR. HAIG: I think it was so in the Canadian northwest. But there are other factors connected with this.

MR. LEUBUSCHER: Would not that be the natural tendency?

DR. HAIG: There are other factors in the situation which work the other way.

MR. LEUBUSCHER: If there are human beings in Vancouver and Edmonton with the same desires as the human beings here, do they differ from those in New York City?

DR. HAIG: They do, sir, in a very essential particular. When you come to New York City they more carefully discount the future. They make more careful use of their assets. They sometimes build in anticipation in order to preserve their title to the increment. If you impair seriously the increment you start a force which discourages buildings. There are, of course, two counter-acting forces and upon the relative strength of these forces all depends.

MR. LEUBUSCHER: Assuming that the experience of Vancouver, Edmonton, and other places in Northwest Canada would be duplicated here, and naturally people would want to have more and better houses, would not the workingman who is a tenant get employment, and, therefore, benefit?

DR. HAIG: I think that would depend upon where the money came from. You are taking away from the income of land owners; before one can answer your question you must answer what the land owners would have done with their income if it had not been taken by the city.

MR. LEUBUSCHER: Is not the lesson of experience the best lesson in the world? If a certain condition produces a certain result in one place is it not probable that it would produce the same result in another place?

DR. HAIG: If you have exactly the same conditions, but you have never been able to have exactly the same conditions in two communities. Moreover, I don't think you can completely isolate factors in this fashion.

MR. LEUBUSCHER: You know from your studies that if you tax any production of labor you make it more expensive and if you remove all taxes you cheapen it. That that is a result—

DR. HAIG: I should agree with that.

MR. LEUBUSCHER: Therefore, apart from those other effects we spoke of—the removal of taxes on the product, namely, in this case, the buildings, would have a tendency to cheapen the building, cheapen the cost of erection of buildings, and, therefore, increase the number of buildings?

DR. HAIG: If you assume in your conditions the absence of these other factors. But I say they are present.

PROFESSOR SELIGMAN: I would like to ask you one last question, which I should not have put had it not been for certain questions by the last speaker. You have made a very careful study of this whole situation and the history of it in Canada and in this country. If the Government of New York City was to come to you and say, "Give me your views—shall we now adopt this scheme which has been proposed for the untaxing of buildings"—"shall we introduce a bill into the Legislature to that effect," would you say yes or no?

DR. HAIG: Under present conditions I should not hesitate to say no.

MR. LEUBUSCHER: You prefer the increment tax to this scheme?

DR. HAIG: I think some of the ends could be better gained by this method.

MR. LEUBUSCHER: But on the whole, you think the tendency of this scheme is in the right direction?

DR. HAIG: I do.

MR. LEUBUSCHER: What do you say to a super-tax on land values in order to meet the increased cost in the budget of New York City?

DR. HAIG: I think it would be a very foolish thing at this particular time and in the situation of real estate just now.

MR. LEUBUSCHER: Would you advocate an increment tax under present conditions?

DR. HAIG: I don't think it would bring in anything just now. It is a matter of looking to the future.

THIRD HEARING,

November 15, 1915, 2.30 P. M., Mayor's Reception Room, City Hall, Professor Edwin R. A. Seligman, Presiding.

TESTIMONY OF MR. HENRY DE FOREST BALDWIN,

Treasurer, Society to Lower Rents and Reduces Taxes on Homes.

MR. BALDWIN: Taxes must be levied. There are two important questions with respect to taxes—who shall pay them, and for whose benefit the proceeds shall be expended. As the tax burden is not always ultimately borne by the people who pay the tax in the first instance, but can be passed on to others, we find that some kinds of taxes are popular in certain circles. A popular tax is one that aids one class of people, and the burden of which is borne by people who do not clearly understand that they are paying it. Examples of popular taxes are tariff taxes for protection and taxes on houses. Taxes on land are unpopular among land owners, because they cannot be passed on. Before this Committee it is not necessary to argue that the incidence of taxation is different when the tax is levied on improvements from what it is when it is levied on land values.

Inasmuch as it has become a habit to designate any proposition to tax land values as distinguished from improvements as "single tax," it is, perhaps, not inappropriate to note here that, if that is so, New York City has always, to a considerable extent, used the single tax in its tax system. A large part of our street improvements has been paid for by special assessments for benefit from the earliest times. Of course, these assessments are nothing but a special tax on land values, and are levied without reference to building improvements. What we propose in reducing the tax on improvements, and in placing a surtax to take care of the debt service on land values, is, in theory and in reality, nothing but an extension of the doctrine of special assessments for benefit. The single-tax philosophy is not more involved in that which we advocate than in assessments for benefit.

It must be perfectly evident to this Committee that the real difficulty with New York City finances to-day is that when we undertook to spend vast sums of money upon transportation, we did not provide that the property particularly benefited by these expenditures should bear the cost of them. Besides the subways, that $62,000,000 that has been spent on bridges and approaches also should have been assessed upon land within the area which, by reason of these improvements, has increased in value many times their cost. We have a big debt incurred for improvements which lead to an increase in rent. Having made the great blunder of presenting to the land owners within particular areas the immediate benefits due to these public improvements, we are now confronted with a situation which requires an examination of our entire tax system and which calls for an immediate determination as to what classes of people should pay for these and other elaborate improvements already made and those yet to be made.

Certain facts which are perfectly obvious should be kept in mind: One, taxes have got to be increased. From some source much larger revenues must be secured. Two, taxes likely to be imposed upon a business enterprise constitute a very large element in determining its action when seeking a location. New Jersey and Connecticut have taken many factories away from New York and have diverted many others from coming to New York by reason of the higher taxes which their managers have felt would be imposed here. Three, between 1906 and 1914, the assessed value of land was increased from three and one-third billion dollars to four billion, six hundred million dollars, which is 36 per cent.; the tax burden on real estate increased from 85½ million to 144½ millions, which is 68 1/3 per cent.; the population increased from a little over 4,000,000 to something over 5,000,000, about 25 per cent. Notwithstanding an increased tax burden land values increased more rapidly than population. But the increase in both appears to have stopped during the past few years. Four, New York's debt was incurred for public improvements of one kind or another made necessary so as suitably to prepare the land within the city limits for human habitation. Land is not fit for permanent city use until the city has spent a great deal of money in anticipation of that use. Streets, sewers, water pipes, pavement, and street lighting, are necessary. Transportation lines, bridges and tunnels, so as to give access to the property, are necessary. These improvements, part of which under our system are paid for eventually out of the general tax budget, and part of which are paid for by special assessments on the property benefited are just as necessary as the buildings which are erected entirely at the expense of the owners. And after the buildings are erected and people living in them it is necessary that the city should provide parks and schools and police and fire protection. For such purposes was our city debt incurred. All such improvements are calculated to add directly to the value of the land, and without them the use of the land for a congested population would be impossible.

A new house which has been erected on land made ready for improvements by those city expenditures is not increased in value by such expenditures. Such a house can add to the value of the land no more than its real cost. Given two lots of equal value, if one were improved with a suitable house, it should be increased in value merely the cost of the house, including, of course, a fair profit to the builder.

The tenant in that part of his rent which is attributable to the land, pays the full present annual value which public improvements have added to the value of the lot, whether the land owner pays for these improvements or not, and irrespective of the taxes levied on the land, but in that part of his rent attributable to the house, he pays the tax levied on the house whatever it may be.

The owner of the land, in his rent, collects a return not only upon the improvements which were erected at his own expense but upon the improvements which were made at the city's expense. The tenant, therefore, pays in his rent his share of these improvements. Any tax on the land cannot be transferred to the tenant. But, in so far as the house is taxed to pay for public improvements that tax can be transferred to the tenant and the tenant is thus obliged to pay for the improvements twice. He pays once to the landlord in his rent the added value which the improvement gives to the bare land and he pays again in the tax upon the house. Tenants receive from public improvements no benefit which they do not pay for in their rents.

Besides improvements, the cost of which is reflected in land values, we have in New York City $100,000,000 in water supply; $100,000,000 in subways, and some millions of dollars in bridges and approaches which are beyond any present need of the city. These improvements have been planned on such a magnificent scale because it was believed that New York would grow, and before very long would need them. But if New York does not grow, then, to that extent they are beyond our needs they are dead loss. For this, as well as for other reasons, we must be very careful, therefore, not to check the growth of New York.

Now, I understand that none of these propositions are seriously questioned by the members of your Committeee. They raise at the outset an all important question: As between landlords and tenants, who should pay taxes to meet the cost of these improvements? The landlords, who, whether they pay or not, will collect from the tenants their annual value to the land—or the tenant who, in any case, must pay their value once to the landlord?

If you seek to make the tenants pay, you are adding, by the amounts of the tax levied for that purpose, a burden upon the great mass of the people, already obliged to pay a higher rent than is paid in any other place in the world. Is that likely to benefit New York as a community? Or is it likely to benefit New York as a city?

Again, as between land owners and business interests, who should be asked to pay the taxes to meet the cost of these public improvements? This is different from the issue between landlords and tenants because business interests can, to a large extent, take care of themselves. If you make it unprofitable to do business in New York, notwithstanding New York's superb location, they will find an asylum in New Jersey, Connecticut and elsewhere. Why should these outside interests be asked to pay for our subways, water supply, and other improvements which were constructed in order to render land suitable for residence and business purposes, and which have resulted in increasing the value of the land to at least twice the cost of the improvements, when the rent paid covers compensation for the advantage each plot has over some other place, including the advantages derived from these improvements? You should ask yourselves very seriously whether the city of New York can adopt in any shape a "pay as you enter" tax and not suffer seriously.

We can offer great advantages to manufacturing establishments and because of that we charge high rents. In return for the high rents, we offer the facility of location here, including the public service for which our city debt was incurred and for which our large annual budget is expended. But if we ask those who have the choice to go elsewhere to pay for these advantages twice, once to the landlord in high rents and again to the tax gatherer, we can be sure that a great many of such enterprises, which would otherwise come to New York, will go elsewhere. A great many of such enterprises already located in New York will do what has been done in many instances heretofore—move away. This means that New York will stop growing. The real estate interests in New York are suffering to-day because New York has—we hope, only temporarily—stopped growing.

How futile it is to expect that outsiders will come here and pay high rents and also a tax to pay for the public improvements which increase the rent, when New Jersey and Connecticut and even Westchester offer excellent opportunities! You can collect a very little after the manner of highwaymen from our present property tax which does not affect big business and rich people, because it requires merely a little carefulness to avoid its burdens, and it bears heavily only on the careless, the weak and the defenseless. But you cannot expect to induce business and large interests to submit to exaction beyond these, which other localities impose, except to the extent that rents are thereby reduced. Taxes upon the laboring classes and upon business to pay for improvements which have increased land values can oppress and demoralize the humbler portion of the community, but they must retard the development of the city. Those who collect the benefit of public improvements should pay their cost. This is expedient, as well as just.

If we had paid for all our public improvements, including subways, bridges and water supply by assessment for benefit, since 1906, we should have still an increase in land values over assessments levied of nearly $500,000,000. If we had done this, would New York be a worse or better place to live? Is it more radical or more unjust to pay for the subway by assessment than to pay for Riverside Park by assessment? The argument against paying for more of our improvements by assessments, which convinced those whose responsibility it was to decide, was that the older portions of the city had not paid for their similar improvements by assessments and that they had an obligation to aid the newly developed districts. Whether this was sound or not, it has been decided in favor of the outlying districts. It is for you to pursue intelligently the logical course which is pointed out by that decision, and to advocate a tax system which will make the land in the older districts pay their share of the development of the outlying districts and not jeopardize the city's growth and oppress its laboring classes by seeking contributions for such purposes elsewhere than from the land. You cannot get the money anywhere else, except at the expense of the city's prosperity. The land cannot move away and business can move. The greatest danger to these real estate brokers who have been so prominent in this tax discussion is to have New York stop growing.

If we adopt a tax system which encourages New York to grow we shall bring into play a power working for a steady increase in land values, which will go a long way towards mitigating the disadvantage to land owners of having the entire debt service placed upon land. On the other hand, if we adopt a tax system which keeps people from locating in New York and drives people out of New York, the land owners must face falling values and also their share of the taxes to pay for several hundred million of dollars worth of improvements at present unnecessary and, for a long time to come, unbeneficial, which have been undertaken with the expectation that the City of New York will grow. We shall have to pay two hundred million dollars for our Catskill water supply, two hundred million dollars for our subways, and seventy per cent. of one hundred million dollars for State Highways and seventy per cent. of one hundred million dollars for the barge canal. The benefit to us from these particular expenditures will be largely deferred, and those for the state roads will be very indirect. To get these expenditures reflected in land values, New York must grow. You can help its growth. Reduce rents by reducing taxes on houses and by placing a sur-tax on land values to take care of the debt service. Let the land, which, in eight years, has increased in value more than one billion dollars, pay for the improvements which have made that increase possible. There is nothing predatory or revolutionary in bearing in mind the use for which the money is raised in classifying property for taxation. New York may grow in spite of anything we may do, but it is better to insure its growth by letting the world know that there is no better place to do business and to manufacture and no better place to reside. We can announce to the world that this is the best place to locate a factory, the best place to dwell, the best place to bring up a family, the best place to do business, because, while rent is high, taxes on individuals and business are low.

It is by a constant rise in the tide of population that New York has surmerged and overwhelmed all of its diffiiculties in the past caused by the errors of judgment and by the corruption of its rulers. In growth lies a sure remedy.

I desire to say one word about what our opponents say with respect to a possible catastrophe in case a greater amount of the cost of the city government and of the debt service is laid on land values. Dr. Haig's investigation shows conclusively that no such calamity has been observed in any of the cities where land values have been more heavily taxed than other kinds of property. But we do not need to go to Canada or Houston, Texas, or Pittsburgh to find competent proof that such fears are groundless. We have an example right here in New York. Twenty years ago it was the rule in the Tax Department to assess unimproved property at one-third of its value, and improved property at two-thirds of its value. If a man had a vacant lot, and desired to put a building on it, he had to figure upon paying a tax on the building and double the tax theretofore paid on his land. This, of course, was a great encouragement to holding land out of use. In accordance with law, the assessment is now made more approaching equality. Unimproved property is assessed at full value, as well as improved property. The change to this method from the old method was a step in the same direction as we ask you to go, and was a far more radical change than that which we ask you now to make. If this change did not cause a revolution or a catastrophe, we have no reason to expect trouble from the plan we ask you to adopt.

It is said that what we propose would tend to bring vacant land into use and cause an increase in building. I have heard real estate men say that New York was already overbuilt. It may very well be that they were right from their point of view. But their point of view is not necessarily the point of view of the public nor the point of view from which to deal with the city's interest. When population is so congested as to cause unsanitary and indecent conditions, we may be sure that such a situation calls for improvements to land. This does not mean merely that there should be no more houses; it may mean that there should be better transportation facilities to take the people who live in the congested part of the city quickly and easily back and forth from their work; it may mean elaborate public work to fit land for houses. From the city's point of view, both as a corporation and as a governmental agent, when we show that living conditions are unsatisfactory, we have shown that some land, somewhere, should be improved. It may very well be that the owner of a lot on the outskirts of the city may consider that his lot is not ripe for improvement because the city has yet to spend a great deal of money in its neighborhood in order to make it possible for the people to use it, while, at the same time, there are parts of the city where people, by force of circumstances, are obliged to live in a crowded and indecent condition. Therefore, the individual real estate owner's point of view is not the point of view which should be taken by the city authorities or by the public in general.

PROFESSOR SELIGMAN: You have spoken of the fact that all the benefit of our revenue system goes to land. Does the benefit of the expenditures for education go entirely to the land owner?

MR. BALDWIN: Yes, sir.

It goes to the people who send their children to school, certainly, but it also goes to the landlord. It is paid to him in the shape of rent. They do not get anything they do not pay for. The benefit of the schools goes to the people who have children and who send their children to school.

PROFESSOR SELIGMAN: Is there any reason why they should not pay for this benefit?

MR. BALDWIN: No; they have got to pay for it.

PROFESSOR SELIGMAN: I say, is there any reason why they should not pay for it?

MR. BALDWIN: I do not see any reason. I think we ought to have public schools where they can go free. But they actually pay for them in their rent.

PROFESSOR SELIGMAN: How about the police expenditures of ten or fifteen millions? Do you think that the benefit of this expenditure goes exclusively to the land owners?

MR. BALDWIN: Yes, it goes exclusively to the land owner; he gets it all in his land. The land owner gets it all back. If we do not have police, the value of land goes down as it did in Chicago where they had the black-hand outrages in a certain quarter of the city; there the rents went down.

PROFESSOR SELIGMAN: Do you know of any connection at all between wages and expenditures of government? If, for instance, we had no police protection in New York City, do you think that wages would be as high as they are?

MR. BALDWIN: They would be lower.

PROFESSOR SELIGMAN: Does the benefit of the police department go at all to the wage earner?

MR. BALDWIN: Of course; everybody gets some benefit. I claim he pays for it in his rent.

PROFESSOR SELIGMAN: Do you think the wages of laboring men are higher because of government expenditures?

MR. BALDWIN: Yes.

PROFESSOR SELIGMAN: Then, is there any reason why he should not pay a certain proportion, according to his ability; or should it all be put upon the land owners?

MR. BALDWIN: I do think that there is reason why wage earners should not be asked to pay taxes for local improvements, because, as I have already pointed out to you, he pays in his rent a full return for all those services.

PROFESSOR SELIGMAN: But, then, if the taxes were taken off buildings would he then pay anything?

MR. BALDWIN: He would pay just the same; yes.

PROFESSOR SELIGMAN: If the taxes were taken off buildings?

MR. BALDWIN: If the taxes were taken off buildings he would pay less rent.

PROFESSOR SELIGMAN: He would pay less rent?

MR. BALDWIN: Yes, but still he would pay in his rent the value of those public services to the plot of land that he occupied. In expressing an opinion concerning the effect of expenditures of government upon wages, I fear that I answered too quickly. How wages are affected by police protection, public schools and expenditures for public improvements, if they are affected at all, I should wish to study carefully before making an answer.

MR. LEUBUSCHER: The Chairman also asked you about police, schools, hospitals, and such like facilities—if there were no hospitals, schools, or police, etc., what would become of the population of New York City, do you think?

MR. BALDWIN: I think it would be in a very much worse condition than now.

MR. LEUBUSCHER: Would it decrease?

MR. BALDWIN: As it would be a less advantageous place to live in, rents would go down and the people would move away.

MR. LEUBUSCHER: Would land values go down?

MR. BALDWIN: If the rents go down the land goes down, too.

MR. LEUBUSCHER: The land owners pass the tax which is levied on their buildings to the tenant and, therefore, they do not pay that tax to the city except as a collector from the tenant—do they?

MR. BALDWIN: In a growing community the tendency is to pass it on to the tenant. Whether it would happen the day after you passed the act or not, I do not suppose it would change the rent that day, but it would tend to bring more land into use, and building would increase and the rents would go down and the tenants would save the amount of the taxes. It would have the same effect if the cost of building material were reduced and the carrying charges of the building were much less.

TESTIMONY OF MR. ALLAN ROBINSON,

President, Allied Real Estate Interests; President, City and Suburban Homes Company.

PROFESSOR SELIGMAN: Is the amount of land actually ripe for building and held out of use a negligible quantity in this city?

MR. ROBINSON: It is; yes.

PROFESSOR SELIGMAN: In your opinion, is speculation in land a good thing or a bad thing for the community?

MR. ROBINSON: It depends on what you mean by speculation. If you mean the purchase of land with a view of holding it out of use and with a view of distant profits, I hardly think such a kind of speculation would meet with my approval. But what I call advanced building is, I believe, a kind of real estate speculation which is exceedingly important to the community. We have a great deal of advanced building, so called, in New York City and it performs very much the service which the advocates of this particular kind of land tax think their plan would accomplish. It is building in advance of the demand and it should by so much assist in relieving congestion and in a number of other things which really benefit the community.

PROFESSOR SELIGMAN: We were told at the last meeting that the expected increase in the value of the land is an important inducement in persuading the poor man, who has to borrow most of his money, to build. Do you think there is anything in that?

MR. ROBINSON: Yes, I think there is a great deal in that.

PROFESSOR SELIGMAN: Does the average builder of a small house own in this city to-day anything more than a slight equity in his proposition?

MR. ROBINSON: Generally speaking, most of the improved property in New York is under mortgage. That is another way of answering your question.

PROFESSOR SELIGMAN: Does the builder hope to pay off the mortgage primarily out of surplus earnings or surplus income, or does he expect to pay it off, in part at least, out of the increased land values when he comes to sell that property?

MR. ROBINSON: It is the expectation that the appreciation of the land value will largely if not wholly balance the depreciation of the building value that leads the majority of the people to invest in land in a large city.

PROFESSOR SELIGMAN: Would the transfer of the tax to land diminish the inducement to build?

MR. ROBINSON: Unquestionably.

PROFESSOR SELIGMAN: Would it be sufficient, in your opinion, to outweigh the advantage which would come from the exemption of buildings from taxation? What would be the net result?

MR. ROBINSON: That would largely depend upon the psychological element; that is, as to whether prospective owners believe that this was only the first step toward the entire socialization of the land, which I believe it to be, or whether it would end right there. If it would end right there, it might have the effect of establishing a new level and advance building might start from that point. The danger is that that would so affect the public mind as to drive people out of that market, which is a market just as much as the grain market is a market and every other commodity market is a market. It would drive people out because they would be afraid that their capital would be confiscated by a further progress towards land socialization.

PROFESSOR SELIGMAN: We have been told on the one hand that this change would cause a more substantial use of the land. We have also been told that it would mean a somewhat more restricted use of gardens and breathing spaces in the suburbs. On the other hand, we have been told by these very same witnesses that this change in taaxtion would mean a lower value of land—a lower selling price of land. I want to ask you whether, in your opinion, the one influence would balance the other, or whether we should have more land to use for gardens, or the same amount of land or less land, as a result of this change in taxation?

MR. ROBINSON: There is no question but that so far as the city is concerned there would be more compactness. That has been the result, as the Haig report shows, in the Canadian cities. They have used that as an argument in fact for the system.

I would like to say I had expected that this movement, of which this is apparently a recrudescence, had about passed its zenith. I felt quite confident that a year or two ago the public interest in it had passed. It is one of the elements which has tended very largely to the decrease of land values in New York City in the last six years.

Three years ago I had occasion to meet the man who decides whether the funds of individuals in Connecticut shall be invested in companies and corporations in New York City and in other cities. He was inclined to discourage investments of Connecticut funds in New York City real estate on account of this single-tax movement. I told him at the time I felt that the movement had reached its zenith, and was going down and that the investors of Connecticut need not fear it. I cite this to show what is likely to happen if this system of taxation goes into effect.

We have had six years of a declining real-estate market. I feel that we are on the verge of improvement in real estate values in New York City. The city needs that improvement—the city needs it in order to finance its various measures. I should be extremely sorry if this Committee should make any move which would tend to give any further impetus to this movement. I believe New York City is on the verge of a large increase in real estate values. You may kill it if you adopt anything like this.

DR. WILCOX: In answer to Mr. Seligman you discussed the question of whether the effect of the plan would be to diminish the holdings for garden spaces inside and also in the outer part of the city—the thing that I want to ask is how can you get an intensity of use both inside and outside, that is at the center, and at the same time, in all the outlying sections?

MR. ROBINSON: You cannot; but you can get the tendency.

I do not say there would be no gardens. I do say the tendency towards compactness in any one given locality in the city will be greater than it is to-day, and as a result the drawing power will be greater than to-day.

DR. WILCOX: Would the effect of this system, do you think, be the shortening of rapid transit lines that run out into the suburbs, so that people could not go so far out?

MR. ROBINSON: Of course; that follows if I am on the right tendency—naturally.

DR. WILCOX: It would not cut off any that are actually built?

MR. ROBINSON: It might seriously affect them.

DR. WILCOX: Can the transfer of tax from the buildings to land ever increase the value of improved land? Neglecting for the moment the indirect effects which arise through the stimulation of other forces, how could the land with the building on it, where the operating expenses chargeable to taxes are reduced, for example, from $2,000 to $1,200—how could it escape from an increase in value? The total tax upon the parcel is decreased, but the tax which the assessor, according to the scheme worked out, writes on his books opposite the land value, has increased. What is the effect of the fact that the total tax upon that parcel has decreased?

MR. ROBINSON: My theory is this: If you increase the tax upon land you decrease the value of the land by the amount of the taxes capitalized. On the other hand, if you decrease the tax upon the land you increase the value of the land by the amount of the taxes capitalized. If the tax upon the land as distinguished from the improvement is a heavier tax the land value will not be higher.

DR. WILCOX: It will not be higher—will it be lower?

MR. ROBINSON: The land value?

DR. WILCOX: Yes.

MR. ROBINSON: Lower—of course it will.

DR. WILCOX: Will rents decrease?

MR. ROBINSON: I presume that theoretically at the beginning —perhaps the first year or so—there will be a decrease of rents as the result of a movement of this sort. I presume that if we had a panic in real estate that real estate values quite generally would decrease and there would be a decrease in rents.

DR. WILCOX: Don't you think that would be presuming too much?

MR. ROBINSON: No.

DR. WILCOX: It is the improvements that make the value of the land and the rents that you get?

MR. ROBINSON: This is another thing that I wanted to say— rents are not what the landlords can get. They are what the tenants will pay. The landlord is a beggar and he takes what the tenant will give, but no more.

MR. LEUBUSCHER: You said the landlord will take whatever the tenants offer him?

MR. ROBINSON: Yes.

MR. LEUBUSCHER: Are you a landlord?

MR. ROBINSON: I am president of the City and Suburban Homes Company, which has 15,000 tenants.

MR. LEUBUSCHER: For your information I will state this: A member of this Committee is a landlord and he will not take what his tenants offer him. If they don't pay the rent he asks he says: "Get out." Now, there is one landlord in New York who will not take what the tenants offer. In fact, I could mention an instance of another landlord, Rogers, Peet & Company, who are the landlords of my offices—where I have an office. When my lease expired I offered them less rent, but they would not accept it. I said I would not pay more and they said they would lease it to somebody else. I stayed and paid the rent they asked.

MR. ROBINSON: You were willing to pay the rent.

MR. LEUBUSCHER: Of course; I had to.

TESTIMONY OF DR. ROBERT H. WHITTEN.

DR. WHITTEN: I am opposed to the proposed halving of the tax on buildings. It would not, in my opinion, be of any value to the rent payer or home owner, but would cause injustice as between taxpayers and would result in an unsettlement of real estate conditions. Both sides to this controversy, I believe, accepted as settled and not open to serious discussion the fundamental assumption that while a tax on land cannot be shifted, a tax on the building tends to be shifted to the tenants. I cannot agree that the tax on the building is paid by the tenant. Generally speaking, I believe that both the tax on the building and the tax on the land are paid out of ground rent and therefore serve to reduce the market value of the land and do not result in the payment of a higher rent by the user of the property. This statement doubtless seems heretical, but its truth or falsity is of such fundamental importance to this entire problem that it may repay careful consideration.

The generally accepted theory in regard to the incidence of the tax on real estate is well stated by Dr. Haig in his valuable report to this Committee. Dr. Haig says (at pp. 125-126):

> It is generally agreed that a charge which is levied upon city land values must be deducted by the land owner from the sum he already receives from his site. He is already, theoretically, collecting all he can collect from the tenant—the equivalent of the advantages his site possesses over others under the conditions obtaining. The heavier tax apportioned according to land values, it may be claimed, would affect these conditions. It certainly will not decrease the number of sites. * * * It follows that land taxes tend to be borne by the payer. There is no shifting. The resting place is with the owner.
>
> The incidence of the tax on buildings is different. The new tax is a charge connected with supplying improvements on land to those who desire them. The person who supplies the improvements is the capitalist. He can place his capital here or place it elsewhere. To place it here he must be given the same return which he should receive elsewhere. Placing his capital here involves the payment of a tax charge which can usually be avoided if he places it elsewhere. The person, therefore, who wishes the improvement on land must meet this charge in order that this option by the capitalist may be as attractive as the other. Taxes on buildings and other improvements which wear out, tend, therefore, to be shifted to the tenant.

The fallacy of this line of reasoning is due to two main causes: First, in failure to recognize that the land and its appropriate improvements cannot be separated in determining the value of the land or the incidence of the land and building tax; and second, in failure to realize the real tactical weakness of the land owner as compared with the builder, investor or tenant in the effort to shift the tax.

Often in considering this question the assumption seems to be that city land has a site value that has little or no relation to its use or to the building that must be erected in order that it may be appropriately utilized. This leads to the assumption that the land and its appropriate improvement are entirely separate investments and need not be considered as a unit in considering the value of the site, and the incidence of the tax on the land and building. Land in a city has value only because of what it can earn for its owner when improved with an appropriate building. The value of a particular plot of land that is ripe for improvement is determined solely by the estimated surplus rental that would remain after paying interest on the cost of the appropriate building, rent collection, repairs, operation and taxes on the land and building. This surplus rental is capitalized as the value of the land. The land is the residual claimant. All expenses incident to the construction and operation of the appropriate building must be deducted and the remainder is capitalized as the value of the land. The market value of land ripe for improvement is determined by estimated surplus earnings when appropriately improved. The market value of land not yet ripe for improvement is determined by anticipated surplus earnings when appropriately improved, discounted by carrying charges, i. e., taxes and interest, until such land will be ripe for improvement. As the land is a residual claimant to profits any taxes that will be levied upon the building essential to its suitable improvement and use must be deducted. The tax on the building is therefore shifted to the land and tends to reduce its market value in the same way as a tax levied directly against the land.

It is true that a tax on buildings cannot reduce the returns on the capital required to provide additional buildings, for in that case capital would seek other forms of investment. It is also true that the builder must see an opportunity for a profit. The two remaining parties to whom the burden of the building tax may possibly be shifted are the future tenants and the present land owners. Which of these possible victims occupies the weaker tactical position? Undoubtedly the present land owner. The present land owner whose property is dead ripe for improvement will lose money unless he sells or improves. If he sells he must sell at such a price that the builder and investor can get a fair return. The tax on the appropriate building will therefore reduce the price he can get for his land. It will not affect the builder, investor or tenant. There is always enough land dead ripe for improvement and enough owners who either realize this situation or that they have other more urgent uses for their money to make the market value of land fluctuate with the estimated net returns that can be anticipated from its improvement. A permanent increase in the tax rate on buildings without corresponding decreases in the tax rate on land means a loss to present land owners in the value of their holdings. A permanent decrease in the tax rate on buildings without a corresponding increase in the tax rate on land means a gain to present land holders in the value of their holdings.

Land as the residual claimant to excess profits from the improvement and use of real estate reach the gain or loss incident to the decrease or increase in the tax rate. There are always builders and permanent investors ready to supply needed accommodations if they can anticipate a fair return on their investments, and there is always land dead ripe for improvements that can be bought at a price that will make it possible to earn this fair return, in spite of any moderate increase in the tax on the improvement.

An increase in the tax rate on buildings cannot immediately affect the tenant, as it does not affect the existing supply of buildings. It does, however, immediately affect the land owner. For owners holding land that is dead ripe for improvement are forced by economic necessity, i.e., the fear of greater loss, to sell at a price that will make possible its improvement with a profit to the builder and a fair return to the permanent investor. The increased tax on the building is discounted at once in the value of the land. Conversely a decrease in the tax on the building will be reflected in an increase in the value of the land.

The land and its appropriate improvement cannot be separated in determining the value of the land or the incidence of the land and building tax. Failure to recognize this has led to confusion. The value of the land is determined by what it will earn when appropriately improved. It is the surplus earnings of the land and the building that are capitalized as the value of the land. Anything that affects the amount of the surplus that can be earned by the land and the suitable building affects the value of the land.

In 1903 the tax rate in Manhattan was 1.41, while the tax rate for the current year is 1.86. During this period there has been a large increase in the population. Yet it is generally stated that during this period of increasing taxes and of increasing population rents have, in general, declined. In the city of Washington the tax rate is about half of what it is in most other cities, owing to the fact that the United States Government pays half the cost of the city government. Rents in Washington, however, are not cheaper than in the cities where the tax rate is much higher.

In conclusion I will say: The present tax on buildings like the present tax on land has been discounted in the market value of the land and, generally speaking, has not affected the rent paid by the tenant.

The transference of the tax from the building to the land would not in general affect rents but would cause injustice as between existing land owners and unless it is gradually effected would cause an unsettlement of real estate conditions.

PROFESSOR SELIGMAN: Do we understand your conclusion to be this: That the theory of incidence which has been usually followed by both sides to the controversy is erroneous; and that, in your opinion, the proposed scheme is a bad one, because it would not help the tenant and would injure the owners?

DR. WHITTEN: I think that is a correct statement of my position.

MR. LEUBUSCHER: Do you think, Mr. Whitten, that experience is a better teacher than all our theorizing?

DR. WHITTEN: Yes.

MR. LEUBUSCHER: Do you think that your theory that there will be no reduction in rents will be somewhat modified if you became aware of the fact that when Houston, Texas, adopted a modified part of this scheme, rents fell from one-fifth to one-sixth.

DR. WHITTEN: If I could be assured that was the only cause that affected rents.

MR. LEUBUSCHER: As I understand it, you run counter to the accepted theory of all economists when you say that the tax on buildings is not shifted?

DR. WHITTEN: Yes, the tax on the building cannot as a general thing be shifted to the tenant.

MR. LEUBUSCHER: I take issue with you on that.

MR. WILCOX: With reference to the harm that this system would bring about to the land owners, I understand that that harm consists in the shifting of values from one person to another.

DR. WHITTEN: Yes. As I have stated, I think that the tax on the building is in general discounted at present in the value of the land. But, as Dr. Haig has shown in his report, the ratio between the value of the building and the value of the land in different parts of the city is different, so that the imposition of the entire tax upon the land would affect different land owners differently, and so result in the shifting of land values to compensate for that difference in the tax burden on different parties.

TESTIMONY OF MISS GRACE ISABEL COLBRON,

Secretary, Women's Henry George League; Vice-President, Women's Society to Lower Rents and Reduce Taxes on Homes; Field Lecturer, Henry George Lecture Association.

MISS COLBRON: On the second day Mr. Leubuscher asked if there were a difference in the value of labor products say, in the price of beefsteak, in the city as compared with the country. As a matter of fact, in smaller towns food prices are higher than they are in New York City. The same is true of prices of clothing, furniture, etc., for goods of equal quality. In other words, the price of labor products is lowered by the growth of population, in contrast to land values, which are raised by the same cause. The return to merchants selling food in New York at a lower cost is, of course, greater because of the larger market; but is not this a clear case of site value, locational value, land value? This point struck me as important because it shows the importance to the purchasing public, to the general public, of any influence of taxation methods on the cost of living.

In New York City we have, through a separate assessment bill, legally recognized the difference between the bare value of land and the value of the improvements thereon. The opponents of the measure now being discussed before the Committee continually reiterate that real estate is already overburdened. We who believe in the proposed measure agree that the **improvement** side of real estate is undoubtedly overburdened. But our opponents do not emphasize the fact, when they talk about it, that we are trying to take the burden off that portion of real estate in which the general public is more intimately concerned. Therefore, when our opponents speak of the burden of taxation on real estate, they should say what they mean. Their unclear statements confuse the public and are unfair in that it puts an extra burden on us of explanation as to what we really propose to do.

I have listened very carefully to what has been said at the hearings but I have not been able to accept any argument as yet given that the reduction of the tax on improvements would not materially reduce rents. If you will, therefore, allow me to accept that premise, I should say that a reduction of rent to the average tenant would prove a very good thing in this city, in fact it would come back to the whole city in increased land values in another way than the way that has been spoken of here. The less rent the average individual pays, the more money he has left over for other expenses. That means bigger business to the food and clothing merchants, a greater incentive for them to settle in more scattered districts, a greater incentive to buy better stock, bringing it back to the wholesaler again, and a greater incentive to the wholesaler to order from the manufacturer. All of this means more business and increases land values, and is, therefore, of benefit even to the land owner. As far as it has been done in Vancouver the land owner has seen this point and is in favor of the present method of taxation, that is as far as the exemption on improvements is concerned. In fact, some of the Canadian towns show higher land values than any other towns of similar size can show here, and this on the basis of the fact that capital invested in productive enterprises will not be taxed.

There has been much talk about the growth of the city. It is true that if you cheapen the price of land you lower its speculative value to the individual, but I do not see how this can lower its *use* value. Anything that tends to bring capital to a city, and certainly the untaxing of capital invested in productive business, and the untaxing of improvements must attract capital, anything of this kind would raise the rental value of city land because it would make that land more desirable. People will naturally flock to a city where their rents are lower and their opportunities of return on capital invested in business are higher.

Naturally, in a new city, which has yet to grow, the city would grow more compact at its center by making it easier to get land and by making it more profitable for capital to put up buildings there. But is that not what every city wants? In New York, we have already built up our center more or less compactly. I have not, as yet, heard any argument refuting my belief that in New York City a very large effect of the new method of taxation would be to spread out, to encourage the building of homes in the periphery of the city, to encourage transit facilities for those living outside of the city, because that, for our city, would be the line of least resistance, the line of natural growth which can be taken under a better method of taxation.

It is a truism, of course, that taxes on improvements tend to restrict improvements, and I have not as yet heard anything to refute this or to refute the assertion that the reduction of the tax on improvements would cause more improvements in this city—something any city desires.

PROFESSOR SELIGMAN: If rents are reduced will wages be reduced?

MISS COLBRON: I cannot think that they would be.

PROFESSOR SELIGMAN: Then you do not think that high rents and high wages go together? You disagree with Mr. Baldwin in that case?

MISS COLBRON: I am afraid that I do—in that case.

STATEMENT OF MR. LAURENCE M. D. McGUIRE,

President, Real Estate Board of New York.

PROFESSOR SELIGMAN: Mr. McGuire, our next speaker, was unfortunately called away. He has left a statement here which I would ask our Executive Secretary to read, in lieu of his testimony.

MR. TANZER (Reading): There should be only one theory as a basis for taxation throughout the whole state. The Committee, in my opinion, should not, under any circumstances, recommend any theory as a basis of taxation which would be different in the City of New York from any part of the state. The Real Estate Board has made a complete statement covering all the points raised by the Mayor's Committee. This answer has been filed with the Committee and I concur in all the opinions expressed. The Mayor's Committee can only recommend. Legislation will be required to put into effect whatever it may recommend. The Legislature has, perhaps a half-dozen times, rejected the theory of removing the tax on buildings and placing it on land. It is to be hoped that the Committee will not include this theory in its report. The theory has not the support of practical persons, who consider it both fallacious and dangerous. It is unfortunate that the Committee has seen fit to emphasize the proposition by giving it such serious consideration as is evidenced by these hearings, for the mere fact that it is being given consideration has a depressing effect upon the real estate market.

All are agreed that the tax burden on real estate is now entirely too high. The Committee can, therefore, best serve the public interests by applying itself to a search for new sources of revenue and recommending that such new revenue as can be found be applied to the general purposes of government, and not used for activities which have no place in a proper governmental system. It seems inconceivable that additional burdens should be considered for real estate when the purpose should be to reduce the tax rate to a fair and reasonable point, that is, two per cent. or less. Two per cent. is the limit real estate in the city should be asked to bear. It is sincerely to be hoped that the Mayor's Committee will include in its recommendations some feasible plan through which those living outside of the city and doing business in the city—the commuting element—will be compelled to contribute a just and fair proportion to the cost of government.

TESTIMONY OF MR. JAMES R. BROWN,

President, Manhattan Single Tax Club.

MR. BROWN: We are at odds with the present method of raising public revenue. We say that there is no principle of business, honor, morality, or of economics, recognized in our present method of raising public revenue. We take private property for public use and we give public value for private enjoyment. Those who do good we punish. Those who do evil we reward.

Taxation is payment for social service. A man ought to pay taxes as he pays for dry goods or groceries. In other words, he should pay for what he gets from society and not for what he does for himself. For instance, under our law if a man paints a house we are supposed to tax him. The law demands that all property be assessed at its full and true value. It is evident to us all that a painted house is of more value than an unpainted house. That brings us into another wrong principle which is involved; for the painting of a house is a service not rendered by society to that individual, but a service rendered by that individual unto himself; and, therefore, to charge a man for services that he renders to himself is dishonest, unbusinesslike, and is nothing but a punishment for doing good.

On the other hand, those things that could be directly regarded as services on the part of society to the individual member of the community, they are all registered in what we call land value, and that, and that alone, is the true measure of the value of social service.

There is no reason for all the consideration we have been giving land speculators. He is not essential in the scheme of things at all. He seeks to gather where he does not sow, to get something for nothing, to profit not by labor on his part, but by a careful development of society and the expenditure of public revenue for public utilities. In other words, by allowing land value to get into private pockets. We are putting a premium on idleness and making payment to men known as land speculators, for holding land out of use, thereby making land artificially scarce and artificially dear and adding to the burdens of labor and of capital.

What is land value? A personal creation? Can even the whole Board of Real Estate Brokers say that they created the land values of New York? Certainly not! It is due to the presence of society and the public utilities that we paid for socially. It is reflected—it is a measure of the advantage of social pressure and service. Get rid of your fire department and what happens to land values? They will go down. Get rid of your police department and land values will go down. Nothing but land values reflect the advantage of social presence and social activity.

Under our present method of taxation what is the result to the business interest of the city and to the capital interest of the city? The assessed value of improvements on land is only three billion dollars. If it earned 5 per cent. to-day, which it is not earning as a fact—the total earning of the capital upon Manhattan Island—Greater New York—would be only $150,000,000. The untaxed value of the lands alone of Greater New York is over eight billion dollars, which, at 5 per cent., would make a tribute or burden carried by capital and labor of $400,000,000. Land value is the value of the opportunity to produce wealth—to do business, and our tax system has encouraged the boosting and booming to the terrible condition where the land values are $5,000,000,000 greater than the sum total of the labor values, the capital and the wealth on the land of this city, what does it mean? It accounts, and it alone can account, for the lower rate of interest on working capital and the miserable revenue for labor. It accounts for the fact that business men have to struggle to keep ahead of the sheriff. Because of the present tax system it makes it more profitable to hold land than to use land. Land values have been boosted to a point where labor and capital can barely live.

We believe that there is no difficulty in obtaining revenue for New York City if we only had the brains and the nerve to go after our own property and take what belongs to the people socially and what they have created socially and which they have given over to the land speculators. What particular advantage to the community are these so-called land speculators? Are they producers? Not at all. Do they cause two blades of grass to grow where hitherto only one has grown? No. Do they put up buildings? No. Do they manufacture goods? No. Do they render any service? No. Not in any way are they an advantage to the community.

Why, we have so much natural revenue here there should be no problem of debt. If the Constitution stands in the way—well, we could very easily fix the Constitution. Law is the most convenient thing ever. What is legal to do to-day is illegal to-morrow. What should be considered in a discussion of the tax problem is the ethics of the situation. If we build our system upon sound ethics it will work out absolutely all right.

What we need here in this city is cheaper land. We have a large amount of it. It ought to be cheap, because there is so much of it and so few of us. It ought to be as cheap as dirt. We have a million vacant lots in New York City. If you want a small piece of land here you have got to pay a King's ransom for it. Remember this, that every cent of land values that goes to a private person is a tribute paid by labor and capital and given to those who produce it not, and who are not in any way related to the development of it.

A simple, plain, comprehensive, effective method of raising public revenue would be this: I would take for the use of society to the last cent that value that society alone produces, the result of presence of society, the social activities and services that society renders. Then, by doing that you would not be charging a man dishonestly but honestly for that service he gets from society. What is the measure of what he gets? The value of the land of which he has sole and exclusive possession is the only and the true measure of the value of the social service. When you charge him on any other basis you are robbing the citizens of private property. When you do not charge him you are giving to that private individual public property.

PROFESSOR SELIGMAN: I would like to know what your theory of taxes is on this point: Do you think that from the point of view of sound ethics it is proper by the introduction of this system to take away from the capital invested by this man in real estate a certain proportion of his property? That is my only point.

MR. BROWN: Yes, for this reason: We are taking for the use of society.

TESTIMONY OF MR. E. A. TREDWELL,

Member, Legislation and Taxation Committee, Real Estate Board of New York.

PROF. SELIGMAN: How large a proportion of real estate is owned by people who have put their earnings into real estate within the last ten years?

MR. TREDWELL: In Chicago they found that by actual statistics that on an average every piece of real estate in the city changed hands every 27 years; so that probably the same relative change would occur here. Recent conditions have been severe regarding real estate. It is not generally considered a desirable security to-day, therefore, values have dropped severely, the income from it has been poor and conditions have been bad. It always seems to have been a target for all kinds of reforms including the idea of halving the tax rate on buildings which is a measure for social reform and, therefore, should not be saddled on the taxing power as that is contrary to every doctrine ever found sound, I think, by economists.

I want to point out to you that the tax on land to-day in the City of New York amounts to what was a war tax in ancient Rome. You will find that the war tax at the time of Trajan was twenty-five per cent. of the net income. It is 35% of the income in New York City to-day. Real estate owners have been referred to as practically grafting on the public. Now the grafting is not amongst the big ones. Real estate men or otherwise, the usual targets of social reformers. You are bringing up a population in New York City to-day where moral fibre is growing so weak, so feeble, that to conquer it is but a boy's task at any time and it is the kind of men you are bringing up here that are going to be a peril to this republic. They are the real grafters.

A man don't value anything that he does not make or achieve through work with his own hands. It is not mere money that we must think of; we must think more in terms of Men. You cannot bring up men when you give them all things free—everybody should know that. Now, I said the real grafter in New York City is not the big grafter. There are grafters up and down the side streets—little grafters—many grafters who are shrieking out loud eternally for you to give—give—free meals, free hospital service, free charity that amounts to full support. Ask any physician what he thinks of the city's free hospital service. Ask any professional man in the City of New York, in any line, his personal opinion about the free gifts of New York City. To you, who do not know, will come a great enlightenment in the intrenched position of the multitudinous little grafters. There are twenty-two hundred organizations in the City of New York giving charity. That is what all this half-tax business is being promoted here for. It is to give more charity to the tired souls that either do not want to work or are so enfeebled that they cannot work. Now, if we must have a separate Letchworth Village for defectives and incapables to put these souls in, let us do it that way and support them altogether under proper restraint and surveillance.

PROFESSOR SELIGMAN: To what extent, do you, as a practical real estate man, believe that people who have invested in land values in New York City have made much more money relatively to their capital than in other walks of business?

MR. TREDWELL: I think a man is foolish to-day who puts his money into land values watching and waiting for them to go up. It is a well-known maxim among land operators and speculators that he who holds land over five years has a loss on his hands after that time and after holding it for five years if they are wise they obey the unwritten law and sell at the market.

There are many lots always to be sold around New York City. I have any number that I would sell now, as low as one hundred dollars per lot. If any gentleman thinks he is deprived in any way of the opportunity to purchase land and make a barrel of money thereby it is a wrong proposition. That man is unaware of the facts because when you have paid taxes, interest, assessments and one thing and another, if you figure it all up then at the end of five years you cannot beat compound interest working against you. There is no profit in holding land against an accruing interest-bearing investment of dollars.

PROFESSOR SELIGMAN: Do you think from practical experience that money earned by the individual, and invested in real estate in New York City, brings in a larger return, relatively, than in other walks of enterprise?

MR. TREDWELL: It does not. It is a matter of common knowledge.

PROFESSOR SELIGMAN: Do I understand you to mean that all these statements that have been made to us about the appropriation of large community-made values by individuals are unfounded? Is it your theory that the real estate men in New York City are not an especially favored class?

MR. TREDWELL: Exactly; if Mr. Astor had taken his money and put it in the Emigrant Savings Bank across the way here at the beginning—he had a large fortune—as a compound interest proposition it would have beaten out his land investments by a large margin. It must be remembered when Mr. Astor put his money into land he was one of the largest merchants of his day and his investing capital was made in merchandising. It was not that rich men made a great deal of money out of land speculation. It was rich men who took the profits out of the commercial hazard of their business. It is not the poor men who can individually put much money into real estate to-day. In bulk or collectively the total is very large but the speculator or operator or investor in real estate is usually a fairly well-to-do man who out of trade put his surplus profit into real estate. The reason why, is: They do not want to put all their eggs in one basket. Real estate spells safety or did until it has become the latter day target for all sorts of social reforms.

MR. LEUBUSCHER: Real estate, as I understand you, is getting increasingly harder burdens than others for some years?

MR. TREDWELL: Declining prices indicate that.

MR. LEUBUSCHER: You do not think that declining immigration has anything to do with these prices?

MR. TREDWELL: Yes; in certain spots.

MR. LEUBUSCHER: Mr. Purdy, President of the Tax Board, has given figures which show that in 1880, real estate, land and buildings together, paid 87 per cent. of the budget.

MR. TREDWELL: Yes.

MR. LEUBUSCHER: And that in 1914, last year—I have not got the figures for this year—real estate paid 75 per cent. of the budget. Now, you say, that is increasing the burdens of real estate?

MR. TREDWELL: Would it not be nearer the fact if you made the statement this way: 97 per cent. of the tax levy, rather than of the budget.

MR. LEUBUSCHER: 97 per cent. of the tax levy?

MR. TREDWELL: Yes. Would not it be a better statement for you to make than the other?

MR. LEUBUSCHER: 97 per cent. of the taxes received?

MR. TREDWELL: 97 per cent. of the tax revenue comes out of real estate.

FOURTH HEARING.

November 17, 1915, 8 P. M., Room 16, City Hall, Professor Edwin R. A. Seligman, Presiding.

TESTIMONY OF MR. DANIEL CAVANAGH,

Organizer, Society of Native Born of the United States of America.

MR. CAVANAGH: It is certainly advisable to take off the tax on improvements and buildings and put it on land values. When a citizen undertakes the responsibility and invests capital to beautify the city and to give employment to idle labor, it is idiotic to penalize him for doing such a meritorious thing. Suppose we increased the license fee on saloons in this town, from $1,500 a year, what they pay to-day, to $10,000 a year, would it not practically obliterate the saloon business? Take the taxes off building and buildings will multiply.

To-day we have in Greater New York 193,077 vacant lots and parcels whose assessed valuation is 618 millions of dollars. The working people are, in the meantime, looking for employment and capital is looking for an opportunity to invest in these valuable locations. People cannot buy things unless they get employment. There are only three ways I know of to make a living, one is to work for it, the second is to beg for it, and the third is to steal it. The people are not allowed to work by the land speculators and they are prohibited from begging or stealing by the police, so what are the working people going to do under such conditions?

We, single taxers, want to encourage capital and labor. We want to stimulate business. We want the people to have money in the only legitimate way they can get it, so that they can buy things. Last winter there was, according to the records of the labor unions, 500,000 people idle in Greater New York. These idle people had no money to buy the products of labor. The City of New York must raise for the year 1916 $212,000,000. If you put this burden on the land speculators, we, who have studied this question for a generation, claim that involuntary poverty will be abolished; that capital will flow to New York; that business will boom as it has never done before; that the crimes that are caused by undeserved indigency will disappear; that labor will be prosperous, happy and contented; that the land speculators, many of whom are aliens, will emigrate; and that the reign of righteousness will obtain.

The very same conditions are rapidly coming to pass right now in the United States that existed in France in 1789 previous to the breaking out of the French Revolution. The rich are getting richer and the poor are getting poorer. When labor is looking for employment, capital should keep them busy. I cannot understand why the rich should keep the poor idle when they get all that the poor produce above a bare living. You would not keep horses in a stable to eat their heads off? Then, why allow the working people to be kept idle? The bees produce the honey and the drones consume it. It would be foolish for the drones to stop the bees from gathering honey. They have the flowers and the fields. The land speculators tell the bees to keep off the flowers. Now, we ask this Committee to get the drones off the fields and flowers and let the bees get busy. The workers must get the rent to pay to the landlord, and it is, therefore, up to the landlord to give the people a chance to earn the money to pay the rent.

PROFESSOR SELIGMAN: How would this change give more employment?

MR. CAVANAGH: If you put the taxes on land values you will get rid of the speculators. They would have to use the land. They would have to erect buildings on it and in that way give employment to labor.

PROFESSOR SELIGMAN: After enough buildings have been erected for the use of the community, what then would these men do?

MR. CAVANAGH: I don't believe there will ever be enough.

MR. SIMON: You made the statement that New York City could never be overbuilt.

MR. CAVANAGH: I mean that. I mean that there never could be enough houses built in the city to satisfy all the people.

MR. SIMON: If the city is not overbuilt, do you still think that rents would come down?

MR. CAVANAGH: Every new house built has a tendency to reduce rents.

MR. SIMON: If you have got just enough apartments, not too many, how would the rents come down?

MR. CAVANAGH: I do not think the people can ever have enough.

MR. SIMON: You said it would never be overbuilt.

MR. CAVANAGH: There would never be enough, positively not.

MR. LINDNER: If the demand is going to keep right up, Mr. Cavanagh?

MR. CAVANAGH: I believe that if the taxes were taken off improvements and placed on land values, we would get rid of the land speculator, and every valuable lot would be used to its fullest capacity. Involuntary poverty would be abolished. The workingmen would have employment. Our young men would get married. The population would increase and create demand for more houses.

DR. WILCOX: Is it your idea when you say that there never would be enough houses that there would come nearer being enough than now?

MR. CAVANAGH: Yes; it would come nearer to being enough than now.

TESTIMONY OF MR. PETER AITKEN.

MR. AITKEN: In my judgment this inquiry gets its chief significance, not from the urgent necessity for the protection of certain speculative real estate investments, nor from the need of this great city for larger revenues, nor even from the effort it represents to save the unfortunate victim of the great white plague, but from its connection with the worldwide movement now in progress to substitute Democracy for Privilege. By Democracy is here meant control by the masses of those natural resources from which man obtains life, liberty, and happiness. By Privilege is meant their control by a restricted class. Such substitution naturally produces friction.

We are told that capital will withdraw if not assured its customary reward and a panic will ensue. Privilege knows the danger involved in thus biting off its nose to spite its face and only employs it in extreme cases, but the masses are frequently frightened by the threat into refusing to risk their half-loaf for the chance of getting a whole one.

Now, we are all Americans and the American idea is democracy. I assume, therefore (certain charges to the contrary nothwithstanding), that this Committee is in sympathy with the desire of the masses of wage workers to get the full product of their labor and will disregard the threats of disaster to follow the enforcement of this moderate demand for the untaxing of buildings. Of course, one is tempted to indulge in counter threats of what will happen if this is not done, but we understand that is bad form—except for Privilege.

An effort has been made by the enemies of this movement to identify it with what is known as the single tax, because single tax is said to aim at common property in land. This, of course, is deliberate misrepresentation. Henry George did not advocate common property in land in the popular sense of that term, which is that a man's farm or garden should cease to be under his control or that what he produces from it should cease to be exclusively his. Such a proposal would, of course, be unpopular with the American people. What Henry George in fact teaches is that a man should be allowed to own all the land he will pay taxes on.

He also teaches that the tax on land should be high enough to insure its proper and profitable use, so that no one could afford to monopolize and hold it idle, thereby throwing men out of work and keeping down wages. This would be popular with the American people for they know that when wages are high and the workers are all busy everybody prospers, except the idler. But it is unpopular with the privileged class who seek to monopolize the earth and the success of whose schemes requires plenty of cheap labor. So their champions distort Henry George's teachings by magnifying the letter which killeth and suppressing the spirit which giveth life.

There can be no doubt that land monopoly is un-democratic and un-American. It is, therefore, safe to assume that no member of this Committee will be so unpatriotic as to thus misrepresent Henry George, who, whatever his mistakes, was the greatest champion of man's rights to the use of the earth and, therefore, the greatest enemy of land monopoly the world has ever seen.

Now, while the single tax will certainly destroy land monopoly in any community having the character, intelligence and courage to apply it, I realize that there are few communities with these qualities sufficiently developed to insure its proper application or even its adoption. The habit of land speculation is a stubborn one. I am not prepared to renounce unreservedly the speculative instinct in any form. All business from the farmers up—or down, is more or less speculative. Perhaps the "lure" of the unearned increment is a harmless necessary stimulant without which human society would languish and die. But, I think not. I think a normally constituted and properly regulated society can survive and progress without either land or race track gambling. I used to be sure but recent events have somewhat shaken my confidence in human nature. I used to think the true laws of social progress were clear, unmistakable and beneficient. But, now, I am willing to accede to a little more experimenting. And so I favor this experimenting of 10 per cent. a year. In fact I would be willing to compromise on 5 per cent., if the sincere co-operation of privilege could be secured thereby. Even that I should wish to submit to a referendum, for I think that unless a majority of the community wants a reform, its success is doubtful.

That there will be some friction encountered in making the change everyone admits—that there will be some householders, as well as vacant lot holders, who will have to pay more taxes is unquestionable and that some mortgages may be inconveniently called—especially if their holders are interested in discrediting the plan—goes without saying, but we believe these evils will be few and ephemeral, while the good results will be general and cumulative.

These exceptional cases will be unjustly treated, so it is said. Changes in the law—if the general community considers that they will be for its benefit—are not frequently retarded seriously by some individual suffering from them. The protective tariff, let us take, for instance. Many men have gone into the protected industries with the idea that their profits would continue to be large, but the change in public sentiment resulted in a change of the tariff and their business was practically destroyed. Now, while we sympathize with them, we do not consider that they have been unjustly treated. The same may be said of race track legislation, where great properties are destroyed and large numbers of men are thrown out of work. We have had a change in the excise laws recently. The taxes were raised from $1,200 to $1,500 a year, and, as a consequence, many saloons were thrown out of use and saloon keepers and bartenders are idle. That did not prevent us from enforcing the law. It seems to me that the question of justice or injustice is somewhat out of place here, in fact, we never know in advance what social justice is. I understand that Herbert Spencer has defined justice as being based on expediency, and the expediency of this measure is the ground on which I ask for its adoption. I believe that the good results of this legislation will be so apparent that before very long there will be a new sense of justice created in the people, which will convince the public's conscience that monopoly of land is wrong, unjust and immoral. There may be something found in enforcing this law that would have an injurious effect. Then we must decide that the measure is unjust, because it injures society.

The effect of a tax upon land is just the reverse of a tax upon buildings, so far as rent is concerned. If it were only applied to one building or to certain buildings it would not so influence rents, for land and building, where property is improved, are inseparable, and, therefore, both taxes will act the same. But, an increased tax on all land will tend to bring land now vacant into use by reducing the selling price of land. It will not reduce its value for use but will tend to reduce the selling price. If the selling price of the land is reduced and the taxes on buildings are reduced, the land will be cheaper and will cost less to carry the buildings. This will be found to reduce rents. That is the general proposition.

I would like to make it clear, that in my judgment, if this movement were to stop with New York City, it would not be worth fighting for. I believe we would soon reach an impasse if we confined it to New York City. But I think it is quite clear that if this fundamental reform showed good results in New York City it would spread to every other country, and in fact would spread all over the world.

MR. SIMON: How will tenants receive any benefit from the change?

MR. AITKEN: It will lower rents because of the decreased cost of carrying the building.

MR. SIMON: And increase the cost of carrying the land?

MR. AITKEN: Not so much. The cost of carrying the land will be spread over a larger area. If you increase the cost of carrying the land you diminish rents because you bring more buildings into use?

MR. SIMON: That would be true if you did not have a certain amount to raise.

MR. AITKEN: I do not consider that the land would, as a whole, depreciate for use. I believe that should be considered. That is one of the bases of this argument.

MR. LINDNER: You do not think that the use value would be depreciated but the selling value would?

MR. AITKEN: That is what I tried to say.

Answering Mr. Simon's question, I think that the use value of the land is a better basis for assessing land than the selling value.

MR. LINDNER: Then you would retain the assessment on the basis of use value.

MR. AITKEN: I should be disposed to do that decidedly. I have often thought of that.

MR. LINDNER: Your idea of this is that this is an interesting experiment which you want to try as part of a world movement?

MR. AITKEN: Yes.

MR. LINDNER: Why try it on the metropolis where the harm, if there is going to be any harm, is going to be the greatest in the United States?

MR. AITKEN: It seems to me that serious harm is so unlikely as to be negligible. If harm became apparent, before long the people would repeal the law.

MR. LINDNER: Why not start the experiment on a smaller scale?

MR. AITKEN: Because it would not do so much good.

TESTIMONY OF MR. GEORGE ALEXANDER WHEELOCK.

MR. WHEELOCK: The gentlemen who are for the exemption of buildings start also off with saying, that the sea, and the moon and the earth, belong to the people. The people of the City of New York have borrowed over a billion of dollars on the land and building values, and these undoubtedly belong to the people.

The owner of property, if he has a mortgage, only has second value. He has an equity. The first mortgage comes first. The first mortgage of 66 2/3 per cent. makes the mortgagee the more than half-owner of every piece of property. The experts have testified before the "Mills Committee" that real estate in the City of New York is over-assessed to the amount of twenty or thirty-five per cent. If that is true, add the over-assessed value to the amount of the mortgage, and you will find that there is only from seven to ten per cent. of equity left to the property owner. The exemption of buildings is going to be a very dangerous experiment. If there is depreciation of any amount, the entire equity of the property owners will be wiped out. As ninety per cent. of the property in the City of New York bears a mortgage, there is only ten per cent. left which can survive the effect.

The object of this step towards the single tax is to reach the very rich men, and they are the very men that are going to escape it. When it is all over the smaller owners will be wiped out.

They also think that the unimproved property owners are almost all dishonest. The people who own unimproved property are the biggest losers in the city. There is not one piece of vacant property in the City of New York that is not a loser on the first investment. It will be a bigger loser should this come in.

The investor and the speculator—they seem to draw a line between the two. The man who invests is all right, but the man who speculates is all wrong. That is a distinction without a difference. Every investor is a speculator. Fifteen years ago, I was an investor. I wanted to put my money into something that would insure me a nice income in my old days. To-day I am a speculator. Why? Because my property does not bring in an adequate return. It does not bring in one per cent.

I say that I am opposed to the single tax. I am for the multiple tax. I believe in taxing everybody and everything that is taxable. Everybody should bear a just burden.

The mortgagee controls the situation entirely. The final word will come from him. They have testified here before you that property would shrink in value. You cannot have any improvements unless they loan you money. Ninety per cent. of the mortgages are controlled by the mortgage trust. Where are you going to get the money? If the lenders will not loan where is the improvement coming in? What you have got to do is to please your lender. They do not like this change. They do not want it. And they are the masters of the situation. They control it entirely.

MR. LEUBUSCHER: You stated that the very men that the propounder of this proposition wants to reach will escape?

MR. WHEELOCK: I did.

MR. LEUBUSCHER: Did you refer to the Astor family, whose holdings consist of seventy-five per cent. land values against twenty-five building values?

MR. WHEELOCK: They would escape entirely.

MR. LEUBUSCHER: Please explain how they will escape.

MR. WHEELOCK: Because even though the rest of the property is confiscated on account of the mortgage and ninety per cent. of it is mortgaged, their property, not being mortgaged, will remain in their hands.

MR. LEUBUSCHER: If the tax is entirely on land values and their holdings consist of 75 per cent. of land value, will they not have a larger tax to pay?

MR. WHEELOCK: They have the wealth to sustain it.

MR. LEUBUSCHER: They will be taxed higher than to-day?

MR. WHEELOCK: I presume so.

MR. LEUBUSCHER: You also stated that if this proposition were adopted that the lenders of money—the mortgagees—would draw in their loans and would not lend?

MR. WHEELOCK: Indeed.

MR. LEUBUSCHER: Do you consider yourself a better authority on that subject than Mr. Hurd, President of the Lawyers' Trust Company, which is the largest lending company in the world?

MR. WHEELOCK: No. He was only one of your witnesses. The others refuted it. The others were against it. He was only one of a number.

MR. LEUBUSCHER: As you have mentioned your property you will pardon me if I ask you a few questions about it. Will you kindly state what kind of property it is?

MR. WHEELOCK: It is residential property which I tried to change to mercantile property. I cannot change because I cannot borrow the money from the institutions. I want a half-million dollars.

MR. WILCOX: You stated that about ninety per cent. of the real estate in this city was mortgaged. We were told that there are about two hundred thousand real estate owners in this city. How many of those two hundred thousand do you think would be wiped out through the foreclosures that would result from this system?

MR. WHEELOCK: I think about one hundred and eighty thousand.

MR. WILCOX: Do you think the ultimate result would be that all real estate would be owned by one person?

MR. WHEELOCK: The law would be repealed before the patient dies. They would use the restorative of change of law.

MR. LINDNER: Would it not be true that the mere entering on the policy would scare people so that you would have an immediate reduction because the people would have to unload?

MR. WHEELOCK: Would have to unload.

MR. LINDNER: No new capital would be available?

MR. WHEELOCK: When the big loaning institutions shut down the smaller ones shut down likewise. They are afraid. And the estates will shut down and they will take their money out of improvements.

MR. LEUBUSCHER: You say that out of the two hundred thousand land owners in New York City only one hundred and eighty thousand would be ruined—that would be about 90 per cent?

MR. WHEELOCK: Yes.

MR. LEUBUSCHER: What percentage of the land values would that one hundred and eighty thousand people own, would you say? What per cent. of the land values of New York at the end of five years would they own?

MR. WHEELOCK: That is a matter of estimation.

MR. LEUBUSCHER: Do you stick to your figures, in view of the fact that the investigations of the Society to Lower Rents show that 99 families own one-ninth of the land value? Do you still stick to your figures?

MR. WHEELOCK: Yes, I stick to the figures.

TESTIMONY OF MR. CORNELIUS N. SHEEHAN,

Secretary, Twenty-eighth Ward Board of Trade, Brooklyn.

MR. SHEEHAN: In the City of New York, in 1910, the rent was just seven hundred and fifty million dollars. Of that seven hundred and fifty million dollars, three hundred and seventy-five million dollars was house hire and three hundred and seventy-five million dollars was land rent. That house hire of three hundred and seventy-five million dollars was just, because the owners of the houses, as owners of houses, rendered service to the tenant, as tenants, equivalent to the three hundred and seventy-five million dollars. Of that three hundred and seventy-five million dollars for land rent, not one cent of it was justified in being taken by the owners, for the reason that the owner, as owner, did nothing in return for it. Of that three hundred and seventy-five million dollars, one hundred and twenty-five million dollars went to taxes and two hundred and fifty million dollars went into private pockets.

Every four years in the City of New York the landlord class takes from the tenant class a sum equal to the war indemnity that Germany exacted from France, and the sum is continuously increasing, so that in 1914 instead of the tenants paying seven hundred and fifty million dollars, it was eight hundred million dollars, in exactly the same proportions.

In the 19th and 28th Wards, where land values are approximately fifteen hundred dollars per lot and houses worth from two thousand to four thousand dollars, the proportion of land values to house values being small, it follows that there is a low rental there. On every dollar that is paid in the Borough of Manhattan for rents, using it in the common sense of the term, 66 cents goes for land and 34 cents goes for improvements. In Brooklyn, out of every dollar paid, 51 cents goes for land and 49 cents for improvements, with the result that in Brooklyn rents are immeasurably lower than in Manhattan and as a consequence of that we have got a very much better community there in Brooklyn than we have in Manhattan.

In the investigation made by the Sage Foundation Fund it was shown, in 1907, taking the average family to be one earning from $500 to $1,800 a year, that out of every dollar earned on the average 25 cents went for rent and 45 cents for food, leaving a balance of 30 cents out of every dollar to go for everything else. It has since risen, so that only 25 cents is left.

You will notice that because rent and food have absorbed a large proportion of the average income, that the spending power of the individual is reduced. Now, under this proposition, what we propose to do is this; as 62½ per cent. of the taxable value of the City of New York consists of land, taking it as a whole, and 37½ per cent. consists of improvements, that wherever a man's property is divided as 37½ is to 62½ the taxes will remain identical. Wherever—I am now taking it upon the whole 50 per cent. reduction—at the end of five years, there would be this change of twice as much taxation upon land as upon improvements, the result would be that in the Borough of Brooklyn there would be a reduction of 9 per cent.; in other words, that wherever the increase in land value was beyond 62½ per cent., for every one per cent. increase there would be five-eighths of one per cent. increase in taxes, and the contrary would be true if they are decreased, there would be a decrease in taxation. So that in the case of a man who would increase his property to equal the value of the land, his tax would be reduced nine per cent. Now, the proposition is this: Under our system of franchise—and land value is a franchise value and nothing else—if a corporation did not exercise its franchise, we immediately, or in theory, do confiscate that. We have now got a Public Service Commission which, in theory, is supposed to inflict penalties upon such a corporation if they do not exercise their franchise to the full interest of the public. Now, we hold that when the land values that are made by the community and made by no one else rises to a given value by productive necessities, that property should be used to the full value. We say it is bad economics when a law is not so framed as to control the use of community-made value. Our proposition is by increasing the tax on land we reduce the taxes on houses. In that way we make it cheaper to build houses. We make it more profitable to build houses. But more true than anything else, by taxing land and permitting a man to use land, which is the essence of all, we make man a free being which he is not to-day under our present system of taxation.

TESTIMONY OF MR. JAMES P. KOHLER.

MR. KOHLER: I agree with this proposed change in the system of taxation. I believe that the land should bear it all. I believe that land can bear it all, and there is no question about it. I believe it will do more for the land owner than anything else. If you look at the tax lien sales in Queens you will see how they are suffering. I think a change in the system of taxation would obviate most of this distress on the part of the land owner himself.

There is such concentration of wealth in the hands of the few that the multitude of consumers are deprived of purchasing power. That would be absolutely destroyed by a change in the tax system, by which the "400"—these land owners—those rich individuals that came in here and bought farms way back—got rich. They are the billionaires of the present day. They are growing rich by the tremendous increase in business here in New York City.

Now, every ten years we have a panic. A change in this tax system would absolutely stop panics. The time for prosperity to come has come. After it has come the real estate boomers will get in all over the United States from the Atlantic to the Pacific. They will swallow up all the business prosperity and the country will be thrown right back in the following panic. If you take the tax off buildings and put it right on the land, you are going to stop this speculation and panic.

Buildings, of course, include factories. Wherever there is a rule of taxation exempting churches, schools, colleges, you multiply that form of building. If you exempt houses, therefore, you will multiply that form, and so on, factories and everything else. Now, who will say that factories are not a good thing. I don't know of anybody that says homes are not a good thing. I cannot imagine how a tax taken off buildings and put on land can work in any way but good for the general community.

TESTIMONY OF MR. M. W. NORWALK.

MR. NORWALK: I present myself as a land owner and as a vacant land owner. I say that the city should return as much of the money as possible that it has robbed the citizens of. There is no reason why the city should come and tell you, Mr. So and So, you have got some money, give me some. Would you allow any highwayman to do that? Where does the city get the right to do it? She is assuming the right.

PROFESSOR SELIGMAN: Your argument is then that we ought to have no tax?

MR. NORWALK: We ought to take that which the people, as a whole, produce. That is the only thing we ought to have—that which belongs to us. Every penny that we take which does not belong to us, whether I do it, or you do it, or anybody else does it, or it is done by our representatives sitting in your chairs there, I say that is robbery. That is what I hate.

PROFESSOR SELIGMAN: Do we understand that you are in favor of taxing land or the improvements on land?

MR. NORWALK: I am in favor of the tax on land values and nothing on buildings.

Now, as I am a land owner I want to make my statement to you. I bought a piece of land on which I concluded to put a residence for myself and my family. I went to the builder and asked him about it and he said: "Well, it will cost you from three thousand to six thousand dollars for a private residence." I consulted the assessor and he said they would tax me about two per cent. on the three thousand dollars and that two per cent. would cost me sixty dollars. That means that the city is taking that much away from me. That is one thousand for every three thousand that I put in because two per cent. of three is six per cent. on one thousand; in other words I will lose a thousand dollars. That is, if I put up a three thousand dollar house (never mind about the land for they will tax me on that too, and that is not the question here). They will be actually robbing me of one-third of the value I put in.

By justice, what is yours is yours. What I earn, what I produce, if I give service and get something for my services, that is mine. If you give services, it is yours. Now, what service does the owner of land as such give? He gives me a permit to work. That is what he gives me. He gives me a permit to go and build. He did not produce that land. He did not buy it from a man who produced it. I might say to you, that coat there, I made it. Or I might say I made the value of it. That would not make any difference. In so far as land is concerned you know no man made it. This coat was made by the tailor. The carpenter made this desk. The builder made this building. You have no right to take one part of it nor have I; but land value has been made by the people at large. The land has been made by nobody and nobody has the right to own land. Man can use land only exclusively. If you want to exclude everybody else from using that land you must pay to the excluded, by paying the full annual rent of it to the people, in the shape of taxes.

TESTIMONY OF MR. BENJAMIN DOBLIN,

Representing the New York State Single Tax League.

MR. DOBLIN: Our tax difficulties seem to require the attention of an investigating committee every year, and some years the attention of more than one committee.

It is evident that our tax system is defective.

Since failure has been the outstanding characteristic of our preceding attempts to rectify tax evils, I take it that this Committee will consider with tolerance principles which lie at the foundation of a just system of taxation, even though they run counter to its predilections. Unless you do, your labors will be as barren as have been the labors of other committees. There are three important threads in the fabric of taxation: The first thread is the valuation of property legally liable to taxation. The second is the budget which determines the sum of revenue necessary to be raised. The third is the tax rate, which is the percentage, or tax levied upon each individual item of assessed property, calculated to provide the amount of money required by the budget.

I take it, that there is no ground for dissatisfaction with the tax rate. If property has been equitably valued and the budget is acceptable, then the tax rate, whatever it may be, which is obtained by a mathematical process, must be as innocent as the multiplication table.

This narrows our study to the two remaining threads. Property legally liable to taxation and its valuation. Valuations or appraisals are made, under the direction of the Tax Commissioners, by deputies. It is true that there is some complaint that the valuations of real estate are inequitable. It is said they are excessive. In support of this allegation a table is submitted, consisting of properties which have been sold with the true considerations stated; we are properly cautioned, however, not to place too much reliance upon this showing, because the exhibit is not an accurate statement of fact.

The deputies charged with the duty of valuing real estate for the purpose of taxation are not limited in their findings by sales at foreclosure. We know that many influences are operative in such sales which may produce sub-normal values. The substantial accuracy of the valuations is, to my mind, clearly established by the table of sales for 1914, which have been cited by the Real Estate Board in support of its claim that property is over-assessed. This table showed that the assessed value exceeded stated considerations by only one per cent. for the whole city; that for the Borough of Manhattan the excess of taxed values over sales values was eight per cent. in 1913, seven per cent. in 1914, and four per cent. in 1915, up to June 24th. As a matter of fact, these objectors to the accuracy of the assessment could prove, most conclusively, before any commission in condemnation, where their individual property was involved, that no reasonable, safe conclusion could be reached by appraising their property at its assessed value, less the excess over average sales prices.

Let us be fair to the assessing officials. I am not asking that tax valuations be established by the rules employed in taking individual holdings for public uses, for that method might lead to over-assessment. Ample provision is made for the protection of the individual owner. If he thinks he is over-assessed, he has the right to prove that fact before the tax officials. If they refuse him relief, then he can appeal to the Courts. We know the Courts are quite solicitous in their protection of property rights.

Assuming that the charge that property is over-assessed is justified, what remedy is proposed? Mere growling will not make matters any better. The Tax Department recently submitted to the legislature an act providing that in all future sales the true consideration shall be stated in the deed, and that the facts be given to the Tax Department. This was designed to inform the assessing officials of the truth regarding nearly all normal transfers. This avenue of knowledge was denied them, however, and the bill was defeated by the hostility of the real estate interests. I submit that it is hardly fair to criticize the work of the assessors when we deny them the facilities they require to make accurate appraisals, based upon all legitimate transactions. No other change is needed to insure more accurate appraisal than the obligatory provision that the true consideration should be stated in all deeds.

A year ago it might have been necessary to thresh out again the futility, injustice and insufficiency of a tax upon personal property. Our present experience has, I am sure, satisfied this generation that the tax on personal property should be discarded. The weight of experience and authorities enforces this disposition of that fool tax.

It is clear that real estate has been, and must continue to be, the chief source from which to gather our revenue.

Real estate, however, is a composite, composed of improvements and land, and you are to determine whether our taxation shall distinguish between them. I believe it should. That they are dissimilar is evident. Improvements are produced and may be prevented by the same incidence of taxation which seeks to prevent the prevalence of dogs by a dog tax, or to suppress saloons by a high license. Land is a natural element, and has no cost of production. The value of improvement is, on the contrary, determined by the cost of production or reproduction. I shall not stop here to discuss the question of upkeep and replacement, except to call attention to another fundamental difference between improvements and land, for we can agree, I believe, that land is not burdened with any overhead charges.

The value of land is clearly and unmistakably a social value. Prof. Seligman contends that it is not the only thing to which a social value, or, as the economists term it, an unearned increment, attaches. Whether it is true of other things or not, the Professor does not contend that improvements on land are equally favored by economic influences—that they gain an unearned increment.

Land is the only taxable property that is now tax free. A tax on a produced article is blended into, and becomes a part of the cost of production, and is passed on with a profit to the consumer. Taxes on land, on the contrary, are a permanent deduction from the selling price, so that the purchaser buys the property tax free. The purchase price of land is determined by deducting taxes from the estimated gross income. The net income is then capitalized at the current rate of interest. This value is its taxable value.

Suppose New York City should find an inexhaustible deposit of gold at the end of one of its new piers from which it could, at practically no cost, dredge each year enough gold to pay all the cost of running the city; in this event it could abolish all the present taxes on real estate. It is obvious that the effect would be to enhance land values by the capitalization of the annual saving in taxes.

Is not this really conceded by the advocates of diffused taxation, who plead that the present taxes on real estate are depressing realty values. The clear inference of their position, I take it, is that if real estate is relieved, land values will rise.

Let me make this proposition more concrete: Suppose a broker submits a parcel of land to one of the gentlemen on this Committee, seeking an investment. The broker presents the data showing the cost of the improvements with the itemized carrying charges, together with the gross rental. This gross rental for the land amounting to $700 annually, at what price do you think the investor would consider the land for purchase? Let us assume that he is content with a modest five per cent., would he pay $14,000 for the plot of land? Certainly not. He would first deduct $200 or thereabouts for taxes, and agree to pay no greater price than $10,000, which at five per cent., must return $500, equal to the balance of the gross income remaining after deducting taxes. I take it, that those on this Committee familiar with real estate transactions will concede the substantial accuracy of this illustration. It is proper to ask at this point who, in this instance, pays the taxes—surely not the buyer; he has already discounted the tax in the purchase price. Let us press this point a little closer, and ask, who will gain if subsequent taxes are less than the $200 per annum agreed upon as a fair allowance? The owner, of course, and, in any subsequent sale, he will capitalize that "velvet." This has been the procedure and the cause of some of our rich landed estates. A representative of the Astor estate testified before the State Legislative Commission that the present taxes were taking a larger percentage of income than formerly. This was a gratuitous statement on their part; the elements that went to the finding of that conclusion were carefully, and I suspect consciously, withheld. It might help our understanding of the situation if they would give us the total amount of rent collected at present, as against the total collected ten, twenty, thirty years ago.

Now, suppose your great, great grandfather had purchased this island at the equivalent of twenty-four dollars; that his descendants had busied themselves since his death with collecting and spending an ever-increasing unearned income, would you consider it unjust to tax this unearned income at its source rather than relieve it from burdens clearly and legally incident to it by taxing onerously investments in bonds held since 1906, which have declined in value 21 points? Here, I want to call your attention that while all other securities have decreased in value the value of lots in New York City has increased.

Can a merchant and his descendants live on the income of inactive goods, and at the end of one hundred or more years leave his posterity far richer than he was?

Improvements, like other merchandise, deteriorate in value and utility; land, on the contrary, is the only property that, here or there, but most certainly somewhere, and all the time, will return wealth to the fortunate holder without effort, and, besides, increase in value—a splendid instance where one can eat his cake and have it, too.

Some testimony has been submitted to this Committee to the effect that rents would not be reduced if all taxation was concentrated upon land values. We may be innocent of economic knowledge without being stupid. If it were true that rents would not decline then the opposition and objections to the proposed shift of taxation from improvements to land values are unreasonable and insincere.

The principle that should guide the judgment of the Committee in the expression of its recommendations is found and successfully applied in the betterment tax. The reasons which justify apportioning the cost of installation of streets and sewers on the benefited land should be as controlling in the levying of upkeep charges and cost of operation of public utilities and services.

We, single taxers, are not primarily concerned about improving the mere mechanics of taxation; we are not striving for a means but an end. It is not the unearned increment tax or even the taxation of land values. What we want is that the land of America shall become the heritage of the whole American people. The single tax would transfer all taxes from private wealth to common wealth and by imposing a tax sufficiently large to absorb the whole of the socially created values for the public good. We announce without equivocation that we mean to achieve this as quickly as possible. For this, we are engaged in a widespread propaganda and when, some day, an informed public decides to reassume its right to the land, the landlord cannot plead surprise.

I take it, this tax reform measure you are considering is an honest effort to make an easy transition. It may be wise to introduce the betterment of our social system with as little disturbance as possible. That is the business of statesmen. Single taxers, however, are not worrying about the loss the beneficiaries of our present unfair system shall have to suffer in the process of establishing just economic conditions.

We single taxers have no patience with the timid high-brow reformers, who would avert calamity by deodorizing economic cancers. Our avowed purpose is to end this agony, at once, if possible, without regard to the outcries and objections of the pets of privilege. If you retard, you cannot prevent our ultimate success. We are pacifists, and desire to see improved social conditions established by the reasoned, calm action of citizens, rather than the frenzied acts of a mob.

TESTIMONY OF MR. ALEXANDER LAW,

Secretary of the Tenants' Union.

MR. LAW: On the first of May, 1906, a meeting was called in Abingdon Square, which well filled the square; at this meeting the Tenants' Union was launched on its beneficent course. The wide publicity which was given to its advent, made the birth of the Tenants' Union an economic event of great importance. Similar unions were formed in many places throughout the civilized world.

The Union holds that through exorbitant rents, the tenants are deprived of one-quarter to one-third of their hard earned wages foı the right to work and be of benefit to the community, thereby depriving their families of much needed food and clothing and other essentials, and are threatened with being thrown into the streets, unless they submit to any exactions the landlords choose to impose upon them. The fact that their health, as well as their lives, are jeopardized by being compelled to live in congested quarters, deprived of sunlight and fresh air, in inflammable disease-breeding tenements, many of them unfit for human habitation, is a disgrace to the great wealthy City of New York, and a reflection on the humanity and civilization of the Twentieth Century.

The Union believes the great need of this city is sanitary, fireproof buildings, equipped with modern improvements, for our tenement population to live in, and lower rents; more employment for its mechanics and laborers, and is convinced that untaxing buildings and increasing the tax on land will materially help to secure both.

The recent destruction of life in both tenement and factory fires shows the imperative need of doing everything possible to encourage the erection of fireproof buildings for people to live and to work in.

Untaxing buildings will encourage the erection of such structures and have a tendency to eliminate the thousands of tenements whose inmates now go to bed every night in danger of being burnt to death before morning and do away with factories whose workers every day face as deadly perils in trying to make an honest living as do the soldiers engaged in the great war now devastating Europe.

In the Bronx, and other parks of our city, all sorts of wild animals, including monkeys, live in houses, built and owned by the city. *They* have all the advantages of Twentieth Century civilization, for which they pay no rent at all. If we can house animals in our parks under such ideal conditions, what can we not do for our citizens, who pay all taxes, including the salaries of our public officials, who make the land values the privileged few now deprive them of, and keep them in hopeless misery and poverty, who hold land out of use while hundreds of the children of the city are sacrificed every year for want of room other than the dangerous and over-crowded streets to play in?

The Union recommends the election of an administration, which, in co-operation with the Board of Health, will condemn unsanitary tenements by the block, and on the block, as a whole, erect sanitary, fireproof dwellings with modern improvements, including roof gardens for playgrounds, the entire centre to be an open court to be also utilized for playgrounds, to be rented at cost of acquiring the property and keeping it in first class condition.

The Union also recommends taking all Long Island in the city limits, as we are convinced the great City of the Twentieth Century will be built there, where there is land enough swept by ocean breezes, with buildings untaxed, and land taxed to the extent of making it unprofitable to hold it out of use, homes can be furnished for the millions who prefer to work for themselves and families, instead of being deprived of their God-given rights for the benefit of those whose only interest in them is to rob them.

TESTIMONY OF MR. LEO KENNETH MAYER,

Chairman, Brooklyn Civic Committee.

MR. MAYER: If the Single Tax had been in vogue for the past decade and had a propagandist appeared, urging the transfer of taxes from land values to labor values, there would be a cry beyond the power of description that the proposed system would be confiscatory, vile and deteriorating. Now, the converse is true. Labor values are taxed and certain persons are advocating relieving labor products and improved property from the burden of taxation and the imposition of a super-tax on land values, created by the presence of society. And now there is a cry that the system proposed would be confiscatory. If man is denied the opportunity to use the natural resources man's mission on earth is futile. He cannot live. The moment that you make it unprofitable to hold land—to hold land for speculation—just that very moment do you force land into use, and by forcing land into use, you give employment to every man in the country. The improvement of land, either building or otherwise, necessitates the employment of diggers, bricklayers, plasterers, carpenters, electricians and a hundred other trades. These people will spend the product of their labor, or wages, and the circulation of the product of human exertion will again be spent by the people who receive it, and so we have the circulation of money, or the means of exchange, which would still cause the employment of men in other walks of life.

What is the cause of crime and poverty? Idleness. What is the cause of most murders? Robbery. And, what is the cause of most robberies? Poverty and hunger. Most men stay on the straight and narrow path until the pangs of poverty take the opportunity and cross the threshold of their door. That man is cornered, and life and liberty for him become a question. Then he kills and that man becomes the scum of society. Is not society, and society alone, responsible for this man's downfall? I say, place a tax upon idle land which would be confiscatory to that land if it remains idle. It would force it into use. It would give employment to men. It would eliminate idleness, poverty and hunger, and you will furthermore get your sufficient revenue to run the city.

TESTIMONY OF MRS. GEORGE ALEXANDER WHEELOCK.

MRS. WHEELOCK: I have two small private houses which some time ago were without tenants. Last winter, during the period of hard times, I allowed some people to live in these houses without paying any rent. One of them had a new baby and he felt his money was insufficient to permit him to live where he had been, so I allowed them to live in my house. Towards spring I had to move them out because they were wrecking my house. I have those two small houses rented now at $50 a month. Mr. Purdy knows that I am taxed on those houses over $1,100 a year each, and so you see what profits I get out of those two houses. Then, I am surrounded by loft buildings all the way around me—the twenty-five-story Vanderbilt Hotel and, in the back, big loft buildings. I consider it would be the rankest kind of injustice to take the tax from the Vanderbilt Hotel and put it on to my little place. The advocates of regulating the height of buildings claim that the tall buildings have stolen the light and air. Now they want to keep it without paying any taxes. They stole my light and air from me and now the game is to keep my buildings down to protect the theft. I consider it an outrage to have me share their taxes and put it on my little piece of ground.

Then about putting people to work: I have been very anxious to improve that property and help out this army of unemployed. I have been very active in the matter. I have been to all the loaning companies and tried to get a loan. I have offered the handsomest kind of bonus, but I have not been able to get a loan. They tell you that the supply is greater than the demand; that, in the last five years, Manhattan Island has been depopulated to the extent of 180,000. Because you make the transit facilities so splendid for the people in the outlying districts, we are suffering right here in New York City to-day. As for putting people to work, it is perfectly absurd because the lending institutions will control that absolutely, and it is only a question of time when the property owner that cannot get a loan is going to be wiped absolutely off.

As to the putting down of the price of building material and the price of building: the market price is there, and, with the architect's fees and all the overhead charges that go with it, it is impossible to make that operation any cheaper than a certain amount.

FIFTH HEARING.

November 22, 1915, 2.30 P. M., Room 16, City Hall, Professor Edwin R. A. Seligman, Presiding.

TESTIMONY OF MR. ROBERT E. DOWLING,

Member, Legislation and Taxation Committee, Real Estate Board of New York.

PROFESSOR SELIGMAN: One of the chief points that has been made in these hearings is that all the benefit of money spent as a result of taxes accrues to the land owner. In your opinion is the land owner the sole beneficiary?

MR. DOWLING: No, not in my opinion.

PROFESSOR SELIGMAN: Will you tell us why not?

MR. DOWLING: In the first place he does not get any immediate increase in rent from improvements. He may have his property leased for five or ten years ahead and by the time the lease expires, there is no benefit and no increased rent owing to those increased expenditures.

We know that in the past five years, seven years or eight years even, there has not been a general increase in rent, but there have been improvements going on all the time. That demonstrates at once that the owner of the land does not get the increased benefit from increased expenditures. He not only does not get all the benefit but, in most instances, he does not get any, that we can find.

PROFESSOR SELIGMAN: If you say that the land owner does not get all the benefit, in what way do other classes get any of the benefit, in your opinion?

MR. DOWLING: The tenants, if they were store tenants, mercantile tenants, doing business in retail lines or in wholesale lines throughout the country, have made very large profits during the period when land values decreased. The owners of land were being subjected to much increased taxation because of improvements that benefited the whole population of the city, but did not increase land values.

PROFESSOR SELIGMAN: If you take thirty or fifty years, of course, land values have increased?

MR. DOWLING: Yes.

PROFESSOR SELIGMAN: Do you think that the same cause which has in general led to an increase of land values, namely, increase of general prosperity, has also contributed to an increase of the income of the community at large?

MR. DOWLING: Yes, I think the income of the community at large has risen in a greater proportion than the income of land owners.

PROFESSOR SELIGMAN: Assuming that other classes, as well as land owners, benefit from city expenditures, would you say that the net result is to have only the land owner win out? If this other class gets a larger income, have they got to pay larger rents for the houses they occupy? Or, would you say that the wages, salaries, earnings in general in New York City are so much higher than in other places in the State that even allowing for the increase in rent there is a margin over for the community at large?

MR. DOWLING: I think that the rents have not increased in proportion to the earning power of the community in the way of wages or income from business. I think that is plainly shown in the great business district south of 23rd Street. I think that you can say safely that rentals in general are not as high as they were in 1900. We know the wages and salaries of all commercial people in large business houses are higher than fifteen years ago. Mechanics' wages are higher; laborers' wages are higher, but rentals are not higher.

PROFESSOR SELIGMAN: Could not, however, someone say that the reason why mechanics' wages are higher is because the cost of living has gone up?

MR. DOWLING: Yes.

PROFESSOR SELIGMAN: If it were true that the lawyer's or doctor's income in this city is entirely swallowed up by the increase of rents that he would have to pay, would there be any inducement for those people to come to New York? How could you explain the immense increase in population in New York unless there was a margin of additional income which is to be found here?

MR. DOWLING: I could not explain that. I am satisfied that the income is not swallowed up by the increase in rents.

PROFESSOR SELIGMAN: If we were to transfer the taxes on buildings to land, would there be more employment for the laborers and more prosperity, and less unemployment?

MR. DOWLING: No.

PROFESSOR SELIGMAN: Do you believe that this untaxing of buildings would lead to a permanent and continuous increase in the output of buildings?

MR. DOWLING: I do not.

PROFESSOR SELIGMAN: Why not?

MR. DOWLING: Most of the building on Manhattan Island—and I presume the other boroughs are the same—is conducted by professional operators and builders. They are obliged to finance their operations by mortgage loans. So far as I have heard from the lenders on bonds and mortgages and what I know myself, the transfer of the tax from the buildings to the land would discourage, for a time, at any rate, the lending of money on bonds and mortgages—and I do not believe that anybody will deny that for a period—a time that I cannot estimate—maybe for years—it may be for from two to three or five years, until they are absolutely satisfied that that system of change of taxation will not hurt them, they will not go into the lending of money on any improvements, consequently there will be less employment of labor in New York in building.

PROFESSOR SELIGMAN: At the expiration of this period, when doubts have been resolved—assuming that there would then be an increase in building operations—would this increase of building operations be a continuous one after the new equilibrium has been attained?

MR. DOWLING: Yes.

PROFESSOR SELIGMAN: Would the change in taxation make this increased demand still larger than before, after the first impulse had spent itself and the population had been housed in this increase?

MR. DOWLING: I do not think it would. I think it would decrease building activity for some time. Then if rents were higher, if there was a great shortage of space and rents went very high, why, if people would be able to pay higher rates for money and could coax people from the other parts of the country to lend money. You understand money will come if you pay a high enough price for it.

PROFESSOR SELIGMAN: It has been claimed before us that because the ordinary merchant and manufacturer will spend less for rent, he will have this additional money to have for other productive employment. What, in your opinion, becomes of the money which is now paid in the way of higher rent? Does it go into the hands of the land owner, who either spends it in riotous living or puts it in the bank? If he puts it into the bank, is it available for productive employment?

MR. DOWLING: Under normal, usual conditions, it is. Yes.

PROFESSOR SELIGMAN: If the merchant in future has to pay in rent only eight hundred dollars instead of one thousand dollars he can put his difference into more luxuries, or with two hundred dollars he can employ more workmen. Would that mean any net increase of employment? Does it make any difference to the community whether the two hundred dollars is employed by the merchant or the land owner, as an economic proposition?

MR. DOWLING: I cannot see that it does.

PROFESSOR SELIGMAN: Is it your opinion that this change in taxation would lead to great social and economic benefits by increasing wages and giving more employment?

MR. DOWLING: I think the reverse. I think it will lead to more unemployment in this city. I cannot see where it is going to reduce rents. I cannot see any possible way of reducing rent by a change of taxation, that is, transferring the tax from the building to the land. We have to raise the same amount from real estate. It will not reduce the amount to be collected.

PROFESSOR SELIGMAN: If you take it off buildings, would there be a tendency not to shift that part of the tax to the tenant?

MR. DOWLING: No. I do not see how taking the tax off the buildings would have any effect. Take a high building—there are so many—take the Woolworth Building if you like, or any other building you are interested in. There is a great deal more value in the building than there is in the land. Which is the argument of the single taxers that would untax the industry. Take an instance where the building is assessed at little more than the land, a few hundred thousand dollars more. If you take the tax off that building and put it on to the land we might save, and will save in that instance, at the present rate, about ten thousand dollars a year.

PROFESSOR SELIGMAN: Would you not pass that on to the tenant?

MR. DOWLING: I certainly would not. The tenants pass on to us additional expenses every day we have to pay for coal. We had to pay more for coal last year and more for wages, and more for porters. We never pass it on to the tenant. We get the same rent to-day that we did in 1907. We would simply say we have saved ten thousand dollars in taxes for the time being. I think it would be a detriment to other properties that I was interested in in other parts of the city where unemployment might affect tenants.

PROFESSOR SELIGMAN: Would the competition of future new buildings not compel you to pass that on to the tenant?

MR. DOWLING: I do not know. We have not been able to pass the increased taxes on to the tenants. There is really an over-supply in business space right now.

MR. LEUBUSCHER: As I understand, you told the Chairman that if this system of taxation is adopted, instead of the tenant benefiting by a lower rent he would have to pay a higher rent?

MR. DOWLING: I think he would; yes.

MR. LEUBUSCHER: If rent is decreased, will not wages be more then and will there not be more left for capital?

MR. DOWLING: It is never done in a practical sense. Wages went up in the City of New York as rents went up. I know know that from actual experience, that the wages of all building labor increased steadily while rents were increasing. Then rents decreased while labor stood at the same price because of conditions of control. We have not a free market in labor. We have a controlled labor market.

MR. LEUBUSCHER: Do you mean union labor?

MR. DOWLING: Union labor has prevented the price that is paid per hour going down. It did not prevent unemployment. Where rent has decreased we must pay the same wages whether the times be bad or good.

MR. LEUBUSCHER: Is there not also a control of the capital market as well as labor?

MR. DOWLING: No.

MR. LEUBUSCHER: It has been alleged that there was a combination of the large money-lending institutions and they could withhold mortgage loans if they desired.

MR. DOWLING: I never heard of it in all my time, and I have been thirty years in this business.

MR. LEUBUSCHER: Some of the witnesses so testified.

MR. DOWLING: I do not care who testified. I testify that there is not. There has never been any control between them. In fact, they compete when they have money, as I do.

MR. LEUBUSCHER: I understand you to say that the adoption of this plan would discourage the lending of money on mortgage?

MR. DOWLING: I think it would.

MR. LEUBUSCHER: Nobody, practically, would lend money?

MR. DOWLING: I stated my own opinion. I would not lend. I do not know anyone else that would. I think that everybody agrees with that.

MR. LEUBUSCHER: Do you agree with Mr. Hurd's statement made before this Committee that mortgage lenders have nothing to fear by the adoption of this plan?

MR. DOWLING: I do not.

MR. LEUBUSCHER: Mr. Hurd, you will concede, is an expert on that question?

MR. DOWLING: He is an expert in the mortgage bond business and selling bonds and mortgages, but he is not an expert in the real estate business.

MR. LEUBUSCHER: You say that rents have not increased as much as wages and profits? You confined that statement to south of Twenty-third Street?

MR. DOWLING: Yes.

MR. LEUBUSCHER: Do you mean to imply that generally throughout the city?

MR. DOWLING: I think that there are some sections where rents went up, owing to special conditions. In the city as a whole rents went down.

MR. LEUBUSCHER: You do not ascribe that to taxation?

MR. DOWLING: No, not principally to that. Of course increased taxation lowers values.

MR. LEUBUSCHER: And you spoke of the skyscrapers?

MR. DOWLING: Yes, I did.

MR. LEUBUSCHER: In which you are interested? In one instance you said you would save ten thousand dollars?

MR. DOWLING: On one building I think it would be about that.

MR. LEUBUSCHER: Do you think the owners of skyscrapers who are interested in any other kind of real estate will benefit by this plan?

MR. DOWLING: I expect that they would benefit. I think I would personally benefit.

MR. LEUBUSCHER: Do you know of any skyscraper owner advocating this proposition for the benefit of his own property?

MR. DOWLING: Only a few individual owners. I do not think that the corporations that own them, the bank, the trust company or the insurance companies have ever thought much about it. I heard the representative of a company that owns a large building say that he thought it would be a very good thing for the property. But he did not think it was a very good thing for the city at large or for us. I said so myself and I say so now here.

MR. SIMON: Mr. Dowling, it has been stated by a number of witnesses called here that there is land being held out of use to-day in the City of New York. Do you know of any cases where people have got land that is ripe for improvement and can get the finances are arbitrarily holding it out of use?

MR. DOWLING: There are very few people that have carried land. There are a few cases like Wendell and Eno. They do not think they can get a proper income out of the property and do not want the trouble of building. It is not business. It is not a general thing at all. It would not pay anybody to do it.

DR. WILCOX: It was testified by one of the witnesses that in his judgment the effect of this change would be to wipe out the equities of substantially ninety per cent. of all the property owners. Do you have any figures on that?

MR. DOWLING: I do not think you can wipe out ninety per cent. of the land owners in this city by any change of taxation except it was by confiscating their land. I do not think that the system of taxation would confiscate it to that extent.

DR. WILCOX: Would the owner who owns his home in the suburb, where the improvement is of more value than the land, be in the same class as the owner of the skyscraper, and would tend to get a benefit rather than an injury directly by this change?

MR. DOWLING: Yes, he would tend to get a benefit. If the tax bill were less on the land he would save that much.

DR. WILCOX: You think, as far as the owners of individual homes are concerned in New York, that they only own a small equity in the property, and that the effect of this change would be to wipe out all of this equity?

MR. DOWLING: I think it would.

DR. WILCOX: You think the tendency, even though he save in operating expenses in carrying his house, would be to decrease the value of the house?

MR. DOWLING: I think it would decrease the value because the saving would be so slight in those expenses that it would mean nothing.

DR. WILCOX: If it is true in the space of fifteen years that there will be an increase from four tracks to thirty-eight tracks crossing the East River, under and over, is it not to be expected that the population of Manhattan will, congested as it has been for a great many years, tend to decrease, and that consequently rents will tend to fall?

MR. DOWLING: I think that the population will probably not increase much on Manhattan Island. All the statisticians have estimated that as a result of these improvements of getting out to other parts of the city. I believe that is true. I do not think that the rent of the dwellings that will be left on Manhattan Island will fall because of that. The cheapest people will go the furthest way from the center —I mean the people who can pay less for rent. As a rule, the poorer dwellers leave the city. The more wealthy go out sometimes to these places, too, to get, as they think, cheaper rent, but I understand that they do not get it. They start for it merely.

DR. WILCOX: That is a very interesting statement; I had supposed that the cheapest and more hard-up of the population were those that stayed in the cheaper center on the west and east side of the city.

MR. DOWLING: That I do not think is true at all. I think that Brooklyn has a cheaper population and also a lower income per capita than New York City. Of course, I do not mean all classes. I mean among the laboring classes that work in the factories of Brooklyn. They get less wages generally at the same employment.

PROFESSOR SELIGMAN: If, as you say, rents will not decrease but rather increase and knowing that in advance, how can you expect that your land value will be seriously or deleteriously affected?

MR. DOWLING: Because of the fact that values are not based on mere incomes, but upon the confidence in the security.

PROFESSOR SELIGMAN: I note you express confidence that the results which other gentlemen have testified will ensue would not happen; and if you have confidence that rents would not come down, and that competition of buildings would not bring them down, why, then, should there be any difficulty as to investments?

MR. DOWLING: You don't see it, but I say it is a fact. Now, that is the business view of it. I am not speaking as an economist. I am speaking as a business proposition. It is just the same as different classes of property. You cannot sell me property in Queens no matter if it pays 15% profit. The capital that goes into real estate does not believe in a change of this kind and, therefore, you will have to change opinions of the investors on it.

TESTIMONY OF MR. WALTER STABLER,

Comptroller, Metropolitan Life Insurance Company.

MR. STABLER: I want it to be distinctly understood that I am not giving any views of the Metropolitan Life Insurance Company. I am giving my own personal views.

The company invested in Manhattan Island in mortgages upwards of $200,000,000 and between $14,000,000 and $16,000,000 in real estate besides. We are as largely interested in real estate in the city as any other corporation and more than any individual.

I have never been able to see what possible advantage could be derived by the city, by the real estate owners, or by the people of the city from the enactment of this idea into law.

In the first place I do not see how we can maintain the city's credit if this proposal should be seriously considered. That I have never heard explained or even any attempt made to explain it. That is the most serious consideration of the whole business.

In the second place, does it not threaten very seriously the largest vested interest in this city, or in the State—the real estate of the city?

If we were a new community the situation might be different; but we are not; we are an old community going on with this present method for two or three centuries. I cannot see how it would be possible to bring about anything of this kind without serious disaster, and in view of the present condition of real estate, I say, that it should not have any more hurdles to cross. I say that this thing should be killed for all time. That is my feeling. I feel very strongly upon that. I do not own a dollar's worth of real estate myself. I do not expect to. I think it would be serious business if anything is done to in any way affect the value of real estate or the readiness with which it may be exchanged or mortgaged.

If this idea goes into effect it is certain to upset values. If it does upset values it will of necessity require lenders of money to call for very considerable payment on their mortgages. It will, in my opinion, make it very difficult for real estate owners to borrow money on mortgage. Now, bring those two things together. Bring those two disasters together and you make a very serious situation.

While I am here I want to answer this gentleman here who asked a question whether there was any combination among money lenders. I say there is absolutely nothing of the kind and that I am in a position to know, because there can be no combination that does not include our company. We never have and we never will enter into any combination or anything that looks like a combination. I do not think any such thing exists anywhere. It could not. Sometimes there is very little money to lend; that is not because there is a combination. It is because conditions are such that people have not got the money to loan.

Now, if this would prevent the borrowing of money on real estate it would prevent the production of buildings, and to that extent the people who are employed in the production of buildings would suffer.

MR. LEUBUSCHER: Mr. Stabler, the fundamental business of your company is that of life insurance?

MR. STABLER: Yes, sir.

MR. LEUBUSCHER: The $200,000,000 that you have invested in mortgages on Manhattan Island are for the investment of policies holders?

MR. STABLER: Yes.

MR. LEUBUSCHER: Would you favor a plan which would decrease the death rate?

MR. STABLER: Would decrease the death rate?

MR. LEUBUSCHER: Yes.

MR. STABLER: We are doing all we can to decrease the death rate.

MR. LEUBUSCHER: Don't you think that is the principal thing for people to decrease?

MR. STABLER: We are doing all we can to decrease the death rate by various plans.

MR. LEUBUSCHER: Any plan which would automatically cause the substitution of new, healthy, modern tenements, for the old rookeries would tend to decrease the death rate?

MR. STABLER: Without doubt, it would.

MR. LEUBUSCHER: Without doubt, the advocates of this proposition claim that would be the result. If your company is convinced that would be the result of this plan, would you adopt it?

MR. STABLER: It would not be possible to convince us of any such thing.

MR. LEUBUSCHER: It would not be possible to convince you of that?

MR. STABLER: No. My mind is not open to any proposition which states that this plan will result in any more erection of buildings than would naturally follow a demand for them.

TESTIMONY OF MR. CHARLES O'CONNOR HENNESSY,

President, Franklin Society for Home Building and Savings; Ex-President, New York State League and United States League of Savings and Loan Associations.

I have been asked, Mr. Chairman, to deal only with that phase of the question which relates to the effect of this proposed plan upon the home seekers and to deal with that question from the standpoint of the Savings and Loan Associations of the city. I should disclaim any intentions to represent any particular loan association here or any particular body of loan associations, but from my experience, I might say that the sentiments which I express here, are the sentiments which are held by building and loan association people generally.

I have no mental reservations whatever in stating that I believe that the adoption of this plan would greatly promote the building of dwellings by people of small means. In this connection I may advert, Mr. Chairman, to the statement that is made (and which I believe), that in the City of New York the number of individual dwellings—small homes—is less than in any other city in the United States. I believe that this is conspicuously indicated by the statistics of buildings in the city. I assume it is not necessary to argue to the Committee that it is a very desirable thing, by any measure of public policy, to encourage the building of small dwelling houses.

I have always thought this work of creating small homes to be the most important work of the savings and loan associations of the United States, and the extent of their work in this direction is, I venture to say, very little appreciated by the people generally and by students of public questions. It is not known, for example, that in those two States, New Jersey and New York, there is something like $200,000,000 invested by these institutons in mortgages upon small dwellings, and that they meet a need and that they serve a purpose that no other class of financial institutions meet or serve. The large insurance companies and our savings banks invest their mortgage money in apartment houses, in tenements, in office buildings and in the larger kind of real estate development, and it is left almost exclusively for the co-operative savings and loan associations to deal with this problem of finding mortgage money for the small home seeker. In the United States when we find that there are over five thousand of these institutions, with resources of over a billion dollars invested in small homes and in promoting small home owning, you will say that I am justified in assuming that it is a very important movement.

Now the appraisement of savings and loan associations in the metropolitan district indicates that the average building of the small home owner in the metropolitan district is worth two and one-half times to three times as much as the land upon which the building is erected. Assuming the tax rate to be two per cent., a slight calculation will show that each $1,000 of building value which is remitted in the tax assessment would be an equivalent to remitting $400 of a permanent mortgage upon the home or dwelling house. Now, the ambition of the small home owner is to pay off his mortgage. It ought to be obvious then, Mr. Chairman, that the present small home owner would be very much benefited if he had his taxes, that portion of his tax which is now assessed upon the building, transferred to the value of the land.

I am quite unable to see, Mr. Chairman, how the untaxing of buildings would upset values or discourage the lending on bond and mortgages. One of the things admitted by Mr. Dowling was, I believe, to the effect that money lenders competed for loans as much as loan seekers competed for money, and I agree with him. The Metropolitan Life Insurance Company, for example, is interested very much in keeping its money out in safe salable bonds and mortgages. Unless it may be shown—and I am quite unable to apprehend how it could be shown—that a slightly increased taxation on land value is going to destroy or seriously damage either land or building values, it is difficult for me to see how security that is substantial in itself is going to be affected by this proposed change in your tax system.

In my capacity as a member of the New Jersey Legislature, I have had the honor for the last four sessions to be the sponsor for a bill that proposes to do for the State of New Jersey what is proposed to be done by this change in the tax system in New York. The bill, which is known as the "Home Rule Tax Bill," proposes that, after approved by a referendum vote, each municipality may, by a gradual process extending over ten years gradually transfer the basis of taxes from real estate, so called, to land values. That bill has received increasing support at each session of the legislature. It is now supported by many substantial organizations in the State. It received at the last session of the legislature the support of nearly one-third of the New Jersey Senate and some sixteen votes in the House of Assembly out of sixty.

PROFESSOR SELIGMAN: In your opinion, would the contemplated plan have any effect at all upon the selling value of land?

MR. HENNESSY: It is my opinion that the application of this plan in the form proposed would not substantially affect the value of land at all. There would be, in my opinion, immediately a stimulation in building operations of all kinds, and this would have the tendency to increase values rather than to decrease them.

PROFESSOR SELIGMAN: In case there was a sudden change, would there be any effect upon the owner of the land and upon the mortgage-lending market?

MR. HENNESSY: I have given no serious thought to that part of the question. I am inclined to think that there would be no substantially different immediate effect whatsoever.

MR. LINDNER: You say that the change that is contemplated would stimulate buildings. In what way?

MR. HENNESSY: The fixed charge on the person who owns the building or who is seeking to put up a building will be made very much lighter by this system.

MR. LINDNER: Would it have any effect upon the speculation of the home owner—his hope for increased land value?

MR. HENNESSY: While I believe that the element of speculative increase in value is taken into consideration to some extent, I want to say that with respect to building and loan association loans, I think the extent to which that is considered is negligible.

MR. LINDNER: There is always present, is there not, in the mind of the man who builds a small home, which is the principal business of the building and loan associations, the expectation of an increase of land value?

MR. HENNESSY: To a less extent is that true than in any other building operation imaginable. The man when he buys his home, buys it for a home. The element of speculative land value enters into it very seldom. He thinks of it as a home site.

Millions of dollars are being loaned in the nearby New Jersey suburbs by the savings and loan associations of this city to small people who labor in New York. The association of which I have the honor to be manager, for example, has some million and a half dollars loaned in Bergen County, which is just across the river, to small home owners. That is true because the type of home that the man of small means is seeking today is not easily found in the City of New York. Conditions may change when your transportation facilities, going across the East River, as Mr. Wilcox described them, bringing within easy reach of the business centers of this city the outlying territory, have been accomplished. Then you ought to do something to stimulate the speculative builder, if you please, to build homes. The proposition that is before you will do more than anything that I can think of to bring that about.

TESTIMONY OF MR. CHARLES H. INGERSOLL,

Vice-President, Business Men's Association to Untax Industry; Chairman, Sub-Committee on Taxation, Congestion Committee; Member of Firm of Robert H. Ingersoll & Co.

MR. INGERSOLL: The Business Men's Association to Untax Industry views the problem of taxation from a business, and not from an academic nor a reform point of view. The power to tax is the power to destroy industry, enterprise, prosperity and employment. We believe the canons of taxation enunciated by Adam Smith are sound today. The four more important are: The patrimony of the State must not be impaired. Taxation must be direct. Taxation must be equal. Taxation must not interfere with business. It is admitted that transferring taxes levied on buildings to land values will reduce rent and taxes on small homes, but it is contended that it will not improve business nor help the condition of the workers of the city.

The wildest and most illogical statement of those who oppose the proposed change is that it will work havoc with legitimate business interests here and produce a panic, and that then the people of the city will proceed to abolish all other taxes and sources of revenue for local purposes, and secure all revenue for local purposes by taking more of the ground rent. The admission of this fear by land speculators, who are the beneficiaries of the present tax system, has doubtless convinced this committee, as well as all impartial students of the question, of the soundness of our proposal and its advantages to practically all the people of the city.

Everyone will admit that prosperity based upon a flourishing traffic in munitions of war, or due to increased export to meet emergency needs of warring nations, financed by loans, is not a sound nor a lasting prosperity. It is equally clear that there has not been general prosperity in this city or country. The taxation of industry, including buildings, the personal property of industry, is the most important cause of the continuous industrial unrest based upon low wages and unemployment for the following reasons:

First, industry and labor pay nearly four-fifths of the total Governmental cost. The revenue for all Governmental purposes, about three billion dollars next year, must be derived ultimately from one or two sources: ground rent or earnings (current or saved). Economists agree that all taxes, except the tax on land values, the income and inheritance taxes, can be shifted to the user of the commodity or service. Approximately six hundred and fifty million dollars is secured for the maintenance of State and local government by taxing ground rents. Taxes on industry, earnings and savings amount to nearly two billion four hundred million dollars. Of this amount approximately forty-one million and forty-six thousand dollars was secured last year from the individual federal income tax, and in 1913, twenty-six million four hundred and seventy thousand nine hundred and sixty-four dollars from the State transfer—inheritance—taxes.

The equity of those two taxes with high exemption, low rates on small incomes and bequests, and rapidly progressive rates on large incomes and bequests may be admitted. The fact remains that the total revenue from both income and inheritance taxes, at present about one hundred and seven million dollars, including the corporation income tax, cannot, I assume, exceed from four hundred million to five hundred million dollars; and governmental expenditures, chiefly due to preparedness, will probably increase by from three hundred million dollars to four hundred million dollars within the next three to five years, before income and inheritance tax rates can be raised to derive sufficient revenue to meet increased expenditures. The existing unfair and injurious burden of taxes on legitimate business and industry will continue, unless present taxes on buildings, at least, are removed and transferred to land values.

Industry pays fifty-five per cent. of cost of city, and sixty per cent. of cost of State government. The city budget of New York, excluding the city's direct tax contribution to the State government was, in 1914, $188,129,261. The tax on land values was only $82,472,576. Other taxes, fees, etc., amounted to $105,656,685. $1,923,025 was received last year by New York City from the State school board. $103,733,660 of the cost of local government last year, therefore, was paid by industry—that is fifty-five per cent.—while land paid only forty-four per cent.

The State Comptroller gives the following chief sources of revenue for the general fund of the State, amounting during the year ending September 30, 1914, to $30,269,689; special tax for court expenses, etc. (direct State tax), $7,701,271; indirect taxes, $38,305,980; the balance is $4,282,427. This balance is from fees, fines, duties, receipts from State institutions, the insurance and banking departments and interest on deposits.

The only charge on land is its proportionate contribution, under the direct State tax. As the value of land and buildings is not assessed separately in most of the cities and counties of the State, it is impossible to state exactly what this tax amounts to. A very close estimate, however, can be made. The equalized assessed value of real estate in New York City was, in 1914, $7,561,076,209. The equalized assessed value of real estate in the rest of the State was, in 1914, $3,399,184,683. In New York City the value of the land was 61.7 per cent. of the total value of real estate. It is not so large for the rest of the State. It is, therefore, conservative to put the charge on land for the cost of State government at sixty per cent. of the direct State tax, i. e., $4,620,762. That is, only nine per cent. (aproximately) of the current expenditures of the State government was paid by taxes upon land. In addition to the tax levy of $4,620,762 on land values, $1,979,970 was secured from sources other than taxation, such as interest ($663,369), institutions for the care of inmates ($867,851). The inheritance tax yielded $11,162,478. The total tax levied upon industry for the current cost of State government was, in 1914, $31,-426,574. This is sixty per cent.—three-fifths—of the cost of State government.

The proportion of the cost of city government paid by industry is steadily increasing. In the report of the Department of Taxes and Assessments of New York City for 1913, the statement is made: "In so far as city taxes alone are considered, the tax burden on real estate had fallen from 87 per cent. to 75 per cent. in the period from 1880 to 1913."

The high selling price of land injures legitimate business industry. New York City has incurred an enormous debt for public improvements, water supply, transit, parks, playgrounds, schools, etc., which have benefited financially only one class of property—land—and less than two per cent. of the population, the land owners. Hardly a dollar of the debt incurred by the city, nor a dollar currently expended, has increased either the profit of business or the opportunity to do business in New York City. On the contrary, by increasing the selling price of land in the city, through the heavy taxes on industry and light taxation on land values, an enormous burden has been placed on legitimate industry and all workers in the city.

The gross funded debt of New York City on June 30, 1915, was $1,304,000,000. The interest on this debt next year will be almost $55,-000,000. The assessed value of land here is approximately $4,650,000,000. This assessed value, or selling price, of land constitutes the first fixed charge upon the industry of the community, under our present tax system, of nearly $300,000,000 annually. This must be paid to land speculators before industry and labor get any return for work.

On the average, the selling price of land in New York City increases $100,000,000 to $125,000,000 a year. With the present tax rate, the increase in the selling price of land here, within the next decade, will be at least $1,000,000,000, on which the net ground rent, at five per cent., would be $50,000,000; that is, there would be $50,000,000 additional fixed charges upon workers of the city for the benefit of local speculators.

Transferring taxes from buildings to land values in the city, during the decade, would mean not only reducing the taxes on the workers of the city by $60,000,000 to $70,000,000 in the tenth year, but reducing in addition the fixed charges levied by land speculators upon legitimate business interests by at least $50,000,000, a total saving to workers of $110,000,000 to $120,000,000 a year.

New York industries are not increasing as rapidly as in competing cities. The census of 1910 gives the following figures for the percentage of increase in the average number of workers in factories, and the value of products from 1899 to 1904, and from 1904 to 1909:

City.	Average Number of Wage Earnings.		Value of Products.	
	1904 to 1909.	1899 to 1904.	1904 to 1909.	1899 to 1904.
New York	19.2	19.6	33.0	30.2
Chicago	21.5	9.4	34.1	19.7
Philadelphia	10.0	6.6	26.2	13.7
Cleveland	32.3	15.7	58.2	23.4
Boston	17.7	11.9	28.8	13.3
Buffalo	18.0	27.1	48.5	39.5
Newark	18.3	18.2	35.0	33.1
Baltimore	9.8	2.3	24.5	11.1
Rochester	23.1	15.3	38.9	35.9
Providence	16.5	3.7	30.7	16.9
Jersey City	25.1	17.0	70.0	20.6

It will be noted that the increase in the average number of workers in factories in New York City actually fell in the second five years—1904 to 1909—while the increase in the value of manufactured products was only about one-tenth more than for 1899 to 1904, although the increase was several times as large in a number of cities. The census figures for the increase in the value added by manufacture also show New York City to be lagging far behind its competitors.

There are several reasons which will operate increasingly in the future to handicap New York City in its effort to maintain manufacturing supremacy.

(a). The city has borrowed heavily instead of paying currently, and the interest charge on the city debt is almost exactly equal to the total taxes levied this year on buildings.

(b). The "pay-as-you-go" policy forced upon the city because it has practically reached the debt limit, will increase city expenditures unprecedentedly.

(c). The shift of population from Manhattan to the outlying boroughs, through the construction of transit lines, and distribution of factories, will necessitate large expenditures for schools, fire and police stations, and other public buildings in those districts, and tend to render useless many public buildings in Manhattan.

(d). Beginning in 1918, there will be interest to pay on subway bonds.

Mayor Mitchel testified before the Joint Legislative Committee on Taxation that, exclusive of any direct tax, the city will have to raise in 1920 $34,554,000, in addition to the present budget. The city budget and our share of the direct State tax is this year almost $200,000,000, so that by 1920 the budget will be $250,000,000 to $260,000,000. It will probably be $235,000,000 within three years, and the major part of the increase, under the present uniform tax rate on land and buildings, will fall upon industry and the workers of the city. No change in the nomenclature of taxes changes this fundamental fact.

It is, therefore, imperative that deserved relief from undeserved burden of taxes should be accorded the legitimate business interests and workers of the city, by transferring taxes from buildings to land values, and so merely requiring the financial beneficiaries of governmental expenditures to pay for what they get, instead of requiring all producers to pay for these expenditures a second time in taxes, after having paid for them once in paying ground rent.

The present system limits employment. High selling prices of land, and heavy taxes on industry and workers and high rents and taxes on homes reduce the amount that workers can spend for manufactured goods, and other commodities. This reduces the demand for commodities and hence reduces employment.

PROFESSOR SELIGMAN: In the comparative statistics that you gave on the relative proportions of taxes on land and industry, do you consider that in the so-called income tax, which you put in the latter category, a large part of that tax is derived from income from lands?

MR. INGERSOLL: Well, I do not remember whether I did specifically.

PROFESSOR SELIGMAN: In view of the fact that a very large part of the inheritance tax is paid from the inheritances that consist of land, did you put that whole amount on the side of labor rather than on the side of land?

MR. INGERSOLL: I was inclined to put that on the side of land.

PROFESSOR SELIGMAN: In view of the fact that a large part of our taxes on corporations comes from the real estate that the corporations own, would you consider it proper to put all the corporation taxes on the side of labor or on the side of land?

MR. INGERSOLL: On the side of labor.

PROFESSOR SELIGMAN: Notwithstanding the fact that this might be a corporation whose entire capital consists of land?

MR. INGERSOLL: If that is a premise it must alter the fact. It is a question whether it comes from land, and in such a way as to be included.

PROFESSOR SELIGMAN: To the extent that it comes from land?

MR. INGERSOLL: I would put it on land, of course.

PROFESSOR SELIGMAN: In the figures that you gave us, you put land taxation on one side and labor and industry on the other side. Now, you say, that in the case of income derived from land, and in the case of inheritances derived from land, the increased taxes therefore ought to go on the side of land.

MR. INGERSOLL: Only such portion as actually came from land.

PROFESSOR SELIGMAN: Then your figures would have to be corrected?

MR. INGERSOLL: If you want to put it on that basis there are possibly some items that do not belong there. That was the fault of the statistician. The figures I have given are so far the best obtainable.

STATEMENT OF MR. WILLIAM H. CHESEBROUGH.

MR. CHESEBROUGH: I have no doubt that the passage of the proposed legislation would greatly unsettle and further impair confidence in the future values of real estate, at a time when the welfare of the community imperatively demands that confidence in them should be strengthened. The tremendous burdens being borne by real estate owners should be lessened by obtaining new sources of revenue. They certainly should not be intensified by enacting into law dangerous and experimental theories which would inevitably further depress real estate values and also cripple the city's borrowing capacity which depends upon their maintenance. The agitation fathered by the advocates of single-tax theories under the guise of halving the rate of taxation upon improvements with a resulting proportionate increase upon land values is but the initial step leading to a practically complete confiscation of the net income from real estate. The aim of many of the advocates of this plan appears to be to first establish the principle, and then, by means of a gradual increase in the rate, to concentrate taxation upon land, with the result of depriving the owners thereof of any substantial net income.

Theoretically, the scheme has an alluring sound, as have had many others equally visionary. It has been plausibly advocated, and has misled many worthy citizens into favoring it who have not appreciated the unfortunate results which its practical operation would inevitably produce. If adopted, it would cause a wholesale calling of mortgages by the holders thereof, including savings banks, life insurance companies, trust companies and others. Real estate held by most owners is mortgaged. Generally speaking, the owners hold only an equity, and do not possess the means to improve their property. The almost complete destruction of confidence in land values which would result from the proposed legislation would render it difficult and, in most cases, impossible for them to borrow money for new construction. To put greater burdens of taxation upon land than now exist would simply break down its value and would not, generally speaking, force improvement of it where there was not demand for occupancy. The argument that it would cause wholesale improvement of land now vacant is fallacious. In New York City, at least, production has almost invariably greatly outstripped demand. The present high rate of taxation with assessments at full value is more than a sufficient incentive to cause improvement where a real demand exists. The effect of the proposed measure would be to concentrate future improvement in the more congested districts by forcing a more intensive use of the land.

I believe that the improvement of land which would be artificially stimulated elsewhere would be less in volume in the aggregate than the reduction of improvement which would result from the increased difficulty of borrowing money upon mortgage for the purpose of improvement. Such amount of building as the proposed law might be likely to stimulate in the less congested districts would consist principally of temporary buildings, largely shacks or "taxpayers," which would impair the future of the neighborhood and retard a substantial and proper development. If such a law had existed thirty years ago, it seems almost clear that we should not now have great and splendidly improved thoroughfares like Fifth Avenue and Broadway. The net result of the proposed legislation would, in my judgment, be some stimulation of improvement where it is least desirable, and a curtailment of the normal and desirable improvement in less congested locations to an extent probably greater than the amount of building stimulated thereby; and labor would, I predict, find comparatively little employment during the painful period of readjustment which would ensue if single-tax theories were incorporated into law.

Such legislation would also produce financial chaos in the city's affairs, and make it at least technically insolvent through a reduction of its assessed valuations. This would probably result in a clamor for the removal or modification of the present legal limitations of the city's debt-incurring power, now limited to ten per cent. of its assessed valuations. Should that safeguard against expansion of debt be removed, a broad road to unbridled public extravagance would be opened which could lead only to eventual and actual financial bankruptcy.

The axiomatic wisdom of not killing the goose that lays the golden egg is peculiarly pertinent to the existing situation, and it is unbelievable that the great State of New York could be guilty of the extreme folly of passing legislation which would inevitably break down the values of its real estate, which have been the most important source of its revenues for taxation and the rock-ribbed bulwark of its credit. There is imperative need to reassure both institutions and individuals who loan money on mortgage that financial hari-kari is not to be committed through the passage of the proposed legislation.

It has been suggested that where the cost of improvement exceeds land value, the owners of such property would be benefited by the proposed legislation. Possibly in a few isolated cases like the towering Woolworth Building, the first effect might be beneficial to them; but in the last analysis it seems clear that the resulting general depression in real estate values would outweigh many times the benefits which a few owners might temporarily obtain.

I believe the adoption of legislation embodying single-tax theories, whether partially or wholly, would be ethically wrong and entirely contradictory to the American spirit of fairness. If the ownership of land were entirely vested in the government, there might be ethical justification for the proposed measures; but remembering that the great majority of the people who now own land have paid for it with their hard-earned money (and probably most of them have paid at least as much or more than it could be sold for today because of the depression in land values of the last few years), it should be obvious that the proposed legislation infringes not only upon the Golden Rule, but would perhaps also constitute a violation of the eighth commandment.

As to the proposed increment tax, while I believe the adoption of this would be unwise, it would certainly be less objectionable than the single-tax propaganda, because the additional tax would fall upon those who are better able to pay it, and would not result in wholesale confiscation. An increment tax to be fair, however, should work both ways and provide for refunds where values fall as well as to impose additional burdens where they rise. In New York City, at least, the nimble tax assessor seems to have made an increment tax totally unnecessary, as it has been the practice to discount the future where it was anticipated land values would rise, and in many cases to overdiscount it. I know of real properties in Manhattan which have been recently sold at about sixty per cent. of the existing assessed valuations.

TESTIMONY OF MR. JESSE F. ORTON.

MR. ORTON: In the time at my disposal, I have thought it most profitable to take up what seemed to me most important in the excellent list of questions propounded by the Committee. I shall assume that the economic distinctions between a tax upon a building and a tax upon land have already been sufficiently emphasized and are recognized by the Committee. I refer to the principles that a tax upon land, according to its selling or rental value, is paid by the owner and not by the tenant or user, while a tax upon a building, being one of the costs of producing the building for the use of its ultimate consumer, the tenant, is paid by the tenant.

Recognition of this principle is not inconsistent with the fact that a tax levied upon an improved parcel of land has, in itself, the same effects, whether we call it a tax upon the building or upon the land, or upon both. The important point is that no tax upon an improved house is a separate thing, to be considered in and of itself. It is a part of a system of taxation by which land, improved and unimproved, is taxed according to its value, and a building, when erected, adds its value to the taxable value of the parcel of which it becomes a part.

In answer to the question whether a transfer of a tax now levied on buildings to land will in any instance increase the value of improved land, I would say that unquestionably the direct effect of such a change will be an increase in the value of the land, where the value of the building, as compared with that of the land, is sufficient to make the tax on the entire property less after the change than it was before the change.

To use the illustration mentioned in the question, if the building be worth $70,000 and the land $30,000, as the total improvement value in the city is less than the total land value, the immediate effect is a considerable reduction in the owner's tax. This reduction will show itself in an increased capital value of the parcel as a whole. But the building, depending for its value upon the reproduction cost of similar buildings, will be worth no more than before; and therefore the increased value of the parcel must be the result of greater value of the land.

To what extent this direct result, an increase in the land value, will be neutralized by the indirect effects of the change, by which other land, formerly unused, is brought into competition with the parcel in question, is a matter which cannot be accurately determined. But I believe that a very large proportion of parcels of adequately improved land will, at least, suffer no diminution in selling value.

In answer to the questions relating to the effect of attracting buildings upon speculation in land, I believe that the direct effect will be to check very decidedly so-called speculation in land, by which I mean the purchasing of land for the purpose of holding it idle until its increased value will return a profit over and above taxes and interest on the purchase price. I would consider this a beneficial result. Speculation in land raises its price above that where it was kept by its present utilities, basing values on expected or fancied utility in the future. It serves no useful purpose to the community, but is a detriment, keeping land out of use because its price is too high to afford a profit for industry under present conditions. It is wholly unlike speculation in the product of labor, which tends to equalize prices over periods of scarcity.

Unquestionably, the direct result of the untaxing of buildings would be to reduce land values, except in cases of parcels so well improved that the land alone, at the increased tax rate, would pay no more than both land and building formerly paid. The indirect effect, assuming that population is not attracted from outside the city, would be to reduce still further land values through the competition resulting from the improvement of land now vacant or inadequately improved. Along with this reduction of land value, would go a reduction in rent, with the result that labor and industry would get a larger share in the distribution of wealth.

As to the effect of the change on the city's revenue, it is plain that taxable land value being reduced in the aggregate, if the city budget were not reduced by this change and if other sources of revenue were not utilized, the increase in the tax rate would be somewhat more than the increase strictly called for by the transfer of taxes from buildings to land.

The objection has been made that the tax rate would have to be so much higher as to cause a failure to obtain the needed revenue. I think we shall see later that one of the results of the change will be to reduce very materially the city's budget below what it would otherwise be. It is also true that other sources of revenue can be found. I believe that other sources should be utilized, if necessary, during the period when conditions are becoming readjusted to the change in taxing real estate.

If the transfer of taxes from buildings to land is made gradually, as proposed, covering a period of ten years, I do not believe other sources of revenue will be necessary, considering the economy in city government which would be possible as a result of the change. There would be forces immediately set to work to sustain the value of land. Cheaper sites invite improvements, invite the starting of industries which would employ unemployed labor and capital already in the city, and, in addition, those sites and untaxed buildings invite the bringing of industries from outside the city. Thus the lowering of land values through taxation tends, in part, to be counteracted by forces set in motion by the reduction itself.

In answer to the question concerning the effect of the change on the tax paid by buildings of the skyscraper class, I believe that, in many cases, the property would pay less taxes than it does now, especially where the value of the building is higher in proportion to the value of the land. But this gain would not necessarily mean that much additional profit to the owner. Since the tax on buildings is in the long run paid by tenants, the actual or potential competition of similar buildings, whose maintenance would involve no charge for taxation, would gradually transfer to the tenants the advantage resulting from the removal of taxes from the existing buildings.

In reply to the questions relating to the effect of the proposed change on the compactness of the city's environments, and on the necessity for restriction of the height of buildings, etc., I would say that the change would undoubtedly cause a more intensive use of land in the central or the business districts. Such land now vacant or inadequately improved would be built upon and the tendency to high buildings might in some localities be increased. It would be advisable, if not necessary, for the city to make suitable restrictions on the height of buildings and on the ratio of buildings to lot area. But this ought to have been done long ago, under present conditions of taxation, for a number of reasons that might be mentioned.

As a result of the more compact development of the city, certain vacant areas which have served after a fashion for breathing spaces or in lieu of parks and playgrounds, would be occupied with buildings. In some cases it might be necessary, as a consequence, for the city to acquire land for some of these public purposes. I believe that this is not to be regretted. It is most unfortunate that any city relies, or attempted to rely, upon these vacant spaces which happen to be left for a time. The result of reliance upon them is that the city neglects to acquire the land needed for parks and other public purposes when the cost of acquisition would be low, and is reminded of its need only when the private owners of the vacant land get ready to improve it; then the city may find it impossible to obtain the required land, or may have to pay a very high price, or, in many cases, may have to purchase improved land and dispose of the improvements before it can make use of the land.

It should also be remembered that if the untaxing of buildings does deprive the city of some breathing spaces which it now enjoys without public expense, and if it does make necessary the acquisition of land as public parks to supply the need of such space, it will at the same time save to the city large sums of money in condemnation proceedings, by which land is acquired for other public purposes. If the speculative element is taken out of the price of land, or if land values are still further reduced, the city will pay much less for the land which it condemns or purchases. I believe the net result on this account will be a gain rather than a loss to the city.

As to the effect of the proposed change upon the maintenance of lawns and gardens in the suburban districts, I have no doubt it will greatly encourage residents of outlying and suburban localities to provide and maintain suitable lawns and gardens. While the effect of the change would be to make the city compact in the high-priced business districts, and to eliminate the magnificent distances over which one must often travel, through vacant or half vacant areas, between business and residence, the effect in the outer portions of the city would be to make land enough cheaper than it is now to enable residents to maintain lawns and gardens where now they cannot afford it. For obvious reasons, I believe, this would be a good thing.

In reply to the general question whether the untaxing of buildings would encourage the making of improvements, whether it would encourage the building of larger and more commodious buildings, whether it would encourage the building of temporary improvements while land is awaiting its permanent use, I think unquestionably the answer would be in the affirmative, and that the building of new and better buildings must gradually, but surely, force the abandonment of old and unfit buildings, just as a cheaper supply of clothing will tend to the discarding of old and ragged garments.

Some persons doubt the possibility of getting capital for the making of these improvements. But the doubt is not justified; capital flows naturally wherever profits may be expected. Under present conditions, capital is constantly being devoted to the making of improvements. It is absurd to imagine that when it is made less profitable to hold land idle than it is now, and more profitable to improve land than it is now, capital will be less willing than now to furnish the money for the operation. Building loans will be made on locations which are favorable for improvement, though the selling value may be somewhat reduced. I do think, however, that some of our friends who are planning so-called self-development improvements on land seventeen miles from nowhere, land which should be used for a long time to come in the raising of corn and potatoes, will find it somewhat harder to obtain building loans than they do now.

The giving of additional employment for labor and industry, in the improvement of land, is only one of the beneficial results that may be expected from the removal of taxes from buildings. Another important result is the relief of congested centres of population, through the offering of cheaper homes than can now be obtained in those parts of the city where space, light and air are more plentiful. General encouragement of industry will follow the change, by untaxing the improvement which is much used and by offering a cheaper site or lower rent for the land which it needs. In a word, the size and number of unearned incomes will be reduced, while the size and number of earned incomes will be increased.

I believe the change will result in great economy of public money, and in certain reductions in the cost of living. The making of the city more compact would undoubtedly reduce the expense of the Police and Fire Departments and some other government services. It will also lower the cost of maintaining transportation lines, the pipes and wires of public utilities, and other services of a semi-public or private nature. Of course, the City of New York cannot get the full benefit of these savings which could have been had by an earlier resort to the measures now proposed. But a large portion of benefit can still be obtained by encouraging the filling in of the unoccupied spaces which now exist, before further expansion and scattering of population occurs. In this way the growth of the city's budget may be checked and the problem how to obtain revenue be made less serious.

The answer to the question whether the untaxing of buildings would attract population and industry to New York from other localities, I think, must obviously be in the affirmative. People are not coming to New York under present conditions for the purpose of residence or to engage in industry.

To deny that cheaper sites and exemption of improvements from taxation will be an added attraction and increase the number of those who come, is equivalent to denying that water will run down hill. Unless other neighboring communities take their cue from the experience of New York and promptly exempt improvements from taxation, this movement toward New York will surely be of considerable importance, and to a certain extent, by increasing the demand for land within the city, it would neutralize the effect of transferring taxes from buildings to land. The opponents of the measure should get at least this comfort out of the situation.

In answer to the question relating to the effect of untaxing buildings on mortgage loans, existing and contemplated, I would say that I believe no confidence should be placed in certain estimates which have been placed before the Committee.

The statement that nearly all parcels of land are mortgaged, and that in most cases the owner has so small an equity that his interest would be wiped out by the decrease in land value, resulting from the proposed change, is so extravagant as to be its own refutation.

Savings banks are allowed, by law, to loan not more than sixty per cent. of the value of improved property and forty per cent. in case of unimproved property. Other loaning agencies, while not subject to this law, follow much the same practice for their own protection. Undoubtedly some equities are being wiped out every year under existing conditions. This always occurs under any system of taxation. The increasing of taxes on lands, which are unimproved or quite inadequately improved, would, of course, accelerate the tendency for equities to disappear in the more unfavorable locations. But, as I have indicated in considering an earlier question, I believe that in case of parcels of land which are adequately improved and in which the value of the building exceeds the value of the land, the direct result of the untaxing of buildings is to increase the selling value of the parcel as a whole.

This direct result may be neutralized in some measure by the indirect effects of the change, the bringing of the land now vacant into competition with the parcels; but I believe that parcels of land which are now adequately improved with buildings, at least equal in value to the land, would be practically free from danger of having the owners' equities wiped out by falling values, except in cases where these properties have been mortgaged with utter recklessness on the part of the mortgagee as well as the owner, or in cases where the shifting of land values, due to causes other than the proposed change in taxation, would have made the loss of the property on foreclosure inevitable under present conditions.

TESTIMONY OF DAVID A. CLARKSON,

Member, Legislation and Taxation Committee, Real Estate Board of New York.

MR. CLARKSON: It is my purpose to consider what would be the effects upon real estate of the adoption of the plan of removing taxes on buildings during ten years and placing them on land until the tax rate on buildings would be one per cent. of that on land. This change is shown by Dr. Haig in his report to the Committee on Taxation, on the basis of the taxes levied for 1914, to increase the amount to be raised on land values in the City of New York from $84,007,000 to $135,988,000, an additional burden on land of $57,000,000 in round numbers; and in the Borough of Manhattan from $56,000,000 to $92,-000,000, an increase of $35,000,000 in taxes on land. The increase in the rate of taxation in this borough, as calculated by Dr. Haig, would be from 1.77 per cent. to 2.86 per cent. on land. This additional burden of $35,000,000 capitalized at 5 per cent. equals $700,000,000, the amount by which land values in that borough would be depreciated unless for other reasons the land values would increase by an equivalent amount. When we consider that these values, as measured by the assessments of the Tax Department, for Manhattan, increased only from $2,600,000,-000 in 1906 to $3,184,000,000 in 1915, an increase of $584,000,000 in ten years, including a change in the scale of valuation in 1911, which accounts for nearly $200,000,000 of the increase, it is inconceivable that land values should not be largely depreciated.

This is the more true if we take into account the probable increase in the rate of taxation for 1916, on the basis of which the capitalized depreciation would be about sixteen per cent. greater, or about $810,-000,000. Is it to be presumed that in the present condition of affairs in the world that any such increase in values can be looked for here? It, therefore, seems assured that by the adoption of the plan of untaxing buildings the value of land would be greatly depreciated.

Let us now consider what effect the untaxing of buildings would have upon rents. While the removal or gradual removal of taxes would seem to encourage building, and thereby lower rents, yet there are other influences which would work strongly against this tendency in New York City. It has not been the custom of owners here to set aside funds for the depreciation of their buildings, as they have looked to the increase of land values to compensate them for this loss; therefore, it is reasonable to presume that rents have been lower than if such depreciation had been charged to the annual income. Buildings have usually, in New York, been erected in anticipation of the demand, and at present there are many only partially rented.

Building operations have usually been carried on here by those who expect to sell the completed and rented buildings. These operations are usually financed by a system of loans by which money is advanced during construction. In the face of falling land values and doubtful ability to sell the finished buildings at a profit, it is certain that neither would these loans be made, nor the operations undertaken on the same scale. These conditions would go far to counteract the incentive to erect new buildings, caused by the removal of taxes, and would, I believe, for years overcome it. Unless new buildings were put up more largely than at present, rents would not tend to decrease. It is most difficult to estimate the result of these conflicting tendencies, but, in my opinion, it would take years for the removal of taxes on buildings effectively to lower rents, while there is no doubt but that it would much decrease land values, especially in the case of vacant lots.

This decrease would cause an entire change in the city's present financial system, which is based on the assessment of land and building values. It would diminish the tax base and, in the face of increasing expenditures, would result in a constantly increasing tax rate, which would tend as constantly to diminish land values. The city's borrowing capacity would be taken away and financial confusion ensue.

MR. JOSEPH L. BUTTENWIESER,

Member, Legislation and Taxation Committee, Real Estate Board of New York.

MR. BUTTENWIESER: I desire to register my strong disapproval of this proposed measure, not only because it will hurt all real estate owners, but also because you will be disturbing the entire financial system. We must not lose sight of the fact that the whole structure of our municipal credit has been built upon the value of its real estate and that over 75 per cent. of the revenue for the support of the city government is derived from the tax on real estate. Vancouver has been repeatedly cited by the other side in support of untaxing buildings. I have just come from across the hall, where I attended the meeting of the Mayor's Committee on National Defense. When I told Mr. Alrick H. Man that I had to leave to testify before your honorable body, he told me that he had only recently returned from Vancouver, and that while riding there in the bus from the depot to the hotel, he noticed a sign "For sale at your own price." He was informed that $2,000 would be accepted for this property, for which but a few years before $44,000 had been offered. That is the true result of this much-vaunted boon to Vancouver.

PROFESSOR SELIGMAN: You are interested primarily in real estate speculation, in building operations or in lending money?

MR. BUTTENWIESER: My line is especially that of the real estate operator and builder. I have built about 300 houses in this city.

PROFESSOR SELIGMAN: From the point of view of the operator would you say that in general the business of the real estate operator is exceptionally prosperous?

MR. BUTTENWIESER: I may say that it has been no more so, and possibly less so, than other lines of business in the City of New York. It is far more unstable, but yet as proper as any regular business.

PROFESSOR SELIGMAN: Do you believe that all the taxes and expenditures of this city go to the sole profit of the land owner and speculator, and that they are the favored class in this community?

MR. BUTTENWIESER: Absolutely no.

PROFESSOR SELIGMAN: The argument made by the gentlemen who took the other view is that while all these things seem to be a benefit to the community at large, in reality they are to the advantage of the land owners, and that the land owners increased the rent because of such improvements. I should like to know what your point of view is?

MR. BUTTENWIESER: These improvements have no more been the cause of the increase in rents than they have been the cause of the increases or developments that are natural in a great and growing city.

PROFESSOR SELIGMAN: In other words, the benefit of the city taxation and city debt accrue to labor and industry no less than to land, because it increases their opportunity of making good?

MR. BUTTENWIESER: I should say more so. They accrue more to labor and industry because the land owner must continue to pay the tax irrespective of whether the prospective profit, which had tempted him to put money into land, materializes or not. Labor and industry can go elsewhere, if disappointed. The land owner must stand by, and continue to pay taxes on his land, or else lose it altogether.

PROFESSOR SELIGMAN: Would you think, Mr. Buttenwieser, that the general tendency of the untaxing of buildings would be to reduce rents?

MR. BUTTENWIESER: It will generally upset things. It may temporarily, but cannot permanently, reduce rents. Of course, in so far as the proposed measure would unsettle conditions, and in so far as it might stimulate additional building during the first few years of the operation of the law, the tendency would be somewhat to reduce rents. No man, however, is fool enough to put his money into any venture where there is no prospect of remunerative return and where he is certain to lose money. Rents would then naturally rise again. The question of rent is governed by the law of supply and demand. By artificial means you may temporarily arrest the operation of this law, but in the end this law must prevail.

May I here interject another remark? It is quite true that every economist, in writing on the incidence of taxation, maintains that you cannot shift the burden of taxation from the land. I hold that this applies primarily to virgin land. When, however, you improve the land and have the building and land as one parcel of real estate, you can no longer be sure of shifting the tax on the building and not shifting the tax on the land. They are a unit—a new unit. It is just the same as if you attempted to keep separate and distinct the tax on the cotton, the labor, the dye, the bleaching, the printing, etc., in a yard of cotton cloth. You have blended them altogether into a new unit, which you must and do tax as a unit. So, too, in improved real estate you have a new unit, and the tax on that new unit can, to a certain extent, be shifted, whether you tax the land or the building or both.

PROFESSOR SELIGMAN: If the tax on land can be shifted, how then would it bring the decreased value of land to which you are referring in saying that the owner is unjustly treated because the tax is shifted or is capitalized into lower selling value?

MR. BUTTENWEISER: I maintain that in the case of improved real estate, if you were to tax the land only, you can shift the tax to a certain extent. Of course, if you unduly tax anything—land or building or anything else—you can no longer shift the tax, but you reach a point where the tax is taken out of the capital, that is to say, you lessen the capital value. That is what will and does happen when you over-tax real estate, be it land or buildings or both. I think you have a fair illustration of that in the present condition of the real estate market. You have piled taxes upon real estate to a point where the tax cannot be shifted, but naturally, therefore, reduces the capital value.

PROFESSOR SELIGMAN: Is there much land held out of use?

MR. BUTTENWEISER: There is very little held out of use simply for speculative purposes. It is held out of use because there is no demand for it.

PROFESSOR SELIGMAN: Do you consider the business of dealing in land in order to build—would you consider that a productive enterprise?

MR. BUTTENWIESER: It is absolutely as productive and as important to the growth of the city and the welfare of its inhabitants as any manufacturing industry.

PROFESSOR SELIGMAN: You would not concede that you represent a class of economic parasites on the community and of those that live on unearned increment?

MR. BUTTENWIESER: With all due modesty, I claim that there is no line of business more directly allied with, or conducive to, the growth of the city than that of the operator and speculative builder, without whose activity we might still be planting potatoes along Broadway and some of the other important streets of this city.

PROFESSOR SELIGMAN: You think that the operator performs the same function as the trader in the stock and produce exchanges and is as necessary to the life of the city?

MR. BUTTENWIESER: Far more legitimate and just as necessary.

DR. WILCOX: I believe you said, Mr. Buttenwieser, that you did not expect that rents would decrease.

MR. BUTTENWIESER: I said that ultimately rents would be determined the same as every other commodity, by the laws of supply and demand. I said and repeat that in the first few years after the enactment of your law, rents may be temporarily reduced, due to the general unsettling of conditions in real estate.

DR. WILCOX: Not permanently?

MR. BUTTENWIESER: No, not permanently, only temporarily.

DR. WILCOX: Then you would think—I assume you would think that the unsettling of values and the harmful effects from the standpoint of the owner of real estate would be only temporary?

MR. BUTTENWIESER: The reduction in rents, if any, would be temporary; the unsettling of values and the general harmful effects would be far reaching and of long duration.

MR. LEUBUSCHER: Are you aware of the fact that real estate in 1880 paid 87 per cent. of the budget, while in 1915 it paid only 75 per cent?

MR. BUTTENWIESER: If that be so, you forget that to-day more activities are being carried on at the public expense and that therefore real estate bears a larger absolute burden than it ever bore before.

MR. LEUBUSCHER: According to the Tax Department, it bears only 75 per cent.

MR. BUTTENWIESER: The expenditures for city government have grown from 1880 to 1915 so rapidly that real estate is more heavily taxed, even in proportion, at 75 per cent. in 1915, than when it paid 87 per cent. in 1880.

MR. LEUBUSCHER: You have given a graphic description of Vancouver and pointed to a piece of land being sold at a high price and later at a very much lower price. Do you not know of any similar instance in New York City?

MR. BUTTENWIESER: I know where values went down in this city.

MR. LEUBUSCHER: Under the present system?

MR. BUTTENWIESER: I know of depreciation under the present system.

MR. LEUBUSCHER: Twenty-third Street values?

MR. BUTTENWIESER: Yes, but nothing like in Vancouver, nothing like the ratio of $44,000 to $2,000.

MR. LEUBUSCHER: How would you say the fortunes of the Astors, the Goelets, the Rhinelanders and the Wendells were built up?

MR. BUTTENWIESER: In the first place, I think, the Astor fortune was first built up by the fur trade. He used his surplus money to invest in one way, in real estate, just as another man did in some other way. Now you cannot take him as an example. He may be one out of ten who have waxed rich by real estate investments. For every one whom you can point out that grew rich by land investments, I will point out twenty who have found them to be a graveyard, as far as profits go.

MR. LEUBUSCHER: Are you aware of the fact that the studies of the Society to Lower Rents have shown that ninety-nine families own one-seventh of the land values of Greater New York?

PROFESSOR SELIGMAN: Is that a fact, Mr. Marsh?

MR. MARSH: One-ninth of Greater New York, or one-seventh of Manhattan.

MR. LEUBUSCHER: If that is true—and I have no reason to doubt it—if that be true, does it not show that the holding of the land of Greater New York is, in fact, a land monopoly or trust to-day?

MR. BUTTENWIESER: Taking it for granted that your statistics are correct, I should say that it would depend largely on what they did and to what use they put the land. If I found that they did not combine to establish higher rents, that they did not keep it entirely vacant, holding it purely for speculative purposes, that the ground rents they charged were on a 4½ per cent. or 5 per cent. basis while many others insisted upon, and got, a much higher rate and while other investments produced a larger return, I should say that they were not a monopoly or trust, and that they certainly did no harm to the rent-payer or to anybody else.

MR. LEUBUSCHER: I call your attention to the fact that, in the case of the Astors, one-fourth of the total valuation is for the improvements, while three-fourths is for the land. If you call the small value of the improvements on their land a proper use of the land, I would say it was not put to the proper use, but to the poorest use.

MR. BUTTENWIESER: What is the ratio of building to land value of other properties located in the same neighborhoods as theirs? Did you take the trouble to make such comparisons? I think you will find they have been as fair in their policy of improvements as any one else. I am quite sure that you will find that in most cases they improved their land, or else ground-rented it to tenants who built. While I hold no brief for the Astors or the Goelets or these other large land owners, I would remind you that if the Astors, out of their large assets, have seen fit to invest in this piece of land, which, if they continue to hold it and pay through all the years heavy taxes and large assessments, may or may not show them a profit, that is no reason for claiming that their policy is to hold land out of use. You must first furnish statistics as to all the Astor holdings. Do you, for instance, think the Waldorf-Astoria a proper improvement?

MR. LEUBUSCHER: It looks like one to me.

MR. BUTTENWIESER: Do you think the New Netherlands is a proper improvement of the land?

MR. LEUBUSCHER: Yes.

MR. BUTTENWIESER: Do you consider the Astor Hotel and the Astor Building at Wall Street and Broadway proper improvements?

MR. LEUBUSCHER: Yes.

MR. BUTTENWIESER: Finally, do you not consider the new building which one of the Astors is now erecting at the corner of Vesey Street and Broadway a better and more suitable improvement than the Woolworth Building, just one block above, and many others which you are seeking to exempt?

MR. LEUBUSCHER: Which do I think the better improvement? TheAstor Building is hardly adequate, while the Woolworth is too much improved.

SIXTH HEARING.

November 24, 1915, 2:30 P. M., Room 16, City Hall. Professor Edwin R. A. Seligman, presiding.

TESTIMONY OF PROFESSOR JOSEPH FRENCH JOHNSON,

Dean, New York University School of Commerce, Accounts and Finance; Member, Commission on New Sources of Revenue; Representing The Merchants' Association of New York.

PROFESSOR JOHNSON: The directors of The Merchants' Association have considered this question of reducing the tax on buildings, and have decided adversely with regard to it, as the result of the report of the Committee on Taxation, of which I am chairman. That committee in its report held that the reduction of the rate of taxes on buildings, since it would be attended by an increase of the rate upon land, would necessarily tend to the lowering of land values, and that any such reduction of land values as the result of a change in the system of taxation would be unjust and would be liable to result in a calling in of mortgages on account of the lessening of land values. The directors of The Merchants' Association were unanimous in their vote that any law having for its purpose the reduction of the rate upon buildings and the consequent increase of the rate upon land should be opposed.

PROFESSOR SELIGMAN: Professor Johnson, the point has been made by several of the speakers in preceding sessions that this fear of the calling in of mortgages has been very much exaggerated, partly because of the fact that mortgage money is loaned up to the extent of fifty or even sixty per cent. of the value of the real estate, and that even on the assumption of a considerable decrease in the value of the land, there would still be an ample margin left as the basis of the security. What do you think of that argument?

PROFESSOR JOHNSON: I should have to know a great deal more than I know about the situation in New York to be dogmatic on the subject, but I understand that many parcels of land have greatly declined in value in the last ten years in certain sections of the city, and I can see very good reason why they should have declined in value. The erection of very tall buildings in certain parts of the city has given a floor space far beyond the expectations of twenty years ago, and then the improved rapid transit facilities have taken people out of the city —out of the downtown section of Manhattan—so, I should be very much surprised if I found I was mistaken in my view that certain parcels of land have declined in value in spite of the increase of the last ten years. Now, any increase in the tax rate upon land is certain to cause a decline in the value of the land. And I should fear it would be disastrous in many cases—in the cases of land which has not increased but has decreased in value as a result of natural forces, at work in the last ten or fifteen years.

PROFESSOR SELIGMAN: Do you believe, in the first place, that all the alleged benefits of the scheme would ensue; and, second, if they did ensue, do you think that it would prevent the value of land from falling?

PROFESSOR JOHNSON: I do not believe those benefits would ensue. I think they are visionary in character. It is possible that if buildings were exempted from taxation there would be a certain amount of additional building in excess of what would come on under present conditions, for two or three years. Then it is certain that the rents of buildings would be a little lower than they are now. I am inclined to think that such an effect can reasonably be expected, that is, more buildings, and then we will have to lower rents. There would be a new level of rents arrived at. But, Mr. Chairman, I do not think that the new level of rents would mean very much to the average man. I do not believe that the difference of rents that were prevailing after the three-year stimulus or boom, if I may call it that, in building, that the difference between rents of the new era and the rents to-day would be enough to attract any attention.

There are so many forces at work, of course, making prices on goods and also rents on buildings, that I do not believe that additional building would be sufficient to bring about any very marked reduction of rents. I grant that theoretically it would be. The tendency would be in the direction of lowering rents. I doubt if it would be in the direction though of better housing, of better quarters, or more sanitary quarters.

Those who have had any experience with landlords in New York City and with builders, know that the man who is putting up a building for rent is anxious to get out of it all he can. In fact, he is compelled to do so by the competition of other buildings. So he puts up a certain kind of building for the people who are able to pay twenty dollars a month, a little different one for those who can pay thirty dollars a month, and so on. I doubt if the quarters in which the people in Manhattan live or in the City of New York live, would be a bit better than they are now as a result of any change made in the tax rate upon buildings.

If New York happened not to increase relatively but to remain stationary in its attractiveness as a city, so that there would be no considerable increase in the population and in the wealth of the city, nor in the earning capacity of the people in the city, I should not be surprised at all if the exemption of buildings from taxation produced no appreciable result for several years in the building trades or upon rents. Even if it did, however, after a few years, as I said before, there would be a new level of rents established. A certain new condition would prevail governing the erection of buildings at a profit, and we would be, to all intents and purposes, as far as sanitation is concerned, where we are now, with possibly this exception: If the land is made to bear the brunt of the taxation and the buildings are exempted, unless we pass a law limiting the height of buildings, I should expect to see more skyscrapers, more tall buildings; I should expect also to see in the outlying suburbs smaller gardens, and smaller yards, because it will be those yards and those gardens upon which the small man will have to pay taxes, and not upon his home.

I notice, Mr. Chairman, that there has been some discussion here as to whether the untaxing of buildings would lessen speculation in land. Am I right, and is that of interest?

I do not think the change would have the slightest effect upon speculation in land if the tax upon land is increased. We will then have land valued by buyers and sellers at a new level. But the same reason will exist as exists now for buildings. The increasing wealth and increasing population of this city will increase the value of land and there would be the same inducement to speculate in real estate or in land that exists to-day.

I think that there would be a tendency to improve parcels of land to the limit and leave certain pieces of land now unutilized still unutilized. I should not be surprised if, by untaxing buildings and placing a very heavy burden upon land, certain owners of certain parcels of land would feel like giving them away rather than pay taxes.

People come to New York to live for a number of reasons: The chief reason is, of course, because in New York City there is a wonderful opportunity to make money and to earn a living. The mere fact that rents of buildings have in some way been changed by a system of taxation and apparently been made a little lower, I think, would not draw more people to New York City. They come now on account of the great opportunities here, the social life, the literary life and opportunites for enjoyment, and, above all, the opportunities to make money, and thus we will bring people to New York in spite of what the people outside of this city call very high rents.

I, personally, if I had money to invest, should not feel like investing it in land in a city, or in a state, in which after centuries, during which a certain tax system had existed, that system had been changed to the detriment of the owner of land. If I were a trustee or executor making investments I would certainly not buy land in a city or a community which showed a disposition to treat any class of property unjustly or unfairly. How much that would affect the value of land, of course, I don't know, because I do not know how many other people feel about it as I do. It seems to me that many must feel the same way as I do.

PROFESSOR SELIGMAN: I understand that you object to the scheme of untaxing buildings chiefly for the reason that the alleged beneficial results are problematical and that the alleged deleterious results are pretty certain?

PROFESSOR JOHNSON: Exactly.

PROFESSOR SELIGMAN: I would like to ask you as to whether your objection to the scheme would be in any way lessened if the increased burden on land values or on a particular parcel of land were brought into relation with the increase in the value of land which might be hoped for under more normal conditions. By that I mean not simply a tax on the increment of land values, but I mean also a greater tax upon land values in general with some relation to its possible increase in value?

PROFESSOR JOHNSON: I should be very glad to see some such plan worked out, for I should most thoroughly approve of it. My objection to this plan of untaxing buildings is that it is an arbitrary reduction of the capital value of land.

TESTIMONY OF MR. ALLAN DAWSON,

Chairman, New York Congestion Committee.

MR. DAWSON: I desire to discuss this question, particularly in relation to the evils of urban congestion. By congestion, I do not mean a mere concentration of population, with geographical diffusion, the only corrective; but rather the conditions that spring from bad living, light and air, and insufficient parks and playgrounds. The problem is not how many persons are on an acre, but how those on an acre live.

A removal of the tax on buildings, with a corresponding increase of the tax on land will lessen the evils of congestion for the following reasons:

First. It will stimulate an adequate improvement of unused or partly used areas; first, because urban land is a complementary form of wealth, and to be fruitful, must be wedded to proper improvements; and, second, because when choice is offered, the tendency of capital is to flow from taxed to untaxed fields.

Second. It will better the quality of tenement houses. When a large number of new structures are erected, the new and more economic buildings tend, according to familiar Ricardian principles, to drive out rookeries previously barely profitable. At the first glance it might seem as if relief from taxation would make for the continued use of poor buildings. But the manufacture of new and better buildings, plus the influence of a heavier tax on land, would overcome this tendency, and competition would push the poorer buildings below the margin of profit.

Third. It will decrease rents per unit of space to the extent of the present tax, now shifted to the tenant, and thus enable a family that now occupies four rooms, to hire, say, five.

Fourth. It will encourage a more harmonious economic development of the city. As one approaches the city's centre, all things being equal, land values rise. With similar improvements, the loss through the inadequate use of land becomes greater with an increase on land values. A heavier tax on land and no tax on buildings will thus lead to a greater relative building activity nearer the centre than on the periphery. This, in turn, will diminish the waste incident to contructing and maintaining miles and miles of streets and sewers, and lessen the cost of educational, water, lighting, police and fire services.

The advantages of harmonious urban development, of comparatively solid building, are insufficiently appreciated. A recent census of a modern, outside court, nine-story West Side apartment house, with sun in practically every room, showed 250 persons in residence. The ground space was a quarter of an acre, giving a density of 1,000 per acre, or 640,000 per square mile. South of 59th Street, Manhattan's area is approximately 13 square miles. At 1,000 an acre, nearly 9,000,000 could live on it. Allow half the ground for streets, parks and playgrounds, the population of New York could be housed south of 59th Street under excellent conditions.

The municipal cost of our scattered development is probably half our debt service, and probably a quarter of the city's annnual budget. The magnitude of our per capita municipal expenditures is not without reason. Other bad effects are obvious. The lost motion from daily shooting millions many miles from homes to business house or factory, is prodigious. Measured in hours taken from sleep and recreation New York's eight-hour day is a ten-hour day. The land speculator wonders what becomes of the increment that so often he does not get. It is swallowed up by the Moloch of waste.

If this waste were eliminated, taking New York as a whole, the consequent increase in market land in the area of intensive urban use would largely offset the loss in market values due to an increase of the relative burden on land. Give New York the harmonious development that the untaxing of buildings would assist and a tax of two per cent. on land values, with little tax on anything else, might easily realize as large a sum as now is realized from land and buildings together.

In conclusion, I would pass to another consideration. The doubling within a decade of the price of building materials and the great increase in labor costs have discouraged building operations and thus increased congestion. To take the tax from buildings would be in the direction of restoring things as they were when taxes on land were 85 per cent. of the total, whereas now they are but 75 per cent. According to accepted principles, a lessening of the relative tax on land is a gift to land owners of the capitalized amount of the reduction. In view of the increase in building, and the practice of assessing new buildings, according to cost, we have at work an influence steadily making for increasing the burden on land payers, and decreasing it on land owners.

My opinion that something should be done to re-establish the old equilibrium is strengthened by the knowledge that in 1890, when land bore relatively a heavier burden than now, many eminent and conservative New Yorkers put their signatures on a declaration which said: "Real estate should bear the main burden of taxation, because such taxes can be most easily, cheaply and certainly collected, and because they bear least heavily on the farmer and the worker." Among the signatories to the declaration were George H. Scott and George R. Read, presidents of the Real Estate Exchange; Spencer Aldrich, F. B. Thurber, Henry A. Hurlburt, William Gordon Fellows, G. T. Christianson, Smith Ely, Amos R. Eno, Hall J. How, James McCreery, William Steinway and John Claflin. The men that have survived all now seem to have recanted.

PROFESSOR SELIGMAN: Do you understand that any or all of these prominent men had in mind the question which we are now discussing?

MR. DAWSON: No, I do not think so.

PROFESSOR SELIGMAN: In other words, that statement has no application to this particular problem?

MR. DAWSON: I think it has. I merely state, as a matter of fact, that that particular question was not before them at the time, but I think it is applicable, however.

PROFESSOR SELIGMAN: The point there was the question of the taxation of real estate versus personal property.

MR. DAWSON: When that question arose a man could discuss it on certain lines of principle which makes it necessarily pertinent to the entire discussion.

I simply said that they are laying down a certain principle.

PROFESSOR SELIGMAN: Which has no application to this particular discussion that we are taking up here to-day. The next point is this, Mr. Dawson: When you stated that, in your opinion, the result of this change would be to enable people who now live in four-room tenements to live in five-room tenements, did you base that opinion upon any studies that you have made as to the probable amount of the reduction in the rentals that the landlord would receive on his property?

MR. DAWSON: I made some studies in that matter. When I said four or five I did not commit myself to any particular unit. I merely spoke of the strong tendency.

PROFESSOR SELIGMAN: Figures have been presented to us by our expert investigator saying that, in the most congested portions of our tenement house district, the net result of the possible decrease in rentals, if there were any decrease, would range from fifty cents a month to a dollar a month in the rentals. Now, my inquiry is, would that lowering of the rentals by fifty cents or a dollar a month enable a man who lives in a four-room apartment now to live in a five-room apartment?

MR. DAWSON: Perhaps four and a half—four larger rooms.

PROFESSOR SELIGMAN: What is the average rental per room in New York City to-day in the congested district?

MR. DAWSON: I am told that it is about $4 a month.

PROFESSOR SELIGMAN: It is about $4 a month, so that the decrease of from 50 cents a month to a dollar would mean as a maximum that he would get from one-eighth to one-quarter of an additional room?

MR. DAWSON: If the argument is correct, in that case he would get four and a quarter rooms.

DR. WILCOX: I think it has been stated very clearly that our expert did not say that the maximum reduction in rentals would be fifty cents or a dollar a month. He said that the maximum available from the direction of the decrease in the tax would be that, and he specifically excluded all the main forces that are being considered here, namely, the forces that result from the competition of new buildings.

PROFESSOR SELIGMAN: You called attention to the fact that a more harmonious building up of the city, as you call it, would lead to a lessening of municipal expenses in various ways. The opinion has been expressed by some of the witnesses here that, in two respects at least, the expenses would be increased; first, because of the larger number of people per acre, due to the more intensive use of the land, the expenses for police would be larger. Second, because of the more intensive use of the land there would be much greater expenditure needed for more parks. Would, in your opinion, these additional expenses, due to the change, counterbalance the lessening of expense to which you called attention?

MR. DAWSON: In regard to police, I think that our experience shows that it takes more expenditure to police 100,000 people scattered over Queens than it does 100,000 in a particularly small neighborhood in New York City.

In regard to parks, I think that there, of course, we would have to add immediately to the city's expense; however, to no degree comparable to the saving.

PROFESSOR SELIGMAN: You spoke about the desirability of the change in order to bring about a decrease in the cost of houses or buildings. It has been stated that there would be an increase in a very material element in the cost of the house, due to the fact of the increase in the rate on mortgage loans, by which, for the most part, houses are financed. It has been claimed that this additional element of cost must be set off against the element of decreasing cost, due to the absence of taxation. Do you think that is a sound argument?

MR. DAWSON: I do not think that is a sound argument with respect to any new erections. A fund of $1,000,000 is available for building loans. A would-be builder buys a site for $1,000,000 and borrows the $1,000,000 in the loan fund. Now, suppose the would-be builder is able to buy the site for $900,000 and has $100,000 left to put in his building. To erect a $1,000,000 building he then needs to borrow but $900,000. The result is that $100,000 is left in the loan fund and the same building created; and normally there should be a fall in interest rates.

TESTIMONY OF MR. FABIAN FRANKLIN,

Associate Editor, New York Evening Post.

MR. FRANKLIN: The questions which, I take it, have occupied a very large part of these hearings, while of high importance, are, in my opinion, of secondary moment in comparison with the underlying question. That question is, for what purpose are we asked to make this great and fundamental departure from our long-standing attitude on the subject of taxation? The reasons are essentially two. The advocates of the change are moved either by the conviction that Henry George's doctrine is right, and we ought to act upon it, or by the feeling that a certain portion of the population ought to be relieved of taxes which they are now paying—in other words, that rents should be reduced for the benefit of the rent-payers or of a certain class of rent-payers. Although these two things are connected, they are by no means the same; and it is important to consider them separately. I am convinced that the backbone of the movement comes from the Henry George idea; but there are advocates of the untaxing of buildings whose advocacy of it is not at all based on that idea, and it will be well to consider first the reasons urged for the measure simply as a means of relief for rent-payers.

For the sake of argument I am going to assume that the removal of a tax on buildings would actually result in a reduction of rents equal to the whole or a considerable part of the tax removed. Now I take it that the relief thus brought about is desired by the advocates of the proposal chiefly for the sake of two classes of people, and not of the whole population. Nobody has come here and advocated this change with zeal and earnestness on account of the rents paid by business men. Nobody cares about the rent of the Woolworth Building. They care about rents on homes; and this divides itself into two parts. The homes of the rich do not come into the consideration any more than business buildings; the relief is wanted for persons in circumstances of moderate comfort and for the poor.

As regards the fairly comfortable class—people who pay, say, from $300 to $600 a year in rent, or who own modest little homes—everybody would like to see them better off, of course; but the question is, is it desirable that these people should feel that they do not contribute to the cost of government? Is it desirable that they should not pay a fairly decent amount towards the support of the government? For my part I think that people of moderate income should feel that they are contributing something worth talking about, and that they have a real interest in the question of whether the municipality is properly administered or not.

Let me make a little digression here. The tendency in our time is to levy all sorts of special taxes, in addition to the existing ones, to meet the constantly advancing cost of government. This is right. There ought to be an income tax. There ought to be an inheritance tax. The increase of governmental expenses is going to continue no matter how economical the administration may be, and this increase is going to be met, and ought to be met, by taxes falling chiefly on the rich. All the more reason that the plain man, the ordinary citizen, who has hitherto paid his share for the support of the government, should continue to pay a reasonable amount. It would be unfortunate if the population were to be divided into a small class upon which every new burden of government was laid, and a large class who felt that it made no difference at all to them what the taxes were. So far, then, as regards the moderately comfortable class, I see no justification for making a radical departure in our whole system of taxation for the sake of relieving them of their present share of the tax burden.

In regard to that class of people who have none of the luxuries of life and are barely able to supply themselves with the necessaries, the question is very different. If under our present system the sum of twenty dollars a year, say, is added to the expenses of such a family by taxation, in the shape of increased rent, it is certainly desirable that they should be relieved of that burden if practicable. It must be admitted that twenty dollars a year is a matter of importance to a family of this class. Yet it must also be admitted that it is not of vital importance. For the sake of bringing about this relief one would hesitate to upset the whole basis of taxation affecting the vast real estate interests of this city. And unquestionably, if it should be decided that this relief ought to be granted, ways could be found of bringing about that result without any such upsetting of the tax system. One such way occurs to me at this moment; I do not offer it as a proposal, but merely as an indication of possibilities. A horizontal deduction of twenty dollars might be made from each tax bill for every dwelling included in it. This would be at least as certain to have the effect of reducing rents as would the proposed exemption of buildings; but it would be manifestly designed as a measure of relief for the rent-payer, limited to the fixed sum of twenty dollars, and would leave the tax system essentially unaltered. Of course, the tax rate would have to be so calculated as to make the total levy equal to what is required after allowing for the deductions. Moreover, it would be easy to make the deduction apply only in cases of property of low value, which would effect the humanitarian object desired with even less disturbance of the present method. Whatever may be thought of this particular scheme, it is certain that the relief desired for poor tenement house dwellers—a matter of very small proportions fiscally—can be attained without upsetting the status of all the real property in this city, the very heart of the economic life of this great nation.

So much for the direct practical ends aimed at by this proposal. But as I have said, the believers in the Henry George doctrine have been the backbone of this movement. When it was initiated some half dozen years ago, a great deal of stress was laid upon the fact that it had no necessary connection with the single tax idea and that many of its supporters were not single taxers. It was proposed to take off only half the tax on buildings, and it was pointed out with great emphasis that even that was to be done very gradually. But those who objected were fully convinced that the proposal to take off half was only a beginning, sure to be followed before long by a move to take off the whole. And, although the original proposal was not adopted, its advocates have reached the second stage already. The proposal now chiefly agitated is that of completely untaxing buildings—for the one per cent. of the tax which is left is, of course, retained merely for the sake of a technicality. This complete untaxing was in the wood all the time; but this is not all that was in the wood. To place upon the land the whole burden of the taxation now borne by land and buildings together is only a step towards a larger end—the end that Henry George had in mind from the outset, and which he expected to get accomplished by this very means.

Let us recall what Henry George said on this subject in the very first edition of *Progress and Poverty*. He declared without qualification that land values ought to be confiscated; but he said it was desirable to avoid the form of confiscation, and attain the substance of it by a tax which would take up the whole value of the land. But, he said, it is not necessary expressly to decree such a tax; all that is necessary is to abolish all other taxes and the thing will take care of itself. With all the taxes falling upon the land owners, none but this small class of the population would be interested in keeping taxes down; and as there is no limit to the possible needs of government, taxes would be put up higher and higher until they absorbed the entire rental value of the land. There was profound political sagacity in this view, and its soundness is even more evident now than it was when Henry George wrote his book thirty odd years ago. At that time the class of things which we now designate by the name of social betterment had hardly come into view. To-day it is perfectly evident that demands upon the government for purposes of this nature can be expanded without limit. No doubt, the tendency is a good one; but the question is whether we are going to accomplish these things honestly, or throw the whole burden upon one class, a class that has been guilty of no crime, but on the contrary has been engaged in a species of enterprise that has been considered—and, I am sure justly considered—as legitimate as any other form of business activity.

The real question, then, that is before us is not any little matter of a quarter of one per cent. difference in mortgage rates, or of twenty dollars a year difference in rents, but the question whether the leading commercial and financial community of the United States wishes to be headed straight toward outright confiscation of land values. Surely before we take such a step we should weigh most gravely its far-reaching consequences. We ought to feel ourselves the guardians not only of the billions of dollars of real estate in this city, but also of the economic soundness of the whole country, for the force of the example which New York sets is absolutely incalculable.

I should like to say a word about a counter-argument that advocates of measures tending towards a full-fledged single tax are in the habit of using. When the proposal to take off half the tax on buildings by installments extending over five years was objected to on the ground that this would prove to be but a first step, its advocates declared that the objection was insincere. If the move was bad, they said, it would be shown to be so at the end of the five-year period, and what the objectors were really afraid of was that it would prove to be a good thing. This argument rests on the assumption that the question of whether a thing is good or bad in a matter of this kind is entirely simple. The truth is that nothing is more difficult to determine. Not only is it extremely difficult to decide whether or not the community as a whole has been benefited, and whether the future results are likely to be good or bad, but there is also the question whether injustice has been done to some while gains have been made by others. You cannot decide matters of this kind justly by a count of noses. Moreover it may easily happen that even if the feeling is general that the experiment has not worked well, yet a very taking cry might be raised that the trouble was that we had not gone far enough. This is a very familiar phenomenon in another field. When democratic institutions have not worked well, and people point to their failure in one respect or another, the favorite slogan of thoroughgoing believers in democracy is—"The cure for democracy is more democracy." And this is precisely the kind of answer that single taxers have repeatedly made to critics who have pointed to the failure of rosy expectations from schemes for the untaxing or partial untaxing of buildings. They have said that the trouble was that these schemes did not get rid of land speculation, which they regard as the root of the evil, and should, therefore, not be counted as disproof of the blessings of the *bona fide* single tax plan. For all these reasons, it would be in the highest degree dangerous to undertake an experiment of the kind proposed. The matter is one that cannot be trifled with. It must be treated on the basis of fundamental principle, and not made the subject of light-minded experimentation.

STATEMENT OF MR. DE WITT CLINTON.

MR. CLINTON: In my opinion our present system of raising revenue is inadequate, unwise and unjust. It penalizes industry and legitimate business and encourages speculation and illegitimate business. I heartily recommend the proposal to gradually reduce taxes on buildings and shift them to land values, as by so doing building lots now wanted for improvement but held at exorbitant prices would be thrown upon the market and industry necessarily fostered.

As land is one of the two indespensable factors in the production of wealth, labor being the other, it is evident that when productive land is held out of use, labor is blocked to just that extent. Therefore those who control access to land control the situation.

From one-third to one-half of the land of our cities and towns is held either vacant or greatly underimproved by owners who are waiting to realize speculative profits. New York is no exception.

Few economists deny that the system of raising revenue from site values and exempting the products of labor would stimulate industry, and applied to building lots of a city, would stimulate building; but they raise a variety of objections such as the following, which I shall endeavor to answer briefly.

Objection A. "Rents would not be reduced" they say. Rents, as with any other commodity, rise when demand has been increased relatively to supply.

Increased demand for building accommodation is caused by increased business, and consequently must be accompanied by increased ability to pay for them, an ability which will keep pace with the rise.

Objection B. The real estate business will be injured. Only such part of it as consists of land speculation, and this should be, for land speculation injures everybody except him who directly profits by it.

Objection C. The city is now overbuilt, therefore, why should land be cheapened to encourage more building. Overbuilding is one phase of the so-called "over-production." Over-production can never truly exist so long as poverty exists, and needs are unfulfilled. Lack of purchasing power, or efficient demand, is at the bottom of this over-production situation and results from lack of opportunity to apply labor to land because monopoly can dictate. If land becomes less expensive and buildings are relieved of taxation burdens, charges for housing accommodations will be less, occupants will begin to come in and fill the vacant spaces and this condition of "over-production" (in our case overbuilding) will disappear.

Objection D. The revenue from land values may be insufficient to meet public expenses, especially in a falling market. The land values of a place reflect its communal advantages. These land values exist because, and are a measure of the conveniences of that place and must, normally, be sufficient to pay for the production of these conveniences.

Objection E. It has been asked if wages in New York City are not higher because ground rents are higher; that is, labor demands and receives more because of these higher ground rents. This is like asking if I cannot give two persons the same dollars. If wages are really higher in New York than in other places where ground rents are lower, how about that other fact well known to economists that wages in new countries, where land values are low, are higher than in older countries where land values are high? There seems to me a contradiction here. But wages are not higher in New York than elsewhere for the same grade of work or ability. If they should be, they could not remain so, because labor would flock in to take advantage of them and the increased demand caused by this would also cause a lowering to the same general level as before.

Objection F. Then it is asked if increased population does not cause increased prices of commodities on account of increased demand, in the same way that it causes increased prices for land. To this I answer, No. The cases are not analogous. Increased demand for products of labor is always met by increased supply of them, whereas increased demand for land cannot be so met since the quantity remains fixed. We all know that prices for the same grade of goods are not higher in large cities than in small ones, as a general proposition, notwithstanding that ground rents are higher.

As an architect, I commend to your favorable consideration the proposal to gradually untax buildings and shift the taxes upon the site values of lots as being consistent with justice and prosperity and as necessarily resulting in an increase in building activity and, therefore, in all other lines.

CLOSING STATEMENT OF MR. BENJAMIN C. MARSH.

NOTE:—The Closing Statement of Mr. Stewart Browne is not printed here, because the substance of it is contained in the brief submitted by him and printed as an exhibit.

MR. MARSH: Gentlemen, a solemn obligation rests upon your Committee, after the investigation you have made and the hearings you have held, to recommend the gradual transfer of taxes now levied on buildings to land values, for several reasons I am going to enumerate in detail.

We thoroughly appreciate the political situation here, in the fact that the administration may not deem it wise to attempt to urge this question or this change in tax system immediately. It seems to us that the thing which is incumbent on this Committee to-day is to regard the situation as a whole regardless of any political aspirations or even exigencies and to recommend this change for the following reasons:

Your own investigator, Dr. Haig, has not only stated in his report that the change promises ultimate benefits of considerable importance to all tenants and to many of the home owners in the outlying boroughs, but before your Committee indicated that it would be a good thing. I feel sure that Dr. Haig must have meant that rents would be reduced. I will quote now from his testimony before this Committee. Mr. Leubuscher asked the question:

> "But on the whole, you think the tendency of this scheme is in the right direction?
>
> "DR. HAIG: I do."

It is not fair for the impression to go out, which was gained from some of the things Dr. Haig has said, that rents will be reduced only by the amount by which the tax on any particular improvement will be reduced. The amount by which the rents will be reduced will not depend upon the total decrease or increase of taxes on any particular property. It will depend upon the number of "To Let" signs in the neighborhood competing for tenants. Take a tenement house where they have to pay $5 for a small dark room and you have to have artificial light in addition during the day time, the rate on this house may be increased, and this would be true of some of the worst tenements even where the land is assessed at $20,000 and the building at $2,000. When Astor has to compete with better tenements his rents will come down. That fact ought to be emphasized. According to Dr. Haig's statement if taxes were reduced $100 on a given improvement, the rent of each of ten tenants could be reduced $10 and still leave the landlord some profit. I don't think that has anything to do with the question whether rents, as a whole, would be reduced or not.

I am glad that the Chairman admits that rents will be reduced. I have the report here of the Mayor's Committee on Congestion.

"MR. MARSH: Would not the reducing of the tax rate more than one-half of the ordinary tax rate tend to reduce congestion?

"PROFESSOR SELIGMAN: It would have that tendency. A tax upon anything produced tends to check the production of that thing. The remission of the taxes tends to encourage the production. A house is produced for what you can get out of it, and if you make it worth while for people to put money into houses, of course, they will do so."

I think the majority of the Committee will agree that the striking thing, Mr. Chairman, is this: I have heard practically every witness and there has not been a witness who appeared before you, who, upon cross examination, has not admitted that rents would be reduced by transferring taxes from buildings to land values. They made the most astounding claims regarding the stringency of the money market, etc., and in the same breath showed their common sense by admitting that rents would be reduced.

I should want to die were I as afraid of the ordinary man as Mr. Franklin, who bitterly opposes submitting this question to a referendum here. This is not a question for your Committee to decide. It is a question to go to the whole people. It is the one big political issue in New York City to-day and from now on. We must oust the traction interests which control the gentlemen who call themselves the Board of Estimate. But we will never oust them until we take the ground rent of the city for the cost of government.

Now, let me quote from Mr. Kelsey's testimony before this Committee the other day. He was asked as to the result of untaxing buildings, and he said—"I am sure it would induce men to build. It would force them to build houses though not needed." "Then, of course, rents are coming down."

Mr. Bright, and every other man knows when he said that you could not get a loan, that this is perfect nonsense. Mr. Bright admitted it in his testimony.

I think every real estate man in New York City to-day, whether his property is improved or unimproved, wishes that we had paid as we went along, instead of piling up a gross debt of about $1,300,000,000. They would rather have had a tax rate on land of $3 twenty years ago, than to be in the present condition to-day with an interest charge of $52,000,000 on the city's debt. Now, the city is facing a worse situation. It faces a crisis, as every informed person knows, with the vast debt we have. The interest on our city's debt amounts to about the total budget of Chicago.

There is a moral question involved as well as an economic question, which we cannot ignore entirely. Either the people of New York City are a bunch of rascals and thieves, or else we have a very bad system here. Our opponents say if we start to untax buildings we will want to go further. There has been no argument before you which reduced to a logical conclusion does not admit that this will be a good thing, or else that the people want to steal. Now, I am not a single taxer. I have called attention to that before. I believe that there should be a rapidly progressive income tax for the Federal Government. We have our own situation here to face. Under present conditions I believe the tax rate by 1920 will be 2.40 with the present sources of revenue and the addition of the state direct tax. It has been proven to you beyond any unbiased doubt that the change we advocate would permanently reduce rents and taxes on small homes by reducing the fixed charges on all adequate improvements. It has been demonstrated that the change would permanently encourage industry and increase employment, by compelling better and earlier use of land.

Of course, the change will not bring in the millennium. No single thing will, but there cannot be any permanent improvement of the condition of the masses without it. I have submitted to you figures showing marked land monopoly. A few thousand families out of about 1,100,000 own the major part of the value of land in the City of New York to-day.

Mr. Richard M. Hurd, President of the Lawyers' Mortgage Company, one of the largest loaning concerns in the city, has shown you that the change can be made in not more than ten years, without in any way injuring the mortgage market; and no one has disproven this self-evident fact.

You know the inhuman housing conditions of the city would be relieved by the change. You know that nothing has been done practically to relieve them, that only about one-fourth of the city's population is living in so-called new law tenements, and they are paying very high rents for them.

It has been made clear that the change would encourage logical and economical development of the city, with a premium upon light and well ventilated buildings, in place of the present straggling, illogical and expensive development, and greater economy for private initiative as well as for the city.

Now, I am sure that Mr. Dawson did not mean that he urged that the population could be housed below Fifty-ninth Street. Personally I am very much in favor of the zoning or districting of the city.

You are urged to postpone this change of taxes on account of the present financial depression. This change is going to take ten years—at least from five to ten years, while the zoning of the city would be done at one time. The zoning system of the City Plan Committee is quite wholly dependent upon present selling prices of land. The change in the tax system which we advocate should precede the zoning of the city to prevent such rapid increase in selling values of land as will follow the completion of projected transit lines even if the city were zoned. There is no sense in having five or six-story buildings in the country—in Queens.

Two men, Messrs. Kelsey and Bloch, have claimed that the "loaning trust" of the city will control loans were this change in the tax system made, and rents lowered. Their statement regarding this trust has been referred to the District Attorney for investigation and action, but your Committee should sift this charge.

We have shown you that the change would merely compel those who are the financial beneficiaries of municipal expenditures to pay a little more of the cost of government, and relieve those who are now taxed twice for this purpose, first, in paying ground rent, and second, by taxation.

Now, it has been said that these public improvements do not improve the value of the land. You know how the hungry hordes of land owners clamor for public improvements from the Board of Estimate because they know they will raise the selling price of the land and they can unload it on the people and reap unearned fortunes.

It is suggested that you do not want to start this system until there is a rise in the prices of land. New York land is pretty well down at par with the water squeezed out of the selling price. There is no better time than now to begin the change. We have lost in the neighborhood of 200,000 population, approximately, recently, and there is going to be an increase of population in the future, and there is no use postponing the starting of the proposed change.

By recommending this change, you can disprove the charge that your Committee is acting merely in the financial interest of a majority of its members. We sincerely hope that you will rise above the selfish interests of a majority of your Committee, but the evidence brought before you will convince the voters of the city of the merits of the proposed change, and that is the essential point.

I want to take up a few of the alleged objections. Someone asked the question why people come here and the answer was, "To make more money." What would New York City be if God had not put the Atlantic Ocean alongside of New York City?

If the manufacturers and other employers of labor in New York City were obliged to pay a living decent wage, a large proportion would go out of business to-morrow, and the Factory Investigating Commission will confirm that statement, if they were obliged to pay the very minimum wage in which a family can maintain a proper standard of living.

I will quote from former President of The Bronx Miller's report on municipal markets. Mr. Bennet who was in Mr. Miller's office made the statement that the land owner gets the produce dealer's profit.

> "If then a retail business proved successful the owners of the property help themselves by increasing the rents as soon as the lease permits and to as large an extent as prudence allows."

Now, when does this affect general rents? I will quote further from Mr. Miller's report:

> "The success of this one business to some extent establishes the business value of the immediate locality and the adjoining rents rise rapidly also."

Now, who gets the benefit? The land owners.

I do not know of anyone who has appeared before you who wants to see the selling price of land in New York City in 1925 or 1926 one dollar less than it is to-day through the transfer of taxes from buildings to land values; less than the present selling price ten years after this measure goes into operation or becomes a law.

Here is a fact which Mr. Ingersoll brought out and which I want to have emphasized. Even if, as it is claimed, one land speculator loses what another makes, the increase in the speculative selling price of land is a net loss and dead weight upon the producers of the entire community. Suppose the selling price of lands should increase a billion dollars in the next decade? It is not going to be of help to a single producer in New York City. Now, that increase of the selling price is a dead weight and a loss. It may not benefit anyone. If one speculator loses and another gains, it does not benefit the community in the slightest degree. But someone is obliged to pay for it.

I am glad, Mr. Chairman, that Mr. Stabler told you the fact about the land monopoly in New York City. He said this is an attack upon the biggest vested interest. Therefore, he objects to it. He objects to it because it is an attack upon the biggest vested interest. I hope that this Committee does not conceive its duty to be to defend the greatest vested interest, as admitted by the beneficiaries themselves.

Every man who has raised the point of the constitutional limit on the tax rate has removed it under cross-examination. We will put up an enormous number of buildings. We have also pointed out that the constitutional provision regarding the debt limit will not be affected by the change.

Privilege cannot be logical because privilege itself is illogical. Every time a beneficiary came before you absolutely thinking that God Almighty intended to have a few good people own the property and to look after the interest of those who did not own any, he could not defend his position. It is fundamentally an ethical question and we have not made a claim that has not been upheld by the opponents under cross-examination. Of course, they did not admit it frankly. They did not come here for that, but they had to do it.

Now, take the case of the little home owner. It has been asserted that a higher tax on land will wipe him out. I grant you that the selling price of land will increase less rapidly, but suppose, instead of inceasing $1,000 it increases only $600. The average little home owner will only save about $50 a year in taxes and 20 times $50 makes $1,000, which is decidedly more exclusive of interest thereon than the smaller increase in the selling price of his lot.

Now, I am going to ask this in conclusion. If the taxes on land can be shifted to the tenant the same as the taxes on the building, why the objection to the proposed change? That question when answered by the real estate people shows the basis for their opposition to this proposition.

APPENDIX.

Correspondence Between Dr. Delos F. Wilcox and Mr. Richard M. Hurd.

Park Row Building.
New York, N. Y.

November 10, 1915.

Mr. Richard M. Hurd,
59 Liberty Street,
New York City.

My Dear Mr. Hurd:

In your statement before the Mayor's Committee on Taxation, Monday afternoon, you said, as I recollect, that the effect of the untaxing of buildings in the reduction of rents would be brought about entirely by the competition of new buildings. I tried to bring out in the questions I asked what I think is the fundamental fallacy in which both the orthodox opponents and the orthodox advocates of the untaxing of buildings agree. They maintain that the transfer of the tax from the building values to the land values would have a *direct* tendency to decrease rents and a *direct* tendency to decrease the selling value of real estate. This, I believe, to be fallacious. I cannot see how the total amount of the tax on a parcel of real estate or any particular distribution of that tax as between the building value and the land value can have any direct effect whatever upon rents, and I cannot see how the distribution of the tax as between the land value and the building value, provided the total amount of the tax on the given parcel of real estate remains the same, can have any direct effect one way or another upon the value of the land. Conversely, it seems clear to me that the reduction of the total amount of the tax levied upon a parcel of real estate will have the direct effect of increasing the selling value of the land even though the amount of the tax levied against the land value itself on the tax roll is increased. This is on the assumption that the selling value of the building as such is not directly affected one way or the other by the increase or the decrease of the taxes or other operating expenses of the building so far as such taxes or operating expenses are a normal and necessary part of the cost of the operation of all buildings of the same character, as the selling value of a building is determined by its construction cost. The necessary general increase or decrease in the operating expenses of the building will have the effect of decreasing or increasing the selling price of the land, for the building is a mere development of the land and the value of the land is based on the net amount of the earning power of the plot when it is appropriately improved and economically administered. If this is so, then the immediate and direct effect of removing the tax from buildings and increasing the tax rate on land value will be to depress the selling value of vacant land and to increase the selling value of improved land where the total amount of the tax levied against the land and the improvements thereon is decreased. Thereafter, if a parcel of vacant land that has been "held out of use" is improved it will recover value that it lost. If the improvement is of such value in relation to the value of the land itself that the tax on the land at the increased rate amounts to less than the tax on the land and the improvement would have amounted to under the previous rate, then the land when improved will be more valuable than it was before the tax rate on land was increased. In all this I am speaking only of immediate and direct effects.

If this is right then the untaxing of buildings so-called would not directly diminish rents, for the people in any case pay all that they may be made to pay for the privilege of living or doing business at a particular spot. The transfer of the tax from buildings to land would not directly affect one way or the other the aggregate selling value of real estate. Otherwise, we reach an absurd conclusion, namely—that the transfer of all taxes from land value to buildings would increase the total selling value of real estate by the amount of the tax capitalized.

It seems to me that this line of reasoning is the necessary support for your statement that the effect of the untaxing of improvements upon rents would be not a direct effect but an indirect one brought about by the competition of additional buildings.

As this point seems to be one of fundamental importance in the consideration of the questions now at issue before the Committee on Taxation, I should be greatly pleased to have your comments upon this line of reasoning. Your testimony greatly impressed the Committee, and I am sure that all the members would be glad to have your mature views upon the matter which I now submit to you.

Yours very truly,
(Signed) DELOS F. WILCOX.

Lawyers' Mortgage Company,
59 Liberty Street.

New York, November 12th, 1915.

Delos F. Wilcox, Esq.,
Park Row Building,
New York City.

Dear Mr. Wilcox:

I have your letter of November 10th regarding the matter of untaxing buildings.

I cannot see that the untaxing of buildings would cause any reduction of rents except where there is competition of new buildings. It seems to me that the lower tax rate on buildings would serve as somewhat of an encouragement to builders to erect new buildings, and would be only one of many factors, the more important one being the judgment of the builder as to whether the new building could be financed, rented and sold. Where the land and building value are the same, I do not see that untaxing of the building, provided the total amount of the tax remained the same, would have any effect on the selling price of the property as long as the existing building remained. When the time came, however, to tear down the building a higher tax on the land might cause a lower selling price for the land, or, what would be more likely, it might check the steady normal advance in land values. I agree with you that permanent buildings are inseparable from the land while they exist and that the ordinary owner and purchaser of real estate will not distinguish in his mind as between what part of the tax on the property is levied against the land and what part against the building. You brought up at the hearing the theoretical case of having all the tax put against the building, under which conditions it might be figured that the land values would increase by the capitalization of the tax remitted. This is practically the situation in England where the income of land is taxed and not land itself. I think the reason that the land value is not increased in a case of this kind is that no income can be obtained from it except under the condition that from the income is deducted the tax on the building. Here again, it makes no difference whether it is called a tax on the land or a tax on the building separately. I agree with you that the general effect of removing the tax from buildings and increasing the tax on land would be to lower the selling value of vacant land, which would be another encouragement to building in addition to the smaller tax collected against the building itself.

I am not sure that I agree with you in your statement that the transfer of the tax from buildings to land would not directly affect the aggregate selling value of real estate. I do not see where the probable drop in land values would be compensated, nor do I think that we should adopt the opposite conclusion, that the transfer of taxes from land to buildings would increase the selling value of real estate by the amount of the tax capitalized, for the reason given, viz., that the land will not remain free from tax as soon as a building is erected on it and this tax charged nominally against the building, but which also necessarily includes the tax on the location, or land value, is discounted in the selling price of the vacant land.

To repeat what I said before the Committee, I think the psychological or sentimental effect of any change that appears radical is usually bad for a time, but I think that, if the rate of taxation should be lightened on buildings and stiffened against land with a view to absorbing a greater part, perhaps, of the unearned increment, and if this were combined with a carefully worked out plan for the limitation of height of buildings, the determination of zones and a thorough town planning viewed more from an economic than an artistic standpoint, the result to the city in the course of ten or twenty years would be most important.

Faithfully yours,

(Signed) R. M. HURD.

Park Row Building,
New York, N. Y., November 22, 1915.

Mr. Richard M. Hurd,
Pres. Lawyers' Mortgage Co.,
59 Liberty Street, New York City.

Dear Mr. Hurd:

I received your interesting letter of the 12th instant replying to mine of the 10th instant in regard to the matter of untaxing buildings.

There is one point which I think requires a little further elucidation. I have not been altogether fortunate in making all of my thoughts clear to Prof. Seligman and other members of the Committee and, perhaps, I did not bring out this particular point with sufficient clearness in my former letter to you. In your letter you say: "I am not sure that I agree with you in your statement that the transfer of the tax from buildings to land would not directly affect the aggregate selling value of real estate. I do not see where the probable drop in land values would be compensated."

My point is this, the transfer of the tax from buildings to land will not have any *direct* effect upon the aggregate burdens borne by the land within the taxing district. It will readjust these burdens among the individual parcels of real estate. In every instance a heavier burden will be placed initially upon unimproved parcels and also upon improved parcels where the ratio of the value of the improvement to the value of the land is less than the ratio of the aggregate value of all the improvements to the aggregate value of all the land within the taxing district. On the other hand, it seems to me clear that the direct initial effect would be to decrease the burden upon all parcels of real estate where the ratio of the value of the improvement to the value of the land is *greater* than the ratio of the aggregate value of all improvements to the aggregate value of all the land within the taxing district. If the burden is less on these parcels, then it seems to me that the direct effect must be to increase the capital or selling value of the property, which means, of course, that the decreased total burden upon land and building will be reflected in an increased capital value of the land.

If this is so then the direct initial effect of the transfer of all taxes from buildings to land would be merely to redistribute the capital or selling value of real estate and not either to increase or to diminish this value in the aggregate.

Of course, I see that the readjustment of burdens as between improved and unimproved property will set in motion other forces which will tend to supplement, check or counterbalance the direct initial effects referred to. If this is so, it seems probable that the result would be to encourage the improvement of vacant land which is ripe for improvement in comparison with other lands already improved. Then until this tendency is in its turn checked there will be an increase in the number and quality of buildings which, through competition, will tend to lower rents, until this tendency in turn is checked by the incoming of additional population attracted by the lower rents.

It is not easy to forecast the net ultimate effects of the proposed change in the taxing system. I think that there would be a tendency through the *indirect* forces set in motion toward a reduction in the aggregate capitalized or selling value of land. I think that this would be brought about through the partial elimination of speculative values. It seems to me that the actual aggregate value of all of the land within the taxing district is no more than the capitalized value of the aggregate net ground rentals actually paid for the use of the land at any given time. This means that, eliminating speculative value entirely, the aggregate value of all land within the taxing district is equal to the aggregate value of the improved land and no more. This is almost a truism. Unused land has no use value. Used land may have an abnormal use value because of the effect of the unused land which is held out of competition with it for speculative purposes. If, therefore, the untaxing of buildings tended to bring additional land into use it would tend to release normal competitive forces and reduce the aggregate value of lands already improved by the value of the additional land brought into use. To make this perfectly clear let us assume that in a city with an area of 300 square miles 150 square miles of land are improved and 150 square miles unimproved. If the transfer of taxes from improvements to land results in the improvement of an additional 50 square miles then, according to my reasoning, the 200 square miles of improved land would have only the same use value and, barring the speculative element, would have only the same value as the 150 square miles had before the change in the taxing system. Of course, this assumes a stationary population and no increase in the total amount of ground rentals paid.

It has been stated by some of the witnesses before the Committee that the transfer of taxes from buildings to land would result in a shrinkage of value sufficient to wipe out the equities of a great number of small holders of real estate. Mr. Browne estimates that there are about two hundred thousand owners of real estate in the city. Another witness was of the opinion that the proposed changes in the tax system would eliminate about 90% of all these property owners through the scaling down of values and the wiping out of equities. This claim, if sound, is a matter of major importance. On the other hand, if my reasoning as above outlined is correct, then the value of all those parcels of real estate, including the modest home of the "small man," where the value of the building is greater in proportion to the value of the land than the aggregate value of all buildings is to the aggregate value of all land, will not only be scaled *down* in selling value, but will be scaled *up* because of the decreased burdens they have to bear. This again only relates to the direct initial effect.

I trust that you will not be bored by my persistence in this matter, but these considerations seem to be of such fundamental importance in dealing with this tax problem that I take the liberty to solicit your further comment upon the subject matter of this letter.

Very sincerely yours,
(Signed) DELOS F. WILCOX

Lawyers' Mortgage Company,
59 Liberty Street.

New York, November 29th, 1915.

Delos F. Wilcox, Esq.,
Park Row Building,
New York City.

Dear Mr. Wilcox:

I have read with great interest your letter of November 22nd and your reasoning certainly seems to me to be sound.

One difficulty in prophesying the effect of a change in taxation on real estate is that the land and building can be seperated only in theory, as they remain in practice inseparable. I think that this is one reason why many people do not estimate that there will be any increase in selling price or value of property where the value of the building exceeds the value of the land and where the tax burden will be diminished. I think that such a result would occur for a short time and this seems to be conceded in part by all those who reason that the untaxing of buildings would lead to an increase of new buildings. As I have stated before, I cannot see any advantage to the tenant in lower rents except through new buildings.

I note your saving clause regarding the improving of vacant land which is "ripe for improvement," and the working out of this experiment would depend largely upon a correct judgment as to what land is or is not "ripe for improvement." I do not subscribe to the theory that any considerable amount of land is held out of the market. My experience has been that practically all vacant land is for sale, although, of course, a difference of opinion as to the selling price of the land between seller and buyer acts as a check on purchase and improvement of such land. I do not think that a gradual change in the direction of untaxing buildings would lead to any wild building boom. Too many forces are involved, especially those engaged in the business of financing new building operations who have so much to lose by any such boom that they would surely check it.

Referring to your statement on Page 3, I have always made the statement that vacant land has no value, but usually has a selling price, which is speculative in the sense that it cannot be surely known what rental will be earned from a new building to be capitalized into land value. I do not follow you in your statement that "the actual aggregate value of all land within the taxing district is no more than the capitalized value of the aggregate net ground rentals actually paid for the use of the land at any given time." What becomes of the vacant land within the taxing district on which taxes are paid on a basis of estimated value for future improvement? Further, I do not see how you can eliminate speculative value entirely in any calculation. What might be called speculative value is really future value, which is the element above or below the "intrinsic value" due to the capitalization of present rents at present interest rates. I think that the average of this speculative element varies from a minor quantity up to thirty or forty per cent. of the selling price of improved land. I should imagine that if New York City should stop growing and it were certain that it would never increase in population again, the total values would fall off twenty or thirty per cent. I know that many owners and lenders on real estate are alarmed at the prospect in the change of the method of taxation. Possibly they are right, but, for myself, I feel that it would be only one of many elements and, if applied gradually and in connection with a far-seeing plan of limitation of the height of buildings and the letting out of zones suitable to a city of ten million population, as Mr. Schiff outlines, I think the whole plan would result advantageously to the city.

Very sincerely yours,

(Signed) R. M. HURD.

BILLS PREPARED BY THE COMMITTEE

BILL FOR ABILITY OR PRESUMPTIVE INCOME TAX.

NOTE.—This bill was prepared with a view to its introduction at the legislative session of 1915, and has not been subjected to revision, excepting that the schedule proposed for the habitation tax has been modified.

The bill, as originally drawn, and as reprinted here, does not contain the provision recommended in the majority report, giving a taxpayer the right to declare and prove his actual income and to have reduced to one per cent. thereof a tax exceeding that amount.

ABILITY TAX.

An Act to provide for additional taxes in the City of New York.

The People of the State of New York, represented in Senate and Assembly, do enact as follows:

Article 1. Definitions.
2. Habitation tax.
3. Occupation tax.
4. Assessment, payment and collection of habitation tax and occupation tax.
5. Salaries tax.
6. General provisions.

ARTICLE 1.

Definitions.

Section 1. Definitions.

§1. **Definitions.** For the purpose of this act, unless otherwise required by the context:

(1) the word "Business" shall be deemed to include business, trade, professions, agriculture and any other gainful occupation, and any other use of real property other than as a habitation;

(2) the words "Business premises" shall mean real property or any portion thereof, occupied or used exclusively for purposes of business. If real property, or a portion thereof, is used both for purposes of business and as a place of abode, such proportion thereof as is used for purposes of business shall be deemed business premises, and such proportion thereof, as is used as a place of abode, shall be deemed a habitation, and the rental value shall be apportioned accordingly;

(3) the word "Habitation" shall mean real property, or any portion thereof, used as a place of abode by one or more persons constituting a single household, or by one or more tenants, guests, lodgers or other persons having no household. The habitation shall be deemed to include all portions of real property to the exclusive use of which, in connection with such habitation, the occupier is entitled, and the

proportionate share of all portions of the real property, to the use of which in connection therewith such occupier is entitled in common with others, such proportion being determined by the share of use to which each is entitled. Real property occupied exclusively for a boarding house, excepting such portion thereof as is the boarding house keeper's personal habitation, shall not be deemed the habitation of the boarding house keeper, but shall as to him be deemed to be business premises;

(4) the words "Habitation tax" shall mean the tax provided for by Article 2;

(5) the words "Occupation tax" shall mean the tax provided for by Article 3;

(6) the word "Occupier" shall mean an owner in possession of a habitation or business premises;

(7) the word "Owner" shall mean any person having any estate or interest in real property or portion thereof, including a tenancy with or without a lease and with or without a definite term;

(8) the word "Rental" shall be deemed to mean such sum per annum as results from a computation based upon all sums agreed to be paid for the use or occupation of real property or a portion thereof during any part of the preceding year ending on the first Monday of November, including all taxes, assessments or other payments paid or agreed to be paid by the occupier in connection therewith, whether paid to an owner or to the public authorities and also including all sums paid as part of the rental for light, heat or other services or conveniences, but excluding sums paid for board;

(9) the words "Rental value" shall, in case of a letting for an agreed sum of money constituting the exclusive payment for the use and occupation of the habitation or business premises, mean the rental computed on the basis of one year. In all other cases the rental value shall be deemed to be seven per centum of the value of the real property as shown on the last preceding annual record of the assessed value of real and personal estate of the borough; provided, however, that the rental value shall in no case be deemed to be less than the rental as defined in subdivision eight of this section. If the habitation or business premises shall constitute a portion of a lot or parcel separately assessed, the apportioned part of the total assessment shall be deemed to be the assessed value of the habitation or business premises, and seven per centum thereof shall be deemed the rental value thereof;

(10) the words "Salaries tax" shall mean the tax provided for in Article 5;

(11) the word "Salary" shall be deemed to include all salaries, wages, commissions, gratuities, emoluments, perquisites, and other compensation of whatever kind and in whatever form paid, received or earned, for services performed for an employer transacting business in the City of New York in or in connection with such business, or performed for the City of New York or the State of New York, but shall not include any sums paid for services rendered to the government of the United States, nor the salaries of judges who are protected by constitutional limitations during the period for which they have heretofore been elected.

ARTICLE 2.

Habitation Tax.

Section 2. Habitation tax.
3. By whom to be paid.
4. Rates of tax.

§2. **Habitation Tax.** There is hereby imposed, and shall be levied, assessed, collected, and paid annually, a tax with respect to the occupation of every habitation in the City of New York having a rental value of six hundred dollars or more.

§3. **By whom to be paid.** 1. Every person who shall, on the first Monday of November, in the year nineteen hundred and fifteen, or in any subsequent year, being the owner in fee or for one or more lives or for a leasehold term of not less than one year of a habitation in said city having a rental value of six hundred dollars or more, be an occupier of such habitation, shall be liable to pay the habitation tax with respect to such habitation.

2. Every person who shall, during the greater number of days in any period of three consecutive months within the period of one year ending the first Monday of November in the year nineteen hundred and fifteen, or in any subsequent year, have been an occupier of one or more habitations in said city having a rental value of six hundred dollars or more, shall be liable to pay the habitation tax with reference to such habitation, or, if there be more than one, with reference to the last one occupied by him during said period, but no person shall be liable to pay said tax who shall not be such an occupier at any time after the enactment of this chapter.

§4. **Rates of tax.** The habitation tax shall be at the rates computed with reference to the rental value of the habitation as specified in the following table:

Rental.		Multiplier.	Presumptive Income.	Taxable Income.	Tax.
$600-	$700	5	$3,500-$2,000	$1,500	$5
700-	800	5	4,000- 2,000	2,000	10
800-	900	5	4,500- 2,000	2,500	15
900-	1,000	5	5,000- 2,000	3,000	25
1,000-	1,100	5	5,500- 2,000	3,500	30
1,100-	1,250	5	6,000- 2,000	4,000	37
1,200-	1,300	5	6,500- 2,000	4,500	45
1,300-	1,400	5	7,000- 2,000	5,000	50
1,400-	1,500	5	7,500- 2,000	5,500	55
1,500-	1,600	5	8,000- 2,000	6,000	60
1,600-	1,700	5	8,500- 2,000	6,500	65
1,700-	1,800	5	9,000- 2,000	7,000	70
1,800-	1,900	5	9,500- 2,000	7,500	75
1,900-	2,000	5	10,000- 2,000	8,000	80
2,000-	2,100	5.1	10.710- 2,000	8,710	87
2,100-	2,200	5.1	11,220- 2,000	9,220	92
2,200-	2,300	5.2	11,960- 2,000	9,960	99
2,300-	2,400	5.2	12,480- 2,000	10,480	104
2,400-	2,500	5.3	13,250- 2,000	11,250	112
2,500-	2,600	5.3	13,780- 2,000	11,780	118
2,600-	2,700	5.4	14,580- 2,000	12,580	125
2,700-	2,800	5.4	15,120- 2,000	13,120	131
2,800-	2,900	5.5	15,950- 2,000	13,950	139
2,900-	3,000	5.5	16,000- 2,000	14,500	145
3,000-	3,100	5.6	17,360- 2,000	15,360	154
3,100-	3,200	5.6	17,920- 2,000	15,920	159

Rental.		Multiplier.	Presumptive Income.		Taxable Income.	Tax.
3,200-	3,300	5.7	18,810-	2,000	16,810	168
3,300-	3,400	5.7	19,380-	2,000	17,380	174
3,400-	3,500	5.7	19,950-	2,000	17,950	180
3,500-	3,600	5.8	20,880-	2,000	18,880	188
3,600-	3,700	5.8	21,460-	2,000	19,460	195
3,700-	3,800	5.9	22,440-	2,000	20,440	204
3,800-	3,900	5.9	23,010-	2,000	21,010	210
3,900-	4,000	5.9	23,600-	2,000	21,600	216
4,000-	4,100	6	24,600-	2,000	22,600	226
4,100-	4,200	6.1	25,620-	2,000	23,620	236
4,200-	4,300	6.2	26,660-	2,000	24,660	246
4,300-	4,400	6.3	27,720-	2,000	25,720	257
4,400-	4,500	6.4	28,800-	2,000	26,800	268
4,500-	4,600	6.5	29,900-	2,000	27,900	279
4,600-	4,700	6.6	31,020-	2,000	29,020	290
4,700-	4,800	6.7	32,160-	2,000	30,160	301
4,800-	4,900	6.8	33,320-	2,000	31,320	313
4,900-	5,000	6.9	34,500-	2,000	32,500	325
5,000-	5,200	7	36,400-	2,000	34,400	344
5,200-	5,400	7	37,800-	2,000	35,800	358
5,400-	5,600	7	39,200-	2,000	37,200	372
5,600-	5,800	7	40,600-	2,000	38,600	386
5,800-	6,000	7	42,000-	2,000	40,000	400
6,000-	6,200	7.1	44,020-	2,000	42,040	420
6,200-	6,400	7.1	45,440-	2,000	43,440	434
6,400-	6,600	7.2	47,520-	2,000	45,520	455
6,600-	6,800	7.2	48,960-	2,000	46,960	470
6,800-	7,000	7.3	51,100-	2,000	49,110	491
7,200-	7,400	7.3	52,560-	2,000	50,560	506
7,400-	7,600	7.4	54,760-	2,000	52,760	528
7,600-	7,800	7.4	56,240-	2,000	54,240	542
7,800-	8,000	7.5	60,000-	2,000	58,000	580
8,000-	8,200	7.5	61,500-	2,000	59,500	595
8,200-	8,400	7.6	63,840-	2,000	61,840	618
8,400-	8,600	7.6	65,360-	2,000	63,360	634
8,600-	8,800	7.7	67,760-	2,000	65,760	659
8,800-	9,000	7.7	70,300-	2,000	68,300	683
9,000-	9,200	7.8	71,760-	2,000	69,760	698
9,200-	9,400	7.8	73,320-	2,000	71,320	713
9,400-	9,600	7.9	75,840-	2,000	73,840	738
9,600-	9,800	7.9	77,420-	2,000	75,420	754
9,800-	10,000	7.9	79,000-	2,000	77,000	770
10,000-	10,200	8	81,600-	2,000	79,600	796
10,200-	10,400	8.1	84,240-	2,000	82,240	822
10,400-	10,600	8.2	86,920-	2,000	84,920	849
10,600-	10,800	8.3	89,640-	2,000	87,640	876
10,800-	11,000	8.4	92,400-	2,000	90,400	904
11,000-	11,200	8.5	95,200-	2,000	93,200	932
11,200-	11,400	8.6	98,040-	2,000	96,040	960
11,400-	11,600	8.7	100,920-	2,000	98,920	989
11,600-	11,800	8.8	103,840-	2,000	101,840	1,018
11,800-	12,000	8.9	106,800-	2,000	104,800	1,048
12,000-	12,250	9	109,800-	2,000	107,800	1,078
12,200-	12,400	9.2	114,080-	2,000	112,080	1,120
12,400-	12,600	9.4	122,440-	2,000	120,440	1,204
12,600-	12,800	9.6	125,880-	2,000	123,580	1,238
12,800-	13,000	9.8	127,400-	2,000	125,400	1,254
13,000-	13,250	10	132,000-	2,000	130,000	1,300
13,200-	13,400	10.2	136,680-	2,000	134,680	1,346
13,400-	13,600	10.4	141,440-	2,000	139,440	1,394
13,600-	13,800	10.6	146,200-	2,000	144,200	1,442
13,800-	14,000	10.8	151,200-	2,000	149,200	1,492
14,000-	14,200	11	156,200-	2,000	154,200	1,542
14,200-	14,400	11.2	161,280-	2,000	159,280	1,593
14,400-	14,600	11.4	166,440-	2,000	164,440	1,644
14,600-	14,800	11.6	171,680-	2,000	169,680	1,696

Rental.		Multiplier.	Presumptive Income.	Taxable Income.	Tax.
14,800-	15,000	11.8	177,000- 2,000	175,000	1,750
15,000-	15,200	12	182,400- 2,000	180,400	1,804
15,200-	15,400	12.2	187,880- 2,000	185,880	1,859
15,400-	15,600	12.4	193,440- 2,000	191,440	1,914
15,600-	15,800	12.6	199,080- 2,000	197,000	1,970
15,800-	16,000	12.8	204,800- 2,000	202,800	2,028
16,000-	16,200	13	210,600- 2,000	208,600	2,086
16,200-	16,400	13.2	216,400- 2,000	214,480	2,144
16,400-	16,600	13.4	222,440- 2,000	220,440	2,204
16,600-	16,800	13.6	228,400- 2,000	226,400	2,264
16,800-	17,000	13.8	234,600- 2,000	232,600	2,326
17,000-	17,200	14	240,000- 2,000	238,000	2,380
17,200-	17,400	14.2	247,080- 2,000	245,080	2,450
17,400-	17,600	14.4	253,440- 2,000	251,440	2,514
17,600-	17,800	14.6	259,880- 2,000	257,880	2,578
17,800-	18,000	14.8	266,400- 2,000	264,400	2,644
18,000-	18,200	15	273,000- 2,000	271,000	2,710
18,200-	18,400	15.2	279,680- 2,000	277,680	2,776
18,400-	18,600	15.4	286,440- 2,000	284,440	2,844
18,600-	18,800	15.6	293,280- 2,000	291,280	2,912
18,800-	19,000	15.8	300,200- 2,000	298,200	2,912
19,000-	19,200	16	307,200- 2,000	305,200	3,052
19,200-	19,400	16.2	314,280- 2,000	312,280	3,122
19,400-	19,600	16.4	321,440- 2,000	319,440	3,194
19,600-	19,800	16.6	328,680- 2,000	326,680	3,266
20,000-	21,000	16.8	353,800- 2,000	333,800	3,338
21,000-	22,000	17	374,000- 2,000	372,000	3,720
22,000-	23,000	17	391,000- 2,000	389,000	3,890
23,000-	24,000	17	408,000- 2,000	406,000	4,060
24,000-	25,000	17	425,000- 2,000	423,000	4,230
25,000-	26,000	17	442,000- 2,000	440,000	4,400
26,000-	28,000	17	476,000- 2,000	474,000	4,740
28,000-	30,000	17	510,000- 2,000	508,000	5,080
30,000-	35,000	17	595,000- 2,000	593,000	5,930
35,000-	40,000	17	680,000- 2,000	678,000	6,780
40,000-	50,000	17	850,000- 2,000	848,000	8,480
50,000-	60,000	17	1,020,000- 2,000	1,018,000	10,180
60,000-	70,000	17	1,190,000- 2,000	1,188,000	11,880
70,000-	80,000	17	1,360,000- 2,000	1,358,000	13,580
80,000-	90,000	17	1,530,000- 2,000	1,528,000	15,280
90,000-	100,000	17	1,700,000- 2,000	1,688,000	16,880

Note.—On rentals over $100,000, multiply by 17, deduct $2,000 and take 1%.

ARTICLE 3.

Occupation Tax.

Section 7. Occupation tax.
8. By whom to be paid.
9. Rate of tax.
10. Certain corporations not liable for occupation tax.
11. Exemptions.

§7. **Occupation tax.** There is hereby imposed, and shall be levied, assessed, collected and paid annually, a tax with respect to the occupation of every business premises in the City of New York having a rental value of six hundred dollars or more.

§8. **By whom to be paid.** Every person who, on the first Monday of November, in the year nineteen hundred and fifteen, or in any subsequent year, shall be an occupier of business premises in said city having a rental value of six hundred dollars or more, shall be liable to pay an occupation tax with reference to such business premises.

§9. **Rates of tax.** The amount of the occupation tax shall be as follows: From an amount equal to seven per centum of the rental value of the business premises, there shall be deducted the sum of twenty dollars in every case, and the remainder shall be the amount of the occupation tax.

§10. This article shall not apply to any corporation organized under the provisions of the railroad law, the transportation corporations law, or under chapter four of the laws of eighteen hundred and ninety-one, entitled, "An Act to provide for rapid transit railways in cities of over one million inhabitants."

§11. **Exemptions.** An occupier of real property or portion thereof which is by law exempt from the tax on real property shall not be required to pay an occupation tax with reference to such real property or portion thereof.

ARTICLE 4.

Assessment, Payment and Collection of Habitation Tax and Occupation Tax.

§13. **Application of article.** This article shall apply to the habitation tax and to the occupation tax.

§14. **Returns.** Every owner of any real property in said city which, or any part of which, is a habitation having a rental value of five hundred dollars or more, or business premises having a rental value of six hundred dollars or more, and every person who shall, at any time during the period of one year ending on the first Monday of November, in the year nineteen hundred and fifteen, or in any subsequent year, have been an owner of any such real property, shall, between the first and fifteenth days of November, in person or by duly authorized agent, make and file with the Department of Taxes and Assessments of said city, a return in writing under oath in such form as shall be prescribed by said department, setting forth the name of every person who shall, at any time during said period, have been an occupier of any such habitation or business premises, the rents agreed to be paid by such persons, and such other information as shall be required by said department.

§15. **Penalty for failure to make return.** Any person required by the provisions of section fourteen to make and file a return with reference to any habitation or business premises who shall fail to do so shall be liable to pay the habitation tax or the occupation tax, as the case may be, with reference thereto, and for the purpose thereof such person shall be deemed to have been an occupier of said habitation or business premises on the first Monday of November, of the year in which he was required to make such return. Such person shall also be guilty of a misdemeanor and shall, in addition to all other liabilities, be liable to a penalty of one hundred dollars and an additional penalty of ten dollars for each day during which the default continues, to be recovered by action brought in any court of competent jurisdiction by the corporation counsel of said city in the name and on behalf of said city.

§16. **Assessments and record thereof.** The department of taxes and assessments of said city shall assess the habitation tax and the occupation tax, and shall cause to be kept in the several offices, established by the said department, books containing a detailed record in such form as shall be determined upon by the said department of the taxes so assessed, payable with reference to the occupation of habitations and of business premises in the several boroughs of said city. Such record books shall be open for public inspection, examination and correction, from the fifteenth day of December until the fifteenth day of January in each year. The said department, previous to and during the time the said books are open as aforesaid for inspection, shall advertise the fact in the City Record.

§17. **Death or erroneous description of person liable to tax.** 1. No tax or assessment shall be void because of the death of any person liable to pay the same after the first Monday of November in the year for which such tax shall be imposed; but in such case it shall be lawful to assess the tax against such person or against his personal representatives, and in either case the personal representatives shall be liable therefor.

2. No tax or assessment shall be void by reason of any error, misnomer or misdescription in setting forth in the record the correct name of the person liable therefor; but in case of a substantial variance in the name of the person assessed no tax shall be collected except from the interest of said person in the real property, except as otherwise provided in subdivision one of this section.

§18. **Application for correction of assessment.** During the time that the said books shall be open to public inspection as aforesaid, application may be made by any person claiming to be aggrieved by the assessment of any tax to have the same corrected. Such application shall be in writing, in such form as shall be required by said department, and shall state the ground of objection. The board of taxes and assesments of said city shall examine the application, and if in their judgment the assessment is erroneous they shall cause the same to be corrected.

§19. **Correcting and adding to assessment record.** On or before the fifteenth day of February of any year, the said Board shall have power, on complaint or otherwise, to correct or add to the said record by correcting, reducing or increasing any assessment or by adding a new assessment; but no assessment shall be increased and no new assessment shall be added without ten days' previous notice to be mailed to the person affected at his last known residence or business address. An affidavit of mailing such notice shall be filed in the main office of said department. Any person affected by the proposed action may file with said department, within five days after the mailing thereof, objections in writing to the proposed action in such form as shall be prescribed by said department. Such objections shall be examined and considered by said Board before taking action.

§20. **Obtaining information and examining witnesses.** The board of taxes and assessments and any member thereof shall have power to investigate and inquire into all matters deemed by it necessary to enable it to prepare, correct or add to the record hereinabove provided for, and to subpoena and require the attendance of witnesses and the production of books and papers pertinent to the investigations and inquiries hereby authorized and to examine them in relation to any such matter. It may delegate to one or more deputy tax commissioners any of the powers conferred by this section.

§21. **Certiorari.** Certiorari to review or correct on the merits any final determination of the board of taxes and assessments made under the provisions of this act may be prosecuted in like manner and upon the same grounds and subject to the same provisions of law as a certiorari to review or correct an assessment of real or personal estate in said city made by said board.

§22. **Preparation of assessment roll and warrant for collection thereof.** Beginning with the fifteenth day of February in each year, the said board of taxes and assessments shall cause to be prepared from the books of record of assessments of habitation tax and occupation tax in the several offices of the said department in the several boroughs, assessment rolls for each of the said boroughs and shall, as soon as such rolls are completed, annex to each of the said rolls its certificate that the same is correct and in accordance with the entries in the said several books of record. Thereafter the said board shall prepare and sign its warrant authorizing and requiring the receiver of taxes of said city to collect from the several persons named in the assessment rolls the several sums set opposite to their respective names and to pay the same from time to time, when so collected, to the chamberlain of said city.

§23. **Delivery of assessment rolls and warrant to receiver of taxes.** The said board shall cause the assessment rolls of each borough when corrected with the said warrants annexed to be delivered to the said receiver of taxes on or before the first day of March.

§24. **Where tax due and payable.** The receiver of taxes, upon receiving the assessment rolls and warrants, shall immediately cause the same for each of the several boroughs wherein he shall have an office to be delivered at and filed in such office and shall thereafter proceed to collect and receive said taxes from the several persons assessed in said assessment rolls.

§25. **Receiver of taxes to give public notice.** The receiver of taxes shall immediately after he shall have received the assessment rolls, give public notice for at least five days in the City Record that said assessment rolls have been delivered and that all taxes will be due and payable at his office in said respective boroughs on the fifteenth day of March next ensuing.

§26. **Tax when due and payable.** The said tax shall be due and payable on the fifteenth day of March.

§27. **Interest upon unpaid taxes.** If any tax or portion thereof shall remain unpaid on the fifteenth day of April, after it shall become due and payable, it shall be the duty of the receiver of taxes to report said taxes to the collector of assessments and arrears of said city, who shall proceed to collect the same and shall charge, receive and collect upon every such tax or portion thereof so remaining unpaid on that day, interest upon the amount thereof, at the rate of seven per centum per annum to be calculated from the day on which said tax became due and payable to the day of payment; and such interest shall be paid over and accounted for by such collector of assessments and arrears from time to time as a part of the tax collected by him.

§28. **Collection of unpaid tax by distress and sale.** If any tax with the interest thereon or any portion thereof shall remain unpaid on the fifteenth day of April succeeding receipt by the receiver of taxes of the rolls, the collector of assessments and arrears shall proceed to issue his warrant under his hand and seal directed to any marshal of said city, and may reissue such warrant from time to time, commanding the marshal to levy said tax with interest thereon as herein provided, by distress and sale of the goods and chattels of the person liable to pay the said tax, and of any goods and chattels in the possession of such person, wheresoever the same shall be found within the said city, and of any goods and chattels which shall have been in the habitation or business premises on the day when the tax shall have become due and payable, and to pay the same to the said receiver and return such warrant within thirty days after the date thereof. Except as herein provided, the warrant shall be in like form and the marshal shall proceed thereunder and all other proceedings in reference thereto shall be had and taken in like manner as in the case of a warrant for the collection of taxes for personal property in said city. Such warrant shall be sufficient authority to proceed in accordance with its terms whosoever may be the owner of or have claims against the property which may be taken in accordance therewith.

§29. **Recovery of unpaid tax by action.** Any tax with the interest thereon or portion thereof which shall remain unpaid on the fifteenth day of April, after it shall become due and payable, may be recovered by the said collector of assessments and arrears in the name and on behalf of the said city in an action in any court of competent jurisdiction.

§30. **Lien of tax and enforcement thereof.** Every tax and the interest thereon shall be from the time when it shall become due and payable, and shall continue to be, until paid, a lien upon the interest of the person against whom the same shall be assessed in the real property or portion thereof with respect to the occupation of which such tax shall be assessed and shall be preferred in payment to all other charges. Any such lien may be sold, transferred, enforced and discharged in like manner as tax liens for taxes upon real estate in the said city.

ARTICLE 5.

Salaries Tax.

§31. **Salaries tax.** There is hereby imposed, and shall be levied, assessed, collected and paid annually a tax with respect to the receipt of all salaries amounting in the aggregate to the sum of $3,000 per annum or more.

§32. **By whom to be paid.** Every person who shall in the year nineteen hundred and fifteen or in any subsequent year, receive a salary or salaries amounting in the aggregate to the sum of three thousand dollars or more, shall be liable to pay the salaries tax with respect thereto.

§33. **Taxable amount.** The aggregate of all sums received by any such person in any calendar year from any and all sources and with reference to which said tax is imposed as hereinbefore provided, shall be known as the taxable amount.

§34. **Exemption.** There shall be deducted from the taxable amount two thousand dollars thereof which shall be exempt from the salaries tax.

§35. **Rates of tax.** The salaries tax shall be at the rate of one per centum upon the amount by which the taxable amount exceeds two thousand dollars and does not exceed five thousand dollars; two per centum upon the amount by which the taxable amount exceeds five thousand dollars and does not exceed twenty thousand dollars; three per centum upon the amount by which the taxable amount exceeds twenty thousand dollars and does not exceed thirty thousand dollars; four per centum upon the amount by which the taxable amount exceeds thirty thousand dollars and does not exceed forty thousand dollars, and five per centum upon the amount by which the taxable amount exceeds forty thousand dollars.

§36. **Tax to be withheld by employers.** Every person who shall in the year nineteen hundred and fifteen or in any subsequent year pay or be or become liable for a salary or salaries amounting in the aggregate to the sum of three thousand dollars or more to any person, shall on behalf of the person receiving or earning the same deduct and withhold from the payment an amount equivalent to the salaries tax thereon and thereupon the person receiving the salary shall cease to be under any further liability to the extent of the sum so withheld. If the person receiving or earning such salary shall not, therefore, have received the benefit of the exemption provided for in section thirty-four, the amount of such exemption, or so much thereof as has not been enjoyed at the time of payment, may be paid over without deduction of tax upon the person receiving the salary making and delivering to the person paying the same an affidavit in such form as shall be prescribed by the department of taxes and assessments of said city showing that the person receiving the salary is entitled to such exemption.

§37. **Return by employers.** Every person required by section thirty-six to withhold any portion of any salary shall, between the second day of January and the first day of February of the next succeeding year, pay to the receiver of taxes of said city all sums which he is so required to withhold, and shall within the same time make and file with the department of taxes and assessments of said city a return in writing under oath in such form as shall be prescribed by said department, setting forth the name of every person from whose salary he is required to make such deduction and such other information as shall be required by said department.

§38. **Payment of tax and return by person liable.** Every person liable to pay a salaries tax, the entire amount of salaries tax payable by whom shall not have been withheld under the provisions of section thirty-six, shall, between the second day of January and the first day of February of the year next succeeding the year for which said tax is imposed, pay to the receiver of taxes of said city the amount of tax for which he is liable, excepting such portion thereof as shall have been so withheld, and shall within the same time make and file with the department of taxes and assessments of said city a return in writing under oath in such form as shall be prescribed by said department, setting forth the amount of salary received by him during the preceding year and such other information as shall be required by said department.

§39. **Penalty for failure to file return.** Any person required by this article to make and file a return who shall fail to do so shall be guilty of a misdemeanor and shall, in addition to all other liabilities, be liable to a penalty of one hundred dollars and an additional penalty of ten dollars for each day during which the default continues, to be recovered by action brought in any court of competent jurisdiction by the corporation counsel of said city in the name and on behalf of said city.

§40. **Obtaining information and examining witnesses.** The board of taxes and assessments of said city and any member thereof shall have power to investigate and inquire into all matters deemed by it necessary to ascertain persons liable or amounts payable for salaries tax, and to subpoena and to require the attendance of witnesses and the production of books and papers pertinent to the investigations and inquiries hereby authorized and to examine them in relation to any such matters. It may delegate to one or more deputy tax commissioners any of the powers conferred by this section.

§41. **Information to be transmitted to receiver of taxes.** The said department of taxes and assessments shall, from time to time, transmit to the receiver of taxes of said city, any information in its possession as to the persons liable and amounts payable for the salaries tax.

§42. **Interest upon unpaid taxes.** If any tax or portion thereof shall remain unpaid on the first day of February after it shall become due and payable as hereinabove provided, it shall be the duty of the receiver of taxes to charge, receive and collect upon such tax or portion thereof so remaining unpaid interest upon the amount thereof at the rate of seven per centum per annum to be calculated from the first day of January in the year in which said tax became due and payable to the day of payment; such interest shall be paid over and accounted for by such receiver from time to time as a part of the tax collected by him.

§43. **Recovery of unpaid tax by action.** Any tax with the interest thereon or portion thereof which shall remain unpaid on the fifteenth day of February after it shall become due and payable may be recovered by said receiver in the name and on behalf of said city in an action brought in any court of competent jurisdiction.

ARTICLE 6.

General Provisions.

§44. **Set off as between habitation tax and occupation tax.** If any person shall be liable to pay a habitation tax and also an occupation tax in any year, he shall not be required to pay both taxes, but upon the payment of the larger in amount of the two taxes, shall be entitled to have the other cancelled.

§45. **Deduction of salaries tax from habitation tax or occupation tax.** If a person liable to pay a habitation tax or an occupation tax shall, within the year next preceding the time when the said tax shall become due and payable, have paid a salaries tax, or if a salaries tax shall have been withheld from him under the provisions of this act, the amount of salaries tax so paid or withheld shall be deducted from the amount of habitation tax or occupation tax for which he may be liable. If, however, any salary with reference to which a salaries tax is paid shall be for work done on premises of the employer, the salaries tax paid with reference thereto shall not be deducted from the amount of occupation tax assessed against the person liable to pay such salaries tax.

§46. **Deduction of taxes payable hereunder from personal property tax.** Any person assessed for a tax on personal property in said city, who shall within the year next preceding the time when the said tax becomes due and payable have paid any tax imposed by this act, shall be entitled to a deduction from the amount of the tax on personal property payable by him, of the amount of all taxes paid by him under the provisions of this act, including the salaries tax withheld from him, during the said period of one year.

§47. **Deduction by member of partnership.** Whenever an occupation tax or a salaries tax shall have been paid by a partnership under such circumstances that if the said tax had been paid by a member of such partnership, he would, under the provisions of this article, be entitled to a deduction or offset of the amount so paid from or against any other tax for which he may be liable, such partner shall be entitled to deduct so much of the tax paid by such partnership as is chargeable against his proportionate interest in the partnership.

§48. **Allowance of deduction or cancellation.** Where any person shall be entitled under the provisions of this article to any deduction from or cancellation of a tax for which he would otherwise be liable, the department of taxes and assessments of said city upon receiving proof of the facts entitling him to such deduction or cancellation in such manner and form as may be prescribed by said department, shall cause the said deduction or cancellation to be noted upon the appropriate record and shall transmit to the receiver of taxes or the collector of assessments and arrears of said city as the case may be, its certificate setting forth under its hand and seal the fact of such reduction or cancellation.

§49. **Board of taxes and assessments to make rules and regulations.** The board of taxes and assessments shall have power to make rules and regulations regarding the assessment, levy and collection of the taxes provided for by this chapter.

§50. **Taxes to be paid into the general fund.** All sums collected by reason of the taxes provided for by this act shall be paid into the general fund of the city of New York for the reduction of taxation.

§51. **Contents of returns not to be divulged; penalty for violation.** 1. Returns filed under the provisions of this act shall not be open to inspection, excepting upon an order for such inspection to be made by a justice of the supreme court in the first judicial district.

2. It shall be unlawful for any officer or employee of the said city to divulge or to make known in any manner whatever not provided by law to any person the contents of any such return or of any portion thereof, or any fact, matter or thing set forth or disclosed therein, or to permit any such return or copy thereof or record containing any abstract or particulars thereof to be seen or examined by any person except as provided by law.

3. Any person violating any provision of this section shall be guilty of a misdemeanor.

§52. **When act to take effect.** This act shall take effect immediately.

INCREMENT TAX BILL.

NOTE.—This bill was prepared with a view to its introduction at the legislative session of 1915, and has not been subjected to revision.

An Act to amend the Greater New York Charter, in relation to additional taxation.

The People of the State of New York, represented in Senate and Assembly, do enact as follows:

Section 1. Chapter XVII, Title I, of the Greater New York Charter, is hereby amended by adding thereto a new section to be known as section eight hundred and ninety-two-b, to read as follows:

§892-b. For the purpose of imposing a tax upon the increment, in addition to the general tax upon real estate, the department of taxes and assessments of the city of New York shall cause to be included in the books for the annual record of the assessed valuation of real estate, kept as provided in section eight hundred and ninety-two of this act, two additional columns, in the first of which there shall be set down in each year the basic value, as hereinafter defined, of each separately assessed parcel of real estate except special franchises, and in the second there shall be set down the amount, if any, by which the assessed value of such parcel for the current year, assessed as if wholly unimproved, exceeds such basic value, which excess shall, for the purpose of this law, be deemed the increment. The basic value of any parcel of real estate shall be the assessed valuation of such parcel, assessed as if wholly unimproved, as the same will appear on the annual record of assessed valuations of real estate for the year nineteen hundred and fifteen; provided, however, that if at any time during a period beginning not earlier than the second Monday of January, nineteen hundred and ten, throughout which period any such parcel shall have been owned by the same person who shall be the owner thereof on the first day of March, nineteen hundred and fifteen, such premises shall have been assessed upon the annual record of assessed valuations for more than the assessed value of such parcel for the year nineteen hundred and fifteen, the highest assessed value during such period shall be the basic value of such parcel. If during such period such parcel or any part thereof shall have been assessed as part of another parcel, the assessed values of such parcels shall be apportioned for the purpose of ascertaining such basic value. Such basic value shall be increased from time to time by adding to the assessed valuation determined as hereinbefore provided the amount of any and all assessments for public or local improvements becoming due after the date of the assessment with reference to which the basic value is determined, and the reasonable cost (when incurred) of bringing the land to the established street level, of making connections for water, light and sewage and street openings, when made at the expense of the owner of the parcel. In case any separately assessed parcel of real estate is divided after the first day of March, ninenteen hundred and fifteen, the board of taxes and assessments shall apportion the basic value thereof in the same manner and in the same ratio as the assessed value thereof as wholly unimproved land shall or may be apportioned under the provisions of section eight hundred and ninety-two-a of this act; and in case separate parcels shall be combined into a separately assessed parcel, appropriate combinations of the resulting basic values and increments shall likewise be entered. The said increment shall be taxed at the rate of one per centum per annum, and such tax shall be levied and collected and be a lien upon the real estate in the same manner as other taxes on real estate. Applications for additions to basic values shall be made to and determined by the department of taxes and assessments at the same time and in the same manner as applications for reductions of the assessment of real estate, and the determination of said department thereon shall be similarly reviewable by certiorari.

§2. Section nine hundred of the Greater New York Charter as amended by chapter four hundred and fifty-one of the laws of nineteen hundred and fourteen is hereby amended to read as follows:

§900. For the purpose of enabling the board of aldermen to impose the annual taxes it shall be the duty of the comptroller of said city to prepare and submit to said board, at least one week before the first day of March in each and every year, a statement setting forth the amounts by law authorized to be raised by tax in that year, on account of the corporation of the City of New York, as hereby constituted, or for city purposes within said city, as created by this act, and purposes for which said city is liable, and on account of the counties of New York, Kings, Bronx, Queens and Richmond, and also an estimate of the probable amount of receipts into the city treasury during the then current year from all the sources of revenue of the general funds, *including receipts from the tax on the increment imposed as provided in section eight hundred and ninety-two-b of this act,* and including surplus revenue from the sinking funds of the mayor, aldermen and commonalty of the city of New York, and of any of the municipal and public corporations, or parts of municipal and public corporations, by this act consolidated with the municipal corporation known as the mayor, aldermen and commonalty of the city of New York, other than the surplus of revenue of any such sinking funds for the payment of interest on the city debt of the municipal corporation known as the mayor, aldermen and commonalty of the city of New York, or the like debts of the municipal and public corporations by this act consolidated as aforesaid, and the said board of aldermen is hereby authorized and directed to deduct the total amount of such estimated receipts from the aggregate amount of all the various sums which, by law, it is required to order and cause to be raised by tax in said year, for the purposes aforesaid, and to cause to be raised by tax such sums as shall be as nearly as possible, but not less than the balance of such aggregate amount after making such deductions, by fixing a tax rate in cents and hundredths of a cent upon each dollar of assessed valuation.

§3. This act shall take effect immediately.

BILLS FOR ADMINISTRATIVE CHANGES

PREPARED BY THE COMMITTEE

BILL NUMBER 1.

AN ACT to amend the tax law, in relation to the exemption of real property of certain corporations.

The People of the State of New York, represented in Senate and Assembly, do enact as follows:

Section 1. Subdivision seven of section four of chapter sixty-two of the laws of ninteen hundred and nine, entitled, "An Act in Relation to Taxation, Constituting Chapter Sixty of the Consolidated Laws," is hereby amended to read as follows:

7. The real property of a corporation or association organized exclusively for the moral or mental improvement of men or women, or for religious, bible, tract, charitable, benevolent, missionary, hospital, infirmary, educational, scientific, literary, library, patriotic, historical or cemetery purposes, or for the enforcement of laws relating to children or animals, or for two or more such purposes, and used exclusively for carrying out thereupon one or more of such purposes, and the personal property of any such corporation shall be exempt from taxation. But no such corporation or association shall be entitled to any such exemption if any officer, member or employee thereof shall receive or may be lawfully entitled to receive any pecuniary profit from the operations thereof, except reasonable compensation for services in effecting one or more of such purposes, or as proper beneficiaries of its strictly charitable purposes; or if the organization thereof for any such avowed purposes be a guise or pretense for directly or indirectly making any other pecuniary profit for such corporation or association, or for any of its members or employees, or if it be not in good faith organized or conducted exclusively for one or more of such purposes. The real proerty of any such corporation or association entitled to such exemption held by it exclusively for one or more of such purposes and from which no rents, profits, or income are derived, shall be so exempt, though not in actual use therefor by reason of the absence of suitable buildings or improvements thereon, if the construction of such buildings or improvements is in progress [or is in good faith contemplated by such corporation or association]; or if such real property is held by such corporation or association upon condition that the title thereto shall revert in case any building not intended and suitable for one or more of such purposes shall be erected upon said premises or some part thereof. The real property of any such corporation not so used exclusively for carrying out thereupon one or more of such purposes, but leased or otherwise used for other purposes, shall not be exempt, but if a portion only of any lot or building of any such corporation or association is used exclusively for carrying out thereupon one or more such purposes of any such corporation or association, then such lot or building shall be so exempt only to

the extent of the value of the portion so used, and the remaining or other portion, to the extent of the value of such remaining or other portion, shall be subject to taxation; provided, however, that a lot or building owned and actually used for hospital purposes, by a free public hospital depending for maintenance and support upon voluntary charity, shall not be taxed as to a portion thereof leased or otherwise used for the purposes of income, when such income is necessary for, and is actually applied to the maintenance and support of such hospital, and further provided that the real property of any fraternal corporation, association or body created to build and maintain a building or buildings for its meeting or meetings of the general assembly of its members, or subordinate bodies of such fraternity and for the accommodation of other fraternal bodies or associations, the entire net income of which real property is exclusively applied or to be used to build, furnish and maintain an asylum or asylums, a home or homes, a school or schools, for the free education or relief of the members of such fraternity, or for the relief, support and care of worthy and indigent members of the fraternity, their wives, widows or orphans, shall be exempt from taxation, and provided also, that the real estate owned by a free public library, situate in any village of the third or fourth class, shall not be taxed as to that portion thereof leased or otherwise used for purposes of income, when such income is necessary for and actually applied to the maintenance and support of such library. Property held by any officer of a religious denomination shall be entitled to the same exemptions, subject to the same conditions and exceptions, as property held by a religious corporation.

§2. This Act shall take effect

BILL NUMBER 2.

AN ACT to amend the tax law in relation to the taxation of corporate stock.

The People of the State of New York, represented in Senate and Assembly, do enact as follows:

Section 1. Section twelve of chapter sixty-two of the laws of nineteen hundred and nine, entitled, "An Act in Relation to Taxation, Constituting Chapter Sixty of the Consolidated Laws," is hereby amended to read as follows:

§12. Taxation of corporate stock. The capital stock of every company liable to taxation, except such part of it as shall have been excepted in the assessment roll or shall be exempt by law, together with its surplus profits or reserve funds [exceeding ten per centum of its capital], after deducting the [assessed] value of its real estate, and all shares of stock in other corporations actually owned by such company which are taxable upon their capital stock under the laws of this state, shall be assessed at its actual value.

§2. This Act shall take effect

BILL NUMBER 3.

AN ACT to amend the tax law in relation to information to be furnished by the State Board of Tax Commissioners for the use of local assessors.

The People of the State of New York, represented in Senate and Assembly, do enact as follows:

Section 1. Section forty-five-a of chapter sixty-two of the laws of nineteen hundred and nine, entitled, "An Act in Relation to Taxation, Constituting Chapter Sixty of the Consolidated Laws," is hereby amended by inserting therein, after subdivision four, a new subdivision, to be subdivision five, to read as follows:

5. The State Board of Tax Commissioners shall at the time of filing the statement required by subdivision one of this section, file with the clerk of each city or town in which is located any real estate other than special franchises owned by or belonging to any person, copartnership, association or corporation, subject to taxation on any special franchise, a written statement, duly certified by the secretary of the board, containing:

(a). The name of such person, copartnership, association or corparation;

(b). An identifying description of each separately assessed parcel of such real estate, stating lot and block numbers in cities or towns in which such property is assessed, in accordance with tax maps;

(c). The value of the land of each such parcel as reported to said board by such person, copartnership, association or corporation, the reproduction value and present value of the buildings on each such parcel as so reported, and the reproduction value and present value of the plant and machinery on each such parcel as so reported;

(d). The valuation placed by said board upon such land, buildings and plant and machinery, showing separately the value placed on each for the purpose of determining the amount to be deducted from the earnings of such person, copartnership, association or corporation by reason of the ownership of such real estate in assessing the valuation of such special franchise.

In the city of New York said statement shall be filed with the department of taxes and assessments, and not with the city clerk. Each city clerk shall, within five days after the receipt by him of such statement, deliver a copy thereof, certified by him, to the assessors or other officers charged with the duty of making local assessments in the said city. Each town clerk shall, within five days after the receipt by him of such statement, deliver copies thereof, certified by him, to the clerk of the board of supervisors of the county, to the supervisor of the town, and to the assessors of the village or villages within the town in which is located any such real estate. The state board of tax commissioners shall obtain, by means of reports required by it under the provisions of section forty-four of this chapter, all information necessary to comply with this subdivision.

§2. This Act shall take effect

BILL NUMBER 4.

AN ACT to repeal section forty-eight of the tax law.

The People of the State of New York, represented in Senate and Assembly, do enact as follows:

Section 1. Section forty-eight of chapter sixty-two of the laws of nineteen hundred and nine, entitled, "An Act in Relation to Taxation, Constituting Chapter Sitxty of the Consolidated Laws," is hereby repealed.

§2. This Act shall take effect

BILL NUMBER 5.

AN ACT to amend the tax law, in relation to information to be furnished by the Secretary of State to local assessors.

The People of the State of New York, represented in Senate and Assembly, do enact as follows:

Section 1. Section two hundred and four of chapter sixty-two of the laws of nineteen hundred and nine, entitled, "An Act in Relation to Taxation, Constituting Chapter Sixty of the Consolidated Laws," is hereby amended to read as follows:

§204. Reports to be made by the secretary of state. The secretary of state shall transmit on the first day of each month to the comptroller, a report of the stock corporations whose certificates of incorporation are filed, or of the foreign stock corporations to whom a certificate of authority has been issued to do business in this state, during the preceding month. Such report shall state the name of the corporation, its place of business, the amount of its capital stock, its purposes or objects, the names and places of residence of its directors, and, if a foreign corporation, its place of business within the state. The comptroller may prescribe the forms and furnish the blanks for such reports. The secretary of state shall make like reports to the comptroller whenever required by him, relating to any such corporations whose certificates have been filed or to whom a certificate of authority has been issued prior to the time when this article takes effect, and during any period of time specified by the comptroller in his request for such report.

The secretary of state shall transmit on the first day of each month to the clerk of each city or town a report of all stock corporations having their principal place of business within the state in such city or town, with respect to which there shall have been filed during the preceding month any certificate of incorporation, copy of an order authorizing such corporation to change its name, certificate of change of place of business, certificate of increase or reduction of capital stock, or certificate of consolidation or merger, or to which, if a foreign stock corporation, a certificate of authority shall have been issued during the preceding month. Such report shall state the name of the corporation, its place of business, the amount of its capital stock, its purposes or objects, the names and places of residence of its directors, and, if a foreign corporation, its place of business within the state; also a general description of the papers filed with respect to such corporation during the preceding month, and in case of a change of name, the former name and the new name; in case of a change of place of business, the former place of business and the new place of business; in case of an increase or reduction of capital stock, the amount of the former capital stock and of the capital stock as changed, and in case of a consolidation or merger, the names of the consolidating or merging corporations and of the consolidated or merged corporation. Each city clerk shall, within five days after receipt by him of such report, deliver a copy thereof, certified by him, to the assessors or other officers charged with the duty of making local assessments in the said city. Each town clerk shall, within five days after the receipt by him of such report, deliver copies thereof, certified by him, to the clerk of the board of supervisors of the county, to the supervisor of the town, and to the assessors of the village or villages within the town in which is located the principal place of business within the state of any such corporation. In the city of New York said report shall be transmitted to the department of taxes and assessments, and not to the city clerk.

§2. This Act shall take effect

www.ingramcontent.com/pod-product-compliance
Lightning Source LLC
LaVergne TN
LVHW020112110826
845151LV00001B/133

* 9 7 8 1 4 2 5 5 4 3 9 1 4 *